D1109636

Imagining Grace

Imagining Grace

Liberating Theologies in the Slave Narrative Tradition

Kimberly Rae Connor

SHANAHAN LIBRARY
MARYMOUNT MANHATTAN COLLEGE
221 EAST 71 STREET
NEW YORK, NY 10021

University of Illinois Press

Urbana and Chicago

OCLC# 41548558
BT
83.57
.C68
2000

© 2000 by the Board of Trustees of the University of Illinois
All rights reserved
Manufactured in the United States of America
∞ This book is printed on acid-free paper.

Library of Congress Cataloging-in-Publication Data
Imagining grace : liberating theologies in the slave narrative
tradition / Kimberly Rae Connor.
p.   cm.
Includes bibliographical references and index.
ISBN 0-252-02530-X (alk. paper)
1. Liberation theology—United States.
2. Slaves' writings, American—History and criticism.
I. Connor, Kimberly Rae, 1957–
BT83.57.I56   2000
230'.089'96073—dc21   99-6615
CIP

C 5 4 3 2 1

The past is, it's a living thing, it's this relationship between ourselves and our personal history and our racial history, and our national history, that sometimes gets made sort of distant. But if you make it into a person, then it's an inescapable confrontation.
—Toni Morrison

In the final analysis the white man cannot ignore the Negro's problem, because he is part of the Negro and the Negro is part of him. The Negro's agony diminishes the white man, and the Negro's salvation enlarges the white man.
—Martin Luther King Jr.

Contents

Acknowledgments

My effort to explore the relationship between the slave narrative tradition and liberation theology has been supported in many ways. The National Endowment for the Humanities (NEH) provided the funds and the context for my ideas to emerge and develop, and I am grateful for its support. William Andrews, who led the NEH seminar in which I participated, remained after its formal conclusion a generous and constant mentor, providing encouragement and careful readings of my work as it progressed. His fine scholarship continues to serve as a model for my intellectual development. Ethel Smith, Anthonia Kalu, Oty Laoye, and Anne Warner, also participants in the seminar, helped me to continue what we began in Kansas, especially Ethel, who gave me the strength to "keep on keeping on."

Institutional funding also included a grant from the Virginia Foundation for the Humanities and Public Policy. The foundation provided support and affirmation at a critical time in my life, when, not long after the birth of my son, Gabriel, they gave me the necessary "room of one's own" and a reason to believe I could complete this book. Glenn Ligon was very gracious in responding to my inquiries about his work and I thank both him and the Max Protetch Gallery for providing me with slides of his work and allowing me to include them here. Anthony Pinn, Eric Sundquist, and Mark Irwin provided invaluable readings of my work as it progressed. Paul Stroble, Tom Hewitt, Jim Dooley, Joseph Brown, Meredith Morris-Babb, and Helen Benet-Goodman, each in his or her own gifted way, restored me to visibility. Thanks also to Carol Anne Peschke, whose careful copyediting brought clarity and precision to my text. I am also grateful to Karen Hewitt, my editor at the University of Illinois Press, for her constructive readings of my text and her encouragement to work on it until I achieved my best effort. Despite my lack of institutional affiliation and a manuscript that did not comfortably rest in any conventional category, Karen accepted the book on its own terms and believed it worthy of inclusion under an imprint that has such a distinguished record of scholarship in African-American studies.

Ed Connor and our son, Gabriel, were both guardian angels, continually affirming the value of my work and supplying me with the essentials beyond what my scholarship could provide. My sister, Deborah Bowers, supplied reassuring care for both mother and son, enabling me to continue my writing without the attendant guilt so many parents experience. Holly Mack and the staff at Woodlands Day School and Lutheran Church of Our Savior Preschool also deserve credit for providing me with many hours in which to write. The spaniels, Ella and Gracie, reminded me what is and what is not essential to salvation. And my friends at the Bay Area Chapter of the NAMES Project helped me to put this achievement in perspective.

This book is dedicated to my parents. Don Bowers revered the power of the word and took seriously his journalistic call to present the truth; in so doing he provided me an important model for my own inquiries. Richard and Virginia Berry showed me by their commitment to their vocations of ministry and nursing that nothing is beneath our concern or above our hope. In their daily witness they revealed to me the responsibility to advance, in ways large and small, personal and abstract, the cause of social justice. Because they "love to tell the story," any story I can tell or any grace I can imagine is because of them.

❦ ❦ ❦

Earlier versions of portions of this book appeared in the following publications:

Chapter 1: "The Ultimate Reality and Meaning of the Slave Narrative Tradition: Literary Acts of Imagination and African-American Liberation Theology," *Ultimate Reality and Meaning* 19.2 (1996): 83–93.

Chapter 4: "'To Disembark' and the Slave Narrative Tradition," *African American Review* 30.1 (1996): 35–57.

Chapter 6: "The Spirituals," in *The Oxford Companion to African Amer-*

ican Literature, ed. William L. Andrews, Frances Smith Foster, and Trudier Harris (New York: Oxford University Press, 1997): 693–96; and "'Everybody Talking about Heaven Ain't Going There': The Biblical Call for Justice and the Postcolonial Response of the Spirituals." *Semeia: A Journal of Experimental Biblical Criticism* 75 (1997): 107–28.

Imagining Grace

Introduction

> Argument provokes argument, reason is met by sophistry.
> But narratives of slaves go right to the hearts of men.
> —Anonymous review of *Life and Adventures of Henry Bibb,*
> *an American Slave, Written by Himself*

As a participant in a National Endowment for the Humanities (NEH) summer seminar at the University of Kansas in 1993, I joined a racially diverse gathering of scholars engaged in exploring the development and significance of the African-American slave narrative from its nineteenth-century origins in autobiography to its contemporary manifestations in fiction. We read the slave narrative tradition holistically, not as solely a nineteenth-century phenomenon, but as the literary and cultural bedrock of much contemporary African-American fiction. We examined how, as social, cultural, and literary priorities have changed during the last 150 years, the slave narrative has been adapted, formally and thematically, so that the traditions of the past might inform and empower the cultural work of the present. This holistic endeavor was an attempt to appreciate more fully what the slave narrative tradition is, what it says to Americans of all ethnicities about the nature of bondage and freedom in our society. As historical fact, psychological metaphor, or aesthetic trope, slavery as discourse is crucial to our worldview as a model of human authority.

Yet as "the historic national sin that no holy water will ever wash away" (McDowell and Rampersad vii), slavery has also been interpreted as crucial to our understanding of divine authority. Bringing my religious studies background to bear on our discussions, I began to appreciate how certain thematic and formal features of the slave narrative tradition were also an important dimension of African-American theologies of liberation in

their modern, academic articulations and their originating forms in abolitionist thought and creative expression that enslaved people developed to
critique, challenge, and transform their condition. As many liberation theologians recognize, theology is a product of a social environment, articulated in the medium of culture and bearing the influence of the culture that
permeates it. Among the most insidious examples of this influence was the
theology upheld by slaveholders in order to justify their economic system.
At the same time, enslaved people were articulating a culturally determined
theology that was in direct opposition to the view endorsed by slaveholders.
Enslaved people articulated their religious sentiments not by "argument"
and "reason" but through stories—in narrative, music, and craft—that
"went right to the hearts of men."

Reading through the slave narrative tradition, I began to appreciate that
the agenda for contemporary liberation theology set forth by James Cone
could also describe the momentum behind the slave narrative tradition. As
he writes, "I firmly believe that the issues to which theology addresses itself should be those that emerge out of life in society as persons seek to
achieve meaning in a dehumanized world" (For My People 28). In their
search to achieve meaning, African Americans have had to confront the twin
abolitionist concerns that inspired and now sustain liberation theology and
the slave narrative tradition: to expose slavery (or racism) in all its guises
and to lay political, intellectual, and spiritual claim to freedom. Furthermore, because "a faith in freedom as the ultimate concern in the black
American experience has revealed itself in non-Christian sources" and because "black belief in liberation is holistic life for an oppressed people [that]
transcends denomination, institutions, personality and movements and
empowers them on the road to freedom" (Hopkins, Shoes 3), I concluded
that there is an ideological bond between the explicitly theological formulations of academic liberation theology and the more creative and secular
but persistently moral and prophetic works of the slave narrative tradition.

Taking my cue from the artists who work within the slave narrative tradition, I became more inclined to view liberation theology as a mode of
interrogation that is not limited to an academic enterprise that, in Cone's
formulation, is addressed to issues that emerge as people seek meaning. A
theology is present in the many forms in which meaning emerges, a meaning
that people locate and describe in ways that are not exclusively systematic or confessional but almost always have a narrative dimension. Narrative, in Mark Ledbetter's formulation, is an act of desire motivated by a
wish for "something 'other than'" what present reality offers: an ordered
and coherent world. Pursing this motivation "leads to a revealing of a

religious virtue," a revelation made possible not because narrative is an "a priori construct" but because narrative "is itself a process not only revealing hidden meanings but also establishing meaning within and by its very structure" (1).

The slave narrative tradition informs us that a liberation theology is expressed in aesthetic and secular modes that may be more random and discursive, but nonetheless are equally cogent calls for liberation. Since its beginning, academic liberation theology has been a contextual theology that tried to negotiate between extremes of sacred and secular communities, Christian and non-Christian influences, theological (intellectual) and religious (experiential) categories. What I am offering here is another example of that effort to negotiate extremes by looking beyond traditional theological sources for meaning. The examples I offer constitute a liberating theology, if not a liberation theology in the academic sense. As Carolyn Jones defines it, theology "is a story about relationship: to self, to community, to nature, and to whatever we consider sacred. . . . [It] begins with located, experiencing subjects telling stories, individually and/or in community, about the meaning of our movements through time and space and about what we believe orients us as we move" (243).

The stories of the slave narrative tradition function in the way Jones sets forth: They dramatize, allegorize, and illuminate the insights offered by liberation theologians, putting flesh and blood on abstract formulations. These texts supply concrete illustrations of praxis so critical in articulating the need for liberation, but they also provide expressions of the will to achieve liberation in its fullest sense: to endure beyond mere survival and to create. Resisting the tendency to circumscribe black life within the experiences of suffering and rebellion is important if one is to appreciate how the slave narrative tradition functions theologically.

If the "content of liberation," as Victor Anderson asserts, is "cultural fulfillment," not just surviving and enduring but creating and appreciating, then liberation theologians need to engage in cultural criticism that "will be both enlightening and emancipatory" (18). Although Anderson does not specify what he perceives to constitute cultural fulfillment, I am proposing that the slave narrative tradition stands as one example of the kind of fulfillment to which his cultural criticism could aim. Because storytelling, as Ralph Ellison observes, "is in itself a small though necessary action in the Negro struggle for freedom" (*Shadow and Act* 142), the storytelling of the slave narrative tradition can be seen as a canon of sacred literature that gives artistic expression to what James Cone calls "the art of survival" (*God of the Oppressed* 2).

African-American theologies of liberation can be extended to serve a wider purpose in advancing social justice if we describe them as liberating theologies that are inclusive of new forms, functions, and messengers. More often than not, people "first perform religiously and then rationalize the process by way of theology" (Rambo 114), and how they perform religiously is often by exercising their imaginations, not by trying to understand God but by encountering God or some essence of divinity that gives meaning and purpose to their lives. As Charles Long reminds us, theology arises out of religion, and often outside the normative framework of Christian theology and apologetics. When we consider that people other than self-proclaimed theologians are "participants in doing theology," then we must also accept that theology must "take other shapes than that of systematic treatises." The "new and appropriate forms" created by nontheologians can "enrich the content and perspectives of theology" (Amirthan 4).

For more than a century, artists working within the slave narrative tradition have been drawing on imaginative, symbolic, and creative language expressed in a variety of modes that relates their own concrete conditions to the cause of liberation. They have been creating on the level of religious consciousness and producing new cultural forms by which to reveal the transformative potential of the creative process. Although performing and identifying themselves as artists, they are also perceiving and reflecting theologically on the world. Their experiential testimonies, when shaped by the imagination, become textimonies and are as authentic as any systematic theology in addressing issues pertinent to liberation.

My aim is to show the creative and powerful link between cultural production and religious expression and to demonstrate that cultural production and religious expression are interconnected and dependent in ways that can move communities toward liberation because they foster a creative imagining of possibility. The link is not just religion per se, or even the fact that black religion could be argued to have a special performative element that suits it to function as a gloss on many differing works of cultural production. Rather, a liberating theology, in a whole spectrum of ways, has been an animating feature of African-American expression from the time of slavery to the present day, particularly in the exhortation and historical recovery within the slave narrative tradition.

Part of my motive in exploring a relationship between the slave narrative tradition and liberation theology is a desire to shift the terms of theological discourse to a new site. Rather than bringing a preordained theological system to bear on cultural production, I hope to show that our cultural life shapes how people theologically reflect on reality and to suggest that the forms in which artists cast their theological reflections may be more effective in advancing social justice because they are more inclusive. The religious and spiritual undertones of cultural production are connected to formal liberation theology in that they recognize social transformation as connected to fundamental existential questions. Both require liberation on individual and communal levels and in actual and transcendent realms of experience.

As the primary model for liberating textimonies, the slave narrative tradition embodies a feature often neglected in theological discourse: a principle that prioritizes the role of imagination in articulating a liberating theology and advancing social justice. Imagination is both the faculty used by an author of a liberating text and the faculty awakened in a reader. As a transformative power directed toward achieving social justice, its potential cannot be overstated. What ensues in the engagement between the author and the reader is dialectic of call and response, where both are imagining grace and experiencing the gracing of imagination.

My decision to identify imagination as one of our most valuable resources for generating tolerance and inspiring liberating action was suggested by my reading of Frederick Douglass's first narrative, in which he proclaims, "To understand it one must needs experience it, or imagine himself in similar circumstances" (144). These lines jumped out at me when I read them and stayed with me as I continued to explore different articulations of the slave narrative tradition. I began to see that promoting the process of imaginative identification was a key motive behind Douglass's (and others') development of the tradition and that this process is reflected in the continuation of the tradition. I concluded that the abomination of slavery and the ongoing implications of racism could be linked to the failure of the imagination of nonblack people who resisted seeing anyone of color as like themselves. Furthermore, I came to appreciate the ways in which the process of imaginative understanding could foster the same goals advanced by theologians of liberation. Although none of the theology I read described the process in the same way I envisioned it, as I was completing this study I found, in a slightly different context, a model for what I was trying to suggest.

In 1996 Michael Berubé, a professor of English at the University of Illinois, published *Life as We Know It: A Father, a Family, and an Exceptional Child*. In this book Berubé struggles to depart from his customary intellectual attempts to make order out of reality because life presented him with a new challenge: the birth of a son with Down's syndrome. Literary theory had trained Berubé to appreciate how "representations matter," but he viscerally absorbed this principle only when confronted with the ethical and aesthetic task of representing his son. The representation of his son mattered to Berubé because it implied a purpose: "to ask about our obligations to each other, individually and socially, and about our capacity to imagine other people. I cannot say why it is that we possess the capacity to imagine others, let alone the capacity to imagine that we might have obligations to others; nor do I know why, if we possess such things, we habitually act as if we do not." His son's life compelled Berubé to ask these questions and to assert, as Douglass did, "how crucial it is that we collectively cultivate our capacities to imagine our obligations to each other" (xix). In his account of raising his son, Berubé cannot resist the urge to theorize, to frame his experiences in a grander scheme of intellectual and social history. But by the conclusion he admits the functional principle that I have come to believe the slave narrative tradition promotes: "For some reason we don't yet understand, we seem incapable of empathizing with other humans in the abstract, and we need to have them represented to us before we can imagine what it might be like to share their feelings and their dreams" (155).

This kind of representation, which moves us to imagine another's feelings and dreams, sustains the slave narrative tradition. And these representations function like a liberating theology because of the ways in which they enable us to imagine grace. If we accept Ralph Ellison's observation that "the basic unity of human experience . . . assures us of some possibility of empathic and symbolic identification with those of other backgrounds" (*Shadow and Act* 123), we can go on to claim as necessary to and achievable for any liberating theology the aim of converting the oppressor toward a disposition of compassion and a desire to reform self and society through imaginative transformation. Slave narrative textimonies continue to advance human liberation because they reveal the oppressor to be anyone who is not conscious of the need for liberation while empowering the oppressed to understand that awakening their own imaginations and the imagination of the oppressor is necessary for any meaningful social change. Ultimately, these textimonies create a space for provisional identities to emerge, where one, in the process of becoming other, adopts a posture that allows different voices to be heard, different acts to symbolize, and different theologies to sacralize the cause of liberation.

There is a considerable body of scholarship on the slave narrative tradition and African-American theologies of liberation, and I hope this study amplifies these contributions to our cultural discourse by tracing the imaginative connections between the two. African-American theologians acknowledge their debt to their enslaved forebears and often include readings of cultural texts in their expositions of theological systems. Likewise, scholars of African-American aesthetics generally acknowledge the role of religious ideas and feelings in the production of African-American culture. But by focusing on the liberating potential and the transformative spiritual effect cultural production can have on the dominant culture as it confronts complex social issues, I hope to demonstrate that the slave narrative tradition bonds people spiritually and sociopolitically without the assistance of, or assent to, a shared belief in a Christian god but also without abnegating a belief in spiritual transformation. The slave narrative tradition can be read as the phenomenological embodiment of a liberating theology that affirms the transcendent potential and fulfilling force of human imagination.

The larger meanings and implications of this work therefore involve a consideration of how liberation theologies can be expanded to include a broader representation of humanity: not just the self-described oppressed and those who share a particular theological (Christian) perspective, but those who, though not experiencing the same conditions of oppression or professing the same faith, may also be partners in the cause of liberation. For liberation, as I conceive it here, is not simply black liberation from bondage or segregation; it is also white and black liberation from racism. As a nonblack who is committed to social justice, I have found in the slave narrative tradition a point of entry into the experience of others who have not enjoyed the entitlements I have received simply because I was born to white parents. So this work stands as my response to the call I heard from the slave narrative tradition. As an attempt to "clarify reality" and "to envision possibility" (Werner xviii), the process of call and response so fundamental to African-American culture is laden with social and theological implications. It enables individuals and communities to define themselves and to validate their experiences while supporting a vision of diversity.

In some respects, I am proposing that the slave narrative tradition supports a pedagogical function similar to the one set forth by Paulo Freire in his classic text *Pedagogy of the Oppressed*. Freire proposes a concept not unlike Douglass's imaginative formulation when he writes, "Solidarity requires that one enter into the situation of those with whom one is solidary; it is a radical posture" because "the oppressor is solidary with the oppressed only when he stops regarding the oppressed as an abstract category and sees them as persons who have been unjustly dealt with, deprived of their voice, cheated in the sale of their labor—when he stops making pious, sentimental, and individualistic gestures and risks an act of love" (31–32).

Although "certain members of the oppressor class" have played an important role when they "join the oppressed in their struggle for liberation," even when "they cease to be exploiters or indifferent spectators or simply the heirs of exploitation and move to the side of the exploited, they almost always bring with them the marks of their origin: their prejudices and their deformations" (42). As Freire maintains, those who authentically commit themselves to liberation must "re-examine themselves constantly" to "enter into communion" or undergo a "conversion . . . so radical as not to allow of ambiguous behavior" because "conversion to the people requires a profound rebirth. Those who undergo it must take on a new form of existence; they can no longer remain as they were. Only through comradeship with the oppressed can the converts understand their characteristic ways of living and behaving, which in diverse moments reflect the structure of domination" (42–43). This kind of change and reimagining of identity, religious in character and degree, is fostered by the slave narrative tradition.

By tracing connections between cultural production and religious beliefs and functions, I hope to enliven conversation between those engaged in theological discourse and cultural studies. I also hope my discussion of examples from different aesthetic genres—narrative (autobiographical and fictional), dramatic (performance), visual (conceptual), and musical (jazz)—will contribute to a broader understanding of specific issues by showing how art functions to reflect and to transform society, based on a particular vision of self and other. I have not set out to criticize or correct those who engage in systematic liberation theology. By linking the work of twentieth-century writers, artists, and performers to a historical tradition and a more recent sociospiritual movement, I hope to endow the slave narrative tradition with a contemporary resonance and to ground the liberation theology movement in a historical matrix. Simply put, I wish to demonstrate that much of what liberation theologians are attempting to do is also being done elsewhere and that their own systems of thought and their own theological and historical principles already validate, to some degree, the work being done by those who do not identify themselves as theologians.

Likewise, because I am more interested in exploring processes than in establishing foundations or advancing a theory, this study is not intended to be a definitive statement about what constitutes the slave narrative tradition. It simply provides several examples of the many ways in which the tradition functions in contemporary cultural and religious discourse and recognizes patterns consistent with liberation theology and the slave narrative tradition. Both emerged from the crucible of oppression and used conventional and customary Christian language and imagery to express ideas about liberation. Both also began not as systematic programs of analysis but as imaginative reflections on experience. But as society moved further from the actual experience and memory of slavery, its invocation in theology and art became less literal and more figurative, serving a metaphorical and symbolic function rather than being an actual indictment of current conditions.

Corresponding to this movement, liberation theology developed into a systematic and academic enterprise that was more removed from direct experience while the slave narrative tradition created new forms of expression that complicated the basic issues it tried to illuminate. At the same time, both enterprises began to broaden their scope, to move beyond often restrictive Christian categories to include a larger spiritual vocabulary that reflected a broad range of black experience. My experience with both the slave narrative tradition and liberation theology instructs me that there is no fundamental contradiction between humanist traditions and theology. Human creative action is a way to come to understand God or whatever one identifies as sacred, and theology is most intelligible and useful when it gives benediction to the creative life.

In choosing the works that I discuss here, I came across a wealth of material that made the selection very difficult. The especially productive literary slave narrative tradition is overwhelming in its scope and variety. In addition to the scores of ex-slave testimonies gathered by historians and folklorists after the war, autobiographies that were not produced as part of the originating genre but emerged from the slave narrative tradition soon after emancipation are numerous and include Elizabeth Keckley's *Behind the Scenes* (1868), Booker T. Washington's *Up from Slavery* (1901), and William Pickens's *Bursting Bonds* (1923). These and other textimonies set the stage for the novelistic treatments of slavery that could continue to be written even though the author had not experienced first-hand the ordeal of slavery.

Nineteenth-century novels of slavery include one by a founder of the tradition, Frederick Douglass, who, in addition to writing three versions of his autobiography, also wrote the novella *Heroic Slave* (1853). His effort was joined by William Wells Brown's *Clotel; or the President's Daughter: A Narrative of Slave Life in the United States* (1853), Frank J. Webb's *The Garies and Their Friends* (1857), Martin Delaney's *Blake; or the Huts of America* (1859), Harriet E. Wilson's *Our Nig* (1859), James Howard's *Bond and Free* (1866), and Frances E. W. Harper's *Iola Leroy* (1892). Early twentieth-century examples include Arna Bontemps's historical romances *Black Thunder* (1936) and *Drums at Dusk* (1939).

In her essay "Negotiating between Tenses: Witnessing Slavery After Free-dom—*Dessa Rose,*" Deborah McDowell remarks, "Judging from the flood of recent novels about slavery by black Americans, Ralph Ellison is not amiss in remarking that 'the Negro American consciousness is not a prod-uct of a will to historical forgetfulness'" (144). McDowell argues that the emergence of "neoslave narratives" gathered momentum especially after the 1960s; following the publication of Margaret Walker's *Jubilee* (1966), "novels about slavery have appeared at an unstoppable rate" (144). This momentum also characterizes the simultaneous production and develop-ment of academic African-American liberation theologies. The literary treatments include Ishmael Reed's *Flight to Canada* (1976), Barbara Chase-Riboud's *Sally Hemmings* (1979), Octavia Butler's *Kindred* (1979), Charles Johnson's *The Oxherding Tale* (1982) and *Middle Passage* (1990), Sherley Anne Williams's *Dessa Rose* (1984), Toni Morrison's *Beloved* (1987), Louise Meriwether's *Fragments of the Ark* (1994), and Lorene Cary's *The Price of a Child* (1995). McDowell observes that even novels by black Americans that "do not focus exclusively on slavery or use it as a significant point of departure, stage characters' necessary confrontation with some story about slavery" (162), as in Paule Marshall's *Praisesong for the Widow* (1983) and Gayl Jones's *Corregidora* (1975).

This staggering list does not even include treatments of slavery in other literary forms, such as poetry or drama. Poetry is not discussed in detail in my study, but its scope and power in representing the slave narrative tradition in works by Melvin Tolson, Robert Hayden, and Michael Har-per constitute an important contribution. Although I do discuss one dra-matist, Anna Deavere Smith, many others could be included. Robert O'Hara's *Insurrection: Holding History* and Robbie McCauley's *Sally's Rape* are recent innovative theater productions that use slavery as a source for dramatic interpretation. And if one goes outside the territory of liter-ary production, as I have done in several examples, the list is even longer.

A discussion of the slave narrative tradition as told in music alone could command an entire volume, spanning musical forms from shout songs to reggae and including Wynton Marsalis's Pulitzer Prize–winning epic ora-torio, *Blood on the Fields,* and Anthony Davis's opera *Amistad. Roots* began television's interest in the topic of slavery, but since then the medium has presented many plays and films on the topic, and slavery was even incorporated as a motive for a contemporary crime in an episode of the weekly series *Homicide.* Alvin Ailey's *Revelations,* Bill T. Smith's *Still/Here,* and Savion Glover and George C. Wolfe's *Bring in 'Da Noise, Bring in 'Da Funk* are dance pieces that further extend the tradition; in film, recent works such as Julie Dash's *Daughters of the Dust,* Haile Germia's *Sankofa,* and Charles Burnette's *Nightjohn* are important expressions of the slave narrative tradition. All of these textimonies assume the same function McDowell ascribes to contemporary novels of slavery. They "witness slavery after freedom in order to engrave that past on the memory of the present but, more importantly, on future generations that might otherwise succumb to the cultural amnesia that has begun to re-enslave us all in social and literary texts that impoverish our imaginations" (160–61).

It is clear from this brief rehearsal of cultural production that there is astonishing breadth to the influence of the slave narrative, and in most instances some version of African-American religious thought has exerted a pervasive and formative pressure on that influence. In deciding which texts or cultural productions best nourish our imaginations, I selected those with a strong narrative component that, however ambitiously expressed, nonetheless depended on some literary text for full expression. I also resorted to the principle of the author's prerogative: I chose the works that I felt most qualified to discuss and that best advanced the theological aesthetic I was trying to establish.

To accomplish my goal of articulating a specific vision of human liberation, I have had to set aside some pertinent issues that would have made my analysis unwieldy. I especially regret that this study does not include a fuller discussion of issues pertinent to women as they work within the slave narrative tradition to advance human liberation. I hope in a future study to focus exclusively on the female slave narrative tradition and to make considerable use of the burgeoning field of womanist thought. That I have not done so here does not indicate a lack of interest in the special concerns of women; it simply indicates my limitations as a scholar. I hope that by including for discussion the work of one female playwright and a novel told from the perspective of a woman, I have made it clear that any discussion of human liberation necessarily includes women.

Imagining Grace begins with a discussion of the landmark works of Frederick Douglass and Toni Morrison that cast shadows forward and backward over all representations of the slave narrative tradition. Although the two exclusively literary texts I consider have obvious precedents in the slave narratives themselves, in the three chapters where I discuss contemporary texts that are not exclusively literary, the final section is reserved for a discussion of an example from the genre under consideration that establishes a precedent for the work being examined. The titles of each chapter are taken from comments made by the artists that situate the work under consideration in the larger context of their moral aesthetic. Furthermore, in each instance, the active verbs I selected to describe their efforts underscore a foundational principle of this study: that each artist is not a passive observer but a vital participant in effecting liberating change. Moreover, privileging of the verb "linguistically accentuates action among people whose ability to act is curtailed by racial constraints" (Mackey 79) and has long been a strategy for African-American empowerment. This same rationale supports my decision to describe these works as liberating theologies rather than theologies of liberation.

Finally, the text is structured in such a way as to implicitly move toward inclusiveness, to make an actual space for those who, though not people of color, have chosen to adopt the radical posture Freire outlines. It begins with an examination of the basic issues that support my analysis of specific works. I explore what we mean when we invoke the principle of imagination as a transformative tool for effecting social change and the problems that arise when one applies this principle to a discussion of slavery and its effects. I also explore the origins and functions of the slave narrative tradition as it has developed over time, delineating the features that highlight a theological or liberation agenda. To this offering I add a selective reading of developments in liberation theology that reinforce the connections I am trying to establish. Here I draw special attention to contemporary theologians who invite reflection in nontraditional or non-Christian ways and who appreciate the role of cultural production in advancing social justice.

My analysis of specific works begins with the autobiography of Richard Wright, whose work is most directly linked to the original source of slave narratives. His autobiography is the most stridently racialized example I offer because it directly indicts the consciousness of nonblack oppressors in a raw and unsparing assessment of racial oppression. Wright's *Black Boy* is a lengthy diatribe against the oppression of a racist society and a stifling and cowardly religion. Wright's recognition of his position in a racist society becomes evident when as a child he makes what he describes as an "emotional" connection between white and black. Wright's complicated and disturbing autobiography gives many examples of those who do not live in deed their religious creed, yet he is no less harsh in evaluating the duplicity of blacks than he is in assessing white failures. By virtue of his writerly extensions, Wright moves the slave narrative tradition away from simple reportage to imaginative reconstruction. His painful journey toward selfhood is one way he attempts to "affirm the unity" of humanity.

Wright's text also reminds us of two important points. One is that despite the de facto end of slavery promised by the Emancipation Proclamation, slavery of a kind continued to exist in America, constantly mutating into new forms of oppression that continued to function like the "peculiar institution." But Wright's text also reminds us of the rejoinder to this fact, articulated by R. Baxter Miller in the following way: "Whenever African American literary art has lost the Emancipation Proclamation as the metaphor from which to face existence, the writing has floundered for lack of imaginative power" (1156).

Juxtaposed to Wright's "fictionalized" autobiography is Ernest Gaines's "autobiographized" fiction, *The Autobiography of Miss Jane Pittman,* a novel cast in autobiographical form that makes a logical connection between the novels that treat slavery and the original autobiographies that engendered the slave narrative tradition. Gaines's text highlights the movement toward inclusion because he personalizes an essential component of liberation that Wright leaves as an abstraction: the presence of a sustaining and cooperative community. The novel faithfully recounts the life of oppression of its black characters from slavery to the civil rights era, but it also celebrates moments of grace and community. Our identification with Miss Jane is accomplished in part because Gaines creates a narrator who, like the readers, listens as Miss Jane witnesses to not just her history, but the history of a people. What Gaines does not specify is the racial identity of his narrator, who has sought the opportunity to record Miss Jane's testimony. This deliberate ambiguity both reinforces and challenges conventions that uphold the slave narrative tradition. Through his protagonist Gaines transforms a private, interior experience into a public, community-building experience and testifies to the many ways in which we can "remember the truth." Gaines's subtle rebuke of white oppression nonetheless acknowledges the complexities of white-black dynamics and shared complicity in oppression and tentatively moves toward reconciliation.

Following Gaines I present the work of the conceptual artist Glenn Ligon, whose use of literary models for visual work demonstrates how even this far into the century, African Americans are still dealing with the legacy of slavery. Ligon has repeatedly turned to sources from the canon of African-American literature to create his multimedia work and, centuries after the Middle Passage, to demonstrate how African Americans are still trying "to disembark." A discussion of the multimedia and multicultural tradition from which Ligon's work emerges is also included. Ligon's art, though deeply personal like the writings of Wright and Gaines, has an intellectual force and analytical power that directly address issues of racial construction. Ligon uses narrative construction in a deconstructive manner to address broader issues of racial identity and construction. Furthermore, he complicates the issues by invoking the additional element of sexual orientation, at one point suggesting, not unlike Freire, that love is where one begins to deconstruct the social structures that so dominate our understanding of who we are, racially and otherwise.

The kind of textimony embodied in the slave narrative tradition is further developed by Anna Deavere Smith, a playwright and performer who stages one-woman shows that use the direct testimony of people in conflict to explore the issues that led to such events and to reveal ways we can "negotiate the differences." Smith's work is supported by a discussion of the Free Southern Theatre that serves as an early model and cautionary tale for what she attempts. Smith takes Ligon's ideas of racial construction even further when she represents on stage the voices of not just African Americans but many nonblacks and other people of color. While reaffirming the role black testimony has played in the slave narrative tradition, this African-American woman transforms herself into any number of racial, social, and sexual identities, revealing not just how to interrogate and break down the social structures that confine us, but also how to begin building new ones. Smith understands that in contemporary American society, being human means being multicultural.

Charlie Haden, the only nonblack artist included for consideration, is a jazz composer and bassist who gathers together in his multiracial and multicultural Liberation Music Orchestra musicians and music culled from various international incidents of fighting for freedom to make a musical statement about how to initiate and celebrate liberating change. The African-American origins of this kind of musical response to oppression are explored in a discussion of the spirituals, a form Haden honors in his recent collaboration with the black pianist Hank Jones. My choice to conclude this study with Haden may indict my own praxis in this effort, but I believe it is historically and theologically sanctioned and provides me the opportunity to accomplish several aims of this study.

First among them is to articulate the role of nonblacks in the slave narrative tradition. Haden functions as white amanuenses and editors did for ex-slave narrators. Haden's Liberation Music Orchestra helps to amplify voices that often go unheard. In this way my study circles back to its origins, a movement also represented by my discussion of the form of American music in which a liberation agenda was first expressed, the spirituals, whose creation actually preceded the slave narrative tradition. I support this decision based on my encounter with radical scholar Herbert Aptheker's study of American abolitionism. In *Abolitionism: A Revolution-*

ary Movement, Aptheker does not hesitate to acknowledge nonblack contributions to the movement.

Aptheker's most formidable example, John Brown, is one that most are not likely to emulate, yet his characterization of Brown is in harmony with the goals of the slave narrative tradition and liberation theology. Brown, Aptheker asserts, "was extraordinary—perhaps unique—in the completeness with which he, his wife Mary Brown, and their children shed concepts and feelings of white supremacy." Aptheker goes on to note that this accomplishment on the part of Brown and his family was "the result of deliberate practice, so that, by word as well as by consistent deed, the Browns not only advocated but lived equality" (123). As Brown wrote in his final statement just before his execution, he was inspired by biblical concepts of justice—the same ones that fired Nat Turner—that taught him "to remember them." Because of his direct identification with the oppressed, Brown can go on to assert, "I believe that to have interfered as I have done, as I have always freely admitted I have done, In behalf of His despised poor, I did no wrong but right" (132).

Although some might argue that recalling John Brown and including Charlie Haden in an analysis of the slave narrative tradition extends the category to the point where it becomes meaningless, this is where my second aim becomes apparent. It is my contention that ideally performed, the slave narrative tradition works toward its own extinction. A provisional step toward ensuring that the conditions of liberation will be so manifest that there will be no slave tradition to narrate involves the inclusion of nonblack voices that echo the imperatives of the tradition and work toward establishing its goals. I see the promise of reconciliation as fully embodied not just in Haden's collaboration with Jones but in Haden's overall posture as a nonblack who performs the music of many people of color while still acknowledging his own entitlements. He takes the transformative potential embodied in Anna Deavere Smith's theater one step further, demonstrating not just how to act in solidarity but how to be solidary. He is radical in the most liberating sense and invites other nonblacks to appreciate what his model can accomplish. Haden's appearance at the conclusion of this study circles back not only to the role nonblacks played in the development of the tradition, but to Douglass's imperative: One can imagine grace because one has imagined slavery.

Even in his most strident early formulation of black theology, *Black Theology and Black Power*, James Cone concludes by considering the role of reconciliation in a theology of liberation. He reminds us that "being black in America has very little to do with skin color. To be black means that your heart, your soul, your mind, and your body are where the dispossessed are" (151). The texts that make up a slave narrative tradition in American arts and letters help us to be precisely where Cone urges us to go—"where the dispossessed are"—and to become, as the authors of these textimonies might suggest, "black like me." The desire to move people to this place of being inspires the slave narrative tradition and extends the work of liberation theology. Through the imaginative leap, as much as the leap of faith, differences can be bridged—not obliterated but crossed over—to produce a renewal of identification with another and a reenvisioning of oneself.

1 Imagining Grace

> While some critics will cry that the American civilization
> is bound to crumble like the tower of Babel from a
> plethora of tongues chattering, we will go on speaking,
> acknowledging that difference encountering difference is
> the American destiny.
> —Thulani Davis

In *Fridays with Red,* National Public Radio host Bob Edwards's affectionate memoir of his friendship with legendary sports broadcaster Red Barber, Edwards includes a chapter titled "Robinson." In this chapter he painfully recounts Barber's confrontation with his own racism, effected by the bold act of Brooklyn Dodgers's general manager Branch Rickey when in 1947 he selected Jackie Robinson to be the first black player in the major leagues. The choice of Robinson was deliberate on Rickey's part. In Jackie Robinson he found a person of singular character and unparalleled athletic talent who had the strength and poise necessary to endure the inevitable criticism, humiliation, and even violence that he would experience in this social drama. But Rickey's decision to integrate the major leagues was the result of an experience he had long before he met Jackie Robinson. Rickey told Barber the story that moved him to act, and this story helped Red Barber overcome his racist beliefs.

In 1904 Rickey was coach of the Ohio Wesleyan University baseball team. His catcher, Charley Thomas, was the only black player on the team. One night, as the team was checking into a hotel in Indiana, the desk clerk would not allow Thomas to register, although he eventually allowed him to take the second bed in Rickey's room. After saying goodnight to the other players, Rickey retired to his room to find Charley Thomas weeping and pulling at his hands while exclaiming, "It's my skin, Mr. Rickey, it's my skin. If I could just pull it off, I'd be like everybody else" (Edwards 90). For forty-one years Rickey could not erase the image of Charley Thomas trying to pull off his skin, so he vowed that once he was in a position of power he would do something to address the racism that led to his suffering.

Red Barber's first response was to quit broadcasting rather than cover a game with a black athlete on the field. But after reflecting on Rickey's story, Barber decided to stay and eventually announced Robinson's entrance in the lineup as he would for any other player, not remarking on his racial identity. The narratives of Thomas, Rickey, and Robinson changed Red Barber; they "made me think," as he succinctly put it. From that moment on he refused to blindly accept the values of his Southern upbringing and became, in the words of the black coach of football at Florida A&M, Jake Gaither, "a converted white man—by that I mean a white man who has made up his mind to be fair." In Gaither's estimation, such a man is "the best friend a black man can have" (Edwards 95).

Whether Gaither's pronouncement about converted white men is ultimately true, his recognition of the transformation that can occur when an entitled white man finally comes to reflect honestly on his condition and how that condition is sustained by the oppression of others points us in an important direction. Having grown up in the South, Barber must have been aware of racial differences, but like many he did not see these differences as equivalent but as hierocratic, allowing him to accept passively the status quo. Many other people react more aggressively to difference, however. They enact defensive postures to enslave or destroy the otherness that so radically challenges their complacency. Even when whites or others in entitled positions preach racelessness as true, they are often blind to how they passively reap the spoils of whiteness while communities of color must struggle to forge cultures of resistance in order to protect their hard-won identity based on race.

Becoming a "converted white man" is not solely a intellectual process. The power of personal narratives and compelling images that effect not just a recognition of difference but an understanding of the experience of difference can "make us think." Although Barber described his process of reevaluation in rational terms, another aspect of his consciousness was surely touched by Rickey's story: his imagination. It took a story for him to change his mind—a simple narrative that described the effects of racism not by argument, but in the poignant image of a young man wishing to remove his black skin. Barber used his imagination to take the perspective of Charley Thomas, an other self. Although in the process he risked the stability of his own self, the resulting destabilization of his formerly rigid identity led to the creation of a new, more tolerant and flexible self.

Barber, in his quiet acceptance of Jackie Robinson as a major league player, and Rickey, in his use of the power available to him, show us ways in which our encounters with difference can lead to meaningful change. For it is not just the encounter with difference that matters but what one does after the encounter.

It is the force of this kind of imaginative response, on the part of Thomas in articulating his suffering and on the part of Rickey and Barber in seeing his suffering and responding to it, that I want to explore here. Although my discussion focuses on black/white relations, much of what I present can illuminate similar instances in which one who enjoys social, cultural, political, or economic entitlement comes to understand the experiences of those who are not so entitled and willingly surrenders his or her intolerant assumptions for a more enlightened perspective. Blackness, even in African-American theology, is not a restrictive term. Rather, blackness encompasses all who are oppressed, whether for reasons of gender, race, or class, and all who take sides with the oppressed by joining with body as well as mind in the struggle for liberation.

In an early formulation of his liberation theology, James Cone uses "blackness" symbolically and metaphorically to represent all victims of oppression (*Black Theology of Liberation* 28). As he writes, "the focus on blackness does not mean that only blacks suffer as victims in a racist society, but that blackness is an ontological symbol of a visible reality which best describes what oppression means in America. . . . Blackness, then stands for all victims of oppression who realize that their humanity is inseparable from man's liberation from whiteness" (*Black Theology of Liberation* 27). Similarly, in his preface to *Black Like Me,* John Howard Griffin warns his readers that although his experiences explored one particular site and historical incidence of intolerance, "the real story is the universal one of men who destroy the souls and bodies of other men (and in the process destroy themselves) for reasons neither really understands. It is the story of the persecuted, the defrauded, the feared and detested. I could have been Jew in Germany, a Mexican in a number of states, or a member of any 'inferior' group. Only the details would have differed. The story would be the same."

Nonetheless, because of the history of the Atlantic slave trade, the dominant paradigm for racism in America remains the black/white dichotomy, as former senator Bill Bradley recognized when he remarked that just "as slavery was our original sin, so race remains our unresolved dilemma" ("Talk of the Town"). Slavery remains the root division in American culture, but its effects are complicated by Alice Walker's observation that all of us are, on some level, "not only the descendants of slaves but also of slave *owners*. And that just as we have had to struggle to rid ourselves of slavish behavior, we must as ruthlessly eradicate any desire to be mistress or 'master'" (*Living by the Word* 80).

The tendency to assume a posture of mistress or master—to unwittingly reinscribe paradigms of authority—can emerge even in the most well-intentioned manner, which is why Martin Luther King offered a model for resolving the American dilemma that held forth black Americans as the agents or characters through which America redeems itself as a nation. King believed that African Americans should act on behalf of their own liberation to convert the unconverted, to wake white America from its entitled slumber, but he also believed that by example, by setting forth images that denote character and a shared humanity, African Americans could persuade others to accept that each person is a full and entitled member of the human community.

Although the disenfranchised do not exist or create solely to move the wicked toward righteousness, the byproduct of living a righteous life and expressing such values in creative endeavors may be the conversion of others. For King and other Christians who embody a theology of liberation, the decisive element in effecting transformation is God. Scripture reveals to them that God is the agent who allows a righteous life to become a redemptive force. But shifting the responsibility to God may leave a moral loophole for otherwise good souls to avoid engaging in liberating acts; also, claiming God as the primary power effecting redemption excludes those who do not assent to God's saving grace from vital participation in liberating acts.

Looking beyond scripture, one discovers in the American canon a slave narrative tradition, stories of liberation that, without promoting a particular theological belief, still function to engage people in redemptive acts. From the antebellum testimonial narratives of ex-slaves to the contemporary photographic portraits of the civil rights era, powerful stories and compelling images drawn from the American experience bespeak the cause of liberation with the hope of raising the consciousness of the American public. They are all part of a tradition that transmits and alters culture for purposes of resistance, survival, and creation and represent various attempts over time to extend, elaborate, and refine the imperatives of African Americans first identified in the context of slavery.

The slave narrative tradition is distinguished primarily by how the trope of slavery functions in evocative ways to turn people toward a perspective that inspires a liberation lifestyle. All this compiled textimony becomes a canon of sacred texts—with all the authority and responsibility accorded sacred texts—for any oppressed people and answers the questions Ralph Ellison rhetorically addressed to a well-intentioned but misguided Irving Howe: "How does the Negro writer participate *as a writer* in the struggle for human freedom? To whom does he address his work? What values emerging from Negro experience does he try to affirm?" (*Shadow and Act* 113). For despite social developments and new trends in theological investigation and aesthetic expression, what has not changed in several centuries of searching for answers and fighting for change is the remarkable evocative power of the image of slavery, the hold it continues to have on our imagination and the service to which countless artist and theologians put it in arguing for the liberation of the oppressed. What I want to do, therefore, is to explore a few representative examples of the discourse of slavery, to show how it engages and affects the same issues liberation theologians address and how it does so through the exercise of imagination and its redemptive potential.

In the foreword to *The Discourse of Slavery: Aphra Behn to Toni Morrison*, Isobel Armstrong notes that "the accounts of race and nation that were implicated in the institution of slavery have not disappeared in a grand narrative which charts emancipation. On the contrary, the metaphors and categories intrinsic to the post-enlightenment imagination, and which shaped the slavery debate, are present in our own thought" (Plasa and Ring xi). The service to which the discourse of slavery can be put is complicated by the problematics of "thinking and imagining the unspeakable nature of slavery for those who have not been slaves as well as for those who have" (xi).

Attempts to appropriately describe or, more perilously, to imagine the unspeakable can lead to the tendency to universalize or misrepresent the condition of slavery. Novelist Martin Amis encountered this problem when writing *Time's Arrow,* a novel about the Holocaust. Like American slavery, the Holocaust has shaped our perspective on reality in metaphorical and categorical ways. Because he is not a Holocaust survivor, or even a Jew, in the essay "Blown Away" Amis describes how he wrestled with the "carapace of verisimilitude" in seeking an artistic passage to the Holocaust: "Nearing the Holocaust, a trespasser finds that his imagination is decently absenting itself, and reaches for documentation and technique. The last thing he wants to do, once there, is make anything up" (48). Yet his imagination is the only way Amis (indeed, most of us) can find a point of entry into understanding events such as the Holocaust or American slavery.

Balancing the requirement for honorable documentation with the aesthetic attempt to understand is addressed by Betty Ring and Carl Plasa when they assert that the discourse of slavery can be an effective way to explore ongoing power valences only if one recognizes his or her own context and appreciates reading as a political act of intervention, determined by and consequential for the moment in which it is performed. By doing such one will better understand history not as thing of the past but as a reflective act with a crucial role in any attempt to counteract oppression in the present. The discourse of slavery can allow us to speak about history of ideologies and to examine how differences are constructed because like the Holocaust, slavery is a brutal, systematic, and far-reaching example. Slavery as a discourse can function as a medium for understanding and articulating other power structures because of the imaginative potential that resides in the metaphorics of mastery and enslavement.

Problems inherent in the discourse of slavery find recent examples all across the country, where the representation of slavery and its metaphoric potential remains an explosive issue. Examples that have caught the public's attention include a debate over white director Steven Spielberg's film about the *Amistad* mutiny, debate over whether schools bearing the name of slaveholders should be renamed and the ensuing revision of historical figures such as Thomas Jefferson, the desire of fans at Old Miss to keep waving the Confederate battle flag at sporting events, and the complaint that the nation's capital has a museum honoring Europeans who died in the Holocaust but no museum or memorial commemorating those who suffered under slavery. But it is in the realm of education—in schools and museums—where the issue becomes particularly explosive and painful.

In 1994, Colonial Williamsburg's curator in charge of the African-American research department staged a slave auction as part of a living history program. Protesters saw the event as a "degradation" and "trivialization" of their heritage, despite the curator's insistence that she was simply trying to "put a face to what happened." In 1995, a school in Conroe, Texas banned Ernest Gaines's novel *The Autobiography of Miss Jane Pittman* from a seventh-grade class focused on "prejudice reduction." Despite one white student's claim that it was the best novel she had ever read to help her "understand the plight of someone who'd been mistreated, who doesn't have privileges," many black parents complained because of racial epithets used by the author.

Even the employees at the Library of Congress rebelled and succeeded in shutting down before it was open to the public a scheduled exhibition, "Back of the Big House: The Cultural Landscape of the Plantation." Drawn from the library's own archives, the exhibit was intended to show, in the words of curator John Michael Vlach, "what was beyond the fence of the Big House garden," specifically the quarters inhabited by enslaved African Americans. But the employees who described feeling "offended," "outraged," and "upset" by the exhibit refused to accept scholarly explanations and the exhibit moved on to its next scheduled location. Most controversial of all, perhaps, was the Walt Disney Company's intention in the late 1980s to build a historic theme park that would include an exhibits that would "make you feel what it was like to be a slave." Criticism of the project—from letters to the governor to editorial page essays—swelled to the point that Disney executives admitted they hadn't anticipated how "emotionally charged" the subject would be.[1]

Most of the criticism leveled at these events came from African Americans. In an essay describing Colonial Williamsburg's incorporation of representations of slave life into its living history program, Rex Ellis reports that from the beginning this and other institutions had difficulty enlisting the aid of African Americans "to help tell the story," a phenomenon Ellis attributes to the fact that "like everyone else, African Americans want to talk about the *virtues* of their culture" and the weary resignation that "contemporary reality [is] a sufficient reminder that the psychological and physical horrors of slavery are still with us" (22). Ellis also reports that most African Americans he observed displayed obvious "discomfort" and many walked away before hearing the presentations. This discomfort extended to black employees of Colonial Williamsburg.[2] Even as living history programs became an expected event at most museums, "the obstacles associated with living in the skin of a slave continued—no matter how accepted the mode of presentation" (24). However, Ellis continues to affirm the importance of representing slavery in terms of characters, asserting that "there are few things more rewarding than watching that light of understanding flick on in the visitors' minds when they have witnessed an informative, stimulating, even provocative portrayal" (25).

The question these incidents raise is not just how or whether slavery should be represented and discussed, but who in power is dictating the course of the discussion and inventing the forms of slavery's representation—who, in the words of Rex Ellis, "put[s] on the skins of their ancestors" (25). Because the original texts of the slave narrative tradition were written by people who had witnessed and experienced first-hand the horrors they documented, the quality of testimony or witness has been established as a criterion for evaluating the effectiveness and credibility of attempts to represent slavery. In 1853, ex-slave narrator Solomon Northup (whose narrative was ghostwritten by a white lawyer named David Wilson) summed up this position when he wrote,

> There may be humane masters, as there certainly are inhuman ones—there may be slaves well-clothed, well-fed and happy, as there surely are those half-clad, half-starved and miserable. . . . Men may write fictions portraying lowly life as it is, or as it is not—may expatiate with owlish gravity upon the bliss of ignorance—discourse flippantly from arm chairs of the pleasures of slave life; but let them toil with him in the field—sleep with him in the cabin—feed with him on husks; let them behold him scourged, hunted, trampled on, and they will come back with another story in their mouths. Let them know the heart of the poor slave—learn his secret thoughts—thoughts he dare not utter in the hearing of the white man; let them slip by him in the silent watches of the night—converse with him in trustful confidence, of 'life, liberty, and the pursuit of happiness;' and they will find that ninety-nine out of every hundred are intelligent enough to understand their situation, and to cherish in their bosoms the love of freedom, as passionately as themselves. (Davis and Gates xi)

The power of texts such as Northup's resides precisely in their documentary status, the fact that they represent to the dominant culture a first-hand proclamation of the humanity of enslaved black people. The literary tradition that emerged after formal slavery was abolished is legitimized by how it bears a "revisionary, or signifying relation of intertextuality" to the original slave narratives (Davis and Gates xiii) or how it continues to offer textimonies for the cause of liberation.

Buried in Northup's testimony is a quality that, though characteristic of the slave narrative tradition, also amplifies the function of the testimonial basis on which it draws its power. His litany of "let them know, let them toil" is an invitation to the reader to consider the act of hearing as an opportunity for engagement and understanding. It is a call not just to see what Northup saw, but to feel what he felt. A very intimate invitation and a call for identification are extended that go beyond the mere absorption of information.

Northup's self/other reference is cast in personal rather than abstract terms and structured by his perception of the complacency of unself-conscious whites and the urgency of self-aware blacks. His comment reveals that the power of the discourse of slavery lies in the way it creates opportunities for encounters—or at the very least a provisional collapse of self/other divisions—and supplies a basis for mutual reckoning wherein new, provisional identities can emerge. Northup and others participating in the slave narrative tradition understood that white America is in need of liberation, too, an issue not often explored by contemporary liberation theologians, despite Jesus' example: "Those who are well have no need of a physician but those who are sick. Go and learn what this means, 'I desire mercy, not sacrifice.' For I have come to call not the righteous but sinners" (Matthew 9:12–13).

Although academic liberation theologians may not address in full Jesus' admonition, corresponding to the slave narrative tradition is a vast textual history of white Americans describing their imaginative identification, their "black like me" moments when they came to experience something like what Red Barber and Branch Rickey felt. A recent example is provided by Edward Ball, a descendant of South Carolina slaveholders who is actively seeking out descendants of the slaves his ancestors owned in order to confront his family's collective silence about the horror of slavery.

Ball turned his own private soul-searching into public discourse about race and history in a series of programs for National Public Radio. In these programs he explored the extent to which any white American can reconcile himself or herself to and be accountable for the pained past that haunts us still. He describes his journey as going to the core of this thing called "whiteness . . . the mother story of us all" (Duke 10). Ball confronted competing narratives of American history: his own family's careful records and the unrecorded stories of slave descendants. At one point Ball ventured an apology to the descendants of slaves his family owned and then regretted it, believing his words were "arrogant" and "inadequate," all the while admitting that the sentiment continues to live within him (Duke 12).

Ball sees his enterprise as part of a larger debate that focuses on analyzing race—not just blackness but the nature of whiteness and what it signifies. "Race," he asserts, "is a masquerade; we are its players . . . whiteness speaks through me like a ventriloquist as it does through you, I think, whatever your color" (Duke 25). He comes to understand that whiteness is not the norm but "might be an 'other' thing, as unto itself as blackness" and not "simply there, like the atmosphere, as unconscious as the intake of breath." Ball locates what many critics and artists who participate in the slave narrative tradition observe: that without the other there would be nothing to distinguish whiteness; whiteness doesn't exist until it comes against difference.

Ball recalls a meeting with Thomas Martin, a descendant of a former Ball slave, as fulfillment of King's dream that one day the sons of slaves and the sons of slave owners will sit down at the table of brotherhood to carve out a sacred space of reconciliation between himself and his family's history, between the whiteness that is in him and the blackness that society has made the "other." Ball writes, "I'm trying to understand how my own identity is connected to catastrophic events of the past in American history—slavery. And rather than merely acknowledging that fact and mourning it . . . I'm trying to act on that component of my identity and transform it, I guess, to make use of it in a way that's productive" (Duke 25).

Ball's enterprise is characteristic of movements to explore racial issues in terms of not just what went wrong for blacks, but what is wrong with whites. James Baldwin was among the first to identify racism as a white problem, not a black one, citing the "willed innocence" of white Americans as that "which constitutes the crime" (*Fire* 16). Baldwin also recognized that what is wrong with whites can be traced back to antebellum times because "the truth concerning the White North American experience is to be deciphered in the hieroglyphic lashed onto the Black man's back" (*Evidence* 47). Baldwin understood that white America's inability to understand African-American oppression was a deliberate act of ignoring what it finds uncomfortable to examine. Baldwin observed that whiteness is not merely a reference to the color of skin; rather, whiteness is a "metaphor for power" and a "moral choice" (Watkins 3). Artists participating in the slave narrative tradition therefore create as both victims of "willed innocence" and responders to it. They appreciate the metaphorics of racism to the extent that they can posit art as able to function in an especially powerful, indeed coercive way, to initiate people to the realities of their experience.

Toni Morrison's *Playing in the Dark: Whiteness and the Literary Imagination* is a more recent example of the phenomena Baldwin addresses. Morrison asserts that although Americans have long considered the calamitous effects of slavery on enslaved people, there has been little serious effort to see what racial ideology does to the mind, imagination, and behavior of slaveholders. Whiteness, she demonstrates, discerns its form only against a backdrop of an imagined, mythologized, or demonized blackness. In discussing Morrison's and similar books for *The Village Voice*, Judith Levine remarks that "whiteness is the most obscure difference of all because it is not considered a difference" (11). Levine quotes Henry Louis Gates as representing the position of many scholars when he remarks, "Race is a metaphor for something else," but as she explains, race is "made concrete in language and in the social and economic relations it seeks to maintain. Reinterpreting histories of slavery and abolitionism, capital formation and labor organizing, forced migrations and immigration policy, as well as contemporary life stories and political events, these writers are figuring out where the quotation marks go around 'white' too. In so doing, they're helping to discover the shame of that 'something else'" (11).[3]

The most famous example of discovering the "shame of something else," which also popularized the compelling description of "black like me," is John Howard Griffin's book. Published in 1961, well before most manifestations of national concern about racial injustice, *Black Like Me* recounts his experimentation with altering his pigmentation and traveling in disguise as a black man in the deep South in 1959. Griffin's title is an allusion to Langston Hughes's lyric "Dream Variations" ("Night coming tenderly / Black like me") and uses the phrase to evoke a both a recognition of exclusion and a sense of spiritual inclusion. In the narrative Griffin specifically recalls Hughes's poem after a month of experiencing humiliation and fear as an African American. At this moment Griffin expands beyond the literal concerns of black and white and reflects, "At such a time, the Negro can look at the starlit skies and find that he has, after all, a place in the universal order of things. The stars, the black skies affirm his humanity, his validity as a human being. He knows that his belly, his limbs, his tired legs, his appetites, his prayers and his mind are cherished in some profound involvement with nature and God. The night is his consolation. It does not despise him" (115, 1962 edition).

In this reflection Griffin is speaking not about what he, as a journalist, has observed of African Americans, but what he has felt as a human being in assuming a black identity. In reversing the process Charley Thomas wanted to effect for himself, Griffin tried to understand what "Black men told me . . . that the only way a White man could hope to understand anything about this reality was to wake up some morning in a black man's skin" (179, 1962 edition). And so he learned "within a very few hours, that no one was judging me by my qualities as a human individual and everyone was judging me by my pigment . . . they couldn't see me or any other black man as a human individual . . . they saw us as 'different' from them in fundamental ways" (179, 1962 edition). Although Griffin began his journey as a "scientific experiment," he ended up filing the data and opting for narrative journal that traces the changes that occur to "heart and body and intelligence when a so-called first-class citizen is cast on the junkheap of second-class citizenship" (Preface).

Like many ex-slave narrators, Griffin observes the contradictions between Christian creed and deed; as he casts it, "if you want to be a good Christian, you mustn't act like one" (43, 1962 edition). He also anticipates a key element in liberation theology when he identifies not just the need for empathy between races, but the fact that it can be accomplished only when those enjoying unacknowledged privileges of the dominant culture come to understand the "truth" of black experience and that even for a "specialist in race issues" like Griffin, the only way to begin to do so was "to become a Negro" (8, 1962 edition). Griffin elaborates on this principle in later writings by using the postmodern language of "otherness" to describe his experience and the belief it engendered: "There is no *Other*, that *Other* is self" (Bonazzi 48). In a 1966 essay, "The Intrinsic Other," Griffin analyzes what was revealed in *Black Like Me* and concludes by declaring that "the wounds I had carried thirty-nine years of my life were healed within five days through the emotional experience of perceiving that the *Other* is not other at all, that the *Other* is me, that at the profound human levels, all men are united; and that the seeming differences are superficial" (Bonazzi 48).

To get to this point, he had to face his own shame at recoiling before the face of the other, even if that other was really himself with altered pigment. He had to confront the disturbing fact that despite his profound intellectual convictions about racism, his commitment to social justice was challenged when he experienced a racist response to the "other Griffin." When he first viewed himself as black, "the transformation was total and shocking. I had expected to see myself disguised, but this was something else. I was imprisoned in the flesh of an utter stranger, an unsympathetic one with whom I felt no kinship" (15, 1962 edition). Griffin experiences a dislocation of self so debilitating that he is appalled and terrified: "I felt the beginnings of great loneliness, not because I was a Negro, but because the man I had been, the self I knew, was hidden in the flesh of another" (16, 1962 edition). Yet it is precisely the death of his old self that led to a transformation more enduring than the one he embarked on for his experiment.

Griffin prophesies in the first sentence of his Preface that "this may not be all of it," and the effect of his book still resonates today in young white Americans like Joshua Solomon, who repeated the experiment some thirty years later and discovered that many of the same hostilities linger. Solomon's experiment was conceived of a latent belief that his black friends blamed everything on color. Despite his overt sympathy for his friends, "secretly, inside, I'd always felt that many black people used racism as a crutch, an excuse" (C1). During his brief experiment Solomon felt racism in the forms of suspicion, avoidance, and unaccountable fear from others and eventually realized that "we haven't come as far as I thought." In symbolic and actual ways that represent the movement of the slave narrative tradition, Solomon, upon his return from an autobiographical enterprise, attempts to better understand his experience by reading Ralph Ellison's novel *Invisible Man*.[4]

However interesting and illuminating these "black like me" moments are, they also raise some troubling questions. Among them is the issue of what constitutes "blackness" or a "black experience." Unpacking what he identifies as a concept of "ontological blackness," Victor Anderson demonstrates not just how flawed white notions of blackness can become, but how African Americans themselves have unwittingly participated in the creation of an ontological blackness that is a "mirror of European genius . . . the blackness that whiteness created" (13). Leveling his charges against the "cult of black heroic genius" that constitutes ontological blackness, Anderson urges both blacks and nonblacks to resist subscribing complete loyalty and admiration to "racial categories and the essentialized principles" that would determine black identity.

Anderson believes that by subscribing to a notion of ontological blackness, African Americans risk losing an appreciation and respect for unique individuals who populate their diverse community and nonblack people succumb to a simplistic and comfortable notion of what constitutes black life. As he explains, ontological blackness "takes narrative formations that emphasize the heroic capacities of African Americans to transcend individuality and personality in the name of black communal survival," thereby calling into question African Americans' interests in "fulfilled individuality" and leaving open for nonblacks an unrealistic point of entry into the experience of what it means to be black in America (15).

Anderson's investigation forces us to further question the dynamics of authorization and appropriation involved in a "black like me" enterprise. Ralph Ellison, in responding to white critics' enthusiasm for *Native Son* as more "true" in depicting black life that his own work *Invisible Man,* chastised them for "designating another, politically weaker, less socially acceptable, people as the receptacle for one's own self-disgust," going on to observe that such a reaction is a "crime of reducing the humanity of others to that of a mere convenience" (*Shadow and Act* 124). More recently, in her essay "The Occult of True Black Womanhood: Critical Demeanor and Black Feminist Studies," Ann DuCille draws attention to what she identifies as "The *Driving Miss Daisy* Crazy Syndrome."

Gathering examples from the published works of several white writers and academics, DuCille demonstrates how "the privileged white person inherits a wisdom, an agelessness, perhaps even a realness that entitles him or her to the raw materials of another's life and culture but, of course, not to the Other's condition." DuCille goes on to explain that such "transformative moves" often occur in the "forewords, afterwards, even apologias white scholars affix to their would-be scholarly readings of the black Other—discussions methinks just may protest too much, perhaps suggest-

ing a somewhat uneasy relationship between author and objectified subject. These prefaces acknowledge the 'outsider' status of the authors—their
privileged positions as white women or as men—even as they insist on the
rightness of their entry into and the significance of their impact on the fields
of black literature and history" (614).

The whole concept of "otherness" has been revealed by Nathaniel
Mackey to be loaded with cultural assumptions. In the essay "Other: From
Verb to Noun," Mackey explodes our comfortable assumption of cultural
diversity by reminding us that such diversity is *cultural,* that is, "a consequence of actions and assumptions which are socially—rather than naturally, genetically—instituted and reinforced" (76). He reminds us that when
we speak of otherness "we are not positing static, intrinsic attributes or
characteristics," so our efforts to promote diversity should "highlight the
dynamics of agency and attribution by way of which otherness is brought
about and maintained, the fact that *other* is something people do, more
importantly a verb than an adjective or a noun" (76).

In drawing this distinction between the grammatical qualities of "other,"
Mackey demonstrates that the process of "othering" occurs in two ways:
in the medium of society and the medium of art. Whereas artistic othering
"has to do with innovation, invention, and change, on which cultural
health and diversity depend and thrive," social othering "has to do with
power, exclusion, and privilege, the centralizing of a norm against which
otherness is measured, meted out, marginalized" (76). Mackey shows that
for the most part it is blacks who practice artistic othering while being
subjected to the social othering performed by nonblacks.

"Black like me" narratives, however well intentioned, can be construed
as a form of social othering, of appropriating the inventiveness of artistic
othering that characterizes the black tradition of textimony. "Black like
me" narratives, even this far removed from antebellum times, still recall
the custom of procuring white testimony to ensure the publication of a slave
narrative. What I want to do, therefore, is to shift my concern toward what
inspired or effected "black like me" narratives in the first place. I want to
try to identify what qualities in these narratives are also present in the tradition of slave narrative textimony that seeks to lead oppressors to a state
Alan Boesak, recalling James Baldwin, calls a "farewell to innocence" (5),
because "at the root of the American Negro problem is the necessity of
the American white man to find a way of living with the Negro in order
to be able to live with himself" (Schnapp 60).

In Ellison's estimation, even "White Negroes" who are predisposed toward racial tolerance "are Negroes too—if they wish to be," but only when

there is a willed affirmation of self "against all outside pressures—an identification with the group as extended through the individual self which rejects all possibilities of escape that do not involve a basic resuscitation of the original American ideals of social and political justice" (*Shadow and Act* 132). For it is my belief that the imagination of African-American artists can inspire the kind of transformative identification Griffin expresses as unconscious grammar when, as his text progresses, he uses *we* to describe himself and African Americans. By focusing on textimonies that keep as central the perspective of the oppressed, perhaps we can appreciate their valedictory function—how they teach people to imagine a farewell to innocence as a unifying and liberating act.

Focusing on the redemptive possibilities of imagination as the central feature of my analysis invites any number of comparisons because of the vast history of discourse on the subject. When I invoke the concept of imagination in relation to the slave narrative tradition, I construe it to be the faculty that enables both writer and reader to transcend the limits of their individuality and attain a holistic (and holy) view of themselves as part of the imminent self, a view held especially since the Romantic era, when the faculty of imagination came to be dignified as suprarational rather than antirational. But I also see it as a self-characterizing concept, where imagination can be construed as the way writers naturalize the unfamiliar and defamiliarize what others regard as natural.

If we remember that the root of the word *familiar* is *familia,* we can begin to consider how imagination works in texts to enable the reader to conceive of the racial "other" as familia. In this sense imagination enables the white reader to reconceive reality (such as slavery, racism, inequality) as un-familia, contrary to family, because the notion of family has been extended by way of imaginative identification with the formerly regarded other. Once this happens, there is a greater potential for the oppressors to willingly concede their entitlements and an opportunity for the oppressed to forgive and accept their shared destiny as the first step in seeking liberation.[5] Although exercising the imagination may seem inadequate for world-changing, I hope to demonstrate that "the imagination plays a critical role in the liberating process" (Hurley 339) by forging narratives of alternative moral vision, what Tom Moylan calls "anticipatory visions" that examine the praxis of oppression, all the while holding out hope that there are effective ways to oppose domination and fight for justice and freedom (104).

But just as the representation of slavery is full of peril, so is the exercise of the imagination, whatever the motive. In 1994, the Modern Language

Association solicited essays for their annual journal *Profession* on the topic "Boundaries of the Imagination." The essays ranged from broad discussions of the nature of imaginative discourse to specific references to writers who have, at some risk, crossed imaginative boundaries. The most oft-cited case was that of Salman Rushdie. Rushdie's problem, as Donne Raffat observed, "is not an isolated phenomenon but, rather, a part of a much larger network of issues that need to be examined" (42), among them the belief that standing up for an artist's imaginative rights is, in the words of Cynthia Ozick, "out of fashion and looked down on among certain multicultural academics; it is considered an intellectual offense against the mores and sensibilities of another culture" (78). In defense of Rushdie and others who seek imaginative entry into the experiences of the other, Margaret Atwood registers the recognition that "it's a paradox of our times that we are more prone to search for truth in works of fiction than in the pages of the daily newspaper" (44).

This observation, Atwood believes, does not indicate that people are longing to escape, but reinforces the belief that fiction renders a truth "we can't find elsewhere" because of both the imaginative faculties a writer brings to the endeavor and what the reader brings to the text under consideration. Atwood writes, "The effect a piece of writing has on its readers is usually silent, inward, individual, and nonmaterial; when people say that reading your book changed their lives, they don't as a rule mean that it paid the rent or helped them to get jobs. But occasionally a piece of writing spills over, grabs hold of—or is grabbed hold of by—something in the material world. Then it can become a reference point, a flagship, an icon for its age" (44). Nonetheless, Atwood is free of the delusion that imagination can have a direct effect in challenging social injustice, that although practitioners of the word would like to think that the word has power—which it may have in the long run—"in the short run I'm afraid the machine gun is more likely to command compliance" (45).

Given this stark realization, Atwood claims one is thrown back on desperate metaphors like "the saving remnant" or "bearing witness" but also concedes that "the very least we can expect is to remind ourselves that we— kindly, liberal 'we'—harbor within ourselves the potential for becoming a repressive 'them' and that one of the first symptoms of this regrettable change, in any society, is the silencing of dialogue and the demonizing of other human beings" (45). What the artist can do is fill the gap between the "barking of orders and the screaming of victims" (47) by using the imagination to open up channels of dialogue. Still, there is no guarantee that the imagination can function to open up channels of dialogue. Just as there are different ways to reach into the past, so are there different pasts for which to reach. When the line between fact and fiction becomes blurred, as so often happens in the slave narrative tradition, the liberties one takes in an act of imaginative license can interfere with the liberty imagination is meant to fulfill.

When he wrote *The Confessions of Nat Turner,* William Styron tried to reach into a past of fact and shape the missing elements with his imagination. In this novel, loosely based on the slave revolt led by Nat Turner in 1831, Styron attempted to flesh out Turner's life from scant historical details and in the process to fashion "an imagined microcosm of the baleful institution whose legacy has persisted in this century and become the nation's central obsession" (Styron 66). This was a righteous undertaking, especially for a white man only two generations removed from slaveholding ancestors. But in choosing to write a first-person narrative of a historical African-American figure, Styron did not enter into his enterprise with the same degree of responsibility to the slave narrative tradition that others considered here display. Rather than risking the kinds of intimate identification, as do the artists considered in this study, Styron tried to keep a comfortable aesthetic distance that revealed how little he, and possibly many other white Americans, actually understood about the slave narrative tradition.

The Confessions of Nat Turner was published in 1967, at the height of the civil rights movement. Styron was initially rewarded with glowing reviews, appearances on best-seller lists, and even an honorary degree from Wilberforce University. Although at Wilberforce Styron was lauded for illuminating slavery's "darker corners," he notes that this event was significant for him not just because he was pleased to receive their acceptance of him but because he had come to an "acceptance of them . . . as if my literary labors and my plunge into history had helped dissolve many of my preconceptions about race that had been my birthright as a Southerner and allowed me to better understand the forces that had shaped our common destiny" (66). Soon, however, Styron was shaken from his complacent assumption that his literary act had assisted him in his effort to "accept" black Americans. What he had neglected to appreciate about his enterprise—which led to what he describes as an "almost total alienation from black people"—was that his art was situated in social and cultural space shaped by the slave narrative tradition.

This tradition calls to us from the other side of a situation of extremity, and our response cannot be to judge it by the simplistic notions to which Styron clung while writing the novel: "accuracy" and "truth to life" (66).

Styron used these terms in the essay "Nat Turner Revisited," composed twenty-five years after the publication of his novel. Still stinging from the indictments leveled at his novel, it appears Styron had yet to appreciate that the slave narrative tradition, like Styron's own novel, is ultimately judged by its consequences, not by our ability to verify its truth. The slave narrative tradition represents attempts over time to mark, change, impress, but never to leave things as they are. Although the later extensions of this tradition are events themselves, not equal to the original documents, they still participate in the same spirit of the original liberating textimonies that changed both our common language about freedom and our individual perceptions about the quality of humanity. Unlike the other artists considered here who continue the tradition, Styron did not appreciate that along with the ability to voluntarily enter into the story of slavery, he must accept the responsibility that goes with it.

Styron's lack of responsibility becomes clear when in his essay he attempts to recreate the conditions that led him to write the novel, hoping to justify his efforts and perhaps even come to peace with his own role. Claiming not to remember a time when he was "not haunted by idea of slavery" or "profoundly conscious of the strange bifurcated world of whiteness and blackness in which I was born and reared," he cites an early "innate sense of moral indignation." He also confesses that he "fell under the spell of negritude" while simultaneously harboring anxiety about his "secret passion for blackness." Styron claims his "early fascination with Nat Turner came from pondering the parallels between his time and my own society, whose genteel accommodations and endemic cruelties, large and small, were not really so different from days of slavery" (67).

But in his attempt to go back to Turner's past, Styron let his imagination "run free," with a disregard for facts that he describes as "a state of grace" (68). Styron nonetheless accepts as fact that Turner "was a person of conspicuous ghastliness," "a madman" who was "singularly gifted and intelligent" but a "dangerous religious lunatic" (68–69) and goes on to imagine several disturbing scenarios to explain Turner's actions. In his defense Styron claims he was striving to "present a complex view of slavery" (70), but the contributors to *William Styron's Nat Turner: Ten Black Writers Respond* overwhelmingly objected to his imaginative play. The language Styron uses to assess this response is strong and unforgiving; he sees the book as an "assault," carrying a "splenetic tone" that is "strident," "crude," "reckless," using "shabby and slipshod rhetoric" and displaying "intellectual squalor" and "overheated absurdity." Styron's summation of this response is that "Nat Turner was not, in this case, an aesthetic object but a political whipping boy" (72). Whether or not Styron's assessment of his critics is correct from an intellectual or aesthetic standpoint, his own harsh descriptions years after the challenge indicate that he may not have come to understand the racial forces that shape American destiny.

His interest in African-American topics, which began as a guilty infatuation with otherness, seems not to have progressed beyond this point, so that now he resembles a jilted suitor who cannot understand why his advances were not welcomed and thus retreats into bitterness. What Styron may have missed is suggested by Thomas Keneally in his remarks on being faithful to truth in fiction. Discussing his novel *Schindler's List,* Keneally remarks, "I knew the truth already and merely tried to enhance it by grace of interpretation" because truth, he warned, "lies in ambush for the fiction writer" ("Faithful in His Fashion" 10). Unlike Styron, who describes disregarding facts as a state of grace, Keneally sees grace as a functional principle, one that guides the exercise of his imagination. Styron appropriated another's story and made it his own, rather than letting the story emerge from its context. In the process he violated the slave narrative tradition because he didn't respect its first imperative: that the oppressed must speak for themselves. The distance between black and white, as John Howard Griffin learned on his brief journey into blackness, is far greater than actual miles (39, 1962 edition).

The most faithful act a nonblack person can contribute toward making this journey is to apply an imaginative grace to his or her creative enterprises that will allow others to emerge out of their hiddenness but still retain authorship over their own textimonies. If the bond between writer and reader that the slave narrative tradition seeks to establish is to serve as a model for all exchange of thought, need, and feeling, it is helpful to view it through the lens of liberation theology, which establishes the pact between reader and writer as a sacred covenant and the texts themselves as a sacred canon of textimony. Artists need not be Christian or even conventionally religious to bring to their enterprises an imaginative memory for articulating the legacy of slavery or the possibilities of transformation, a point repeatedly affirmed by Nathan Scott over his long career investigating the religious dimensions of literary art. As he writes, "The religious dimension is something intrinsic to and constitutive of the nature of literature as such" (*Negative Capability* 132).

Many artists can serve as constructive sources for theology or, at least, come to the same kind of disposition liberation theologians urge us to acquire because they exercise and endorse what Carolyn Jones describes as a "moral imagination" that "reimagines and requires a constant interrogation of our positionalities" (252). Imagination, Jones continues, is faith, for "making meaning is making God" (253). If we cease to view artists simply in evangelical terms—as promoting the adoption of a particular faith stance—we can appreciate how they include those marginalized from traditional theological discourse, inviting them to be partners in achieving liberation and advancing the goals of social justice. By expanding our notion of what constitutes a sacred canon and surrendering the impulse to identify Christian motives and answers in each situation we strive to understand, the slave narrative tradition can continue to function as it once did in advancing the abolitionist agenda.

Today the need for an abolitionist agenda is as great as it was in antebellum times. For as Griffin predicted in the 1977 epilogue to the second edition of his book, "In the past, hope was based on the moods of the majority—a fragile and slippery basis. That is gone now, and a realism—harsh, full of contradictions—has replaced it as something more solid on which to build" (208). How solid that foundation remains is challenged by August Meier in *A White Scholar and the Black Community, 1945–1965: Essays and Reflections*. Meier, an activist in the civil rights movement and a scholar of African-American culture before it was recognized as essential to curricula, spent the bulk of his career teaching at historically black schools. He describes how he became the "heir of a rich but bitter-sweet experience" (38) when, by virtue of his race, he was alienated from a political role while his scholarship took on new influence with the rise of the black power movement.

Meier now views the state of American race relations as not "part of the world I was hoping to help build" and claims that his recent experience "has eroded the liberal optimism with which I started out at Tougaloo nearly half a century ago" (220). Still, he reaffirms the strategies of Dr. King, which acknowledge that exploiting the historical or personal guilt of white people is not sufficient for liberation of the oppressed unless it is accompanied by a belief in and an insistence on their redemption. Because he saw spiritual belief as an animating force, King could challenge the dominant culture to live up to its professed values while still affirming its redemption. King could open our eyes to a racist hell on earth while motivating us to imagine a paradise of unity and to activate its possibilities. Reinvesting imagination with its power to transform, rather than viewing it as a depleted and corrupted resource, was the original impulse behind the slave narrative tradition, one of the first ways "difference encountered difference" in the American experience.

ⓠ ⓠ ⓠ

Full low at thy bidding thy negroes may kneel
With the iron of bondage on spirit and heel;
Yet know that the Yankee girl sooner would be
In fetters with them, than in freedom with thee.
—John Greenleaf Whittier

At the time of their publication, ex-slave narratives were widely read and appreciated by a public that had "itching ears to hear a colored man speak, and particularly a slave" (Gates, *The Classic* xi). These writings constituted a unique genre of literature and were viewed as both powerful works of literary art and persuasive tools for articulating and advancing the abolitionist agenda. They offered convincing evidence of the humanity of people of African descent by setting forth a particular image of ex-slaves that emphasized commonly admired human traits and virtues. As Lucius C. Matlock wrote in 1845,

> Naturally and necessarily, the enemy of literature [American slavery] has become the prolific theme of much that is profound in argument, sublime in poetry, and thrilling in narrative. From the soil of slavery itself have sprung forth some of the most brilliant productions, whose logical levers will ultimately upheave and overthrow the system. . . . Startling incidents authenticated, far excelling fiction in their touching pathos, from the pen of self-emancipated slaves do now exhibit slavery in such revolting aspects, as to secure the execrations of all good men and become a monument more enduring than marble, in testimony strong as sacred writ against it. (Gates, *The Classic* xi)

The dynamics of the production and reception of ex-slave narratives were underscored by their distinctively intertwined literary and thematic features. Robert Stepto identifies freedom and literacy as the dominant issues set forth in the narratives, cast in the form of a quest from enslavement to liberation. Acquiring literacy skills became for enslaved people a vehicle for obtaining freedom. Because enslaved people were denied by law literacy training and education, once they achieved it in freedom they used this skill to take down the very institution that forbade it. Stepto's analysis—which finds the quest articulated not only in the formal literature of the slave narrative genre but also in tales, sermons, and songs—anticipates the future development of the tradition and invites the application of the slave narrative model to other genres.

What the slave narratives accomplished provided the form by which future artists would participate in the tradition as a way of achieving social justice. Demonstrating proficiency in language arts became a form of resistance, a literal and a literary way to articulate the humanity of black Americans. The narrators challenged readers to confront the elements of essence and social context that make up the formula by which we customarily construct identities. They proclaimed their essential humanity by manipulating and repositioning themselves in a different social context. In essence, each writer was an artist whose medium was identity. In fashioning their own liberated identity, they gave readers a passageway into their experience by introducing them to another world on the margins of American society. The result was the creation of literary art that was greater than the sum of its techniques because after the works were read they continued to resonate in experience as models of resistance.

Furthermore, these narrators added the element of transcendent reality to the formula for identity construction. Attendant on the personal and political implications of slave narratives is the broader implication of theological truth. As William Andrews emphasizes, ex-slave narrators traced freedom to an awakening of "their awareness of their fundamental identity with and rightful participation in logos, whether understood as reason and its expression in speech or as divine spirit" (*To Tell* 7). These narratives, or "testimony as strong as sacred writ," also served as symbolic representations of the biblical power of the word. Because the act of abolishing slavery was seen by many abolitionists as a sacred cause, these narrators are "models of the act and impact of biblical appropriation on the consciousness of the black narrator as bearer of the Word" (Andrews, *To Tell* 64). Appropriating biblical language and appealing to religious sentiments was a profound way to overturn Southern apologies for slavery, which depended in large part on appeals to religious sanctions derived from scriptural narratives.

Yet Andrews also observes that in order to achieve their aims, ex-slave autobiographers had to develop a writing voice that could negotiate a potentially hostile discursive environment. They did so by creating, in effect, a sympathetic audience. To achieve their goal of liberation, writers had to attract an audience with access to the sources of institutional power, which must be altered if there was to be any substantial change in society. Adopting the language of scripture and offering appeals to readers' moral sensibilities was a political and rhetorical strategy as much as a profession of faith. But to deny that the authors' religious sentiments were sincere would be to misread not just the theological foundations of black culture but the larger social and cultural context in which these texts were created.

Many slave narratives were created, sustained, and promoted by abolitionists as sacred texts in the fight against slavery. Although there is some scholarly debate over the role abolitionism and its adherents played in the eradication of slavery—whether abolitionists were principled humanitarians or calculating economists—in *Radical Abolitionism* Lewis Perry sets the context for appreciating the role of slave narratives as sacred texts. Perry argues for understanding abolitionism as a radical liberation movement that tended toward an anarchist vision because "abolitionism had at its core a definition of sin based on a view of God's sovereignty and human accountability with potentially radical implications" (xi). Any claim to be "master" over another, therefore, was challenged by abolitionists who also exposed other forms of "slavery" found in the church, government, society, and family and offered in their stead new models for shaping these institutions that honored the sovereignty of God in human affairs.

As Herbert Aptheker notes, however, abolitionists were not adherents of any particular religious doctrine. But in the context of a rapidly changing antebellum religious culture, abolitionism functioned for many to connect theological assertions of liberation principles with changes in human consciousness made visible by ex-slave narratives that described the arguments they faced and the events they lived through. According to Aptheker, the role of religion in the abolitionist movement was twofold: "In its priestly guise, religion was a bulwark of the institution, but in its prophetic aspect, it served as a goal and inspirer" (xvi). Aptheker goes on to suggest that the religion of abolitionism "differed little from what today is called the theology of liberation" (xvi). Although Aptheker does not elaborate on this opinion, the ways in which he characterizes the abolitionist movement bear striking parallels to the ways in which liberation theologians have articulated their position.

African-American liberation theology as an analytical and systematic academic enterprise formally began in the 1960s. Its immediate and catalytic origins can be traced to the civil rights struggle and the black power movement as theologians strove to ground these influences in faith. It grew out of similar movements in Latin America that focused on the relationship between faith and socioeconomic issues, analyzing systems of oppression in terms of sinful behavior. In African-American terms this meant identifying white racism as the demonic force behind all unjust political and social systems. At its core liberation theology proposed that solutions to injustice would require more than economic or political action. What was required was a change in heart: for the privileged to relinquish their power and position and for the victims of exploitation to rise up and demand change. Praxis—action informed by reflection—was identified as the principal strategy that could achieve the kind of material and spiritual redemption envisioned by liberation theologians. A faith in transformation and a willingness to embody a vision of justice are the tasks liberation theology challenged people to embrace.

This task involves the participation of both African Americans and the dominant culture. A depiction of black humanity that recognizes and upholds human dignity and value must be acknowledged by nonblacks. This basic principle underlies the liberation theology that was understood and promoted in abolitionism. Like contemporary liberation theology, abolitionism was a movement begun and sustained by African Americans, but throughout its existence abolitionism strove to be inclusive and democratic in its goals and activities. In their jeremiad against slavery, abolitionists identified the peculiar institution as the embodiment of sin, construed as a state of consciousness in which individuals exist only for themselves and transform people and goods around them to objects of use under their control. Ex-slave narratives related the social consequences of this sin or the concrete conditions of oppression.

Many abolitionists who were not ex-slaves became forceful champions for liberation because they had achieved, by hearing the testimony of ex-slaves, a capacity to see them as being like themselves. They chose to bear the weight of the sins of the society and willingly to identify with their enslaved siblings. In the process they not only challenged the systemic order of oppression but also radically transformed their identities. Slave narratives helped abolitionists to overcome one problem inherent in their vision. In their emphasis on self-liberation abolitionists displayed an uncommon devotion to righteousness and a corresponding trust in individuals' private judgment about what constituted righteousness. Given this open-ended possibility for individual transformation, slave narratives provided a necessary demonstration of the character of one seeking righteousness. And as textimonies that characterized the righteousness of humanity, they provided an important model for self-transformation.

Although in *A Black Theology of Liberation* James Cone observes that oppressors encountering black thought will judge it irrational because "not understanding the enslaved condition the enslaver is in no position to understand the methods which the slaves use for liberation" (214), understanding the enslaved condition is precisely what the ex-slave narratives enabled abolitionists to do. The sacred literature or textimony that engendered the slave narrative tradition was created out of both the negative experience of oppression and the concrete praxis of abolitionist reformers, who provided a theological system for articulating the cause of liberation and an actual model for modes of action—resistance and community building—necessary to advance the agenda of liberation.

Despite the attempts of Southern slaveholders to find spiritual justification for their claims, their beliefs rested primarily on their desire to preserve their economic interests and their assumption that blacks were inferior beings. This kind of attitude was summed up by one of history's most notorious defenders of slavery, John Wilkes Booth: "This country was formed for the *white,* not for the black man. And looking upon *African slavery* from the same standpoint held by the noble framers of our Constitution, I, for one, have ever considered it one of the greatest blessings (both for themselves and for us) that God ever bestowed upon a favored nation" (Neely 190).

It is precisely this general assumption of the character of people of African descent that abolitionists and ex-slave narrators so effectively challenged. Realizing that all African Americans would be judged on the evidence they presented in their narratives, they wrote about their experiences to accomplish twin goals. Based on what they reported about the actual conditions of enslaved people, they could create consensus in the nation that slavery was immoral and should be abolished. By the act of writing and demonstrating their achievement of "higher" skills and thought, they could convince white people that the authors (and by extension all black people) were indeed human and worthy of freedom.

Many scholars have pointed out that these slave narratives came to resemble each other in both form and content. In his essay "'I Was Born': Slave Narratives, Their Status as Autobiography and as Literature," James Olney distinguishes the formal dimensions of slave narratives by what he describes as their absence of "patterned significance," or any indication on the part of the narrator as a creative and active shaper of his or her text. Indeed, Olney goes so far as to list characteristics of slave narratives that constitute the preformed mold into which all slave stories were poured. According to Olney, Henry Louis Gates Jr., and others, a "process of imitation and repetition" created a cumulative effect of each narrative being part of a "communal utterance, a collective tale rather than merely an individual's biography" (Gates, *The Classic* x).

From at least the early 1840s, readers remarked on the tension between the "I" used by all narrators and the "we" of all people held in slavery. The autobiographies emphasized the collective character of enslaved people when the community became encased in a singular pronoun. But it is important to appreciate that community was construed not just as fellow slaves but as anyone willing to identify with them, a response John Sekora points out as being encouraged by a preexisting consciousness: "Radical individualism in its evangelical New England Protestant guise proved a highly serviceable philosophy for abolitionists after 1830. Teaching the sacred value in God's eyes of every individual soul, it made a persuasive potent political point as well as a valuable literary one" (621).

Yet because a distinct sense of individual identity was perceived to be hidden in a general proclamation of human identity, for nearly half a century some scholars evaluated slave narratives as exhibiting something less than literary quality. They dismissed or did not fully appreciate the transformative power of the collective identity. Seizing on the formulaic quality of the narratives, they denied the presence of any aesthetic shaping on the part of the authors (Davis and Gates 148). Once ex-slave narratives were no longer necessary to sustain abolitionist arguments, little effort was made to promote each writer as a singular artist or to distinguish these narratives as literary works, and they vanished from the canon of American literature.

Also problematic for appreciating slave narratives as aesthetic achievements was the polemic use of the narratives that insisted on defending the veracity of the texts. As Albert Stone remarks, slave narratives were written "to describe the experience of being chattel and then *not* being one so vividly that the white reader would be moved to destroy the oppressive institution. To this end, the most effective means was to create a convincing impression of historical veracity and verisimilitude" (194). In postbellum analyses, veracity became complicated further by scholars' conflicting definitions of what constitutes authenticity in a slave narrative.

As Laura Tanner points out, some "focus on the former slave's attempt to manipulate the form of his or her narrative to achieve authentication of that narrative as historical evidence worthy of use in a political argument," whereas others define authenticity "by the ex-slave's effort to remain true to his or her own unique history and consciousness by focusing on the effort of presenting him or herself in that narrative as an authentic human being" (424). Indeed, the text I have chosen as my model for how the slave narrative tradition articulates liberation theology—Frederick Douglass's first autobiography—has been shown by John Sekora's persuasive analysis not to be a "true, full autobiography" (610) but a text shaped as much "by the American Anti-Slavery Society [led by William Lloyd Garrison] as by its author" (620). This leads us to another problem: the dominant culture's appropriation of the voice of the oppressed. As Sekora explains, while Douglass takes Garrison's writings as his lesson, "Garrison takes Douglass's life, his being, as *his* text" (610), thereby forcing Douglass to create multiple versions of his autobiography to resist what Sekora calls being "a black dummy manipulated by white ventriloquists" (612).

Yet whatever distortions resulted, ex-slave narratives represented a genuine response—indeed, a challenge—to the specific social and political context that engendered them. The same postbellum analyses that lead us to puzzle over authenticity also uncover shared tropes and themes, a quality of intertextuality between the narratives and recent black fictional forms that demonstrates the "nature of narrative" and what it can reveal "about the urge of the human will to transcend the very chaos of experience with imposed literary figures and structures" (Davis and Gates 147). In other words, the truth of these texts lies outside their historical veracity and can be located in how they function as textimonies, for what they contribute by way of imagination to our ongoing cultural dialogue.

It is not surprising that we now see an emphasis on the narratives as a source of history not because of what they offer in terms of the particulars of a specific life, but because of the way in which they show a self characterized and what this means in terms of revising canons of American history and literature. Contemporary literary theory and historical analysis have encouraged us to read these texts a new way, one that appreciates both the context (the circumstances of their making and expression) and the text (the aesthetic or universal qualities that contribute to the endurance of these narratives as artistic forms). Slave narratives have transcended the circumstances of their making and their expression and are considered profound artistic achievements because they continue to provide a source for ongoing moral reflection on the human condition and for aesthetic analysis of how we image humanity and construct identities.

Because slavery was not abandoned as a topic in the works of African-American writers after Emancipation, there is an ongoing recognition by African-American writers that there is something ultimately incomprehensible about slavery and its aftermath that compels them to create new textimonies or fictions that allow the voiceless to speak as emotionally true or authentic alternatives to history. As Arna Bontemps explained in 1966, slavery is part of black literary ancestry that continues to influence African-American artists: "From the narrative came the spirit and vitality and the angle of vision responsible for the most effective prose writing by black American writers" (Gates, *The Classic* x). The slave narrative tradition in American arts and letters includes not only the original documents of the antebellum genre but also postbellum formations that take slavery as a topic of concern or use slavery as a symbolic vehicle by which to discuss broader issues of identity and liberation.

During the Civil War General Sherman promised each slave "40 acres and a mule," and this broken pledge became a symbol to African Americans of the system that held them down and America's empty promise of justice. There has been talk since Reconstruction of the need for social and economic reparations (most recently in a bill introduced by Representative John Conyers of Michigan) and even an attempt initiated by Representative Tony Hall of Ohio to have the federal government issue a formal apology for slavery. But all along the same concern has continuously been amplified in aesthetic modes, especially by artists participating in the slave narrative tradition. Assessing the damage inflicted by slavery is nearly impossible, but these textimonies point a way. The slave narrative tradition writ large effectively negotiates between claims of essential, sociohistorical, and transcendent reality to convey a whole vision of reality. What facilitates a connection between these claims is imagination, where art does not happen to society as a whole or all at once but happens one mind to one mind.

Imagination functions in two ways in the slave narrative tradition. It is the faculty the individual artist brings to and uses in her literary effort that makes it a work of art and distinguishes the creator as fully human because a complete claim to humanity involves not just the ability to report and survive, but also to create and appreciate. As Albert Stone observes in the case of Frederick Douglass, "the more clearly and fully we see the man and the writer—the man revealed in the act of discovering and recreating his own identity—the more we acknowledge the force of his argument for an end to slavery's denial of individuality and creativity" (197). Imagination is also the faculty the narratives elicit from and encourage readers to exercise in order to understand what is presented.

In this context, imagination is a link created by metaphor—to see the self as the other or to experience an idea of humanity through a particular image of humanity. Although the slave narrative tradition is dependent terrain, linked historically to the original experience of an oppressed people and theologically to the idea of the freedom of souls, metaphorically the tradition serves as a point at which one can gain entry to the experience of oppression. Artists who participate in the slave narrative tradition by creating new textimonies give readers an imaginative road to travel toward seeing what they cannot see and hearing what they cannot hear, thereby providing unique access to the circumstances and conditions from which emerge constructs of identity.

The narratives achieve this through an interplay of character and characterization that allows the reader to witness the life of an oppressed person who is characterized not as the sum of her oppressions but as a human being of dignity and character. A narrative character, as Mark Ledbetter observes, "intensifies our own self-awareness if for no other reason than we are relating to lives and interpreting ourselves in relation to these lives" (15). We adopt for ourselves the virtue embodied in the character who has been newly characterized, thereby moving to a kind of religious experience of revelation in which our worldview becomes that of the character's. Doing this involves personal and even textual struggle.

In the case of Douglass, for example, the reader must reconcile Douglass's past as a dependent slave and his present as an independent author. This interplay between character and characterization was noted even in the earliest readings of the slave narratives. In an 1849 review of Ephraim Peabody's narrative, the reviewer notes, "There is that in the lives of men who have sufficient force of mind and heart to enable them to struggle up from hopeless bondage to the position of freeman, beside which the ordinary characters of romance are dull and tame" (Davis and Gates 19). The reviewer goes on to describe the "combination of qualities and deeds and sufferings most fitted to attract human sympathy in each particular case" (19), later observing that "they give, doubtless, a just idea of what slavery is to the slave" (21).

More recently, bell hooks has affirmed the imaginative components of the slave narrative tradition and the role of imagination in raising consciousness in the essay "The Magic of Our Moment." In describing her own experience of reading her poetry before audiences, hooks points to what she calls "the magic of our moment" wherein people can expand their capacity as spiritual and artistic beings to hold difference and contradiction in balance by appreciating that "we are never static souls, but always in the process of unfolding" (30), thereby intensifying our capacity to live passionately and to commit to the struggle for liberation. Creating and learning from these moments, hooks laments, is unappreciated in American culture.

As she writes: "We do not talk enough on the Left about the relationship between creativity—the capacity to imagine—and our capacity to change and transform society. Most artistic practice is, in fact, a process of transforming experience and materials into something else, almost an alchemical process" (10). What this process can evoke, hooks claims, is communion: "The artistic practice draws me further into what we often call forth in religious experience: a sense of communion of spirit, a sense of not being alone." In this experience of communion lies "tremendous power, a vision of art that is redemptive. Such a vision sees art not as an individual process of creating a product to own and hold but as a movement from the unitary self into a more expansive, transcendent process of empathy" (10).

She goes on to assert that our art, like our theology, must be intimately connected with our pain because "the power inherent in art is that power to imagine for ourselves and the process of transformation on which we then embark." Furthermore, access to this imaginative power is not bound by limitations of class, race, or gender because whatever deprivation one suffers, "the great power of art is that all people can create" (11). Participating in this process of imaginative transformation, hooks says, is "both our true spiritual quest and the archetypic quest—to embrace difference and sameness at the same time without feeling the need to negate one or the other" (30). Embracing this perspective, hooks concludes, will "illuminate our struggles for justice and our visions for love and peace" (30).

From Frederick Douglass's early insistence that "to understand it one must needs experience it or imagine himself in similar circumstances" (*Narrative* 144) to Toni Morrison's prescription that "the only grace they could have was the grace they could imagine" (*Beloved* 88), imagination has always played a role in developing strategies for survival and resistance. It reveals how to create and appreciate life, demonstrates how to articulate the cause of liberation, and assists in the construction of identities of both the writer and the reader. The writer constructs an identity by characterizing himself or herself a specific way and readers are enjoined to construct a new identity through their identification with the characters portrayed. Indeed, even Abraham Lincoln recognized the potential inherent in this kind of imaginative identification when he remarked, "I never knew a man who wishes to be himself a slave. Consider if you know any good thing, that no man desires for himself" (Neely 118–19).

When he published the first narrative account of his life in slavery in 1845, Frederick Douglass was still a fugitive slave. The trials Douglass endured, the risks he took, and his suffering under the system of slavery are all well documented in this familiar narrative. His effort to establish for public record a summary of his experiences was also a courageous and symbolic act. Indeed, not long after the publication of *Narrative of the Life of Frederick Douglass, An American Slave,* Douglass had to flee to England for safety because of the threat of reenslavement. Friends eventually purchased his freedom in 1846, but the risks he took in publishing his account reveal a courage that cannot be diminished.

Douglass's efforts to free himself did not end when, under disguise, he boarded a ship north. Nor did they end when his own freedom had been legally secured. Douglass's sense of his own freedom was inextricably bound to his commitment to the liberation of all enslaved Americans of African descent. As he describes his position, by writing his *Narrative* he "subscribes" himself to a "sacred cause" (159), thereby entitling "himself to become the subscriber of his own biblical text" (MacKethan, "Fugitive Slave" 69). Douglass's efforts toward liberating his people are effected both by his characterization of himself and other enslaved people and his own personal character, which is demonstrated in the act of writing.

To further the cause of liberation for his people, Douglass constructed a narrative that invited its readers to share his representative experience of slavery. As he explicitly expresses, it was an attempt to urge readers to "place himself in my situation. . . . I say let him be placed in this most trying situation,—the situation in which I was placed,—then and not till then, will he fully appreciate the hardships of, and know who to sympathize with, the toil-worn and whip-scarred fugitive slave" (144). Here Douglass is referring to the tenuous and anxiety-ridden condition of being a fugitive slave, but he alludes, through the images of "toil-worn and whip-scarred," to his prior condition of slavery. In both instances he insists that his readers not just take up his cause but in a sacramental way feel his pain and understand his oppression. As William Andrews points out in *To Tell a Free Story,* "in this statement Douglass, for the first time in Afro-American autobiography, declared a new and crucial role for the imagination as a mode of mediation, not distortion and deception" (137).

Twenty years later, as the Civil War loomed, Douglass was still insisting on this kind of imaginative identification when he warned a sympathetic audience in New York City that much of the drive behind the abolitionist movement seemed to be derived not so much from "the outgrowth of high and intelligent moral conviction against slavery as such, than because of the trouble its friends have brought upon the country." Douglass proceeded to assert that "a man that hates slavery for what it does to the white man stands ready to embrace it the moment its injuries are confined to the black man, and he ceases to feel those injuries in his own person" (Aptheker xvi).

Nearly a century and a half later, the novelist Toni Morrison reaffirmed the role of imagination as a mode of mediation in understanding the experience of slavery when she wrote *Beloved* (1987), the story of a fugitive slave named Sethe who, when threatened with recapture, chooses to murder her children rather than return them to a life in slavery. Before *Beloved* Toni Morrison wrote four novels that explored the conditions of African Americans during various episodes of their history and in diverse settings. But in *Beloved* she finally returns to the experience of slavery in an attempt to understand its ongoing implications. As she explains in interviews, the story on which the novel is based is an actual event, but Morrison found customary historical sources inadequate to understand the conditions of slavery that would lead a woman to express her maternal love through infanticide. Morrison concluded that "if they could live it all of their lives, I could write it" (Kastor B12).

Through her character of Baby Suggs, Morrison offers up imagination as a mode of mediation when Baby Suggs preaches to the community: "She did not tell them to clean up their lives or to go and sin no more. She did not tell them they were the blessed of the earth, its inheriting meek or its glorybound pure. She told them that the only grace they could have was the grace they could imagine. That if they could not see it, they would not have it" (88). Baby Suggs further clarifies the role imagination plays when she insists that it must be informed by love: "'Here,' she said, 'in this place, we flesh; flesh that weeps, laughs; flesh that dances on bare feet in grass. Love it. Love it hard. Yonder they do not love your flesh. They despise it. . . . *You* got to love it, *you*!'" (88).

What Toni Morrison offers us is a characterization of a people's mode of survival through their ability to have grace by "seeing" it and an affirmation of the humanity or character of African Americans who are "flesh that dances on bare feet." At the same time she invites her uninitiated readers to understand the legacy of slavery by asserting how the power of an imagination informed by love can lead one to a state of grace. As Morrison explains, her literary explorations in empathy are meant to be invitations to white readers to undertake their own: "To read imaginative literature by and about us is to choose to examine centers of the self and to have the opportunity to compare those centers with the 'raceless' ones with which we are, all of us, most familiar" (Hulbert 46). Indeed, John Hope Franklin expresses the belief that if Americans would read *Beloved*, "perhaps they could gain some perspective on the plight of this country as it gropes for a solution to its oldest social problem" (Franklin 90).

Toni Morrison's theology of imagination arose out of her awareness of and participation in the culture generated by the slave narrative tradition. Just as James Cone did in his development of a black liberation theology a century after Douglass, Frederick Douglass identifies his God as the "God of the oppressed" (*My Bondage* 265). Indeed, Douglass's theology—which judges slavery as a crime not just against humanity "but against God" (*My Bondage* 231)—foreshadows the black theology of liberation developed by Cone and can be used as a paradigmatic form by which to assess the relationship between the slave narrative tradition and liberation theology.[6] Despite the problems attendant to white editorial intrusion, or even Douglass's own need to continually rewrite his autobiography, the first narrative, as Sharon Carson observes, sets forth a liberation theology that "shakes the foundation" of American culture with "subtle to explicit claims of religious authority" that "invites white Christian readers into familiar territory, then radically rearranges the theological landscape" (19–20). He achieves his aim not simply as an autobiographer relating the events of his life but as a creative writer and "a prophet commenting upon American history from a supramundane viewpoint" (Couser 53).

Like liberation theologians who emphasize the need for salvation and liberation in the context of human history, Douglass begins and ends his narrative situating himself by name, date, and place—attaching himself to history and showing no wish to escape it. As liberation theologians promote an activist over a reflective theology, so too does Douglass, who repeatedly makes distinctions between creed and deed—between southern slaveholders who espouse Christianity and make "the greatest pretensions to piety" (*Narrative* 97) and northern abolitionists who live it with "vigilance, kindness, and perseverance" (*Narrative* 144). Or, as he remarks, "Between the Christianity of this land, and the Christianity of Christ, I recognize the widest possible difference" (*Narrative* 153). Corresponding to liberation theologians' activist imperatives, Douglass emphasizes the personal initiative that grew out of his battle with the slavebreaker Covey and challenges other slaves who would wait passively for the Lord to deliver them to have a hand in their own liberation, to experience a moment as he did, when "my long-crushed spirit rose, cowardice departed, [and] bold defiance took its place" (*Narrative* 113).

As liberation theologians use political and sociological analyses to investigate the roots of oppression, Douglass describes the evils of slavery in systemic terms of the institution. He shows how those in power seek to divide and conquer, set different factions of the oppressed against one another, as when he is abused by fellow apprentices at a shipyard who "began to feel it was degrading to them to work with me" (*Narrative* 132). He also reveals how the oppressor tries to break the will of the oppressed through violence, neglect of physical, emotional, spiritual, and intellectual needs, or addictive distractions and intoxicants introduced to render the oppressed further passive and powerless and ultimately "disgust the slave with freedom, by allowing him to see only the abuse of it" (*Narrative* 11). Douglass describes the situation ethics of liberation theology, which prescribe, under conditions of oppression, a different code of morality when one is forced to "steal a bag which was used for carrying corn to the mill" (*Narrative* 71) to use as a sleeping pallet on a cold, damp floor.

But Douglass also holds out hope for the redemption of those who subscribe to the system when he concludes his narrative by praying that his book "may do something toward throwing light on the American slave system, and hastening the glad day of deliverance to the millions of my brethren in bonds—faithfully relying upon the power of truth, love, and justice, for success in my humble efforts" (*Narrative* 129). The liberating theology that emerges from the slave narrative tradition is written "not only to record the author's conversion but to precipitate or confirm that of the reader" (Couser 60). Thomas Couser argues that Douglass and other ex-slave narrators consciously modeled their narratives on the traditional form of conversion narratives because it enabled them to present something with which the audience was not directly familiar—the experience of slavery—in terms of something with which they were presumably familiar, thereby encouraging the reader to "expand his sphere of moral concern" (61). In this way an ex-slave narrator such as Douglass invites readers "to walk a familiar landscape, then shifts the ground beneath their feet" (Carson 25), creating a way to include the reformed oppressor as an agent of liberation.

Ex-slave narrators understood that in order to understand praxis, the circumstances under which oppressed people survive, one needs the experience of confronting and familiarizing otherness that the narratives supply by their interplay of character and characterization. In these narratives, words do things and actions say things.[7]

As Toni Morrison observed in her Nobel lecture, "oppressive language does more than represent violence, it is violence; does more than represent the limits of knowledge, it limits knowledge" (16). Correspondingly, "The vitality of language lies in its ability to limn the actual, imagined, and possible lives of its speakers, readers, writers," and in so doing points us "toward the place where meaning may lie" (20). Furthermore, the act of committing experience to creative expression is itself an act of liberation, affirmed in two regards by Ralph Ellison. In a generic sense, Ellison observes, "the work of art is important in itself . . . it is a social action in itself" (*Shadow and Act* 137). But a work of art is important in a specific historical sense, too, as in the case of ex-slave narrators who used the medium from which they were excluded to fiercely embrace a new identity, providing a model for later writers who understand that "being a Negro American has to do with the memory of slavery and the hope of emancipation" (131).

The slave narrative tradition therefore shows us how we could construct a canon of sacred texts or textimonies for liberating theology, a canon that would make reference to the dominant experience of African-American oppression, the experience of slavery. Although canon formation is not my exclusive concern, the process raises issues I want to consider in developing imagination as a liberating tool and narrative as a critical dimension of liberation theology. In African-American theologies of liberation, one indisputable fact is that the dominant source for its emergence derives from the experience of slavery. As Gayraud Wilmore remarks, from the beginning, black theology and black history have been inseparable. "The world has been a stage, and the slaves and masters—the Black underclass and the White establishment—have supplied the *dramatis personae* for God's struggle in behalf of his oppressed Black Children. Black History, therefore, must be understood as sacred history and Black theological thought as eventful theology" (Wilmore and Cone 4).

Perhaps the first concerted effort to describe the qualities of a canonical slave narrative tradition was undertaken by the English Institute in 1987 when they invited papers on the slave narrative tradition that were eventually published as *Slavery and the Literary Imagination*. This volume is especially helpful in identifying recurrent motifs, but it is also remarkable for its lack of attention to the religious dimensions of slave narratives. But this volume does acknowledge that slave narratives "provided the basic paradigm for virtually all later fiction and autobiography by black Americans" (McDowell and Rampersad ix).

In other words, the literal text of slavery became the literary text as writers moved further in history from the experience of slavery but still identified a cognitive and emotional need to understand the experience. Hortense Spillers, in her essay included in *Slavery and the Literary Imagination,* describes this problem in the following way: "In a very real sense, a full century or so 'after the fact,' 'slavery' is primarily discursive, as we search vainly for a point of absolute and indisputable origin, for a moment of plenitude that would restore us to the real, rich 'thing' itself before discourse touched it. In that regard, 'slavery' becomes the great 'test case' around which, for its Afro-American readers, the circle of mystery is recircumscribed time and again" (29).

This circle of mystery is not just for African-American readers. A key function of narratives of liberation continues to be to speak not only to the oppressed in order to validate their experience, but also to the "unconverted," to those who may not experience oppression in the same mode, but, once awakened, may be willing partners in liberation. In the African-

American mode of call and response, the call extended and the response required are meant to be heard and spoken not only by the oppressed but by the oppressors as well.

Eric J. Sundquist points out in *To Wake the Nations: Race in the Making of American Literature* that the call extended by African Americans in various cultural forms has always been responded to, if not acknowledged, by the dominant culture. Using the spiritual "My Lord, What a Morning," chosen by Du Bois as an epigraph in *The Souls of Black Folk,* Sundquist reveals how the spiritual announces "the (re)awakening of present generations of black Americans to their own hidden history in slavery and beyond," and how it serves as a call to "wake the nation"—not only black Americans but the United States as a whole (2). Once we are awakened to the need for liberation, it is difficult to pretend we are unaware of social injustice because as witnesses we assume a responsibility. As the slave narrative tradition of textimony so effectively demonstrates, witness can beget witness, and each person can find his or her own role in the process of working toward liberation, whether one is experiencing the oppression, recording the experience, or listening to and acting on the voiced needs of the oppressed. One need not be a liberation theologian to embody a liberating theology.

ର   ର   ର

> But be doers of the word and not merely hearers who deceive themselves.
> —James 1:22

The role of the slave narrative tradition in shaping a liberating theology is underscored by an observation James Cone made in the first volume of a documentary history of black theology edited by Cone and Gayraud Wilmore and published in 1979. There Cone recognized that white theologians' response to or participation in black liberation theology began only in the early 1970s, when the cumulative and ongoing effect of reform and liberation movements made it impossible for them to ignore the theological relevance of the black experience. In this same volume, Peter C. Hodgson cites the reason for this lack of participation: "There is an authentic role [in the creation of black theology] only if white theologians sense their own survival to be at stake as well. I believe this to be the case, for American democracy cannot survive if liberation of blacks and other ethnic minorities is not completed" (Wilmore and Cone 2). Thus it is not surprising that Cone's repeated emphasis that "one's praxis in life inevitably shapes one's theological perceptions" (Wilmore and Cone 138) corresponds with a point made by nearly every white theologian Cone and Wilmore include in this volume: a recognition that all theologians, black and white, must take primary account of the realities of black experience in constructing a theology.

Helmut Gollwitzer goes so far as to suggest that a white theologian must try to "become black. . . . This is the concrete form of the metanoia by which he sees himself challenged—cutting deeper into his lifestyle than any metanoia he had previously imagined" (Wilmore and Cone 152). Because Gollwitzer believes that theology and proclamation are responsible not only for what they mean but also for what they effect, he challenges white theologians to become black by undergoing a practical metanoia wherein guilt is confessed as shared with white Christian ancestors and is exposed and examined as to its causes. This should be followed by a recognition and acknowledgment of the daily social, institutional, and personal entitlements white people enjoy. Finally, white theologians must express solidarity with exploited masses.

The slave narrative tradition points a way for white theologians to undergo the metanoia Gollwitzer describes, and its influence is alluded to in the work of Cone that articulates the narrative dimensions of liberation theology. In his 1975 essay "The Story Context of Black Theology," Cone is specific in citing "the slave-experience" as the dominant shaping force in evaluating the African-American experience. In this article Cone explicitly states, "The theme of liberation expressed in story form is the essence of black religion. Both the content and the form were essentially determined by black people's social existence. . . . They did not debate religion on an abstract theological level but lived their religion concretely in history" (144).

More recently, James H. Evans's 1990 article "Deconstructing the Tradition: Narrative Strategies in Nascent Black Theology" picks up on Cone's emphasis on the dialectical relationship between form and content, where "story was both the medium through which truth was communicated and also a constituent of truth itself" (Cone, "The Story" 147), when he identifies two important literary tasks of a black theologian: recording the unwritten raw material of black theology and writing as a political act of liberation grounded in the will to be free. Evans concludes that as writers, early black theologians served the dual purpose of edifying and preserving the religious resources of the black community and boldly confronting the structures of oppression.

Evans elaborates his position in *We Have Been Believers* when he writes, "African-American religion is not a static phenomenon, but is the result of a dynamic interaction of the remembered past, the experiences present, and the anticipated future. It reflects the changeable character of African American experience in the world" (24). African-American theology therefore becomes "the explanation, defense, and critique of the religious practice and interpretation of the black community" and, as a consequence of this understanding, narrative is the necessary form of African-American theology because the form of black religion is story.

But it was Cone who pioneered the recognition among black theologians that "the form of black religious thought is expressed in the style of a story and its content is liberation" (*God* 54), with an emphasis on the actual telling of the story as bearing equal importance to the content of the story. In this regard, the interplay of character and characterization typical of the slave narrative tradition assumes a theological significance. According to Cone, ex-slave textimonies that described the actual situation of African Americans in their state of oppression gave voice to a "truth for and about black people that . . . emerge[s] out of the context of their experience" (*God* 17). The narrators' stories depict not only the actual misery of slavery, but also elements of hope for liberation so that the story functions as both a mirror of the present and an indicator of the future.

Although this kind of storytelling may assume secular proportions, if there is one enduring and explicit link between Christianity and the slave narrative tradition it is the model established by Jesus—not just that he "did good things" (Acts 10:33), but how he conveyed his message. Jesus' style was invitational. Instead of telling people what to do or what to believe, he encouraged them to see things differently, confident that if they did so their behavior would change accordingly. This called for working with people's imaginations more than with their reason or will and resulted in Jesus' parables, the stories that helped people to perceive what they saw and to understand what they heard (Matthew 13:13–17).

Whether it was by conscious design or not, a survey of the writings of James Cone reveals that his own theology has been continually refined in terms of story. His first book, *Black Theology and Black Power* (1969) is best described as a theological manifesto; in his second book, *A Black Theology of Liberation* (1970), Cone emphasizes in a systematic way the content of theology and Christian doctrine; but in his third book, *The Spirituals and the Blues* (1972), Cone moves away from systematic arguments and toward story in this theological interpretation of slave and blues songs. In *God of the Oppressed* (1975), Cone demonstrates how a black theology of liberation is the necessary imperative of the sermons, songs, and stories produced by the black experience. While arguing for a story dimension as essential to the formation of black theology, Cone also demonstrates the function of story through his frequent allusions to stories culled from a variety of sources.

From his 1975 article to his 1991 book, *Martin and Malcolm in America,* which is the story of men who lived in deed their respective liberating creeds, Cone draws our attention to the rich narrative sources for liberating affirmation. He quotes from Zora Neale Hurston's folktales gathered in *Mules and Men,* sermons collected by Langston Hughes and Arna Bontemps, and spirituals and work songs preserved in oral traditions and sung in the church of his youth. But he also makes reference to contemporary narrative sources such as lyrics from a song sung by Roberta Flack, the poetry of Countee Cullen and Mari Evans, and the novels of James Baldwin and Richard Wright. In fact, his book *For My People* (1984), a theological interpretation of the civil rights movement, takes its title from a poem by Margaret Walker that Cone includes in the text. In 1982 he published *My Soul Looks Back,* an autobiographical reflection that situates itself, in form and the act of demonstration, squarely in the slave narrative tradition of textimony.

My Soul Looks Back blends personal experience with public testimony to reveal how experience—the legacy of slavery—generated not just a life but a theology. Cone's book was written as part of a series on "journeys of faith," and he takes his title from a Negro spiritual whose lyrics suggest the journey motif from oppression to liberation that is characteristic of the slave narrative tradition:

How I got over
How I got over
My soul looks back
And wonders
How I got over.

The text is explicit in not just wondering, but identifying how the author "got over." Like Douglass and those after him, Cone had a kind of conversion experience. After the assassination of Martin Luther King, Cone describes experiencing a radical shift in thought and belief that allowed him to intellectually make the connection between his lived experience as an African American and his learned experience as a theologian. It was then that he identified his fate as tied into the fate of all oppressed people.

Throughout the narrative Cone describes how he suffered moments of shame and frustration in trying to understand his encounters with an oppressive, racist society. He identifies everyday people who are agents of change and models for inspiration. He demonstrates how racism is present in all levels of American society, and he is full of anger and confusion as he tries to decode a way out of life as he knows it and toward a life that reflects the Kingdom of God. But by his act of textimony, by making his story accessible to others, he is participating in a tradition of storytelling, instructing his readers how to keep faith while giving himself "'a little extra strength'" to 'keep on keeping on'" (14). Cone reasserts the power of story and the role the slave narrative tradition continues to play in drawing us into identification with the oppressed by showing that people naturally make their entry into the struggle for liberation at the point where they are personally hurt the most. This text and Cone's overall body of writings demonstrates that at some point a theology of liberation must move toward story in articulating its form and content.

Following Cone's narrative directive, several significant extended works have emerged that broadly treat the slave narrative tradition as a resource for liberation theology. They were preceded by Benjamin Mays's *The Negro's God as Reflected in His Literature* (1938), in which the author shows how ideas of God are interpreted in literature to support a growing consciousness of social and psychological adjustment required by African Americans. William R. Jones's *Is God a White Racist?* (1973) and Cornel West's *Prophesy Deliverance!: An Afro-American Revolutionary Christianity* (1982) make many references to or discuss in some respect African-American creative writers in formulating their theologies. Feminist theologians such as Katie Cannon in *Black Womanist Ethics* (1988) and Delores Williams in *Sisters in the Wilderness: The Challenge of Womanist God-Talk* (1993) have drawn our attention to the narrative resources found in modern black women's writings, and James H. Evans Jr. in *Spiritual Empowerment in Afro-American Literature* (1987), identifies in the writings of Frederick Douglass, Rebecca Jackson, Booker T. Washington, Richard Wright, and Toni Morrison ways in which African-American religion and literature express and define the struggle for liberation.

In *Shoes That Fit Our Feet: Sources for a Constructive Black Theology* (1993), Dwight Hopkins engages in a systematic liberation theology rooted in literary resources that begin with slave narratives and spirituals and move to include the fiction of Toni Morrison, traditional trickster folktales, and the writings of W. E. B. Du Bois, Martin Luther King Jr., and Malcolm X. Yet as a resource for the kind of analysis I am undertaking in this study, Hopkins's volume is problematic. Although Hopkins invites the use of non-Christian sources in constructing a black theology, he always cites these secular examples as evidence of God's power because "God liberates where

God chooses to liberate" (3). Hopkins seems sincere in his goal to create "a closer working relationship between black church and non-church segments of the African-American community" (9), but his readings of secular cultural production are so dominated by his Christian convictions that he misses much of the power of these texts, which by imagination and design resist too easy a Christian interpretation. Likewise, his belief that his Christian analysis can "strengthen black and non-black relations by pointing out the necessity for non-blacks to grasp the importance of justice . . . that permeates the diverse segments of black politics, culture, and spirituality" (9) is exclusive and uninviting to non-Christian whites who also stand in need of redemption.

The same problems are present in a volume Hopkins edited with George Cummings, *Cut Loose Your Stammering Tongue: Black Theology in the Slave Narratives* (1991). This work is an attempt to ground contemporary black theology in the cultural resources present in the historic black community and examines slave narratives exclusively as a source for black liberation theology. The authors included in this volume try to take seriously the indigenous sources of their enslaved ancestors—the narratives, spirituals, blues, sermons, prayers and other stories of struggle and survival—and to accent non-Christian liberation by recognizing that the slave narrative tradition often involves a critique of Christianity. Proclaiming a collective strength in "literally developing black theology from the actual voices of poor, enslaved African Americans" (xiii), Hopkins's introduction identifies four foundational elements for the creation of a constructive black theology of liberation that derive from the slave narratives under consideration.

First they "tell us to hear and heed the life-language of our chained forebears" (xvi). Second, "black slaves remove obstacles from our 'God-talk' by imbuing us with their unique liberation practice, world view, language, thought patterns and theological common sense" (xvi). Third, "the slaves' language, thought, and practice show us how God presents God's particular self in the constrained, marred lives of a faith-freed, beautiful black people" (xvi). And fourth, slave narratives "provide a theological abundance of religious experience from non-Christian bearers of God's freeing spirit" (xvii).

Although this volume greatly contributes to our understanding of an enslaved person's perceptions of his or her liberating presence in the world, it does not discuss in literary critical terms how these texts can generate that feeling of identification Douglass draws our attention to in his narrative. The authors have limited themselves to a specific definition of a slave narrative, relying mainly on forty-one volumes of interviews with former slaves recorded in George P. Rawick's *The American Slave: A Composite Autobiography*, and they do not discuss the ways in which a slave narrative tradition as a conscious aesthetic form was developed and continues to be developed. Furthermore, despite the authors' recognition of the relevance of non-Christian narrative sources for liberation theology, Cummings and Hopkins either ignore or have difficulty understanding these non-Christian resources in terms other than theistic ones, often forcing them into inappropriate categories. Their implication that black materials are religious because they all point to the workings of God fails to take seriously humanistic strands of black expression.

Victor Anderson challenges this approach as a dangerous "hermeneutics of return" that serves an ideological function that is not theologically illuminating but culturally apologetic for a notion of ontological blackness. The consequences of such a hermeneutic, Anderson warns, "is that whatever claims are made for African American identity in terms of black subjectivity . . . are subsumed under a black collective consciousness definable in terms of black faith" (99). By forcing black sources such as slave narratives to fit into a rigid Christian design, "the theologian as storyteller has a difficult task of overcoming the vicious circularity between oppression and liberation" (102). What is lost in this kind of enterprise, Anderson believes, is possibilities for "cultural transcendence." He asks, "On what does transcendence depend? At what point do thriving and flourishing enter the equation of suffering and resistance? An existence that is bound existentially only by the dimensions of struggle and resistance or survival, it seems to me, constitutes a less that fulfilling human existence. We all want more than to survive; that is a minimal requirement of a fulfilled life. We also want to thrive and flourish" (112).

Although I certainly agree with Anderson's goals for cultural fulfillment, I believe there is some merit to the hermeneutics of return if we take seriously the imaginative implications of the sources under investigation. What is flawed is not the attempt to retrieve slave narratives as a source for theological reflection, but the insistence that these texts must serve a Christian theological agenda that identifies suffering and resistance as the only forces at work in these cultural productions. Slave narratives and especially the ongoing tradition they engendered give more than ample testimony to the human quest for cultural fulfillment that extends to include thriving and flourishing. That they do so in ways that are not exclusively Christian does not diminish their effectiveness for promoting a theological enterprise or advancing social justice. In fact, it is precisely the unconventional, imaginative theology embodied in the tradition that makes it a valuable resource for promoting liberation in its fullest multicultural sense, as the examples I provide in subsequent chapters make evident.

What I am suggesting here as a direction for liberation theology is succinctly illustrated by the documents collected in the two volumes of Cone and Wilmore's *Black Theology*. Among all the scholarly treatments and doctrinal statements, only one clearly points a way for understanding the imaginative potential embodied in the slave narrative tradition as a resource for liberation theology: Alice Walker's landmark essay "In Search of Our Mothers' Gardens." In this essay Walker lovingly pays tribute to her mother's legacy of weaving the sacred and the profane in her approach to life and for handing down by example, "respect for the possibilities—and the will to grasp them" (441). What Walker reminds us is that the imaginative components of African-American religious formulations cannot be dismissed because theology, as Leon Watts reminds us, "is informed not only by revelation, scripture, and tradition, but also by culture and history" (26). The canon, like the cause of liberation, is ongoing in its formation as artists continue to identify in imaginative terms the spiritual resources available to humanity.

The most obvious place to begin developing a canon for a liberating theology is with scripture because liberation theology asserts that scripture records the actions of a living God on behalf of God's oppressed people. Indeed, any nonscriptural source for a liberation theology reflects scriptural concerns in allusion and tone, if not in actual citation, because God-language, however it might have been corrupted by slaveholders and other oppressors, still draws attention to the source of the black community's identification with divine presence.

The texts preferred by contemporary theologians and antebellum slaves are the same: Moses leading his people out of bondage, Jesus and his ministry to the poor. Liberation theologians repeatedly make reference to Christ or other biblical figures as storytellers. Christ, in particular, is recognized for telling parables about the weak, the oppressed, the humiliated and exploited, which in essence contain the concentrated elements of black experience. But these stories also contain glimpses of hope for change and liberation. Christ's stories and his actions display the resistance to existing and dehumanizing conditions that liberation theologians promote. In the figure of Christ, liberation theologians reveal Jesus as a character. They remove him from the realm of being an ideological concept or mental ideal and present him as a active liberator who willingly demonstrates his character in his identification with the oppressed.

Black theology, in addition to examining black cultural forms, introduces a reexamination of fundamental scriptural texts, even those that served a specific role in slave theology. Although enslaved people viewed the Book of Revelation as a key text, most contemporary liberation theologians focus on biblical texts that give examples of human agency, not divine agency, in effecting liberating change. The apocalyptic strains and strong reliance on transcendent forces to shape human history presented in Revelation are viewed as less relevant than stories of enslaved Hebrews overthrowing Egyptian oppressors or Jesus' conscious and deliberate decision to be an emancipator of people's bodies as well as their souls.

Whether or not Jesus' death on the cross was a genuine act of redemption for oppressed people is challenged by Delores Williams, who suggests that for black women in particular the redemption of humanity is accomplished not by the death of Jesus on the cross but rather by the ministerial vision of righting relationships that he implemented in his life ("Black Women's Surrogacy"). Similarly, Jacquelyn Grant urges theologians to abandon or at least reconsider the language of servanthood that underscores so much religious testimony because "this language has undergirded many of the structures causing pain and suffering in today's world" (38). To nurture the process of liberation, Grant suggests that we "adopt and emphasize a language that challenges the servant mentality of oppressed peoples and the oppressive mentality of oppressors" (39). The language she offers in its place is the "language of discipleship" because of the way it functions to break down traditional and exclusive understandings.

Liberation theologians appreciate that the Bible has been and continues to be manipulated for any number of desired interpretations and used to defend circumstances of oppression rather that serving as an inspiration for agents of liberation, even if one is speaking from a biblically sanctioned theological perspective. But the language of discipleship Grant describes is embodied in the slave narrative tradition, whose existence reminds us that just as we need to reinterpret biblical resources, so too should we turn to other texts that may speak more directly to human experience as recorded in history or that recast scriptural truths in a new story.

Anyone who is not moved by the plight of the ancient Israelites or the courage of first-century Palestinian Christians can look beyond traditional Christian forms and obvious theological narratives to more imaginative works, often the creation of artists and activists who, although not Christian, are partners in constructing theology and promoting social justice. As the slave narrative tradition suggests, one can stand outside the conventions of this particular faith stance and still advance the goals of liberation theology. An awareness of other "sacred" texts that still participate in the spirit of the gospel imperative may be more effective in initiating modern skeptics into acting on behalf of the cause of human liberation.

For despite the fact that many texts of the slave narrative tradition lack, in the words of James Cone, the presence of "God as a symbol of victory over suffering and pain" (*God* 26), their theme remains identical with those that do contain "churchly expressions" (*God* 22): persistence, survival, creation, and overcoming the odds in an oppressive system. Consequently, the black experience in white America, however secular its expression, can be seen as a major foundation of theology as "a source for its starting point" (*God* 18). In *Is God a White Racist?* William R. Jones addresses this foundational principle when he sets forth and promotes a "humanocentric theism" or a humanistic approach toward constructing a liberation theology.

Humanocentric theism, Jones maintains, offers a more realistic and relevant interpretation of black experience and model for liberating change. Jones sets out to demythologize religious studies as a reflection on an eternal being and to see it more as a cultural product. He asserts that we should take into account the influence of humanists who "rejected the biblical and Christian models for explaining black suffering, who were unafraid to doubt God's intrinsic goodness relative to blacks, who questioned God's existence and relevance in the black struggle for freedom" (xv).

In advocating the "functional ultimacy of man" (xxii) in redressing oppression, Jones not only opens wide the arena for humanity's involvement in liberation concerns, but also tackles the problem of theodicy by minimizing God's responsibility for the crimes and errors of human history and placing the challenge of liberation in humanity's hands. Jones believes that what is required to persuade humanity to be active in liberation comes from sources other than God or scripture and that if we recognize this we may begin to eliminate the potential for anyone to find a moral or theological "escape clause" to refuse participation in liberation agendas. Another voice in African-American liberation theology that is picking up where Jones left off is that of Anthony Pinn. His book *Why, Lord?: Suffering and Evil in Black Theology* (1995) takes strong exception to the notion of redemptive suffering, regarding it as a roadblock to liberation. Turning to the tradition of black humanism, Pinn locates (as I try to do here) resources in literature and music that provide new motivation and hope for African Americans. Pinn, like Jones, is attempting to reveal forms of black religious experience that often are ignored by Christian theologians who examine African-American religion. He suggests ways in which one can view the African-American religious landscape from a perspective that considers anything that provides ultimate orientation religious.

In rethinking the canon of African-American religious experience, Pinn is not entirely without precedent. Frederick Douglass structures his narrative in such a way that non-Christian influences coming from noncanonical sources are given prominence and authority as determining factors in his liberation. The fact that *The Columbian Orator* is the text that launches his sacred quest for literacy is one instance in which a secular text functions in a religious capacity. Although he never explains how he came to possess this significant text (and many theologians no doubt would conjecture the movement of grace), once he had it he read it constantly.

This text helped Douglass gain basic tools of literacy and develop a critical sensibility wherein he could interpret both the text and the subtext of slavery. As he writes, "These were choice documents to me. I read them over and over again with unabated interest. They gave tongue to interesting thoughts of my own soul, which had frequently flashed through my mind, and died away for want of utterance. The moral which I gained from the dialogue was the power of truth over the conscience of even a slaveholder. . . . The reading of these documents enabled me to utter my thoughts," and increasingly to "abhor and detest my enslavers" (*Narrative* 84). Another non-Christian "text" is introduced to him when he meets Sandy on his way to a confrontation with the slavebreaker Covey; Douglass accepts Sandy's offer of a "root" for protection and in so doing affirms a religious authority that is outside a Judeo-Christian framework and portrays the root as a possible source—"from whence the spirit came I don't know" (*Narrative* 112)—for his determination to challenge Covey.[8]

Still, whatever empowering source they locate, the critical element that makes texts of the slave narrative tradition so compelling is their insistence that the oppressed, not the oppressor, define the terms of their theology and experience. Black theology, as Cone insists, is first and foremost "a theology of and for black people, an examination of their stories, tales, and sayings. It is an investigation of the mind into the raw materials of our pilgrimage, telling the story of 'how we got over'" (*God* 18). But in the same book, Cone also asserts that "in order for the theologian to recognize the particularity of black religion, he must imagine his way into the environment and ethos of black slave, probing the language and rhythm of a people who had to 'feel their way along the course of American slavery,' enduring the stress of human servitude, while still affirming their humanity" (11). I suggest that Cone's reference to "theologians" should be read as "all people." The imaginative disciplines of writers of the slave narrative tradition are used to remind readers that their command of the powers of definition and description can initiate all their readers into an experience of conversion to the cause of liberation.

This role of the slave narrative tradition in liberation theology is affirmed by James H. Evans's essay "Toward an African-American Theology," in which he develops three tasks for contemporary black liberation theology. First is to "clarify the contacts—historical, sociopolitical, cultural and intellectual"— in which faith is affirmed (28). The second task is "to articulate, interpret, and assess the essential doctrinal affirmations of African-American faith" (31) for the contemporary community of faith. The third task is "to examine the moral implications of that faith" (32) for witness in the world.

These tasks correspond to the criteria I have discussed for appreciating the liberating theology that emerges out of the slave narrative tradition. The contacts or context is the slave narrative tradition itself, in both its original formation and its recent development. The content is the affirmation of experience expressed through a writer's creation of a protagonist or one who has been characterized and with whom a reader is drawn into sympathetic or sacramental identification. The intent, or the moral implications for witness in the world, are demonstrated through the character of the writer and his or her liberating act of testifying, of creating a textimony, in the hopes of converting the oppressed.

The necessary qualities for a text to become canonical for a liberating theology are not those found in its Christian testimony or justification; they are the creative elements suggested by Douglass in his insistence that the reader must imagine himself or herself in the circumstance. The literature must powerfully draw a reader into an experience of oppression and make the reader care about the fate of the protagonists. Although this does not necessarily require that the author experience first-hand the oppression being detailed, one must at least believe that the author is, by his or her act of imagination, participating in the liberation struggle by attempting to identify with the life of the oppressed. How a writer achieves the effect of helping the reader to identify with the protagonist is the primary distinguishing characteristic of the slave narrative tradition as it functions for a liberating theology.

A narrative component therefore is consequential for a liberating theology and it is especially suitable to awakening readers to the cause of liberation through demonstration, not instruction. This is not to suggest that there is a dichotomy between demonstration and instruction, but that instruction or edification is evident or implicit in the act of demonstration—

in this case in the act of creating textimony. The awakening is achieved by the interplay of character and characterization: identifying, as slave narrators did, an authoritative and credible authorial voice of character responsible for the creation or the telling of the story (itself an act of liberation and a liberating act) and creating or characterizing a protagonist with whom the reader is compelled to identify. The second characteristic is perhaps the more easily understood. Understanding it involves using standard literary critical terms by which to establish the aesthetic achievement of a particular story. The first criterion (the character of the author who stands behind the characterization) is more complicated, at least in postbellum formulations of the slave narrative tradition.

The writing acts of ex-slave narrators such as Douglass clearly establish in our contemporary consciousness the character of the authors. But to explain the character of contemporary writers as courageous and their writing as a liberating act involves more subtle appreciation of the act of literary construction, or in the case of the slave narrative tradition, literary reconstruction. One way of identifying the character component of contemporary narratives of liberation is to focus on the recurrent motif of slavery and its role in shaping the literary imagination of African-American writers.

As Toni Morrison describes in her essay "The Site of Memory," by using the resources of memory and imagination she can begin to approach her ancestors' experience of slavery and show "awe and reverence and mystery and magic" (111). She does so because she understands that "This is not a story to pass on" (*Beloved* 273), the dual meaning of this passage implying something about both the pain involved in remembering slavery and the responsibility to confront slavery. Yet by returning to the origins of the slave narrative tradition and by tracing its development in African-American consciousness and form, we may begin to wash away the debris of our historic national sin.

To demonstrate how a liberating theology is articulated in the slave narrative tradition, I examine how, from the context of slavery as the dominate example of praxis, several artists set forth a specific content or characterization of the oppressed or other with the intention of promoting a recognition of and respect for the character of the oppressed. Themes or tropes set forth by Douglass that recur throughout narrative formulations of the slave experience begin with a moment in the life of the protagonists when they recognize their difference and the condition of their oppression. Descriptions of the circumstances of the oppression are critical because they establish firmly in the reader the reality of the experience.

From this moment of recognition, the protagonist draws the reader into a consideration of the distinction between creed and deed—between what people say and what they do. In considering this critical difference, the reader, who often is implicated as an oppressor in this distinction, is then drawn into an identification with the protagonists in their experience of oppression. Finally, the reader becomes a partner in the pilgrimage from oppression to liberation because the story is situated in a journey motif in which freedom is affirmed in the protagonist's actual arrival at a state of grace, a state iterated by the reader in his or her own experience of conversion to the cause of the oppressed.

What propels the plot and generates the protagonist's movement from oppression to liberation—represented in the slave narrative tradition as movement from slavery to the North, Zion, or Africa—is a vision of home or a place of grace. Ex-slave narrators and their successors actually write their way home. The geographical movement from the South to the North serves as "a conscious metaphor for the fugitive's personal and social movement from anonymity to identity, from self-contempt to self-respect, from ignorance to enlightenment, and from sin to salvation" (Butterfield 27). But in the slave narrative tradition home is a concept that carries a variety of associations and meanings. There is no home without a journey away from it, and the customary alien place away from home is precisely where former slaves hoped to create true homes. The slave narrative tradition inverts our customary understanding of home, just as it is meant to invert other binary formulations. In doing so it signifies on America itself as "the idea of an ever recreated new home, indeed 'a new Heaven and a new Earth'" (Sopher 135). The vision of a future homeland sustains the slave narrative tradition, a homeland that, paradoxically, may be created even at the site of one's most profound oppression.

This vision begins in a private mode of confession as described by each character's own particular experience, but it is transformed into a public mode of textimony when cast in narrative form. The reader, in turn, reinteriorizes this public discourse and makes it private through her identification with the oppressed. The result is the initiation—in terms of vision, if not actual fact—of the ultimate goal of both the narratives and a liberating theology: the creation of a human community in which a private place one can call home is available to all. The slave narrative tradition and our attempts to understand its ongoing development continually recapitulate the energies that engendered it, helping to transform us by enabling us to understand others and thereby come to a deeper understanding of ourselves. Contemporary representatives of the slave narrative tradition and the public to whom they speak try through their imagination to take the same journey ex-slave narrators took: "the 'passing over and returning home,' the journey to self-knowledge through empathetic intuition (admittedly imperfect and vicarious) of the experience of others. In this journey we encounter difference not as something alienating but as simply different. Ideally, the journey . . . leads not only to experience but to compassion" (Raboteau, "Praying" 321).

All the works I discuss in this study continue to issue the abolitionist call in the hope of generating a response, even though that response has been judged by history to be less than effective. Indeed, Albert Stone observes that despite the abolitionists' belief that slave narratives were their most powerful weapon in the fight against slavery, "though hearts were indeed moved, minds disabused of much misinformation, and imaginations fired by vivid pictures of slavery and of the black man's actual and potential achievements in coping with slavery, nevertheless American political behavior was not fundamentally altered" (211).

One is forced to conclude that though widely read, the slave narratives effected no vital change in American attitudes. Aesthetic power is not translated readily into political action, and those already predisposed by social, economic, and religious outlook to be open-minded are most likely to be affected by the slave narrative tradition. But the ongoing dynamics of the tradition indicate that measuring the effects is not the sole reason for creating; the solution may not be the solution, but the process of trying to arrive at a solution can be a solution.

Just as black theology demands of white theologians a radical response that forbids neutrality and demands that one take the side of those on the margins of society, so too does the slave narrative tradition. None of us can have direct access to the experience of slavery, but the slave narrative tradition began and continues as an effort to bring others, through the exercise of their imaginations, to the struggle for liberation by revealing where African Americans hurt the most: back in slavery and even now in racist encounters that reinscribe the master/slave paradigm.

These texts encourage others to make a sacramental identification with African Americans so that others' liberation is bound up in a commitment to the liberation of all. As James Baldwin observes, the common inheritance of humanity imposes on all of us "the necessity of treating each other as sacred" (*Evidence* 51). Liberating acts of imagination are not only efforts to keep at bay an awful reality, but actual attempts to transform individuals and the communities they create. These acts of textimony may begin with yesterdays—the legacy of slavery—but as Paul D. remarks near the end of *Beloved*, "we got more yesterday than anybody. We need some kind of tomorrow" (273).

NOTES

1. These examples were gathered from accounts in *The Washington Post*, including Donna Britt's column "Book Debate Twists, Turns on Race" (24 January 1995), Courtland Milloy's "Slavery Is Not Amusing" (14 November 1993), Tamara Jones's "Living History or Undying Racism" (11 October 1994), and Linton Weeks's "The Continuing Hurt of History" (22 December 1995).

2. A notable exception to the generalization Ellis cites is the activities of Donna Wyant Howell. An African American freelance editor in Washington, D.C., Howell discovered the Work Project Administration interviews with ex-slaves while doing research at the Library of Congress. She was so moved and so appalled that so few Americans knew of the existence of the interviews that she began publishing them in fifty-page booklets that she sold at trade fairs and educational conferences for $5.95 each. Her goal was to make these texts widely known and available. See Ken Ringle, "Out of the Mouths of Slaves: Woman Brings Stories from the Archives to the People," *The Washington Post* 28 October 1996, D1.

3. In the same article Levine discusses the role played by the recently established journal *Race Traitor: A Journal of the New Abolitionism*. In articulating their reasons for starting the journal, the editors assert that the white race is a "club" but that if enough people "defect"—that is, refuse to follow the rules and value the privileges of being white over their "class, gender, or other interests"—whiteness will cease to predict their behavior and this "will set off tremors that will lead to the [white race's] collapse." Although this agenda is commendable, Levine warns against the tendency to be romantic and patronizing, to see blackness as "a faith into which one may be baptized; whiteness as the sin that floats off in the holy water" (15).

4. The dynamics of the slave narrative tradition were played out even further when Oprah Winfrey devoted an entire show to the "black like me" experience, going so far as to test the principle in reverse with black men cosmetically transformed into white men so that they could experience the unacknowledged privileges whites enjoy every day. Among the guests was Grace Halsell, who experimented with living as an African American, a Latina, and a Native American. Halsell participated as an audience member and was not invited to share in detail her experiences, which, considering their diversity, may have added interesting complications to the enterprise.

5. I am indebted to William Andrews for providing this insight on the nature of imagination.

6. Although Douglass's was not the first book-length ex-slave narrative published, I chose his text as my paradigm because of the status it has been accorded in the American canon and because of the way in which it lent itself as a model for the

analysis I wanted to undertake. I chose James Cone as the primary representative of African-American liberation theology for similar reasons.

7. Readers may recognize this reference to the relationship between words and actions in the recent arguments of attorney Catherine MacKinnon, who uses the notion of the interchangeability of speech and action as a legalistic ground for challenging pornography as unconstitutional. See MacKinnon's *Only Words* (Cambridge, Mass.: Harvard University Press, 1993).

8. In her essay "Malcolm X and Liberation Theology," Nancy Tenfelde Clasby shows how *The Autobiography of Malcolm X* and the Muslim beliefs expressed therein are also sources for and representations of liberation theology.

2   Affirming the Unity: Richard Wright

> What moves a writer to eloquence is less meaningful than
> what he makes of it.
> —Ralph Ellison

In 1939 Billie Holiday recorded "Strange Fruit," the song that would
become the pivotal vehicle of her career. A ballad that depicts a "pas-
toral scene of the gallant South," the song centers on the image of "a
strange and bitter fruit"—the lynched bodies of black men—swaying from
poplar trees in the Southern breeze. It contrasts the scent of magnolias with
"the sudden smell of burning flesh." Although her biographer Donald
Clarke and others claim that Billie Holiday didn't know what to make of
"Strange Fruit" when she first heard it, Holiday claims in her controversial autobiography *Lady Sings the Blues* that she "dug it right off" (84).
But most agree that once she did get it, when "suddenly the impact of it
hit her," as composer Arthur Herzog explains, "she put herself into the
song" (Clarke 163).

When she first performed the song at Cafe Society, owner Barney Josephson remembers how spontaneous tears began to flow down Holiday's
cheeks, leaving the audience profoundly moved. In fact, Josephson recalls
that every performance of the song was "unforgettable" (Clarke 164). To
"let it sink in," Josephson arranged special conditions for Holiday's performance of "Strange Fruit." It would be Holiday's last number and would
not be followed by a bow. The stage would be blacked out except for a pin
spotlight on Holiday's face and no interruptions for service of patrons were
allowed. The impact created by Holiday's performance of "Strange Fruit"
was summed up by one patron as "a moment of oppressively heavy silence

followed, and then a kind of rustling sound I had never heard before. It was the sound of almost two thousand people sighing" (Clarke 167).

A lynching scene similar to the one depicted in "Strange Fruit" is also the subject of a poem written several years earlier by Richard Wright. "Between the World and Me" narrates the story of someone who accidentally stumbles across the aftermath of a lynching and finds its "sooty details . . . thrusting themselves between the world and me." Throughout the following lines the narrator, shocked and dazed, recounts the "sooty details." Soon, however, his shock turns "frozen with cold pity for the life that was gone," and he states, "The dry bones stirred, rattled, lifted, melting themselves into my bones." In this sequence the observer becomes the victim and identifies with the experience of lynching, reliving it in his own mind: "And then they had me, stripped me, battering my teeth / into my throat till I swallowed my own blood" (18–19).

Wright brings the individual narrator's experiences as the shock of an observer to that of someone else, a black man being lynched. This broader identification, as Robert Coles points out, "not only fuses two identities but—most importantly, by recreating the violence directly through the narrator entering the flesh of the victim—brings the audience closer to the experience as well" (391). As the narrator recreates the scene, which now affects him directly as the victim, the audience loses its observer status and is pulled closer to the experience, in effect eliciting from the reader the kind of response evoked by Holiday's performance of "Strange Fruit." This technique, Coles suggests, is "fundamental" because "it acts as a method by which Wright, in artistic terms and within the structure of his art and creative process, uses a method to draw together seemingly separate experiences and identities" (391). By pulling together the identities of victim, observer, and audience, Wright demonstrates, in Coles's words, that "the fundamental dynamic of Wright's art is constantly moving toward unity" (391).

Coles's description of Wright's aesthetic of moving toward unity by creating circumstances in which a reader is drawn into vicarious identification with a protagonist is characteristic of the slave narrative tradition from which Wright emerged and attains a particular immediacy and poignancy in his autobiography *Black Boy,* published a decade after "Between the World and Me." Writing his autobiography served the same purpose for Wright that singing "Strange Fruit" did for Billie Holiday: It created a platform from which he could pronounce a judgment on the racist environment that led to such episodes of lynching. Furthermore, the genesis of "Strange Fruit" and the legend that surrounds it is symbolic of both the continuities and the discontinuities of the slave narrative tradition as Wright and others extended it after the antebellum era.

After observing the initial impact of Holiday's performance of "Strange Fruit," Josephson realized that the song "became such a personal thing with her, so identified with her, that I guess she began to think she wrote it" (Clarke 164). Holiday admitted that the lyrics derived from a poem by Abel Meeropol (a.k.a. Lewis Allan), but contrary to the recollections of other involved parties she also claims that she helped to compose the music.[1] As she asserts in her autobiography, the song "became my personal protest." Despite the fact that it depressed her and reminded her of tragedies in her own family, she insisted she had to keep singing it, in part because "it has a way of separating the straight people from the squares and cripples" (*Lady* 84).

Like the original ex-slave narratives, "Strange Fruit" became an aesthetic call for liberation. Its ability, in Holiday's words, to separate "straights" from "squares," reflects the impulse behind and the effect of ex-slave narratives that attempted to personally awaken people to issues of social injustice. Like ex-slave narratives that were prohibited in the slaveholding South because their transformative power was instantly recognized, "Strange Fruit" was banned from most radio stations, and Columbia, the company that produced Holiday's records, refused to touch it. As ex-slave narratives became intimately identified with the extraordinary people who created them, Holiday's performance of the song became so definitive that jazz aficionados can scarcely bear to hear it sung by anyone else. And just as the production of slave narratives had an ultimately numbing effect and probably contributed very little toward concrete social change, so too did "Strange Fruit" come to be chic and distanced from the very context out of which it emerged. Audiences would call for it to be sung like it was a dance favorite, and despite Holiday's poignant relationship to the song and its contents, "Strange Fruit" became the pivotal vehicle in her career, launching record sales and garnering her picture on the cover of *Time*.

But as a product of imagination a century after slavery, it hardly matters that Holiday's version of the song's creation has been proven to be untrue. Holiday's autobiography was written with Bill Dufty, a journalist at the *New York Post,* thereby placing her in a long line of black narrators who needed a white amanuensis to tell their stories. But the singer participated fully in the creation of her own myth because she understood the ways in which it could sustain her actual life. The creation, reception, and myth-driven history of "Strange Fruit" serves as an instructive model for considering postbellum articulations of the slave narrative tradition such as Richard Wright's *Black Boy*. Wright's autobiography has been revealed by biographers and Wright himself to have many fictionalized episodes. Nonetheless, it was hailed by critics as a genuine portrait of Southern black life that "really makes you realize how it felt to be a Negro in the South" (Reilly 127). Wright's highly selective memory may recall only the most pathological incidents in his life, but in the words of Timothy Dow Adams, "*Black Boy* should not be read as historical truth, which strives to report those incontrovertible facts that can be somehow corroborated, but as narrative truth" (82–83).

The fictionalized aspects of Wright's work, like those of "Strange Fruit," are aspects of structural design that reveal an important motive. In each case, unspeakable horrors are presented in a package so lyrical that the reader or the hearer is swept into confronting a reality he or she might otherwise have avoided. Ellison's analysis of *Black Boy* describes the same quality embodied in each creative effort: "the impulse to keep painful details and episodes of brutal experience alive in one's active consciousness, to finger its jagged grain, and to transcend it, not by the consolation of philosophy but by squeezing from it a near-tragic, near-comic lyricism" (*Shadow and Act* 78).

The song and the autobiography each testify to the certainty that in aesthetic production for the cause of social justice, whatever is actually fact or fiction is not as important as the greater truth that is represented and the reality that is finally given form. In the cases of Holiday and Wright, the blurred distinctions between autobiography and fiction are generated for a specific purpose that is a central feature of both the slave narrative tradition and a liberating theology: the process of humanizing the other. The arousal of the conscience of oppressors, whose "willed innocence" was shaped by an unjust entitlement, and the self-realization of the oppressed, who were shaped by an unjust prejudice, characterize this process. Whether they are secular or religious in tone, at the core of every liberation text are elements typical of both an autobiographical and a fictional enterprise: an individual experience of the search for the self and a communal journey toward an unknown.

From its beginning, the slave narrative tradition, which voices previously unheard stories of the search for self through the other, has achieved a narrative truth through its characteristic blend of fictional and autobiographical qualities. In his analysis of the narrative of Frederick Douglass, Albert Stone observes that this text and other ex-slave autobiographies "occupy the territory between history and art, biography and fiction, memory and imagination" (194). Stone goes on to argue that if one accepts that all history is a deliberate artistic creation, one can appreciate how slave narratives and the literary tradition that emerged from them exhibit a variety of literary devices for recording a past, persuading belief, and motivating action, thereby blurring the line between autobiography and fiction.

The combined effect of plot and moral in ex-slave narratives exploited the natural focus of autobiography on private experience, thereby paradoxically providing a fictionlike perspective. Thus, the veracity on which slave narratives depended to support their polemical function also supports postbellum articulations, where the existence of actual life histories authenticates what the novelist has imagined. As writers moved further away from the actual experience of slavery, the fictional elements necessarily dominated their endeavors. But this fictionalizing actually was a technique provided to them by their ancestors, who understood, in the words of F. R. Hart, that "in understanding fiction one seeks an imaginative grasp of another's meaning; in understanding personal history one seeks an imaginative comprehension of another's historic identity" (488).

Richard Wright's *Black Boy* (1945)[2] is one example of the attempt to imaginatively comprehend a historic identity—to fictionalize self in autobiography. What unites the autobiographical and fictional enterprises is imagination. Although Wright's autobiography shows him as shaped by the oppression that was "the historic inheritance of his people" (Scott, "The Dark" 153), it also reveals him as the heir of a slave narrative tradition that displayed a "reverence for the imaginative,"[3] a recognition of the role imagination can play in the process of defining self and humanizing the other. Wright believed the exercise of imagination was a powerful strategy for survival, not a luxury the oppressed could not afford but an essential constituent for all human growth and development.

When he cites *Black Boy* as Wright's supreme achievement because of how it reveals his special talents—"the eye of a skilled reporter, the sensibility of a revolutionary poet, alert to varied forms of injustice, and the sense of symbolic meaning carried by the rituals of ordinary life" (425)— Charles Davis helps us to appreciate how Wright's "fictionalized" autobiography demonstrates for liberation theologians that the most effective attempts to deal with the complexities of racial experience do not necessarily come from a theoretical perspective. Wright's text opens up a theological space in which numerous voices can speak, numerous acts can symbolize, and numerous artifacts can represent and evoke ultimate meaning.

Wright's autobiography contributed to America's consciousness a new dimension of experience because in writing it he "accepted his own individual responsibility for seeing to it that America become conscious of it-

self" (Ellison, *Going* 215). Wright's burden as an heir to the slave narrative tradition was also his passion, and *Black Boy* is another example that
affirms creativity as an appropriate survival response and the exercise of
one's imagination as a form of liberating activity. Remarking on the existential strain in Wright's work, Nathan A. Scott Jr. observes that "the fundamental reality about which it has very often wanted to speak is that of
the 'extreme situation'—the situation, that is, in which man's essential dignity is radically challenged by an unconscionable subversion of justice and
an intolerable distance between master and slave. And this is precisely the
reality that stirred Mr. Wright's imagination into life" ("The Dark" 149).

   Black Boy has assumed an important position in the development of African-American autobiography precisely because of its relationship to the
liberating energies of the slave narrative tradition and the way in which
the author fictionalizes his life for the specific effect of achieving full authenticating status in reporting on his post-Reconstruction experience of
oppression and survival. The narrative rests uneasily on two assumptions:
that readers need not take it literally, but also that this is the life of an actual
person, not an invented Bigger Thomas who could be dismissed as a literary device. Although W. E. B. Du Bois considered *Black Boy* "creative writing" rather than "a record of life," and thus terribly overdrawn and not
convincing in the total picture it presents (Reilly 132), another contemporary reviewer, Isidor Schneider, noted that the fault Du Bois cites is the
same found in most autobiographies. As "a picture of the Negro people,"
Schneider comments, "it is a distortion; but as a document of the psychological patters of race tension it is unique, powerful, and of considerable
importance" (Reilly 149).

   Ralph Ellison interprets the fictionalizing elements as Wright's attempt
to "endow life's incidents with communicable significance" (*Shadow and
Act* 78). So much of *Black Boy* is exaggerated precisely because Wright was
trying to dramatize the complexity of racial experience as he knew it and
had lived it and because editing the raw material of life "required the use
of controlling principles that are invariably fictional" (Davis, "From Experience" 427). As Ellison explains, "the fictional techniques were not there
in order to 'con' anyone, but to drive home to Americans, black and white,
something of the complexity and cost in human terms, in terms of the loss
to literature and to art, and to the cause of freedom itself, imposed by racial discrimination; the cost, that is, of growing up in a society which oper-
ated on one side of its mind by the principle of equality while qualifying
that principle severely according to the dictates of racism" (*Going* 213).

   Wright describes his motive as an attempt to "show exactly what Negro life in the South means today, the total effect, a kind of common denominator. I've used what I lived and observed and felt, and I used my imagination to whip it into shape to appeal to the emotions and imaginations of other people, for I believe that only the writing that has to do with the basic issues of human living, moral, political, or whatever you call it, has any meaning. I think the importance of any writing lies in how much felt life is in it: It gets its value from that" (Kinnamon and Fabre 4). What the reader gets from *Black Boy* is an actual rendition of a life not as it was lived but as it was felt.

In an interview that came out not long after the publication of his autobiography, Wright explains this distinction: "Of course, an autobiography is the story of one's life, but if one wants to, one can make it more than that and I definitely had that in mind when I wrote the book. I wrote the book to tell a series of incidents strung through my childhood, but the main desire was to render a judgment on my environment. I wanted to render that judgment because I felt the necessity to. . . . That judgment was this: the environment the South creates is too small to nourish human beings, especially Negro human beings" (Kinnamon and Fabre 65). Although Wright coyly admits that "some may escape the general plight and grow up," knowing full well that the publication of his autobiography establishes the fact, he concedes with a humility not characteristic of his autobiographical reflections that "it is a matter of luck and I think it should be a matter of plan. It should be a matter of saving the citizens of our country for our country and I don't think it should be put on a narrow moral plane of a good white person helping a poor Negro" (65).

Wright crafted his text so that it would resist readers' tendencies toward narrow moralizing, but he still assumed an ambivalent posture toward the social efficacy of his work. By Ellison's recollection, Wright was bemused that his folk history *12 Million Black Voices* could move his white readers to tears, seeing this as an evasion of the intended impact of his vision and "a betrayal of the struggle for freedom" (*Going* 211–12). Although Ellison claims that Wright failed to grasp "the function of artistically induced catharsis," when he relates aesthetic catharsis to the shouting that occurs in many black churches—where the ritual generates the power to cleanse the mind and redeem and rededicate people to forms of ideal action— Ellison was perhaps being too harsh in judging Wright's response. Wright understood fully the spiritual power described by Ellison, and however ambivalent he was about the ways in which people exercise that power, he appreciated and relied on its universal properties. As he explained not long after *Black Boy* was published,

I know that the scalding experiences of *Black Boy* are alien to most Americans to whom education is a matter of course thing, to whom food is something to be taken for granted, to whom freedom is a heritage. Yet to those whites who recall how, in the early days of this land, their forefathers struggled for freedom, *Black Boy* cannot be a strange story. Neither can it be a strange story to the Jews, the Poles, the Irish, and the Italians who came hopeful to this land from the Old World. Because the hunger for freedom fills the hearts of men all over this war-ravaged earth today, I feel that Negroes in America have a moral duty, a sacred obligation to remind the nation constantly of their plight, their claim, their problem. And when you hear the voice of the submerged Negro in America, remember that it is but one of the worldwide chorus of voices sounding for freedom everywhere. (Kinnamon and Fabre 82)

Wright may even have seen himself as functioning out of a biblical prophetic mode—not to predict the future but to rebuke the powerful—that he secularized for his purposes but exploited nonetheless because he appreciated the ritualistic power that role conferred on him. As he observed, "The artist is a revolutionary figure. The serious artist grapples with his environment, passes a judgment on it. He helps to deepen people's perceptions, quicken their thought processes. He makes them conscious of the possibility of historical change—and in that way he facilitates change" (Kinnamon and Fabre 67). Wright's belief in his creative ability to facilitate change is why *Black Boy*, although much of it reads as a lengthy diatribe against the oppression of a racist society and a stifling religion, can still function as textimony for a liberating theology. Like his predecessor Douglass, Wright identifies as the culprit of racism not individual whites but the systemic complicity of a society that, in collaboration with its religion, allowed the design of slavery to renew itself in the South.

In a 1953 interview, Wright proclaimed that "the church, fundamentally, does little and stimulates not at all. Religious activities do not occupy themselves with the oppression of the Negroes. There exists a definite fundamental idea, an observable interpretation of the Christian faith, but its influence on the relation between Negroes and whites is very little. The activities of the church—if they ever were important with regard to the Negro problem—have never brought about a favorable change" (Kinnamon and Fabre 157). Wright's harsh indictment of the institutional church is distinct from his views on religion, however, and can be interpreted as a kind of family fight, a tough-love response to religion's distorting effects that is tempered by his deep respect for what faith can accomplish, which he admitted late in his life when he remarked, "The religious spirit always endures. Up to now, man has always been a religious animal and secular art is a sublimation of the religious feeling" (Kinnamon and Fabre 210).

In his biography of Wright, Michel Fabre explains how "Wright had perhaps used his special experience as a universal example of cultural poverty, when it may have been caused largely by his particular family relationships and atypical religion" (280–81), suggesting that for very personal reasons—because of the oppressive role of religion in his childhood—he tended to consider religious beliefs shackles to individual freedom. But by choosing lines from the book of Job and lyrics from a spiritual as epigraphs for the two sections of his autobiography, Wright demonstrates how he sublimated his religious feeling in secular art.

That this sublimated religious feeling may have emerged as criticism is wholly appropriate in advancing the agenda of a liberating theology. Wright's invocations of religion provide an important challenge to the complacency often fostered by religious faith and an appropriate indictment of the complicity of religion when, in institutional forms, it ignores or obstructs liberating thought and action. Wright gives many examples of those who do not live in deed their religious creed and he is no less harsh in evaluating the duplicity of blacks than he is in assessing white failures. As a resource for liberation theologians, therefore, *Black Boy* offers a compelling critique of traditional and institutional forms of religion as a way to begin addressing oppression and social justice concerns in order to create "the social atmosphere in which other black boys might freely bloom" (Ellison, *Shadow and Act* 80).

Although Wright's autobiography offers an instructive model for promoting black liberation, it is also a cautionary guide. The very skill that set him apart and helped him to survive—his unrelenting sense of individuality—is also what has the potential to damage liberation, both his own and that which he seeks for his race. That Wright pays insufficient attention to the achievements of others and the community's role in his own personal and creative liberation is but one of many exaggerations that the author purposely uses, in this case to emphasize his brutal realization that many of the promises of Emancipation proved empty. Wright's autobiography gives compelling testimony to Ralph Ellison's assertion "that whatever else the environment contained, it had as little chance of prevailing against the overwhelming weight of the child's unpleasant experiences as Beethoven's Quartets would have of destroying the stench of a Nazi prison" (*Shadow and Act* 82). Wright wanted precisely to challenge the complacency of the black community and their reliance on preexisting cultural forms and traditions, including religion. He emphasized his self-reliance and movement away from restricting social categories to demonstrate not that these forms were inherently corrupt and ineffective, but that they needed to be radicalized for the present challenge.

Wright's ambivalence about his spiritual and political role is reflected in the self-portrayal he creates in *Black Boy*. The protagonist embodies the paradoxical characteristics of ex-slave characters because he is both exemplary and representative, a condition Wright once used to describe himself: "One of the things that makes me write is that I realize that I'm a very average Negro. Maybe that's what makes me extraordinary" (Kinnamon and Fabre 66). Facing the twentieth century, Wright understood that "the human predicament and the compositional problem are one" (G. Taylor 342). As he strives to create a character of human individuality, he is also hoping to identify the personal with the race's general condition, revealing that the "'truth' central to the autobiographer is also that sought by the novelist" (G. Taylor 349).

Thus, when he identifies Richard Wright's autobiography as the first representation of the slave narrative tradition that reveals the creative shaping of the author himself and is not the product of a collaborative and polemical document used by abolitionists, James Olney underscores how Wright's "fictionalized" autobiography tells us much about the impulses behind autobiography and fiction and their implications for a liberating theology. Olney recognizes that although "slave narratives do not qualify as either autobiography or literature" ("I Was Born" 65), it is undeniable that the African-American literary tradition takes its start, in theme certainly but also often in content and form, from the slave narratives.

Citing *Black Boy* as Wright's supreme achievement, Olney also sees it as the perfect example of his argument for the foundational aspect of slave narratives. "In effect, Wright looks back to slave narratives at the same time that he projects developments that would occur in Afro-American writing after *Black Boy*" ("I Was Born" 65) The crucial difference between *Black Boy* and its predecessors is that it is "not under guidance of any intention or impulse other than its own," and thus provides "a nexus joining slave narratives of the past to the most fully developed literary creations of the present: through the power of symbolic memory it transforms the earlier narrative mode into what everyone must recognize as imaginative, creative literature, both autobiography and fiction" ("I Was Born" 67).

Robert Stepto shares Olney's observations and those of other scholars, such as Charles Davis, Sidonie Smith, and William Andrews, who have shown how Richard Wright's autobiography assumes a secure place in the slave narrative tradition. Motifs or traits that Wright's autobiography shares with ex-slave narratives are a vision of the trajectory of his life as pointing toward freedom, in all cases envisioned as the North; an identification as an autodidact whose life did not lead in a specific direction but was shaped by random choices that led to liberation; a textual emphasis on episodes of violence, descriptions of gnawing hunger, and other physical and societal deprivations that led to isolation; a skeptical view of Christianity as it is practiced by both blacks and whites; portraits of black families attempting to maintain a degree of unity; and a quest for literacy or a mode of creative self-expression. Although critical of the ways in which Wright "suppresses his own extraordinary human spirit by rendering himself a black biological fact," Stepto asserts that his "founders set aside a large space for confused men" like Wright and that Wright counters "relentless passages" of biological determinism with moments of self-assertion that reveal the "presence of a questing human being seeking freedom and a voice. Here, a hostile environment is modulated by an emerging, extraordinary figure, and the resulting narrative establishes a place for itself in the continuum founded by the slave narrative" ("I Thought" 199–203).

Wright's text reveals that as African Americans moved further from the actual experience of slavery, their character continued to be developed in ways that characterized them as both average and extraordinary, trying to hold in balance responsibility to self and to the other, to see themselves as both shaped by and against historical pressures rooted in race. His autobiography continues to promote many of the same concerns of the antebellum tradition, but with unique variations that continue to demonstrate the need for humanizing the dominant society by insisting on the unbounded possibility for transformation. Unlike Ernest Gaines, who creates a fiction he titles as autobiography, Wright's text must function as and call itself an autobiography in order to achieve its purposes of representing his race's experience.

This kind of duality, even multiplicity of purpose attached to Wright's text, is further reflected in the composite portrait of the protagonist or literary character Wright created, who represents himself both as child and adult. In his essay "From Experience to Eloquence: Richard Wright's *Black Boy* as Art," Charles Davis identifies three voices of narration that underscore thematic emphasis in the autobiography. These voices include the simplest child's voice that records recollected events with a clarity that illustrates basic emotions and psychological dimensions and underscores the theme of survival; a second, more complicated and lyrical voice that underscores the making of the artist; and a third didactic voice that offers

explanations of the matter recorded by the other two voices for the purposes of educating the reader. With this elaborate narrative strategy,
Wright's text can function as art and as polemic—as textimony.

In the process of creating the character Black Boy, Wright's personal
enterprise becomes representative of the contemporary African-American
search for form and self-definition and of the autobiographical process itself
that explores, from the perspective of a representative of "the oppressed,"
the nature of subject/object relationships in American society. In the estimation of John Hodges, "Wright knew well, of course, that those responsible for inflicting crimes upon blacks in the South were not likely to be
moved to correct their abuses unless they could somehow be forced to see
themselves not only as the perpetrators of those crimes but as their victims as well" (432–33). Because the reader is given several Richard Wrights
with whom to identify—a struggling young boy charting his developing
consciousness, a lyrical writer imposing his interpretive consciousness, and
a political agitator insisting on the adoption of a social justice consciousness—the reader is provided little opportunity to escape the recognition
that "if the atmosphere in white America was to be conducive to the black
man's growth . . . the white man, the oppressor, would have to cooperate"
(Ochillo 52).

By presenting his experiences through the bewildered consciousness of
a young boy, Wright forces both blacks and whites to examine long-held
practices and customs that impeded human development. As Black Boy's
consciousness grows, so too does the reader's, thereby eliciting an "emotional bond between the author and his audience" (Ochillo 52). Wright's
recognition of his position in a racist society becomes evident when as a
child he makes what he describes as an "emotional" connection between
black and white. He had always observed color difference but also had not
concerned himself much with the difference because he never came in close
contact with white people. As he describes it, "For the most part I never
thought of them; they simply existed somewhere in the background of the
city as a whole" (BB 27).

This posture points exactly to the position texts of the slave narrative
tradition attempt to address, where one is so distanced from the reality of
others that one has no idea of how they think and feel. Wright's benign
assessment seems oddly characteristic of a conventional stance of most
white Americans who claim not to understand black Americans. By casting his impressions this way, he craftily draws his reader into identification,
whereupon he proceeds to detail in excruciating ways exactly what the lives
of black others are like. This is why Ralph Ellison identifies as Wright's

important achievement in *Black Boy* the conversion of both black and white Americans. He transforms "the American Negro impulse toward self-annihilation and 'going-under-ground' into a will to confront the world, to evaluate his experience honestly and throw his findings unashamedly into the guilty conscience of America," thereby forcing white Americans to awaken from their entitled slumber (*Shadow and Act* 94).

Wright's text "call[s] into question those injustices which blacks and whites, because of habit and custom, dismiss all too perfunctorily. In short, the boy, in wearing the mask of the author, forces those about him—and Wright's readers as well—to examine the deeper implications of their actions" (Hodges 421). As Ralph Ellison describes it, Wright attempted "to discover and depict the meaning of Negro experience; and to reveal to both Negroes and Whites those problems of a psychological and emotional nature which arise between them when they strive for mutual understanding" (*Shadow and Act* 77). Thus the "generic ambiguity" (Adams 69) of *Black Boy* that has the potential to be a source of confusion for readers is in part what makes the book so powerful. Wright presents the kind of truth he wants readers to respond to and in the process develops what Timothy Adams identifies as an "elaborate system of signifying" in order to "narrow the gap between the narrative and authorial audiences; the reader of *Black Boy* must strive to be like the narrator of *Black Boy*, must keep what is happening at a particular moment and the entire history of black-white relations—the content and the context—together in his or her mind. Wright's context includes the need to speak simultaneously as an adult and as a child and to remove everything from his story that, even if it happened to be true, would allow white readers to maintain their distorted stereotype of southern blacks" (79).

Stereotypes are exploded and the multiple Wrights are held together in the text by a motif of migration. Like his ex-slave ancestors, Wright makes a slow and painful journey north and even to the end he reminds his readers, through his persistent hunger, which he is unable to satisfy—"all my life I had been full of a hunger for a new way to live" (BB 452)—that the struggle for liberation is ongoing, on both personal and public levels. Part One of *Black Boy*, "Southern Night," ends in 1927 with the eighteen-year-old Wright leaving the South for Chicago, seeking relief from the "pressure of southern living" which has made it seem impossible "to be real." Part Two, "The Horror and the Glory," ends in 1937, with Wright leaving the Communist party and launching a literary quest for both self-fulfillment and fulfillment of the social values that had drawn him into politics. By the end of the autobiography he has come to appreciate how his writing creates opportunities for "significant living"—on a personal level and on a public level—because he has come to understand the relationship between imaginative expression and social action, "between prospects for personal fulfillment in America and for America's fulfillment of its social promise" (Taylor 349).

Together the two parts take on the form of biblical scripture. The first part, which begins with an epigraph from the book of Job ("They meet with darkness in daytime / And they grope at noonday as in the night") is full of Old Testament law and story, detailing the struggle to escape, as Job did, an undeserved and unjust oppression and the harsh requirements of religious doctrine. The second part begins with an epigraph that recites the lines of a Negro spiritual:

> Sometimes I wonder, huh,
> Wonder if other people wonder, huh,
> Sometimes I wonder, huh,
> Wonder if other people wonder, huh,
> Just like I do, oh, my Lord, just like I do!

It hints at the possibility of grace, or New Testament gospel "good news," as Wright discovers in black culture and in himself the power of creative "wondering" that will help lead him to fulfillment. Because this fulfillment is only hinted at, Janice Thaddeus notes a crucial difference between Wright's text and those of his ex-slave predecessors. *Black Boy,* she observes, is "more tentative and open. . . . He is deviating from the model of the black slave narrative, which moved teleologically from slavery into freedom, from dehumanization to fulfillment" (208), reminding us that the struggle for liberation is ongoing.

By choosing "the labyrinth of complexity over the straight road of simplicity . . . the darkness of ambiguity over the lightness of clarity" (Smeltsor 102), Wright's narrative becomes self-consciously cryptic, recapitulating his boyhood search for when "the moments of living slowly revealed their coded meanings" (BB 8). Among the coded meanings Wright attempts to unravel are the mysteries of scripture. In an ironic reversal of the ways in which ex-slave narrators used scripture as a symbolic shorthand to convey eternal truths in conventional discourse and to appeal to sympathetic readers, Wright describes how as a child he found that "some of the Bible stories were interesting in themselves, but we always twisted them, secularized them to the level of our street life, rejecting all the meanings that did not fit into our environment" (BB 96).

Here Wright reveals a lesson passed on through his folk tradition—where biblical texts were used to illuminate the conditions of slavery—that is pertinent to contemporary liberation theologians seeking to advance social justice. Just as enslaved people created new identities for themselves out of the images and myths of the Old Testament, Wright understood that the codes of scripture or any other expression of religious sentiment must be shaped to reflect black life. Although Richard Wright and liberation theologians share a similar motive—to decode scripture and history for a liberating presence—Wright engages us in a journey toward understanding that goes through the secular to arrive at the sacred.

Wright's autobiography demonstrates what his title announces: that racial stereotypes persist in denying African Americans the opportunity for full human development. Boyhood and blackness are states to be overcome, but one can begin to be liberated, and liberate others, through imagination, which "offers the magic power to lift an imposed circle away from the imprisoned self" (MacKethan, "*Black Boy*" 134). The deliberate openness and tentative hope that characterize the conclusion of *Black Boy* demonstrate how the oppressed are still searching, through the distortions of a twentieth-century perspective, for a different vision of the Promised Land, energizing and giving new voice to the abolitionist call for liberation.

ꙩ ꙩ ꙩ

> God, Satan, and Mississippi notwithstanding . . . I was going to be free.
> —James Baldwin

In the scheme he develops in *From Behind the Veil,* Robert Stepto confidently identifies *Black Boy* as a spiritual document because it is a "narrative of ascent" that, like ex-slave narratives, is as much a cultural document as a personal one. The autobiography "valorizes the enduring importance of slave narrative . . . as a genre for understanding the insights and aspirations of the oppressed" (Graham and Ward 112). As such it becomes "the voice of a self transformed by an autobiographical act into a sharer in the general public discourse about slavery" (Davis and Gates 253). But years removed from the actual fact of slavery, this public discourse is reinteriorized by Richard Wright, reclaimed as an individual vision and eventually offered to the reader in a very personal act of risk as a way for the reader to privately enter into a public discourse about racism.

When we examine his text from the perspective not of "the private act of a self writing" but of "the cultural act of a self reading," we can see how his text illuminates the situation Janet Gunn describes as a collaborative interpretive act between the autobiographer and the reader, both of whom read the life presented. This reading takes place "by selves who inhabit worlds," however different they may at first appear to be (Gunn 8–9). Like ex-slave narrators, Wright, despite his wish to escape his oppressive circumstances, still very much invested himself in the world in which he lived, acknowledging his temporal experience as a vehicle of meaning. He encourages the reader to do the same because of the ways in which he positions his autobiographical text in a participatory mode, "as an occasion of discovery: of seeing in the text the heretofore unexpressed or unrecognized depth of the reader's self—not as a mirror image, nor even as a particular manifestation of same shared idea of selfhood, but as an instance of interpretive activity that risks display. . . . In a word, the reader discovers the possibility of selfhood through interpretation" (Gunn 19–20), a selfhood that is enlarged beyond the confines of simple racial stereotype.

The possibility of selfhood Wright explores in *Black Boy* begins in his early childhood and concludes after he has escaped to the North only to find that "for the more modern slave narrator, the dogs of the overseer still pursue, though they have assumed the qualities of a more general fate" (S. Smith 130). The reality of the world Wright inhabited in post-Reconstruction Mississippi differed little from the antebellum conditions faced by his enslaved ancestors. Sharecropping was but a variation on the theme of slavery and its legacy was overwhelming in Mississippi. His textimony is viewed by most readers as an almost unrelieved picture of a young personality thwarted by a brutal environment, but each episode Wright selects to relate becomes a significant and determinative event in his life. The portrait of the environment Wright draws exposes this bleakness, and although it may be seen to dwell excessively on the brutality of this environment, his "exaggeration beyond the typical," one reviewer believed, was "necessary to wake up white America" (Reilly 137). Furthermore, this brutality is contrasted by the way it is presented initially through the fresh responses by a sensitive child whose startling memories recall in tone the kind of rhetoric usually reserved for a slave narrative.

Wright's childhood experiences confirmed in him the feeling that most of the support customarily gathered from the traditional matrix in his community totally negated his identity as a human being. Even as he matures and moves toward other external avenues of support, he is disappointed. His family denies him, religion disgusts him, and the Communist party abandons him. These factors give sufficient justification for Wright's predisposition toward extreme individualism, self-reliance, and nonconformity. They also structure his literary perspective so that the autobiography presents his life as a series of compelling and frightening episodes that "focus his imagination on a single incident or aspect of the total experience" to epitomize his environment (Skerrett 87).

These episodes take on a parabolic quality of almost scriptural design wherein Wright instructs his reader through story. As they do for the reader, for Wright these episodes "altered the look of the world" to the point at which he did not need to experience brutality directly to "give my entire imagination over to it." This response "blocked the springs of thought and feeling in me, creating a sense of distance between me and the world in which I lived" (BB 203), but giving his entire imagination over to the horror that surrounded him also provided him the disassociation of sensibility he needed as an artist, enabling him to control his terror and find a way to communicate its reality to others. Or as Ralph Ellison has observed, "Wright was able to free himself in Mississippi because he had the imagination and the will to do so" (*Shadow and Act* 116). Playing subject to his own objectification, Wright rejects the options of accommodating oppression or becoming a destructive and self-destructive rebel and instead, through writing, learns how to resist and find a space "where integrity, balance, and wholeness might be achieved" (Graham and Ward 111).

In *Black Boy* Wright's imagination helps him to decode the complexities of one great force that both gave and withheld liberation: religion. Wright singles out religion as a unique force that personally affected his own efforts at selfhood and liberation. One significant change in postbellum articulations of the slave narrative tradition that is especially pertinent when viewing it as a textimony for a liberating theology is that the representative author's critique of institutional forms of religion could be more pronounced and graphic. Likewise, the individual author was more likely to challenge religion not just as it affected society, but as it influenced him or her personally, often leading to what John Barbour identifies as a "deconversion," a change that involves doubt or denial of the truth of a system of beliefs. Barbour notes that in the autobiographies of people of color, "the loss of faith in the identity between Christianity and the white man's religion—is a central goal" (85). He continues, "From the very start black autobiography has involved a mixed assessment of Christianity, invoking the norms of this religion as an ideal yet criticizing the constant and widespread failure of Christians to practice what they preached" (86).

As literary narrative, "versions of deconversion" in Barbour's analysis represent a series of events arranged as a plot and a decision that the writer tries to justify. More profound than simple secularization because of the way they affect the creation of narrative, deconversions are stimulated primarily by ethical considerations, when an autobiographer deems religious beliefs as harmful or hypocritical. Furthermore, the experience of religious deconversion can become a metaphor for other kinds of personal change and initiate liberating changes outside religion. Barbour cites Frederick Douglass's first narrative as a paradigmatic example of black deconversion that shapes the agenda and rhetoric of many later autobiographers. As an archetypal example of both black autobiography and the tradition of the American jeremiad—prophetically criticizing a departure from an ethical norm—Barbour reveals that the central aim of Douglass's text is "not to destroy the religious faith of his audience but to contribute to the abolitionist cause" (88).

To do this Douglass appeals to white Christians to put in practice what they profess to believe and, in Barbour's estimation, posits his narrative as a "call for conversion, for genuine commitment to the ideals of Christianity (as well as to American democratic ideals)" (88). In its focus on the reader's need to reject the white man's religion, Douglass's narrative challenged two of the most pervasive and firmly entrenched beliefs of nineteenth-century southerners: that Christianity sanctioned slaveholding and that white people were inherently superior to blacks. To accomplish his aim, Douglass presents testimony to undermine these convictions because he realized that "before white readers could recognize the full humanity of black persons they would have to lose faith in the religious basis for their claim to innate superiority and for the institution of slavery" (Barbour 88).

But Wright's developing loss of faith and ultimate deconversion go beyond even that of Douglass, who only hints at his own deconversion without explicitly claiming a loss of faith. However ambiguously, Douglass continued to see "some positive resources for social justice in Christianity," structuring his narrative so that it would become "a paradigm for many later autobiographers not only in the deliberate attempt to deconvert the reader from 'the white man's religion' but also in the veiled, indirect ways that the writer's own doubts about Christianity must be expressed, given the circumstances of a minority writer in America" (Barbour 89). Wright's deconversion went beyond an ambivalent relationship to Christianity and became a full-fledged assault on institutional religion. At the same time, he was also reassessing his relationship to many aspects of American culture. Characterized by his moral criticism of the actions, practices, and way of life fostered by religion, Wright's deconversion brought him emotional upheaval and eventually led him to reject the community to which he belonged.

Thus Richard Wright resembles more the Douglass of *My Bondage and My Freedom*, where the author's doubts about Christianity are more

strongly suggested. Wright is the heir to the more complex and ambivalent Douglass, who exhibits, according to William Andrews, "a rebellious
shadow" that "comes to the fore . . . only when all his gods and fathers
fail and he must become his own self-authorizing presence in a world be-
reft of legitimate structure or sanction" (*To Tell* 229). Because of the social context in which he published, Douglass's deconversion appears in
"disguised or covert way and with considerable ambiguity because of the
author's wish to appeal to the audience's Christian values" (Barbour 92).
But what was unacceptable for publication in the nineteenth century does
not apply to Richard Wright, who goes where Douglass could not. Where
Douglass began to signify on the hypocritical nature of Christianity, Wright
is blunt in revealing the ambiguous role of religion in African-American
experience, thereby forcing his reader to examine more critically the central terms of religious discourse.

As a "version of deconversion," therefore, Wright's text accomplishes
three things necessary for liberation: It challenges complacency, indicts
complicity, and encourages the exercise of creativity as response to oppression. The most obvious and pronounced trait Wright's text shares with
liberation theological analysis is a sustained critique of the institutional
church and the corresponding theology that not only tolerates but also
undergirds racism. But as Peter Dorsey notes in *Sacred Estrangement*,
Wright textually belies his disdain for religious contexts when his deconversion takes the customary form of a conversion narrative. Despite his ab-
horrence of the tyranny of conversion structures in black religious life, he
depends on the form he rejects to free himself from a repressive identity,
and conversion becomes both the mechanism by which his cognitive
changes take place and the model readers are led to adopt. Because of the
ways he challenges social institutions to be more responsive to and reflective
of the needs of the oppressed, Wright's secularization of black culture serves
as a constructive resource for articulating a liberating theology and as a
true descendant of the slave narrative tradition of textimony.

The oppression Wright depicts is real, affecting body and soul of not just
the oppressed but, in the act of reading, the oppressor as well. But to get to
this point of conversion, Wright does not take us on a familiar or comfortable journey. Whether black or white, those who continue to assent to the
saving virtue of religion and its communal institutions will be discomforted
by what he reveals. The rejection of traditional religion as a solution to personal problems that occupies much of *Black Boy* is underscored by his rejection of religion as a solution to social problems. In "Blueprint for Negro Writing," Wright defines the African-American consciousness as rooted

in two sources: the black church and the folklore of black people. Considered the most complete, coherent, and profound statement of Wright's theories on writing, this essay, like much liberation theology, blends Marxist literary approaches with interpretations of black life and culture.

To explore black social consciousness, Wright steered African-American artists toward the church and folklore as the "channels through which the racial wisdom flowed" (40). However, Wright established folklore and religion in oppositional terms, viewing folklore as synonymous with the collective life experience of African Americans, which embodied the "memories of . . . struggle[s] for freedom" (41). It is this liberating quality of folklore that allows Wright to reject and condemn the very institution that has traditionally been regarded (and regards itself) as the source of salvation from oppression: the church. Christianity, Wright believes, was intended only to satisfy metaphysical hunger, and the hunger Wright describes in himself is more vast: It is emotional, intellectual, and most vividly physical.

So Wright rejects what he perceives as Christianity's emphasis on assuring liberation in the hereafter rather than in the here and now because that kind of liberation only guarantees the status quo of oppression. The black church becomes in his mind the very root of black suffering because it "was through the portals of the church that the American Negro first entered the shrine of western culture" (39). As they had come to practice it, Christianity was not indigenous to blacks, but a substitute for their African spiritual heritage, allowing the white ruling class to justify their oppression as it "began to serve as an antidote for suffering and denial" (39).

But the longing for self-realization—the hunger—that Wright describes repeatedly yokes physical hunger with psychological and spiritual yearning. Wright's sense of religion's incompetence at dealing with spiritual and actual hunger takes concrete form during a family dinner to which the preacher was invited. Wright's first estimate of the idea of religion is thrown out of balance by the actions of a preacher. "The preacher had finished his soup and had asked that the platter of chicken be passed to him. It galled me. He smiled, cocked his head this way and that, picking out choice pieces. . . . There were already bare chicken bones on his plate and he was already reaching for more. . . . 'That preacher's going to eat all the chicken!,' I bawled. . . . The preacher tossed back his head and roared with laughter, but my mother was angry and told me that I was to have no dinner because of my bad manners" (BB 31).

In this episode the preacher becomes symbolic of the institutional church's lack of awareness of and compassion for the hungry in their congregations. Although Wright's recollection of this episode is typical for a young boy, combined with other revealing incidents related in *Black Boy* it demonstrates how his whole outlook on religion could have been distorted. From this moment on Wright builds a stoical sort of resentment in the boy's spirit, and in the process reveals a constant danger in organized or institutional religion when it becomes staged or bound to traditional practices, when religious education becomes routine and prayer perfunctory and worship becomes an end in itself.

The religion young Richard was introduced to was far from its antebellum roots, where believers affirmed spontaneous identification with the liberating potential found in scripture and found solace in ritual practice. All the young protagonist saw was a community that looked to the church for answers and found temporary relief in doctrines that demanded that they accept suffering and pain and suppress emotions. Wright came from a home where "feelings were never expressed, except in rage or religious dread" (BB 256) and where important news about his family he discovered only "through Granny's informative prayers" (BB 162). As a child he was subjected to a harsh religious regimen in his Granny's home: prayers three times a day (at which he had to kneel painfully), Sabbath and weekday worship, and the occasional all-night prayer meeting. Ultimately, therefore, Wright shrinks from religion "since it denies the self, applauds the selfless and promises heavenly fulfillment, devalues the needs of the oppressed blacks in the here-and-now and counsels them to be content with their social position" (S. Smith 131). All the experiences with religion he relates in *Black Boy* lead Wright to conclude that religion is incompatible with black liberation.

For not only does religion fail to relieve his physical hunger, it also stands between Richard and his imaginative hunger. Recalling the effect *Bluebeard and His Seven Wives* had on him when it was read to him by his family's lodger, Ella, a schoolteacher, Wright reveals himself as occupying the same place readers of his own text are meant to occupy, a place where the "slow and meaningless" (BB 183) Bible stories could not take him: "The tale made the world around me be, throb, live. As she spoke, reality changed, and the look of things altered, and the world became peopled with magical presence. My sense of life deepened and the feel of things was different somehow. . . . My imagination blazed. The sensations the story aroused in me were never to leave" (BB 45).

When Ella is rebuked by his grandmother for reading him "Devil stuff," Richard protests to no avail, only angering his grandmother to the point at which she exclaims, "You're going to burn in hell" (BB 46). Here religion becomes disconnected from the vital life of the imagination, and the "sense of emptiness, loss" that the young boy felt at being denied knowledge of the ending of the story was countered by his resolve to read all he could when he was older; the threats of his pious family had "no effect whatsoever," and Richard came to understand that religious texts would not give him what he had learned from a secular book: that words could be "the gateway to a forbidden and enchanting land" (BB 47).

His experiments with language begin in earnest after this episode, leading to more conflict-ridden encounters with his family and to a disturbing event of taunting Jews, whom he had been taught "at home and in Sunday School" were "Christ killers" (BB 71). As the author explains, "to hold an attitude of antagonism or distrust toward Jews was bred in us from childhood; it was not merely racial prejudice, it was a part of our cultural heritage" (BB 72). Here Wright again draws attention to religious instruction as having a corrupting influence and highlights its complicity in maintaining the historical relationship fostered by oppressors, who would set the oppressed against one another. Yet at this point he is still able to distinguish between the stern doctrinal issues of his grandmother and the religiously imbued language of black folk wisdom as he further explores the "magic possibilities" (BB 83) of language by toying with the sound and sense of phrases such as "If I walked in my sleep, then God was trying to lead me somewhere to do a good deed for him" (BB 85). Artful language is what stirs his imagination and helps him to see that "because I had no power to make things happen outside of me in the objective world," he could make "things happen within" (BB 85). His repetition of many such folk phrases recalls again the folkloric roots of black religious expression rather than its doctrinal constraints, becoming for the young boy a kind of hoodoo conjure that carries him into a new world.

But one thing his imagination could not counter was a fear of whites. Fantasies of revenge against them became "part of my living, of my emotional life; they were a culture, a creed, a religion" (BB 87); despite the fact that he had never been abused by whites, he had "already become as conditioned to their existence as though I had been the victim of a thousand lynchings" (BB 87). He observes how both black and white boys began to play "traditional racial roles as though we had been born to them, as though it was in our blood, as though we were being guided by instinct" (BB 96). Here Wright moves toward the conviction that he can change and not be guided by instinct and reflexive cultural responses. His efforts to change involve a profound recognition of the nature of his suffering and how it is connected to others, but they also lead to his deconversion from the very faith that promised to deliver him from suffering. When he comes to appreciate a deeper sense of communal responsibility, that "the meaning of living came only when one was struggling to wring a meaning out of meaningless suffering" (BB 118), he does so without the assistance of religion.

The ways in which this revelation is juxtaposed with his most scathing indictment of institutional religion as it was practiced in his family suggests that this is how the church must change. Wright challenges the church to do what he has already begun to do, to "seek those areas of living that would keep [meaning] alive . . . to make me skeptical of everything while seeking everything, tolerant of all and yet critical" (BB 112). He also shows how the church can direct its gaze toward more compelling and instructive sources for enlightenment. Like Wright attempts, the church could "lay open to the core of suffering," not through doctrine and theology, but through psychology, fiction, art and politics—secular "stories" that could open up and keep alive "that enthralling sense of wonder and awe in the face of the drama of human feeling which is hidden by the external drama of life" (BB 112).

What follows this revelation is a sequence of episodes in which the author relates how religion functions as one of the external dramas that hides human feeling and imaginative spirit. That he eventually comes to reject religion is not surprising because all of his encounters with religion display it as ignoring the "common realities of life" to which he believed it should be wedded (BB 134). Wright admits he was "pulled toward emotional belief," but only by the "sensual caress" of hymns (BB 130). He listened "indifferently" to the harsh sermons about cosmic annihilation because as soon as he left church the words encased in the ritual performances were used as a weapon against him. Wright begins his assault on religion by cataloguing, with a relish he applies also to descriptions of nature, the vivid aspects of his family's theology that he heard described by preachers:

A gospel clogged with images of vast lakes of eternal fire, of seas vanishing, of valleys of dry bones, of the sun burning to ashes, of the moon turning to blood . . . a salvation that teemed with fantastic beasts having multiple heads and horns and eyes and feet . . . a cosmic tale that began before time and ended with the clouds of the sky rolling away at the Second Coming of Christ; chronicles that concluded with the Armageddon; dramas thronged with all the billions of human beings who had ever lived or died as God judged the quick and the dead. (BB 119)

Very soon these theological features take on a special dread and poignancy when they are used against a young boy.

Raised in a Seventh-Day Adventist household, Wright reveals how the psychological consequences of a stifling faith can inhibit one's growth toward liberation. Harold Bloom describes Adventists as a sect that began in opposition to the American vision, defining themselves as a negation of the American dream of unlimited material and spiritual progress. Adventists identified the nation as in league with the devil and its achievements doomed to destruction. Unique to their particular "imaginative" articulation of religion was the way they assigned a "crucial role to Satan" (Bloom 156). In Adventist theology, Satan unwillingly takes upon himself the sins of the world, giving believers what Bloom identifies as a "Satanic Atonement" in which the vicarious nature of the Atonement passes from Christ to Satan.

A satanic scapegoating leads to horrid figurations of the end of time, whereupon those who have failed to raise children to keep the Seventh-Day Sabbath will bring upon them the Mark of the Beast, thereby making the children scapegoats as well. It is the dark psychological consequences of Adventist belief that eventually deconvert Richard Wright when he comes to accept his role as the household scapegoat, "a blood relative who professed no salvation and whose soul stood in mortal peril. Granny intimated boldly, basing her logic on God's justice, that one sinful person in a household could bring down the wrath of God upon the entire establishment, damning both the innocent and the guilty" (BB 120–21).

In addition to the psychological violence Richard comes to associate with religion is the actual violence that follows religious instruction, as when his aunt who conducts the religious school he attends singles him out for special punishment. The adult Richard Wright who can pontificate about the hypocrisy of religion emerged from a terrified little boy who grew up where there were "more quarrels in our deeply religious home that in the home of a gangster, a burglar, or a prostitute, a fact which I used to hint gently to Granny and which did my cause no good. Granny bore the standard for God, but she was always fighting. The peace that passes understanding never dwelt with us" (BB 159). The fights even occurred over minor points of doctrine or some imagined infraction of their moral code. Thus Wright comes to associate religion not with liberation but with anxiety because "wherever I found religion in my life I found strife, the attempt of one individual or group to rule another in the name of God. The naked will to power seemed always to walk in the wake of a hymn" (BB 159–60).

Wright sums up his feelings about religion by making distinctions between its aesthetic and its doctrinal elements characteristic of the way he juxtaposes folklore and religion in his essay "Blueprint for Negro Writing."

Many of the religious symbols appealed to my sensibilities and I responded to the dramatic vision of life held by the church, feeling that to live day by day with death as one's sole thought was to be so compassionately sensitive toward all life as to view all men as slowly dying, and the trembling sense of fate that welled up, sweet and melancholy, from the hymns blended with the sense of fate that I had already caught from life. But full emotional and intellectual belief never came. Perhaps if I had caught my first sense of life from the church I would have been moved to complete acceptance, but the hymns and sermons of God came into my heart only long after my personality had been shaped and formed by uncharted conditions of life. I felt that I had in me a sense of living as deep as that which the church was trying to give me, and in the end I remained basically unaffected. (BB 130–31)

Here, as in his other comments about religion outside the autobiography, Wright reveals himself as very ambiguous about religion. His disclaimers that he was already too formed to change strike the reader as disingenuous from a man whose entire life was turned over to the possibility of transformation. Religion remained a part of Wright's consciousness and was an integral part of the social aesthetic he developed. That he strives so vigorously to deny its influence can only be explained by how emotionally traumatized he was by religion as a young boy, when it failed to supply him with the comfort he needed.

Not only did religion fail to supply young Richard with emotional reassurance, but the ways in which it was foisted upon him caused him great emotional conflict. When his family and their friends try to make him attend a religious revival, Wright finds himself in the uncomfortable position of choosing between his own position and hurting his family's feelings, and even surprises himself by remarking, "I don't want to hurt God's feelings, either" (BB 134). In this spontaneous confession, Wright reveals that what he lacked in his introduction to religion was the very personal quality affirmed so deeply by his ancestors. Wright's exposure to religion cast God in the same one-dimensional way in which society and his family cast him. Thus Wright reduces God to a deus ex machina, just as he himself was reduced to Black Boy.

Wright had no model for a relational concept of God or self that would resist and dissolve such static concepts of identity and from which could emerge tentative structures that permit diversity and freedom in human life. Even his emerging creativity could not help him to "imagine God pausing in His guidance of unimaginable vast world to bother with me" (BB 134). In order to cling to the creative mechanisms he was developing to survive, Wright could not risk feeling "weak and lost in a cosmic manner," a decision he based on his own experience with religion and its effects: "Before I had been made to go to church I had given God's existence a sort of tacit assent, but after having seen His creatures serve Him at first hand, I had my doubts. My faith, such as it was, was welded to the common realities of life, anchored in the sensations of my body and in what my mind could grasp, and nothing could ever shake this faith, and surely not my fear of an invisible power" (BB 134–35).

Although his Granny warns him that he would "burn forever in the lake of fire," Richard is determined not to surrender. But he is also torn by how his own rejection of religion "wounded Granny's soul" (BB 136). He doesn't want to hurt or humiliate her, but that is precisely what he does when he comes upon a scheme he believes will keep her hoping for awhile. Claiming he needed proof to believe, that he "could not commit myself to something I could not feel or see" (BB 136), he suggests that he is like Jacob and that if he saw an angel he would believe. Although this plan is imagined with the purpose of "salving . . . Granny's frustrated feelings toward [him]," his words are misconstrued. His grandmother thinks he has seen an angel.

Her joy over his revelation leads to his being dragged out of his pew by an elder to proclaim his faith. But he will not submit and eventually admits the confusion, still insistent that "I knew more than she thought I knew about the meaning of religion, the hunger of the human heart for that which is not and can never be, the thirst of the human spirit to conquer and transcend the implacable limitations of human life" (BB 139–40). Although he promises and tries to pray to appease his grandmother, he feels ridiculous because he has already learned a more effective way to transcend his limitations—by exercising his imagination. As he explains, "I took the Bible, pencil, paper and a rhyming dictionary and tried to write verses for hymns" (BB 140). Although he fails to produce any religious literature, he does create instead a story about Indians, an act that finally allows his family to give him up for lost.

Even after they cease to strive to save his soul, the arbitrary dictates of religious faith the family clings to deny Richard to opportunity to work on the Sabbath, even though he could have made good money. Once more religion interferes with his attempts at self-liberation. He eventually agrees to attend the Methodist church with his mother, where his imagination is stimulated anew and he once again catalogues all he observes in this "new world":

Prim, brown, puritanical girls who taught in the public schools; black college students who tried to conceal their plantation origin; black boys and girls emerging self-consciously from adolescence; wobbly-bosomed black and yellow church matrons; black janitors and porters who sang proudly in the choir; subdued redcaps and carpenters who served as deacons; meek, blank-eyed black and yellow washerwomen who shouted and moaned and danced when hymns were sung; jovial, pot-bellied black bishops; skinny old maids who were constantly giving rallies to raise money; snobbery, clannishness, gossip, intrigue, petty class rivalry, and conspicuous displays of cheap clothing. (BB 178)

Even though he feels detached from the congregation and admits that "I had been kept out of their world too long ever to be able to become a real part of it" (BB 178), his aroused senses are seduced by what the congregation offers and he responds to the call to attend a revival. There eager deacons try to convert him and Wright describes a dramatic sequence in which he is persistently confronted with the need for his salvation through "familiar techniques" that left him "filled more with disgust than sin" (BB 179–80). Even though he relents and follows the crowd toward candidacy for baptism, the "terrifyingly sweet" hymns and shouts do not stimulate his aesthetic sensibilities this time and he feels only that "this business of saving souls had no ethics" (BB 182).

Because of the entreaties of his mother and his desire to express what he "had in common with other people," he wearily assents to an eventual baptism. But in effect this leads to the final episode of his deconversion. He doubts that his lack of belief will ever mature, as his mother suggests, but he submits anyway, resulting in what James Olney describes as "his disgust and bitter anger as an individual at being forced and violated by the community" ("The Value" 61). When he is baptized and shakes the preacher's hand, the ritual courtesy indicates "not what he has in common with the community" but the strength of the community that is alien to him and forces him to submit. The community violates his individual, private self, his "real self," which only he knows and which his autobiography "is dedicated to realizing for Wright and his reader alike" ("The Value" 63).

What continues to generate "awe" for Richard is not church but suffering, either abstract in fear of whites or concrete as he witnesses his mother's physical decline. He survives without the customary familial and communal supports; instead, "by imagining a place where everything was possible, I kept hope alive in me" (BB 199). This hope was generated not by his participation in public religious ritual but by his own private ritual of reading. As his vision of emancipation develops, it ultimately leads him away from religion and into isolation. Cut off from the community, he embarks on an existential journey outside religious parameters.

But what he finds outside his community is the ultimate fact of his skin color that, even more than the religious and familial pressures he has endured, seeks to stifle his development. When his companion, Griggs, tries to school him on how to deal with white people and avoid confrontation, Richard resists, exclaiming, "I can't be a slave" (BB 218). When he tries to adopt Griggs's strategy and secures a job at which he performs well, even his performance of the part of a good slave is insufficient; a white coworker's jealousy leads to his dismissal and his unmistakable realization that he had "been slapped out of the human race" (BB 225).

Despite his efforts not to regard himself as a slave, he is powerless to stop whites from regarding him as precisely and only that. These and other confrontations force readers to evaluate the unexplored dimensions of their entitlement, a condition wherein a black boy, in dealing with whites, is "conscious of the entirety" of his relations with them, but "they were conscious only of what was happening at a given moment" (BB 231). By Wright's estimation, the problem lay not only with the willed innocence of whites but also with the complicity of "black boys [who] acted out the roles that the white race had mapped out for them. Most of them were not conscious of living a special, separate, stunted way of life" (BB 232).

Worse than the silent accommodation were the ways in which African Americans he observed retreated into expected deviant behavior such as stealing and justified it with a peculiar ethical standard born of oppression. Although in many instances liberation theologians remark on the particular situation ethics one needs to adopt to effect liberation, in this case Wright sees his fellow African Americans as simply accommodating white racist assumptions and sustaining a system of relationship in which "southern whites would rather have had Negroes who stole work for them than Negroes who knew, however dimly, the worth of their own humanity" (BB 236). Although unconvinced, Richard allowed himself to reason that stealing would not violate his ethics, and finally he earns and steals and saves enough money to leave Mississippi and make something of his life.

Wright's first discovery upon returning to Memphis is that "all human beings were not mean and driving, were not bigots like the members of my family" (BB 247). But his prolonged encounters reveal the city to be like the entire South, a place where African Americans "bowed silently" to white men's power (BB 271). When he links a customary religious posture of reverence to the oppression of the dominant class, Wright demonstrates how religion and racism are inseparable in his consciousness. He extends this relationship further when he uses the scriptural design of a gospel parable to relate a particularly painful episode in his life. An anecdote describing how he and another black man were set up to fight by the lies of their white bosses unfolds like a parable and calls the reader into engagement in order for its full meaning to emerge. When the two black men discover the hoax and agree to let things pass, their white supervisors prod and arm them and finally agree to pay them to fight bare-fisted. Although the "fighters" plan to pull punches and take the money and run, eventually they must be pulled apart after having beaten each other senseless.

As Roger Rosenblatt observes, "The point of this story, in fact and parable, is repeated regularly; a black man seeking recognition in the white world must be brutalized to the extent that when recognition comes, it will be to him as an animal. If he decides not to fit this pattern at the outset, its designers will push him until he becomes violent in protest. Should he become violent enough, he will be considered an animal and so satisfy his predetermination just as effectively. Either way he will be functioning according to external dictates that run counter to his will, and despite the fact that he is sane and reasonable, he will only be judged so by joining a world that is unreasonable and fundamentally mad" (172–73). The pathology of victimization this parable relates only enhances the dilemma wherein the dominant culture, assisted by religion, ensures its preferential status by pitting the oppressed against the oppressed and avoiding any confrontation with the status quo. But ever ambivalent, Wright also betrays his submerged religious sensibility when after the fight he admits "that I had done something unclean, something for which I could never properly atone" (BB 287).

Wright's process of atonement takes shape not in religious acts but in acts of the imagination. Soon after the deflating fight he discovers through the writing of H. L. Mencken that he could "fight with words." The ways in which religious language had been used to wound him in the past prepare Wright to exercise his own ability to use words as weapons. Reading and writing become for Wright "ways of living" (BB 328) that enlarge his vision by allowing him to connect his own experiences with a vast range of other experiences, demonstrating for him that when used skillfully, words could be powerful tools against racism, just as they had been used by his religious family against heathenism.

Although Wright chooses not to dwell on the fact, his introduction to the writing of Mencken and other white authors reinforces the presence in society of some whites who possessed a conscience and who spoke out. The pivotal role they play in Wright's development establishes them as models for the white reader. Furthermore, the symbolic literary function of these writers is made concrete in Wright's own life by the presence and actions of Mr. Falk, an Irish Catholic white man who, also despised by southerners, lends Wright the library card that allows him entry into the segregated library. Despite Falk's generosity in lending him a card, Wright's success in securing books is not possible unless he also acts on his own by forging a note for the librarian that he makes "authentic" by describing himself as a "nigger boy" fetching books for the white cardholder. What Wright reminds his readers here is that charity alone does not create justice; still he must improvise, claim the power that is his to "subvert the discourse of the dominant culture and bring it to terms of his own control" (Graham and Ward 112).

After borrowing and reading many books, as he does on so many occasions, Wright makes a list of what stirs his imagination, this time not of the preacher's apocalyptic metaphors, which failed to satisfy his hunger, or of the faithful congregants in his mother's parish to whom he cannot feel connected, but a list of all the new books for which he hungered that showed him "new ways of looking and seeing" (BB 294). As when he was trying to read the Bible in order to write hymns, the experience of reading makes him attempt to write and in the process he discovers "what being a Negro meant. I could endure the hunger. I had learned to love with the hate. But to feel that there were feelings denied me, that the very breath of life itself was beyond my reach, that more than anything else hurt, wounded me. I had a new hunger" (BB 296). To satisfy his hunger he considers and rejects several available possibilities, all of which continue to present themselves to the oppressed as the only available means of liberation: organizing rebellions with other blacks, submitting to the life of a "genial slave," transferring self-hatred to others with a black skin, or finding release in sex and alcohol (BB 298–99).

Eventually he raises the courage to go north, "precisely to change" and flee the terror and culture from which he sprang with a resignation that an unknown terror could be no worse than the one with which he was already acquainted. The din of Chicago overwhelms him at first, but no more so than his recognition that immigrants to America could still find a better life than African Americans do. "When I contemplated the area of No Man's Land into which the Negro mind in America had been shunted I wondered if there had ever existed in all human history a more corroding and devastating attack upon the personalities of men than the idea of racial discrimination" (BB 312).

He proceeds to describe the devastating impact of such discrimination, particularly as it renders the black man "lonely and afraid," hating "in himself that which others hated in him" (BB 313), so that "each part of the day would be consumed in a war with himself, a good part of his energy would be spent in keeping control of his unruly emotions, emotions which he had not wished to have, but could not help having. Held at bay by the hate of others, preoccupied with his own feelings, he was continuously at war with reality" (BB 313). Realizing that "Negro life was a sprawling land of unconscious suffering," Wright concludes, "there were but few Negroes who knew the meaning of their lives, who could tell their story" (BB 314).

At this point, Wright, who has decided to live "by hard facts alone" and to "put God out of [his] mind" (BB 335), still does not see himself as the writer who could tell the story of his people. But he moves toward becoming that man when he is introduced to other groups that offer what religion cannot, including literary societies and Garveyites. Yet it is his encounter with the Communist party that seems to hold the most hope for filling the hunger that religion could not satisfy. Attracted by their "emotional certainty" and an "access to a fund of knowledge denied ordinary men" (BB 347), he nonetheless is disturbed by their "ridiculous overstatements" (BB 349), citing a speech by a black Communist whose words he judged "downright offensive to lowly, hungry Negroes." In particular Wright objects to how the speaker inveighs against religion by taunting and mocking God, challenging God to act. When no divine response is forthcoming the speaker rants, "'I'll tell you where to find God. When it rains at midnight, take your hat, turn it upside down on a floor in a dark room, and you'll have God'" (BB 349).

Wright realizes that this approach is no different from the religious exhortations that so disgusted him, observing that this "was not the way to destroy people's outworn beliefs. . . . They were acting like irresponsible children" (BB 350). Furthermore, he realizes that the Communists, for all their talk of raising the masses, did not understand or appreciate the complex nature of black life. Communists rejected the state of things as they were, which was the necessary first step toward "embracing a creative attitude toward life," but they did not understand what they were rejecting or why, and had supplanted it with no compelling alternative vision.

Although Wright still rejects religion, his analysis of the shortcomings of Communism betrays his ongoing fascination with and even respect for religion. In issuing an analysis of what America needs to solve the "Negro problem," he uses concepts characteristic of the slave narrative tradition as it articulates a liberating theology. His language casts the role of liberation on the oppressed but acknowledges that "the Negro could never solve his problem until the deeper problem of American civilization had been faced and solved," even suggesting, as King did, that African Americans are uniquely qualified for this redemptive role because unlike any other group in America, the black "was the most cast-out of all the outcast people in America," and thus "no other group could tackle this problem as well as the Negro could" (BB 350). Again betraying how steeped he is in the religion of his cultural upbringing, Wright compares the task before African Americans to a "miracle," using scriptural imagery to pose the rhetorical question, "Could the Negro accomplish this miracle? Could he take up his bed and walk?" (BB 351).

As he waits for employment at a relief station, Wright further reflects on the conditions in America, and once again his analysis reads very much like a liberation theology text. He applies the analytical tools he acquired from the Communist party, and with vivid memories of Southern oppression and the present conditions of Northern poverty he is able to both diagnose and prescribe. The oppressors, he observes, are unaware of what they are doing in "trying to save themselves and their class," for by establishing conditions wherein the poor gather together as they must to receive assistance, they also create the opportunity for them to come to a "new realization of life" as they talk to one another. This new vision is the master's tool that would take down the master's house because "once this new conception of themselves had formed, no power on earth could alter it" (BB 354). Although surely talking about his own future and his confidence in his own transformation, in this instance Wright is acknowledging that his extraordinariness comes from being like ordinary blacks, people who in Wright's estimation are those whom the oppressor should most fear, those in whom an unconscious revolution has already taken place.

The same could be said for Wright. He continues in his menial labor supplied by relief assistance, including one painful job that is ripe with parabolic meaning. As a medical research assistant, he is assigned to care for dogs that, for no purposes of research but simply for human relief, are devocalized, barking wildly and silently for attention. His description of the animals' plight matches in poignancy his childhood experiences, wherein innocent creatures become the pawns of those in power. Furthermore, by juxtaposing the conditions of blacks with those of laboratory animals he creates another parable for white readers who value black life as "close kin" (BB 370) to animal life.

By comparing the dogs to his co-workers, who also bark to no avail, he demonstrates how the impulse to cry out, even if it isn't heard, stems from a chronically frustrating way of life that persists as a vague psychic pain.

Like the animals, African Americans are "locked in the dark underworld of American life" (BB 370). There they survive by their own code of ethics, values, and loyalty, which has devastating consequences for the dominant culture that they cannot even see, a point dramatized in Wright's parable when co-workers turn on each other for no significant reason and their fight results in the escape of the laboratory animals. The careful research of the white men that is supported by slavelike labor is destroyed when the oppressed turn on each other. But they never notice the haphazard efforts of the workers to make the lab look like nothing was disturbed and continue their research unaware of how it has been violated, just as many nonblack people live with the comfortable assumption that their lives are not affected by the violence perpetrated against people of color.

With the Communist party Wright begins to develop sustaining and abiding relationships, seeing as he did in his mother's church a community to which he wants to belong. His initial conversion to party politics is without the trauma that attended his enforced baptism, for rather than shoving him toward a public act of confession, the party provides him with literature that he can read privately, writing that confirms "in this world an organized search for the truth of the lives of the oppressed and the isolated." Unlike the church that demanded that he conform to preexisting patterns of identity, his first impression of the party is of a group that unites "scattered but kindred peoples into a whole" (BB 374).

Soon, however, Wright comes to appreciate the shallowness of the party's profession of unity, and his criticism of the party's deficiencies rings like his criticism of the church, including people "who had been misled so often . . . were afraid of anybody who differed from themselves" (BB 390). What the party and the church both lack is what the slave narrative tradition provides and liberation theology hopes to accomplish: a way to break down the barriers that would objectify the oppressed and reveal to the oppressor the human lives at issue. "In their efforts to recruit masses, they had missed the meaning of the lives of the masses, had conceived of people in too abstract a manner." Wright's goal therefore becomes the same as that of his enslaved ancestors: to "make voyages, discoveries, explorations with words and try to put some of that meaning back" (BB 377).

So rather than wrestle with family, God, nation, or the Communist party, Wright begins to "wrestle with words," which gave him moments of "deepest meaning" (BB 402). Because the party demands that he suppress the very quality that goaded him towards liberation—"an individuality which life had seared into my blood and bones" (BB 428)—he comes to see it as not unlike the religion in its paradoxical characteristics, its inability to perform in deed what it expresses in creed. It is but another institution inspired by the "loftiest impulses, filled with love for those who suffer, urged toward fellowship with the rebellious, committed to sacrifice" but also filled with "hate, suspicion, and bitterness" (BB 434).

The party's response to Wright's creative prescription for society is the same as the church's. When his Communist friend Ross breaks down and begs forgiveness of the party that has judged him as a transgressor, Wright feels for him the same thing he felt at his own forced baptism. He ironically casts his impressions in terms that recall in tone and language a great religious anthem of liberation: "This, to me, was a spectacle of glory; and yet, because it had condemned me, because it was blind and ignorant, I felt that it was a spectacle of horror" (BB 441). This spectacle is extended and intensified in its figurative relationship to Wright's forced baptism, when, rather than being bodily pulled toward commitment, he is bodily denied participation in the May Day parade.

Humanity could only learn from its mistakes, as Wright would do in writing *Black Boy,* "by marching down history's bloody road. He would have to purchase his wisdom of life with sacred death. He would have to pay dearly to learn just a little" (BB 451). That bloody road is the same route taken by his enslaved ancestors, who created the slave narrative tradition and to whose ongoing function Richard Wright contributes a new textimony. In particular, Wright's textimony reveals the ways in which the slave narrative tradition demonstrates that in order to be effective in witnessing to the need of liberation, whites must understand that they are "as miserable as their black victims. . . . If this country can't find its way to a human path, if it can't inform conduct with a deep sense of life, then all of us, black as well as white, are going down the same drain" (BB 453).

Wright's response to the call for liberation once again affirms imagination as an effective agent for change. When he picks up a pencil and holds it over a white sheet of paper—figuratively demonstrating the way in which black experience is inscribed on white history—Wright is ready to begin to "build a bridge of words between me and that world outside, that world which was so distant and elusive that it seemed unreal. I would hurl the words into this darkness and wait for an echo, and if an echo sounded, no matter how faintly, I would send other words to tell, to march, to fight, to create a sense of the hunger for life that gnaws in us all, to keep alive in our hearts a sense of the inexpressibly human" (BB 453).

Thus Wright learns how to tell the story of voiceless African Americans' story by telling his own. As Horace Porter suggests, it is the power of words and their transforming and redeeming abilities that "lead to Wright's salvation and redemption" (61), thereby establishing as his ultimate liberation the ability to face the dreadful experiences and to record them. Through the interplay of character and characterization in *Black Boy*—by characterizing himself as a representative yet extraordinary Negro and by his act of character in recollecting the past—Wright becomes the agent of his own drama and a symbol of the liberated lifestyle he hopes to effect in others. Although the conclusion of *Black Boy* is tentative and the promise of the narrator becoming an artist is uncertain, such uncertainty remains so only until the reader recognizes that "what we have read is not simply the statement of a promise, its background and development, but its fulfillment" (C. Davis 438).

Wright still has many trials to face before he becomes the writer who establishes the fact of his liberation in textimony. The process by which he arrives at this state and the skills required to attain it are symbolic of the process his readers are meant to undergo: "For white America to understand the significance of the problem of the Negro will take a bigger and tougher America than any we have yet known" (BB 320), true in 1927 and still true today. The way in which Wright becomes tougher is the same prescription he offers America, which is "frightened of fact, of history, of processes, of necessity" (BB 321). As he has wrestled with understanding his past in *Black Boy*, so too must America abandon its shallow past and face the same paradox all African Americans face: finding itself "at war with itself, convulsed by a spasm of emotional and moral confusion" (BB 320). In other words, America, like Wright, must find its place in the slave narrative tradition. And the way in which America can begin to find its place is by being "drench[ed] with a sense of a new world," by reading *Black Boy*—a text characteristic of the tradition because of the way in which the author sought to "fasten the mind of the reader upon words so firmly that he would forget the words and be conscious only of his response" (BB 330).

❧ ❧ ❧

> The accident of race and color has placed me on both sides: The Western World and its enemies. If my writing has any aim, it is to try to reveal that which is human on both sides, to affirm the essential unity of man on earth.
> —Richard Wright

Wright's position in the slave narrative tradition and his role in advancing a liberating theology are evident not only in the ways he forces readers to confront the awful realities of racism. In conjunction with the searing criticism he applies in his social analysis, he offers a vision that points toward a belief in unity and a way to realize that unity in community. In his essay, "In Search of a Common Identity: The Self and South in Four Mississippi Autobiographies," William Andrews discusses how *Black Boy* "has sought or signified a peculiar kind of selfhood and community" (47). Reading the autobiography as Wright's means of "psychic survival, a way of giving form and meaning to a sense of selfhood" (48), Andrews notes that exploring concepts of difference are a crucial part of developing notions of corporate identity, which is why Wright crafted *Black Boy* to include a recollection of a time early in his life when he viewed the racial other through the undifferentiated perspective of childhood.

As demonstrated earlier, Wright's discovery of difference comes early in childhood, creating a sense of disjunctiveness and unexplained mystery in his most intimate world and undermining all his relationships. Because difference can be explained only as arbitrary, capricious, and repressive, Wright turns to his own imagination and creates a "culture, a creed, a religion" out of which he can fashion an ideal of selfhood that is liberated from opposition to otherness. For as Andrews points out, both whiteness and blackness are oppressive forces in Wright's life, and his antagonistic response to both his family and the dominant culture was motivated by "a fundamental need throughout his youth to view his world wholly, as a community, and to negotiate his world not through images and roles but as an authentic personality" (58).

Although Wright abandons any possibility for community in the South, he finds in his emerging identity as a writer the possibility for a communal identity. As Andrews explains, Wright's retreat into literature does not seal his alienation but "liberates him from it by enhancing his powers of imaginative identification. He begins to recognize himself in and through others, even the once terrible other, by way of their common Americanness" (58). What he has been rebelling against in the South he comes to understand as part of a larger American environment that writers, even white writers, were trying to reshape "nearer to the hearts of those who lived in it," leading Andrews to assert that "in this community the black man from the South believes he can become a self-wrighter" (59–60). Even though in the North he does not find the community in personal, political, or artistic terms that he imagined, Wright's autobiography "testif[ies] eloquently to his hunger for an identity realized in community" (60). Because his autobiography does not "picture his achievement of a communal identity in an historically locatable place and time," Andrews reads Wright as sending a double message of both optimism and skepticism about the possibility "of the black southerner's achieving a fulfilling sense of identity and community in America" (60).

From the perspective of what the slave narrative tradition and liberation theology hope to accomplish, Wright's autobiography functions effectively to engage the reader in a community of intimate discourse that is intended to defy the history he personally experiences, in which efforts to engage others are frustrated. The impact of this discourse is to force the reader to make a choice of identification, to confront his or her own otherness. This open-ended story, Andrews concludes, "calls on the American reader to identify with the narrator in a national community of moral commitment so that together they can seize the pen of history and write the future in common" (64). This is the same call extended by ex-slave narrators, who spoke with a voice of such unique authenticity and power that they personally engaged readers. Wright directly challenges his reader in deeply personal terms, the same personal terms by which he elaborates his own declensions of guilt and fear, fantasy and desire. Just as he had to do in writing *Black Boy*, Wright compels his audience to look at suffering without blinking while he asserts the claims of imagination in facing the forces that would deny it.

As a liberating strategy for survival, writing gave Richard Wright the freedom to envision a world that was fair, complex, and balanced. As he expressed it in a 1955 interview, "Writing is my way of becoming a free man, of expressing my relationship to the world and to the society in which I live," that allows others when they read his texts to exercise their own imagination, "to know what is happening to other people," thereby establishing the conditions for creating unity, "to build a bridge between individuals" (Kinnamon and Fabre 234). Imagination is a critical faculty not just to exercise but to discipline and use in appropriate ways. As Wright's parables in *Black Boy* so effectively demonstrate, "there is a lot of distrust between the two races and this creates a distance. This can be explained somewhat strangely by the fact that, on both sides, there is a wish to protect one's own personality. Black people have tried to establish a protected self. With the white man, the same feeling prevails: he is afraid; he does not understand exactly what happens in a black person" (Kinnamon and Fabre 211). And the only way a white person can begin to understand "what happens in a black person" is to redirect his or her imagination away from characterizations that engender fear and "set limits to the existence of Negroes" and toward more meaningful characterizations of blacks that denote character and a shared humanity.

Despite the challenges and criticisms he levels at religion, Wright still uses its language appropriately to describe his own creative efforts and the responsibility he feels, the "sacred duty" he has as a creative artist "to speak and write ceaselessly about this problem" (Kinnamon and Fabre 211). But to write about it is not enough. One must also write well, following the precedent set by ex-slave narrators, who understood what was at stake. As Lionel Trilling points out in a contemporary review of *Black Boy* for *The Nation,* "our literature is full of autobiographical or reportorial or fictional accounts of misery and oppression" that, though they may serve a good purpose, also may generate emotions that are not enduring but serve "the liberal reader as a means of 'escape.'" By escape he does not mean relief or diversion, but a specific "moral escape" that can be offered by accounts of suffering and injustice where one can "sit in one's armchair and be harrowed" and let that experience pass for a moral or political action. As he explains, "we vicariously suffer in slippers and become virtuous: it is pleasant to exercise moral indignation at small cost; or to fill up emotional vacancy with good strong feeling at a safe distance; or to feel consciously superior to the brutal oppressor; or to be morally entertained by poverty, seeing it as a new and painful kind of primitivism which tenderly fosters virtue, or if not virtue, then at least 'reality'" (Reilly 152).

Trilling exempts Wright's account because the dignity and integrity of the book that resists generating easy and inexpensive emotions is born of the author's not wholly identifying himself with his painful experience. Using the same literary interplay of character and characterization typical of ex-slave narratives—where the young Wright protagonist of *Black Boy* is characterized as being more than the sum of his oppression and the adult writer of *Black Boy* establishes his character in writing the narrative—Wright does not become "a mere object of the reader's consciousness, does not make himself that different kind of human being, a 'sufferer.' He is not an object, he is a subject; he is the same kind of person as his reader, as complex and as free." Because Wright possesses the "objectivity that comes from refusing to be an object," his is able to advance the belief that oppression has done something more than segregate his people. "He dares, that is, to take the oppression seriously, to believe that it really does oppress" (Reilly 153).

It is not surprising, therefore, that when *Black Boy* was published reviewers described it in terms similar to those applied to reviews of ex-slave narratives. George Streator, writing for *Commonweal,* cites the publication of the autobiography as "another milestone in the road to emancipation" (Reilly 145). Over and again reviewers remark on how the text accomplished Douglass's imperative "to imagine oneself in similar circumstances." Writing for the *Philadelphia Bulletin,* John Cournos notes how the autobiography could "wring the heart and stir indignation," describing the book as "challenge of a thinking sensitive Negro to his fellow human beings, the white man" (Reilly 129), a sentiment nearly duplicated by R. L. Duffus in the *New York Times Book Review* when he calls *Black Boy* "a challenge and an occasion for searching of hearts" (Reilly 135).

In *Negro Story,* F. K. Richard even remarks on the universal quality of Wright's depiction of oppression, in language that prefigures John Howard Griffin's description of his "black like me" experience. Richard suggests that "the cruel experiences which happened to Richard during his boyhood did not happen to him only as a black boy. They may happen to many other poor boys of any minority group. I could tell many a story of white friends who went through similarly tragic childhoods, who were shuffled around by others, mistreated and rejected. In those cases another excuse was found—another label was tagged on to them, like 'Dago,' 'Hun' or 'Jew'. Richard Wright's book speaks therefore, for any minority group of our nation, and its value and importance grows through this new aspect" (Reilly 170).

In many instances reviewers suggest a salvific effect of the book on white readers, as when John D. Paulus, writing for the *Pittsburgh Press,* challenges readers, "If you can watch this desperate, trapped, beaten and hopeless fellow human without a tug in your heart—you need salvation" (Reilly 118), a sentiment affirmed by Amy Croughton in the *Rochester Times Union* as she advances the belief that the autobiography could "clear away the thoughtless indifference that caused such an indictment to be written . . . there is plenty in the book to make white readers think, and be ashamed that any human being, of any race or creed, could be made to feel as Wright must have felt at some time of his life in order to be able to write this hard, bitter arraignment" (Reilly 131).

The "bitter arraignment" presented in *Black Boy* is tempered elsewhere by Wright's respect for nurturing aspects of black culture and his belief in the possible transformation of society. In *12 Million Black Voices: A Folk History of the Negro in the United States,* a pictorial analysis of the life of blacks from rural South to urban North published three years after *Black Boy,* Wright evokes through descriptions of the conditions of African Americans the strength embodied in their reactions to these conditions, merging literary expression with the need for social and political change. The study is a respectful and appreciative portrayal of black folk culture, including religion, which Wright praises for the ways in which it sustained African Americans by emphasizing the triumph of oppressed peoples over exploitation and subjugation. In the conclusion to *12 Million Black Voices,* Wright asserts, "The differences between black folk and white folk are not blood or color, and the ties that bind us are deeper than those that separate us. . . . We are with the new tide. We stand at the crossroads. We watch each new procession. The hot wires carry urgent appeals. Print compels us. Voices are speaking. Men are moving! And we shall be with them" (146–47).

Thus, as Ralph Ellison reminds us, Wright absorbs and expresses more of his culture than he identifies or admits, including the religious dimensions of that culture. Wright's life becomes, in Ellison's reading, the example through which the author could probe what "qualities of will, imagination, and intellect" are required to possess meaning in life, and the autobiography that results reveals a conflicting pattern of identification and rejection, both with his own world and culture and the larger Western culture. Just as *Black Boy* recasts traditional conversion narratives in the form of a deconversion, both honoring and rejecting the influence, Wright, for all his critical analysis, recognizes the beneficent role religious institutions have played in the survival of his people. Ellison explains Wright's paradoxical posture by joining the imaginative and spiritual strains of their shared cultural inheritance as two chief means of resisting oppression and advancing social justice:

> We were an assertive people, and our mode of social assertion was artistic. But there was also the Negro church, wherein you heard the lingering accents of nineteenth-century rhetoric with its emphasis upon freedom and individual responsibility; a rhetorical style which gave us Lincoln, Harriet Tubman, Harriet Beecher Stowe, and the other abolition-preaching Beechers. Which gave us Frederick Douglass and John Jasper and many other eloquent and heroic Negroes whose spirit still moves among us through the contributions they made to the flexibility, the music, and the idealism of the American language. Richard Wright was a possessor of that tradition. It is resonant in his fiction and it was a factor in his eager acceptance of social responsibility. (*Going* 209)

In resisting society's attempts to negate him, Wright turns his own self into a mirror that reflects the negation back at the oppressive hegemony. He crafts his autobiography so that each racial incident can be understood in light of the entire social, political, and ideological system of racism and slavery. In the process he represents the slave's dialectical overcoming of his condition by bringing to consciousness the structures of his social death in the symbolic realm of literature. His autobiography becomes not only a site of freedom for himself, but the place where he effects a revolution in the collective consciousness of America.

After writing an autobiography that explores in poignant detail his own childhood experiences, it is not surprising that Wright should claim as part of his mission the responsibility to give voice to those not traditionally heard and identify as his primary audience young African Americans searching for a sense of character. Wright asserts that he "wanted to lend, give my tongue, to voiceless Negro boys. I feel this way about the emotionally and economically deprived Negro children of the South." He continues by quoting Whitman: "'Not until the sun ceases to shine on you will I disown you.' That was one of my motives. I wanted to give voice to that, to make it known" (Kinnamon and Fabre 64–65).

Echoing Whitman was a canny choice for Wright, indicating simultaneously how much he gained from absorbing the best of what the dominant culture had to offer and his recognition that his primary audience is white. He accepts the responsibility of that role because he is aware that "our life is still invisible to whites. It still remains outside the pale of whites' preoccupations. I'd like to hurl words in my novels in order to arouse whites to the fact that there is someone here with us, Negroes, a human presence. . . . When I write I have a white image of my audience. This is natural because my audience is white, and I want to make them aware of the fact that there exists a black life with the same dimensions" (Kinnamon and Fabre 224–25).

By revealing shared human dimensions, Wright functions like a liberation theologian but in the guise of a secular artist and social critic who seeks to understand how human beings actively and imaginatively interrogate and make worlds. For all the challenge he offers to traditional religion as an agent of social change, Wright's autobiography participates in the same spirit and "sense of self-discovery and exaltation which is implicit in the Negro church" (Ellison, *Shadow and Act* 214) and demonstrates to theologians agitating for liberation that art, whether it is judged as secular or sacred, still has the ability, as Ellison wrote, to "create within us moments of high consciousness; moments wherein we grasp, in the instant, a knowledge of how transcendent and how abysmal and yet affirmative it can be to be human beings." In Ellison's estimation, "it is for such moments of inspired communication that the artist lives" (*Shadow and Act* 212). It was for such moments that Richard Wright lived and in such moments that his religious spirit endured. Because once he found the language for articulating the mysteries of human existence, Wright knew he could liberate not just himself but his readers as well by providing in *Black Boy* engaging ways for us to think about how our lives are shaped by law and custom and to experience how they can be reshaped by imagination.

NOTES

1. Abel Meeropol was a Jewish schoolteacher from New York City. In addition to writing the lyrics to "Strange Fruit," he is remembered for raising the two orphaned sons of Julius and Ethel Rosenberg and for writing the lyrics of "The House I Live In," a paean to tolerance sung by Frank Sinatra in an Oscar-winning short subject in 1945. Meeropol was inspired to write the lyrics to "Strange Fruit" after seeing a photograph of a ghastly lynching. See David Margolick's article "Strange Fruit" for more details about the composer and Holiday's role in the song's development.

2. Although most published scholarship relates exclusively to the first published edition of *Black Boy*, for this analysis I am using the 1991 restored text established by the Library of America, *Black Boy (American Hunger)*, which includes two parts: "Southern Nights" and "The Horror and the Glory." It was prepared from a complete set of page proofs dating from the spring of 1944, before Wright agreed not to publish *American Hunger* in 1945. All quotations from *Black Boy* are designated by the abbreviation BB.

3. This remark is drawn from Wright's dedication of *Native Son* to his mother, who "when I was a child at her knee, taught me to revere the fanciful and imaginative."

3   Remembering the Truth:
Ernest Gaines

You had to decide: Am I going to change the world, or am
I going to change me? Or maybe change the world a little,
just by changing me.
—Sadie Delany

C hanging the world by first changing oneself has been a prominent strategy for human liberation ever since Frederick Douglass announced
in his autobiography, "You have seen how a man was made a slave; you
shall see how a slave was made a man" (107). This elemental effort has
been undertaken and endorsed by many who lacked Douglass's literary
talent and whose stories are told not in words but in deeds. Rosa Parks is
one such person, and although she is properly celebrated for her historical role as the mother of the civil rights movement, she is also more than
the symbol she inevitably became. She represents not just the character who
performed a single act of unassisted heroism, but a person of character
whose lifetime of acting on behalf of liberation is characteristic of many
other ordinary and determined people.

In "Rosa Parks and the Making of History," Walt Harrington emphasizes two elements customarily not included in canonical civil rights lore.
Her refusal to move to the back of the bus in 1955 did not initiate the
boycott or the civil rights movement, as the prevailing myth suggests.
Neither burst forth from any single symbolic act, but both were the result
of the brave activities of many people who contributed to creating the
conditions in which Rosa Parks's act could become historic. Furthermore,
her actions that day were not the spontaneous reaction of an exhausted
and meek seamstress. Despite the racism she experienced while growing
up in the segregated south, Rosa Parks was instilled early on with a deep

sense of pride, strength, and confidence that propelled her toward that act of nonviolent resistance. It was no accident but something she, like many others, had been preparing for all her life.

Her decision was a long time coming, as she relates in her 1992 autobiography, *Rosa Parks: My Story*. At the time of her arrest, Rosa Parks had been active in the NAACP for more than a decade and was already radicalized to the movement. She wasn't physically weary; she was weary of injustice. "I just felt that as a person I didn't want to be treated like a second-class citizen. I didn't want to be mistreated under the guise of legally enforced racial segregation and the more we endured that kind of treatment, the worse we were being treated" (Harrington 29). As she waited for the police to arrive after her refusal to relinquish her seat, she was thinking about a night when she was a girl and sat with her grandfather, shotgun at the ready, while the KKK rode the countryside. The humiliating segregation of Montgomery's buses was also on her mind, particularly a sequence of harassments recently experienced by her friends. Although a lifetime of experiences led to the moment of her resistance, her simple reply to the police officer who interrogated her before he arrested her, "Why do you all push us around?" became part of the legend that she had just had enough and in one sudden act that she describes as "set in motion by God" refused to relinquish her seat (Harrington 26).

Described variously as an angel or a saint, Parks demurs at first, saying she is "just a person who wanted to be seated on the bus" (Harrington 29). But she also admits, "I consider myself a symbol of freedom and equality, and I wanted to let it be known that that was what I believed in" (Harrington 29). The truth of what Rosa Parks accomplished, therefore, is grander and more heroic than is customarily appreciated. Although he is uncomfortable "deflating the myth" of what Rosa Parks did, Aldon Morris, sociologist and author of *Origins of the Civil Rights Movement,* suggests that "what Rosa Parks did is really the least significant part of the story." Morris goes on to explain that we have taken her action and "elevate[d] it to epic proportions, but all the things that happened so she could become epic, we drop by the wayside. . . . That she was just a sweet lady who was tired is the myth. . . . The real story of Montgomery is that real people with frailties made change. That's what the magic is" (Harrington 14).

Rosa Parks's role as a symbol, and the myth that supports it, carries a deep cultural resonance about America's own self-image. In protecting her image we also celebrate and reaffirm core values for ourselves as Americans. For blacks, Rosa Parks gives evidence that they could be empowered to force change. For whites, Rosa Parks gives evidence that they were willing to change. Rosa Parks played her role, but many others did, too, something Morris reaffirms when he says that "the message is ordinary people doing extraordinary things" because "the power exists with the collectivity" (Harrington 30).

Locating power in the collectivity and representing it through the life of one ordinary person is the impulse behind Ernest Gaines's novel, *The Autobiography of Miss Jane Pittman* (1971), whose protagonist Miss Jane, like Rosa Parks, is at once simple and complex, heroic and ordinary. Miss Jane also appreciates what conditions are necessary for people like Rosa Parks to emerge: "People and time bring forth leaders . . . leaders don't bring forth people. The people and the time brought King; King didn't bring the people. What Miss Rosa Parks did, everybody wanted to do. They just needed one person to do it first because they all couldn't do it at the same time; then they needed King to show them what to do next. But King couldn't do a thing before Miss Rosa Parks refused to give that white man her seat" (MJP 228).[1]

In creating Miss Jane, Gaines records a history of the people and the times that bring forth leaders. Although in *Black Boy* Richard Wright remarks that "there were but few Negroes who knew the meaning of their lives, who could tell their story" (BB 314), in *The Autobiography of Miss Jane Pittman,* Ernest Gaines dispels this notion and suggests that narratives such as Miss Jane's embody the history of those who had no one to record their stories. Unlike Wright's autobiography, which was challenged for its veracity, Gaines's novel was always acknowledged by the author as fiction. Yet Gaines's novel rang so true to readers that the author reported many instances of incredulity on the part of readers who mistook Miss Jane for an actual person. Librarians featured the book as nonfiction and reporters and reviewers asked Gaines for a picture of Miss Jane to accompany their articles (Gaines, "Miss Jane" 23). Former New York governor Hugh Carey included Miss Jane on a list of historical black women, and *Folklore and Literature in the United States* lists Jane Pittman in the author index (Gaudet, "Miss Jane" 24). In "Image Making: Tradition and the Two Versions of the Autobiography of Miss Jane Pittman," John Callahan even reports how a popular monthly magazine wanted to serialize Miss Jane's story, until they found out it was a novel and decided against it.

As Callahan suggests, this question of authenticity is a variation not only on the question of what truth is but on who should tell the truth. Provocative questions are raised when the claim is made that Miss Jane and her document are less authentic because the story flowed from the imagination of a novelist rather than being the story of a historical person. Callahan asks, "Does it mean that at least some white Americans will accept their racial history as true if it comes to them with conventional, literal authenticity . . . but not if that same history takes it form from the mind and traditions of a black artist?" ("Image Making" 55). The judgments about reality and imagination and the role each plays in accounts of oppression may explain, in part, why Gaines took such care in rendering his story, framing Miss Jane's life against a backdrop of conventional historical facts.

In the essay "Miss Jane and I," Gaines reflects on the composition of the novel, suggesting that he began many years before the novel's actual literary formation, simply by sitting on the porch in Louisiana and writing letters for old people. He got from them some idea of what their lives were like, but he also knew he didn't have enough knowledge to fill in the historical gaps. He sought the help of Alvin Aubert, asking him to list ten or twelve significant things that had happened in Louisiana since the mid-nineteenth century. The list Aubert derived included the obvious, such as the Civil War, Reconstruction, and the civil rights movement, but it also included local events such as the floods of 1912 and 1926, the construction of spillways to control floods, the role of Huey Long, and the arrival on the scene of sports figures such as Joe Louis and Jackie Robinson.

Gaines used these events to shape the background of the novel, but to draw the foreground, a portrait of the people and their immediate lives, Gaines asked questions of old people in his hometown and librarians in local and state libraries, who led him to read period histories, biographies, and autobiographies. He even read *The Diary of Anne Frank* to see what a young girl would think about when alone (Doyle, "A MELUS Interview" 63). To further craft a realistic portrayal of former slaves, Gaines took as a model *Lay My Burden Down,* a collection of WPA interviews of ex-slaves. "I used that book to get the rhythm of speech and an idea of how the ex-slaves would talk about themselves" (Rowell 46–47). He absorbed anything that would help him get to his character, Miss Jane, being careful to take all that historical information and "to digest it and then give it back to a little lady who is illiterate—very intelligent—brilliant, but illiterate. She's never read a book; she cannot write. So that was a problem; I had to get all this information, and then I had to come back and get a language for her (Doyle, "A MELUS Interview" 63–64). He read just enough books on a particular subject so he would know what he wanted Miss Jane to know. All this was undertaken in an attempt "to find a straight line" throughout many circular narratives (Gaines, "Miss Jane" 35).[2]

Gaines's search for authenticity involved an effort to ascertain not just the language used by ex-slaves, but also what might have been their vision of the world. Furthermore, the painstaking historical research Gaines undertook to lend authenticity to his novel was an important development in the slave narrative tradition. As William Andrews remarks in "The Novelization of Voice in African American Narrative," the authenticating conventions used by ex-slave narrators established the "precedent and justification for a vital tradition in the black American novel" (33). Using Douglass as a model, Andrews demonstrates that Douglass's idea "of black history as a necessary, that is liberating, fiction underlies the experimental historical narratives of the twentieth century" (33) that began with Arna Bontemps's *Black Thunder* (1936) and evolved to include *The Autobiography of Miss Jane Pittman*. By telling Miss Jane's story "in accordance with an idea of authority rooted in authenticating acts represented in fictive discourse" (33), Gaines explores new potential for expression within the conventions of the slave narrative tradition as it moved away from the actual experience of slavery.

Because his text unintentionally raises unanswered questions of where fact begins and fiction leaves off, Gaines keeps open the possibility of a broader and more empathetic interpretation of the narrative. He locates a new space for African-American empowerment in the cause of liberation that isn't dependent on strict historical veracity for authenticity but points us toward the margins, to the unwritten stories of unheralded people, represented by people like Miss Jane, that underscore much of the African-American experience. Gaines confidently walks the fine line between fact and fiction, conscious of his role as both a creative artist who manipulates literary techniques and a historian of African-American culture who respects the reality from which his story derives. Miss Jane embodies Gaines's accomplishment because of the way he "roots her moral being in stubbornly particular, elemental, objective phenomena" (Callahan, *In the African-American* 202). Her recollections reveal her to be both pragmatic and imaginative: Although she may not remember the exact date an event occurred, she will remember it was hot (MJP 16).

To further bolster the authenticity of Miss Jane's version of truth, Gaines introduces his tale with an explanation of how the story came to be told. A history teacher seeks out the 108-year-old Miss Jane to interview because of his desire to expand his lessons to include aspects of the past that heretofore were excluded or misrepresented. When asked "What's wrong with them books you already got?" the editor explains that "Miss Jane's not in them" (MJP vi). Gaines remarked in an interview that a historical backdrop to his story was necessary—"I must bring in some kind of reality to what my narrator is talking about" (Gaudet and Wooten 10)—but he also wanted to be certain that the story came across not as the narrator's account (i.e., the interpretation of a trained historian), but as Miss Jane's story. He wanted her to tell her own story her own way. The narrator functions primarily as a stimulant to take Miss Jane out of the present and to "make her get back there. And once he got her mind working, she would get back there, she would live that past" (Gaudet and Wooten 31).

In one respect the "autobiography" reverses the great value placed on literacy associated with ex-slave narrators, who celebrated their achievements in literacy, because Miss Jane remains illiterate her whole life. Although she is like ex-slave narrators because she depends on a sympathetic and interested "editor" to have her story told, her editor respects the integrity of her text and seldom intrudes. It is only her voice we remember, and the misgivings many contemporary critics express about the validity of historical ex-slave narratives paradoxically vanish in Gaines's fictional creation. For Gaines, "the most important aspects of the past can be fully conveyed only through character. History is character, he seems to say, but the character of little people rather than the great movers of events that inhabit formal history books" (Bryant 861). Therefore, it is not surprising that critics such as Jerry Bryant identify as one of Gaines's great talents an ability to create "a character who has a broad visceral appeal—who embodies a wide range of complex historical meaning while at the same time speaking to a heterogeneous audience on a highly personal level in an eccentric but profoundly moral language" (851).

As the editor tapes and edits Miss Jane's reflections and shapes them into her textimony, he explains that her narrative recapitulates the stories of many others: "I should mention here that even though I have used only Miss Jane's voice throughout the narrative, there were times when others carried the story for her. . . . This is not only Miss Jane's autobiography, it is theirs as well. . . . Miss Jane's story is all of their stories, and their stories are Miss Jane's" (MJP x). Herman Beavers finds this feature of the novel especially significant because "Miss Jane's and the teacher/editor's narrative collaboration exists in a communal matrix that essentially 'saves' information from being lost" and demonstrates that history "is participatory and inclusive" (146). Thus the radicalization of "the folk" through education, religion, or social action, which Wright omits from *Black Boy,* is balanced by the perspective of Ernest Gaines. In his writing Gaines extends to all of his characters what Wright allows only for himself, recognizing, in the words of Ralph Ellison, that "possibilities of human richness exist for others" (*Shadow and Act* 112). In *The Autobiography of Miss Jane Pittman* Gaines affirms what Wright denies, writing in folk speech a narrative that gives birth to a character who becomes as real as any of the ex-slave protagonists who wrote their own life stories. Miss Jane represents the vital spirit that was always present in the harsh history Wright exposes, and she embodies a collective voice that attests to the need to apply collaborative energies for survival and creation.

Caught in the movement of changing times, the characters in the novel must make choices that result often in tragedy. Some of the characters maintain from the past proven ways of surviving; others try to adapt themselves to keep pace with society's changes. Gaines's historical perspective sees the need for both change and continuity. His ultimate concern is with dignity of the individual. In the world he sketches, his characters possess a spirit flexible enough to survive and change because they understand that "tradition and kinship . . . are not fixed conditions. They require rigorous acts of shaping and discovery" (Callahan, "Image Making" 54). But it is Miss Jane and the great force of her personality that in many respects enable others to be themselves, whichever identity they assume.

The future she engenders for the community is borne through her moral authority and her ability to recognize when it is appropriate to move on and when it is imperative to stop and take a stand. Rather than traveling to find her liberation in the North, as Wright did, Miss Jane creates it where she is. As the novel traces her circuitous movement back to her origins, it also dramatizes Gaines's concept of freedom and progress. "She returns 'home' because, in his view, true liberation and the progress it engenders are not an abstract, such as the notion of 'freedom,' or a spatial entity, such as 'the North,' but rather a spiritual entity, deeply rooted in a person's character, dignity, and knowledge of his or her history and place" (Babb 85).

Both Gaines and Wright offer their readers portraits of black life, represented in its human dimension. But whereas Gaines offers up something in place of what he removes—a communal or social structure—Wright offers only the example of himself. Both aspects are critical for the process of humanization, and together these texts demonstrate how one contour in literary history occasions another in antagonistic cooperation. Each vision is fundamental to building the kind of society envisioned by liberation theologians, a step toward the ideal of community that lies beyond the paralyzing tendencies of interracial and intraracial discourse. Whether fiction or autobiography, these texts embody the recognition that liberation is a process rather than an achievement.

Who is to participate in this process and how they participate is complicated by a peculiar ambiguity that Gaines leaves unresolved in the novel. Gaines did not identify the schoolteacher's racial identity until a 1994 interview with John Lowe. In that interview Gaines says that the schoolteacher is black and that his racial identity allows him to uncover aspects of Miss Jane's story that she would not have revealed to a white man. Recalling when ex-slaves were interviewed during the 1930s, Gaines remarks, "If a white writer went in there and asked the same people the same thing, they'd give him some information, but they would not give him as much that was revealing as to the black who interviewed them. They'd still be talking about the same thing, but the shading is a little different at the time" (Lowe 313). Yet it is curious that in nearly all the criticism on the novel published to date, no one seeks to clarify the ambiguity of the narrator's racial identity, or even admit that its exists, despite the fact that a specific identification of the narrator's racial identity is essential to their interpretation. Scholars advance their arguments on a presumption that the narrator is either white or black but do not even acknowledge that an ambiguity (or, given Gaines's pronouncement, a misinterpretation) exists. They confidently assume that their interpretation is the correct one.

The critical shading Gaines cites as an aspect of Miss Jane's historical narration becomes important when one examines the narrator's role as a point of entry into the text. Taking a specific position on the racial identity of the narrator leads to two competing interpretations that reinforce larger themes that dominate the novel. If the history teacher is a young, college-educated black man, then he becomes symbolic of the need for African Americans to be responsible for preserving their past. In this respect he can be seen as standing in for the author himself, the guise Gaines assumes to get his story told. He becomes one who returns and resanctifies the old ways often lost in the progress of the race. Moreover, the credibility of his tale is strengthened, as Gaines's statement to Lowe makes clear. As an African American, he would be privy to aspects of the story black people might not reveal to a white man.

However, not only could this interpretation distance white readers from the text, but in some respects it subverts the conventions of the slave narrative tradition out of which the novel emerged. Were the narrator white, we could see him assuming the role many in the past performed as amanuenses, assisting those less empowered to have their stories heard and thereby conferring the validation of the dominant culture, claiming the story not just as true but as necessary for all of society to hear. Although in some respects this customary role has granted credence to white compassion toward black liberation, it also may reinscribe paradigms of authority, making whites the legitimizers and in some respects the saviors of the black race.

That Gaines does not make the racial identity of the narrator important, that race is not a key element in how readers interpret Miss Jane's response to him or the relationship he develops with her, may therefore be more important than if Gaines had identified his race one way or another. I think Gaines sees the promise and the peril attached to either identification, and by leaving open the issue of the narrator's racial identity, he creates new opportunities for both black and white readers to enter the story on their own terms, but to leave it with an understanding that racial identity does matter. It is important that African Americans claim a unique perspective on historical events, and it is significant that in this instance that perspective is freely offered to the dominant culture as a gesture of reconciliation. As Jerry Bryant observes, "He asks us through Miss Jane to respond to his characters as one human being to another, not as representatives of a race or an ideology" (864). In the process we learn a critical truth: "that any adequate grasp of history, and hence of our life in the world, must rest upon the ability to love, to sympathize with the people in their pain, rejoice with them in their triumphs, respect them in both their weaknesses and strengths" (Bryant 864).

What is important is the story and Miss Jane herself, who sees both whites and blacks clearly and completely. None are perfect, all are capable of cowardice and heroism. As Blyden Jackson suggests, this is part of Miss Jane's message, meant for all "who have ears to hear about their own salvation" (272–23). Like Wright, Gaines is especially concerned that his work will first and foremost reach an audience he identifies as "the Black youth of the south" (Doyle, "A MELUS Interview" 61). But when pressed he also affirms a hope that his books will help both black and white youth to achieve an understanding of who the other is. As he explains, "I would want the black youth to say 'Hey, I'm somebody.' And I would want the white youth to say, 'Hey, that is part of me out there and I can only understand myself truly if I can understand my neighbor.' That's the only way one can understand himself, if he can understand other things around him . . . every little piece of things around us makes us a little bit whole . . . so that's what I'd want: the white kids to understand what the black kid is, and the black kid to understand who he is" (Gaudet and Wooten 14).

The novel has been called a "chat with the reader" and part of "that rare category of American novels which talk to the reader" (Beckham 108), becoming a "ritual of sacred significance" (Callahan, *In the African-American* 194) because of the way it embodies the principle of call and response.

Miss Jane's story is called for, and eventually history and circumstance respond by calling her. This same pattern of call and response, embodied in the novel's autobiographical structure, is extended to include a relationship between the storyteller and her audience as "she responds and changes storytelling from a secondary to a primary act. Her voice, her life, her story and her last civil rights action fuse with her people; individually and together, they influence 'the scheme of things' in the quarters and, through the history teacher's good offices, the world beyond" (Callahan, *In the African-American* 194). This creates for the reader the kind of intimacy one imagines was experienced by the people gathered on Joe Clark's porch in Hurston's Eatonville. Like Hurston's memorable characters, the readers of Gaines's novel are invited to listen in and even participate in the "lying" sessions, learning as the novel progresses how to distinguish not just what is essential to the story, but what makes the story's telling essential. In the process reader and characters alike come to discover the difference between the anonymity of a stereotype and the individuality that comes when one grasps one's own humanity and that of the other.

All along Jane assists her community of listeners and readers to "just feel it" (MJP 199), recapitulating a desire expressed by Gaines himself when he commented to an interviewer, "Maybe what I need to do, is sit in a chair on a stage and just tell people stories rather than try to write them down" (Rowell 41). Thus Gaines exploits the potential embodied in oral history but brings it up to date for a contemporary audience because he realizes that only through the artifice of the written word can he introduce strangers to his story. "Paradoxically, he shifts from speech to print, from oral storytelling to fiction so that readers may hear his people's voices and experience imaginatively their oral culture" (Callahan, *In the African-American* 191). Just as the creators of the spirituals measured their own experiences against a larger historical framework of biblical narrative, Miss Jane's story reveals connections between past and present episodes of oppression and liberation. "The past ain't dead," Gaines is fond of paraphrasing William Faulkner, "it ain't even passed" (Rowell 41).

What has not passed is the trope of slavery and how, even after emancipation, its structure and insidious influence remained largely intact in the South. All black Americans share the central conflicts in the novel that are also Jane's particular problems. They derive from the same source liberation theologians cite as destructive: a system of oppression to which whites continue to contribute. Although this system is no longer called slavery, the long course of Miss Jane's life reveals how the contours of the system of oppression continue to be played out in American life. When the novel begins with Miss Jane's description of her life in slavery, we come to appreciate through her matter-of-fact tone ("They couldn't tell if I was white or black, a boy or a girl. The didn't even care what I was" [MJP 4]) that the dominant culture's disavowal of a slave's humanity was routine, a posture that exercises its influence throughout Miss Jane's life. Coupled with Miss Jane's account of slavery are her comments and analyses that depict slavery's inhumanity and the manner in which slaves sought to overcome dehumanization. Every facet of slavery, in all its historical manifestations, is individualized in Jane's narrative, and historic wrongs against a mass of people that might have remained abstract in other historical documents become keenly felt. Gaines reinforces this pattern of systemic oppression and individual redemption in the way he structures his novel.

Although the novel takes its shape in part from slave narratives in its movement from slavery to freedom, it shows this as a constant and repeated movement; as the forms of enslavement change, so must the forms of freedom. Also present are the same devices for coping with oppression that appeared in the antebellum narratives: accommodation and acceptance, rebellion and flight, and a middle ground Keith Byerman calls "strategic resistance . . . characterized by a refusal to accept the imposed definitions of black life, but a simultaneous refusal to rebel openly" (*Fingering the Jagged* 88). Like slave narratives, Gaines's novel exposes us to the realities of racial oppression and people's reaction to it.

Each of the novel's four "books" spans a period of roughly 25 years and represents an era of Miss Jane's life: her movement from childhood, maturity, and seniority to old age (Doyle, "The Autobiography" 96). A corresponding structure has been identified by Herman Beavers as a movement from "dispersion to intimacy, a journey from the disconnectedness of the post-slavery moment to the transformation of the quarters into a community displaying agency" (147). In each era or book Jane functions differently, but all along she shapes the reality she observes with increasing levels of involvement. For as Miss Jane develops, so too does her race. As her life unfolds, so too does African-American history since emancipation; each book contains episodes epitomizing the character of that span of time and illustrating the essence and dynamics of black life. Valerie Babb observes that "Jane's narrative shows her life to be a microcosm of the vast panorama of African-American culture—its people, its history, its myth, its vision. She is a personified archive that . . . records the African-American past and her place in it" (93).

As Jane reveals the details of her history, she makes larger American history an animated presence. Important figures of the American past are remembered not as two-dimensional portraits but as human beings whose actions have a direct impact on the lives of others. Through the interplay of character and characterization typical in slave narrative textimonies, Jane shows how words do things and actions say things. The ideas of leaders such as Frederick Douglass, Booker T. Washington, and even Huey Long are shown to have been absorbed and translated into social change, just as heroes from other areas of life, especially sports figures such as Joe Louis and Jackie Robinson, are embraced as setting examples and giving hope to people as they negotiate their way out of slavery.

Jane's discussion of formal slavery makes up a small part of the book and spans only two days in the first book, "The War Years." It is marked by the hope embodied in the symbolic act of claiming a new name and Jane's aspiration to claim freedom by traveling North. In the second book, "Reconstruction," Jane's narrative reveals the dynamics of the reconstruction of black character in new forms and sentiments, but that reconstruction leads to a white supremacist backlash. The third book, "The Plantation," carries the story up to the late 1930s and reveals the ways in which plantation life after slavery differs little from how it was before Emancipation. The last book, "The Quarters," tells of Jane's experience up to and including part of the time she tells her story. As Jane relates her story in the first three books, the editor punctuates her tale by creating short-titled chapters of her reminiscences, choosing a word or phrase spoken by Jane to illustrate the story's theme. Made up of set pieces, typical episodes include Jane's meditations on history (as in the tragic end of Reconstruction, "A Flicker of Light; and Again Darkness"), religion (as in "The Travels of Miss Jane Pittman"), and nature (as in "Of Men and Rivers").

By the time Miss Jane reaches "The Quarters" on her narrative journey, the titles fall away because here the storytelling is not arranged as reflection but transformed into action. In the Quarters, it is not just historical or heroic figures whose words do things and whose actions say things. As the most personal and intimate section of the narrative, "The Quarters" embodies Jane's liberating theology, encompassing everything she has learned about leadership and deliverance for her community. Her textimony becomes truly liberative as she "summons biblical folk tones and rhythms of prophecy" and transforms her testament from the "old" law record of the past to a "new" grace vision for the future (Callahan, *In the African-American* 205). As the novel's voice and storylines work back to the Civil War, Jane moves forward to the continuing present, where, before her death, she puts her eloquence to work for change in a small but significant act of social justice, one she may not have anticipated when she began to tell stories, but one for which she, like Rosa Parks, had been preparing all her life.

How Miss Jane prepares is the essence of the novel. Keith Byerman suggests that Jane's success is due largely to the role she plays throughout her life as a mediator, as one in the middle who can move comfortably between black and white worlds, the past and the future, the folk and society—between those who defend existing rules and the status quo and those who rebel and are willing to die to break out of the system's limitations. Poised in the middle, Jane comes to represent the complex attitude toward folk culture that Gaines's entire text embodies—an attitude that sees in folk culture possibilities for resistance to oppressive conventions of the dominant culture but also insists that the folk community itself, with well-established mores, can become an imprisoning force (*Fingering the Jagged* 67). In Byerman's estimation, the successful characters are those who negotiate their way amid forces of racist repression and folk parochialism and who survive by "accommodating themselves to the existing system without sacrificing their dignity and by living on the psychological edge of the folk community, near enough to absorb the genuine wisdom of that experience but not so close as to fear change and resistance" (67).

Thus it is appropriate that the novel ends with Miss Jane testing her own experience, which is the combined experience of many people on either side of her middle stance. In her long life she has gained many insights, but not until she is near death does she turn her knowledge into concrete social action. What changes in between is what upholds the entire novel and all the efforts toward liberation that precede Miss Jane's final act: a recognition that although success is never guaranteed and the same social contingencies abide, what makes a difference is one's willingness to confront the world despite the odds. Storytelling becomes for Miss Jane what writing is for Ernest Gaines: an act of remembrance, creation, and performance that sometimes leads to acts of change once the significance of the story is understood.

To get to this point of understanding, however, there are no rules. Miss Jane tells her story on her own time, and she acts accordingly. But the intervention of the editor, just like the act of Gaines himself in writing about Miss Jane, demonstrates how we can help to initiate such liberating impulses. As a contemporary historian, the editor does for social justice what Gaines does for our imagination: He advances the possibilities for transforming history to be responsive to the vision of a liberating theology. Because his novel is so firmly rooted in the slave narrative tradition, Gaines's subject is human universals that transcend the temporary concerns of the politics and social problems of an era and invite anyone concerned with social justice—black or white, young or old, conservative or progressive—to follow Miss Jane's example and write their own narrative of liberation.

❧   ❧   ❧

> One man asks: What is to come?
> The other: What is right?
> And that is the difference
> Between the free man and the slave.
> —Dietrich Bonhoeffer

In her articulation of a postmodern theology, Carolyn Jones repeatedly draws our attention to the ways in which the sacred is disguised in the secular, especially in the stories we relate that help to situate and orient us as we move through history. Drawing on the insights of Cherokee poet Marilou Awiakta, Jones demonstrates how the story and the people who tell it are one because "what happens to either happens to both" (248).[3] In the process Jones breaks down customary distinctions not just between the sacred and the secular, but also between word and action, reminding us of the intimate ethical relationship between what we do and what we say that engenders a life of faith. As she writes, "Faith is a combination of the capacities to narrate and to act, both alone and with others." Furthermore, where the action takes place need not be located on any grand historical scale, but is more often than not found in the simple act of "'housekeeping' that makes the world a home" (250). In his portrayal of Miss Jane Pittman, Ernest Gaines creates a character who embodies this kind of faith. His novel further embodies a constituent element of Jones's theology because of the way in which he exercises his memory—through the creation of Miss Jane's memory—as a kind of duty, where memory is method, "not only an internal activity, but a storehouse of meaning and a way of beginning to reinvent the self in relation to the world and the past. In short, memory, both personal and cultural, is a tool for telling one's story both as a recovery and as a movement forward" (C. Jones 246).

Jones identifies music as providing the form for this movement forward because as a metaphor, music allows one to articulate a "concept of self that is relational, fluid, mutable, and performed and narrated," a redefinition Jones, using the words of Dietrich Bonhoeffer, identifies as essential in a world that does not need "recourse to the 'working hypothesis' called 'God' which exists in its compartment marked 'Religion'" (246). Therefore, it is not surprising that Gaines claims that much of what he learned about writing about his people came from listening to music, especially African-American forms such as the spirituals, blues, and jazz, which "all have fired my imagination as much as anything in literature" ("Miss Jane" 31). From this music Gaines developed the formal aspects of his writing that help him to get his point across, including a sense of pace and style that emerges from qualities such as understatement (playing around a note) and repetition (a recurrent head tune around which musicians improvise).

In her study of Gaines's fiction, Gayl Jones links these musical elements with elements also present in oral forms of literature, noting that Miss Jane "has a quality N. Scott Momaday ascribed to storytelling: 'whole and consummate being,'" in which one's own voice is established without diminishing the voices of others (162). Gaines's use of the musical elements of storytelling allows him to develop a spiritual concept of identity that is fluid, relational, performed, and narrated. He embodies this concept in both the way he portrays Miss Jane and the way she tells her story. Jane's musical storytelling technique creates the impression that the listener is present; she gives advice, moves easily between past and present, anticipates events, and offers revelations of their outcomes before they occur. Sometimes she sings ahead of the beat, sometimes behind, but because she dislocates and relocates time and place, she creates "a sense of the moment, of the processes—continuity and discontinuity—of awareness" (G. Jones 168). This awareness that Miss Jane possesses both shapes the style of her narration and underscores a theological concept of self as embodied in relationship and existing in process. Because Miss Jane is concerned with the full humanity of everyone, Gaines facilitates through her a link between the teller and her audience, a link that is further reinforced by the presence of the editor, who "validates the folk or oral historian, the relationship between autobiography and history, and the autobiographical approach to history" (G. Jones 162).

In this respect, Miss Jane's narrative validates the historical significance of the slave narratives. As in slave narratives, whose very publication established the fact of freedom, for nearly every important incident in her life, Miss Jane divulges the outcome before it happens. For example, we know from the editor's introduction that Miss Jane has already died, yet this does not keep us from wanting to know how she lived her 108 years. To learn this we must go with Miss Jane all the way back to slavery, where we are introduced to a world corroborated by the original texts of the slave narrative tradition.

Jane's narrative describes a similar journey from slavery, but rather than concluding with an arrival at a de facto liberation ensured by the Emancipation Proclamation, it continues where slave narratives end, taking the characters to a recognition of what freedom actually entails. Also like the narratives, Jane's story begins in struggle, but unlike the narratives it ends in struggle, too. In this way, her narrative makes the same ideological connection between current racial problems and the past of slavery that liberation theologians agitating for present social change make. Her entire text demonstrates why liberation theology was constructed in our time as a critical discourse but also how it emerged from liberating impulses that were always present in the long history of African-American oppression, despite the distortions of religion that accompanied its development.

Gaines not only illustrates the objectification of black humanity that was present in the way Jane and other slaves were treated, but reminds us of the insidious role religion played in supporting the Southern system of oppression. Ticey, as Jane was called when she was a slave, quotes confident Confederates who insisted, "'We the nobles, not them. God put us here to live the way we want to live, that's in the Bible.' (I have asked people to find that in the Bible for me, but no one's found it yet.) 'And he put niggers here to see us live that way—that's in the Bible, too. John, chapter so and so, verse, right now I forget'" (MJP 4). While betraying the role of religion in oppressing enslaved Africans, these remarks also demonstrate how certain religious beliefs were not necessarily scriptural, as Jane observes, but devised to bolster a corrupt system and to disguise the genuine liberative spirit of scripture. Nonetheless, the effects are staggering, even for a clever young girl like Ticey.

When Yankees ride through her plantation and one corporal tries to speak to her, Ticey responds meekly and with downcast eyes, continually referring to this white man who has no actual claim on her as "Master." Although she is reluctant to tell him about her treatment under slavery, he eventually coaxes the admission he was seeking and announces to her that she should have a new name. This action on the part of the Union soldier to alter a label of slavery tempers the denial of personal identity that slavery tried to instill and shows Jane a new world of possibility, one in which the power of the slaveholder is not final. When he presents her with the name *Jane* she demurs, but eventually she announces to her mistress, "My name ain't no Ticey no more, it's Miss Jane Brown" (MJP 9), and accepts the beating that follows. By demanding to be called not only by a new name but also by the title *Miss,* Jane demands respect and recognition of her existence apart from that of slave, and in the words of Keith

Byerman, becomes an icon of freedom (*Fingering the Jagged* 82), symbolic of the ways in which an identity can emerge out of resistance.

Claiming a new name precedes the moment when she and her fellow slaves are read the Emancipation Proclamation, whereupon they begin singing and clapping. Their euphoria is quickly tempered by the reality that freedom is more than a concept, it is a lifestyle for which they are unprepared. Uncle Isom, the community's spiritual leader, who is about the same age as Jane when she tells her story and who "knowed alot about roots and herbs" (MJP 12), leads everyone in prayer and then begins to prepare the people to face their situation. His actions prefigure a role Jane will later play in her community, both as a leader and as a cautionary guide. Despite his warnings about the problems she will face if she leaves the plantation, Jane is determined to head North, to find the benefactor who gave her a name and to begin a new life in Ohio. Jane reasons along with other slaves that "niggers hearts been broke ever since niggers been in the world," and they "can't be pained no more than they already been pained" (MJP 14).

Thus Jane initiates a pattern that William Andrews sees recurring throughout the novel. As he explains, "One sure mark of heroism among the characters is a refusal to 'go back' either willingly or by force. All of the admirable characters in the novel subscribe to Jane's intuitive progressivism—'I knowed I had to keep going,' she says as a child. But the manner and goal of the 'going' determine whether true progress, individually and in terms of the larger mass, can be made to come about" ("We Ain't Going" 146).

First, however, Jane must cast off her naive assumption that freedom and its fulfillment can be identified spatially, rather than psychologically and spiritually. In order to do this, she must face a series of disillusionments, beginning when she and a company of fellow freed slaves head North with a few apples and potatoes and a lot of hope. Their leader this time is not the cautious Uncle Isom but Big Laura, who is described in much the same way Sojourner Truth described herself in her famous "Ain't I a Woman?" speech: "She could plow, chop wood, cut and load as much cane as any man on the place" while also raising an infant daughter and a son (MJP 16). To occupy themselves while they traveled, the others adopt Jane's example and begin choosing new names. Walking until all are exhausted, eventually they stop and, with pieces of flint and iron she carried with her, Big Laura builds a fire and they finally rest.

Big Laura is the first in a series of rebels in Jane's story who establishes a basic pattern the rest will follow: An act of resistance is led by a heroic figure who ultimately is killed by forces she opposes. Despite bold resistance, Big Laura and all the others except her son, Ned, and Jane are murdered when they are discovered by a band of patrollers, whom Jane describes as "poor white trash . . . soldiers from the Secesh Army . . . the ones who made up the Ku Klux Klans later on" (MJP 21). Although still a child herself, Jane adopts the responsibility to care for Ned and establishes the pattern she will follow throughout the novel. She will be the one who remains to preserve whatever gains have been made by others, including keeping alive the legend of heroes of biblical stature, such as Big Laura, and preparing a new generation of rebels to follow her example. This commitment is symbolized in Big Laura's flint stones, which Ned carries and refuses to relinquish; the stones represent the liberative flame Big Laura lit and Ned's own role as keeper of that flame. It is "on these rocks" that Ned will later build a "church" for his people (Matthew 16:18).

Preserving the past is not sufficient for liberation, however, as Jane observes when she comments, "We couldn't let what happened yesterday stop us today" (MJP 24). And so they travel on, thinking they are moving North, but actually heading deeper South. In a series of picaresque episodes, Jane comments on segments of Southern society she encounters along the way and each becomes symbolic, teaching her the difficulty of freedom: A black hunter who is seeking his father symbolizes the fragmentation of families in a context where Jane learns freedom "ain't North" (MJP 54), an eccentric old white man further reveals the elusiveness of the freedom Jane seeks when he demonstrates how it will take her a lifetime to get North, and a poor white farmer who had refused to fight for the Confederacy symbolizes an ongoing and deeply rooted class conflict in the South that Jane cannot escape even in her black world. As Jane's observations about the similarities between slavery and freedom become more precise, she finds herself reconciled to the fact that she won't get North and must make a life on yet another plantation.

"Reconstruction" begins with Jane reconciled to living in the South, even grateful for such opportunities as the chance for Ned to go to school. But the small opportunities exist in a wider context of oppression in which local politics inhibit even white efforts at human progress and "secret groups" such as the Ku Klux Klan emerge to inflict terror and humiliation on the black population. These and other forces lead many in the black community to realize that "it was slavery again, all right," and they consider leaving for the North. But Jane understands that the promises of a better life elsewhere are empty and "this time" she becomes "one of them who stayed behind," reasoning that "I would stay right here and do what I could for me and Ned" (MJP 69).

However, Ned eventually leaves. Quiet and serious as he was during his travels with Jane, when he barely said a word and held tightly to his mother's flint stones, Ned never describes for Jane what he is thinking. But when he begins to participate in efforts to monitor the status of blacks in the South and changes his name to Ned Douglass, after Frederick Douglass, his actions say what is on his mind. Already anticipating that Ned will leave so he can become a great leader like Douglass, Jane is not surprised when the plantation owner, Colonel Dye, roughs her up to try to get Ned to stop his activities, thereby setting in motion Ned's inevitable departure. Ned begs Jane to leave with him, but she refuses, insisting, "This is not my time . . . people don't keep moving, Ned" (MJP 75). Although Jane will not be moved by vain ideals or despair, as William Andrews points out, "It is important to recognize . . . that this decision, while appropriate for Jane, is not established as a rigid standard for Ned to follow as he approaches his own restless years" ("We Ain't Going" 147).

Indeed, Jane consoles Ned by reassuring him that he can't give up what he is going to do: "Things like this you got to make up your own mind" (MJP 76). Jane's agreement that Ned must leave shows that "she understands the essential psychological nature of his quest; she sees that he needs to break the ties of home, to become his own man, to leave the South rather than go back to a slave status or voluntarily stop black progress" (Andrews, "We Ain't Going" 147). Although their forced separation becomes yet another variation on the effects of slavery, it also indicates the promise of progress because, as Ned observes, when one is enslaved, one must keep moving toward liberation (MJP 75).

Jane's own movement progresses in a different way when she takes up with the widowed Joe Pittman and helps to raise his daughters as she had raised Ned. Unable to bear her own children because of beatings she endured as a slave, Jane continues to occupy a maternal role she will hold in the community throughout her life. In this section Jane also shares with her reader folk beliefs and rituals practiced in her community that help them to endure, even resist, oppression. Yet she introduces these customs in a context that demonstrates that because they are indexed culturally to slavery, they are not entirely effective in shaping life in freedom. For example, Jane considers joining Joe in observing the marriage ritual of jumping the broom until Joe refuses, insisting that they didn't need to do that because they were not slaves anymore.

Jane's ambivalence about the effectiveness of old ways is also present in her assessment of other sources of support, as when she provides examples of white people who both deny and assist African Americans in achieving social progress. Jane learns from letters from Ned in Kansas that some "white people who liked him" had assisted him. "They saw how much he cared for his race, and they thought he could help them much more" (MJP 79). Meanwhile, Joe's efforts to advance—to leave the plantation and take a position breaking horses—are frustrated by Colonel Dye, who cheats him out of a financial agreement that would have settled their score.

Eventually Joe and Jane free themselves of their "obligation" to Dye and for 10 years live happily as a family, with Joe performing work that satisfies his body and soul. In another example of folk customs' interference with progress, Jane lets her recurrent nightmares of Joe's death so take over her consciousness that she seeks out the advice of a hoodoo woman when the black stallion of her nightmares appears on the ranch. Despite her insistence that she doesn't believe in superstition, Jane tries to sort out her feelings with the help of Madame Gautier, a rival of the famed Marie Laveau. Jane evocatively describes the mood and power generated by the hoodoo woman, revealing why such practices might gain the support of people cut off from other forms of empowerment.

But Madame Gautier does not give Jane a simple solution. Instead, she insists that she cannot stop the inevitable. Just as she could not and would not prevent Ned from leaving, she must let Joe ride to be a man, even if it kills him, because that is the way he would want to die: like a man. In her desperation Jane begs for some potion to prevent Joe from taking on the black stallion, but through a series of inadvertent actions she leads him to a deadly confrontation with the horse. Joe's encounter with the stallion is clearly symbolic of a pattern Gaines establishes throughout the novel, as the stallion becomes an incarnation of hostile forces that keep African Americans from social progress. But by making the stallion black, Gaines does not succumb to a simplistic allegory of equating white with bad or black with good. "Instead Gaines recognizes that the obstacles confronting the black man are not reducible to the whole white race" (Wertheim 225).

Jane keeps Joe's memory alive by retaining his name, but moves back to Louisiana just in time for "Professor Douglass" to return with his family. Ned's fate is as predestined as Joe's, and Jane announces his return and his death at the same time. Returning with a message of immovable determination and preaching the social gospel of his namesake, Ned explains his reasons for returning—and his own awareness of the risk he is taking— in much the same way the editor/teacher justifies his interview with Miss Jane. Both return to teach, establishing their method as an important effort toward achieving social justice.

Ned's efforts to introduce the community, through the education of their children, to the ideas of Booker T. Washington and Frederick Douglass, is quickly met with resistance by the white community. Even the local black church refuses to help him. The agent of Ned's demise is Albert Cluveau, a Cajun with whom Jane has spent many hours fishing and chatting. Jane has heard Cluveau brag about how many men he has killed and isn't surprised when he warns her that he has been hired to kill Ned. Jane tries to challenge Cluveau, person to person, in much the same way the entire book challenges the reader, but her efforts are in vain. When he says he will kill Ned, Jane describes feeling like she "was in hell and he was the devil" (MJP 106), and the reader is then confronted with choosing sides, identifying either with Jane, in her oppressive hell, or with Albert, the devil.

Ned is aware of the threat on his life, but he vows to stay and eventually delivers "The Sermon at the River," an act of social justice that hastens his death because it articulates basic themes of a liberating theology advanced by the novel. The crowd Ned addresses is like the audience Gaines hopes to reach in his writing, mostly children. In complicity with the whites who want Ned to "go back," the adults stay home, thereby repeating, as William Andrews points out, "a familiar language of resistance to progress which all defenders of stasis in the novel repeat" ("We Ain't Going" 109). As Ned's own life has repudiated the invalid equation associating freedom with a place outside the South, in his sermon he redefines progress toward freedom in intellectual and spiritual terms. Speaking with a conviction Jane vividly recalls, Ned reminds the people that "This earth is yours and don't let that man out there take it from you. . . . It's yours because your people's bones lays in it; it's yours because their sweat and blood done drenched this earth. The white man will use every trick in the trade to take it from you. He'll turn you against each other. But remember this . . . your people's bones and their dust make this place yours more than anything else" (MJP 107). Without references to God or any traditional religious concepts, Ned succeeds in establishing the sacredness of the people's past actions that consecrate their existence, pointing a new direction for a liberating theology. He then goes on to explain what the present requires.

His subtle analysis does not simply blame whites. "You got some black men, that'll tell you the white man is the worst thing on earth . . . but let me tell you this, if it wasn't for some white men, none of us would be alive here today." He admits that a white man probably will kill him, but insists he "won't blame all white men. I'll blame ignorance. Because it was ignorance that put us here in the first place. Ignorance on the part of the black man and the white man." In his sermon Ned leaves open the same imaginative space ex-slave narrators did, revealing where whites can enter into the cause of liberation. But he also insists, as ex-slave narrators did, that blacks take responsibility for their own liberation, a point he emphasizes by giving an excruciating account of the history of slave trade, pointing to the complicity of both Africans and white slave traders, insisting that "the white man never would have brought us here if we was together" (MJP 109).

How they get together and stay together is suggested by Ned in the adoption of a corporate identity, not as blacks but as Americans. Just as Jane and other ex-slaves began the process of creating new identities by changing their names, Ned insists to the children that they need to adopt a new identity, but one more expansive than an individual identity. He exclaims, "I'm as much American as any man; I'm more American than most." He includes in his list of what is American "red, white, black. . . . America is for all of us and all of America is for all of us." But to get to this point, he understands that they first must "be men. Look inside yourself. Say, What am I? What else beside this black skin that the white man call nigger?" He refuses to accept oppression as a justification to abandon hope, insisting that "A Black American cares, and will always struggle. Every day that he get up he hopes that this day will be better. A nigger knows it won't" (MJP 110).

In urging resistance to all efforts to oppress body, mind, and soul, Ned's words achieve the effect about which he preached. In a proud demonstration of a mind that fights back, one child challenges him about his opinions on "Mr. Washington" and his contributions to black progress. Clearly pleased, Ned pushes his students to imagine a future even beyond what Washington envisioned. Although he admits that whites will continue to kill resisters, as they did his own mother, he challenges them in terms he eventually fulfills himself: "But if you must die, let me ask you this: wouldn't you rather die saying I'm a man than to die saying I'm a contented slave?" (MJP 111).

When Ned does die, it is at the hands of Albert Cluveau, acting on behalf of the entire white community. Another dream warns Jane that this will happen, but this time she doesn't capitulate to hoodoo but chooses a different form of empowerment. She motivates the rest of the community to ensure that Ned's school is kept open and that the land where he is buried is preserved as a memorial, "for the children of this parish and this State. Black and white, we don't care. We want them to know a black man died many many years ago for them. He died at the end of the other century and the beginning of this century. He shed his precious blood for them" (MJP 113). Poised at the liminal time between centuries, the blood Ned shed stands in contrast to the Secesh blood shed that Miss Jane's former mistress so dearly lamented.

Having inherited the strength and spiritual stature of his mother, Ned returned to his people as prophet. Because Jane builds no suspense about Ned's fate, she shifts the reader's attention to his sermon and the reaction of the people to his life and death. Like Jesus' Sermon on the Mount, Ned's sermon outlines "a new testament, a new vision for his listeners" (Wertheim 226). It encompasses a breadth of vision that transcends racial antagonism, deemphasizing the differences between blacks and whites and affirming the need to stand together as Americans. The biblical proportions of Ned's sermon and its importance as a textimony for a liberating theology are further reinforced by the way Gaines indexes Ned's identity with Christ. Ned's death becomes laden with symbolic importance, as the trail of his blood never washes from the road and people preserve the lumber similarly stained. The people's reaction to Ned's murder differs from their response to previous tragedies because they show that "they have learned the necessity of conserving a usable past on which to build a viable future. To memorialize Ned's example is to begin the fundamentally progressive process of creating a black American heroic tradition. Instead of rejecting their past as something shameful from which to flee, the black folk preserve their martyred ideals and ground the roots of their growing folk consciousness in them, the better to hold fast to hope" (Andrews, "We Ain't Going" 147).

They do this despite the fact that the white authorities resist any efforts to bring justice to the murderer they themselves employed for the task. But a different kind of justice finally does have its day when Cluveau, trapped between his humanity and his racism, is driven mad by his own internal demons and eventually dies a mysterious death. Cluveau believed that Jane had cast a hoodoo spell on him when she predicted that the "Chariot of Hell" would take him away. But Jane simply lets Cluveau's conscience do its work. By structuring the narrative this way, Gaines demonstrates the effectiveness of the kind of power exercised by people working within the slave narrative tradition, both Jane's power and his own. Jane may not be able to change the circumstances, but she has shown her oppressors that their very act of destroying resistance inspires new forms of resistance within the oppressed community. Furthermore, it is significant that at this stage of her development Jane undertakes a reassessment of her spiritual life and in so doing opens herself up to even greater forms of empowerment.

Book Three, "The Plantation," introduces how Jane's understanding of progress becomes more spiritual and personal after Ned's death. Whereas her journey to Ohio was "completely mediated by the material world, Jane's spiritual journey covers her whole life" (Beavers 152). When she moves to the Samson plantation and has a conversion experience, she recounts it in travel imagery borrowed from the Bible and recalls figures from her past. As she relates, she had been fighting with her conscience ever since Ned was killed. Although raised around church people, she never thought too much about joining until a decade or more after Ned's death when she "knowed I had nothing else in the world but the Lord" (MJP 134). Her conversion comes only after many others are swept away by sudden acts of "getting it," and after Jane expresses doubts about whether she is even "fit for Glory" (MJP 136). Then, at last, while she is walking to the fields to work, "a big load just fell off my shoulders" (MJP 136). That night Jane testifies to the community, describing what she calls her "travels." She begins her spiritual journey with a burden she can cast off only by crossing a river between her and her savior. Satan, who takes variously the form of Ned and Joe, tempts her, but she resists these compelling images and turns her burden over to Jesus: "I put my feet on solid ground and the Savior was there. He smiled at me and took the load off my shoulder. I wanted to bow to His feet, but He told me rise I had been born again. I rose and I felt light and clean and good" (MJP 138).

Throughout her account of "coming through," Jane describes figures associated with her own past and personal history, including Albert Cluveau sitting on the horse that killed Joe, and ends her narration evoking the past of her people when she describes how the church sang a spiritual about getting over at last. But her travel account also points to the future. In describing her encounter with Jesus, she depicts him as a savior who instructs her not to assume a posture of humility but to stand tall. Jesus corroborates the same advice Ned gave the people, thereby revealing how much of Jane's religious testimony reflects her absorption of Ned's liberating theology. In her conversion account she translates Ned's ideals into traditional and fundamental spiritual values on which both her individual development and the community's survival depend. She accepts the necessity of giving the church figurative reconstruction of her life, but she also "celebrates those psychological and spiritual qualities which are prerequisites to progress, to black people's 'coming through' their social as well as religious trials" (Andrews, "We Ain't Going" 148).

Jane has arrived at the point at which she does not seek escape from her burden but is determined to carry it, independently, throughout her life, demonstrating a "self-reliance and acceptance of life as a spiritual struggle from which there can be no escape, no vicarious victory" (Andrews, "We Ain't Going" 148), a lesson others in the community, both black and white, have yet to learn. The sad saga of Tee Bob and Mary Agnes represents how people still succumb to the attractions of escape while providing a sober reminder of external racism that internal conversion alone cannot eliminate. One of two sons of plantation owner Robert Samson, Tee Bob is favored despite his fragile health because he is the "white son," even though his brother, Timmy—the product of Samson's indiscretion—is much more like his father in personality and form. Tee Bob becomes attached to Jane and turns to her for counsel, especially when he cannot understand why Timmy is sent off the plantation for not "keeping his place."

His own father cannot provide him a satisfactory account of why the brothers should be separated, believing he "didn't have to tell Tee Bob about these things" (MJP 147) because "they was part of life, like the sun and the rain was part of life, and Tee Bob would learn them for himself when he got older." But as Jane further observes, "Tee Bob never did. He killed himself before he learned how he was supposed to live in this world" (MJP 147). Once again, Jane divulges the sad ending of the story she will soon relate about Tee Bob, accepting the outcome of this social/family drama as a fact of nature, like "the sun and the rain." But she coyly undermines the inevitability of Tee Bob's fate when, before continuing his story, she interjects a story that describes actual natural forces that humanity cannot control, shifting the locus of power both away from irresponsible humanity and toward it at the same time.

"Of Men and Rivers" describes a period of high waters and the damage it caused. Jane directly condemns the destruction as an example of when "Man had just gone a little too far" (MJP 150). However, Jane's story about the high waters ends in hope because she believes "that same water that Indians used to believe in will run free again. You just wait and see" (MJP 150). In contrast to this example of systemic pride that was insufficient to control nature, Jane introduces in her narrative a white man who accommodates and even initiates change: Huey Long. Jane credits the governor of Louisiana with the following: "Nothing better could 'a' happened to the poor black man or the poor white man no matter what they say" because although he may have said "nigger" when referring to African Americans, he told them to "read a book," not to "pick cotton" (MJP 151). Jane's broadening understanding of liberation and the forces that prevent it are revealed further by her understanding that the economic oppression Long fought was as destructive as the racial oppression she had encountered all her life. It was rich people, Jane believed, who killed Long for helping the poor—both black and white—and so she mourns his death and describes it in religious language, equating through metaphor the actions of Huey Long and Ned Douglass: "Look like every man that pick up the cross for the poor must end that way" (MJP 153).

After these digressions, Jane returns to the recurrent theme of racial oppression when she introduces Mary Agnes Le Fabre, a Creole teacher on the Samson plantation. Mary Agnes came from New Orleans, trying to escape a Creole culture as prejudiced and confining as what Jane's community experiences. Jane observes Mary Agnes's shame but recognizes that her attempts to escape it are doomed. She was "trying to make up for the past—and that you cannot do" (MJP 58). Tee Bob falls in love with Mary Agnes. In the process he becomes, like Mary Agnes, a victim of the same pathology of trying to escape a past that is still deeply entrenched in the present. As Tee Bob's feelings for Mary Agnes grow from initial enchantment to near obsession, Mary Agnes confesses to Jane that she is aware of his feelings, but claims she is not afraid of Tee Bob and the consequences of his attachment to her because she believes he is decent. But Jane challenges her to recognize that individual decency is insufficient: "Is this world decent, Mary Agnes?" (MJP 169). Mary Agnes's stubborn insistence that Tee Bob is "more human than white" is again countered by Jane, who knows the world won't let him stay like that.

Tee Bob's family grows increasingly suspicious of his infatuation with Mary Agnes, and in a biblical turn of phrase his father suggests the problem's origin is ontologically elemental. When his mother exclaims that she doesn't want any more "Timmy Hendersons," Robert Samson replies, "Whoa Eve, don't touch that apple." As has happened so many times in Jane's story to date, his mother dismisses what Jane calls the facts of nature, proclaiming, "Eve or no Eve, he's my only child" (MJP 170). Jane believed Tee Bob's love for Mary Agnes was genuine because "he didn't look at her the way you think a white man look at a nigger woman" (MJP 171). But she also saw in his face that he was "ready to go against his family, this whole world, for Mary Agnes" (MJP 171). The denial by his family and even his best friend, who warns him that "Africa is in her veins" (MJP 173), lead Tee Bob to finally confront Mary Agnes with his feelings.

Although she was not present, Jane relates what transpires between Mary Agnes and Tee Bob as if she were there, for the first time in her narrative making up a story she did not witness herself. Gaines has her do this, in part, to contextualize a later recitation of events offered by the Samson family friend, Jules Raynard, who picks up the story where Jane leaves off. Although no one was privy to what went on, the combined tales of Jane

and Jules, black woman and white man, reveal the dynamics of race relations in the South and suggest the possibility that the races are moving
toward telling the same story.

Jane tells the reader that Tee Bob asked Mary Agnes to marry him and
run away. She describes his desire in terms relevant to her own experience
of recreating an identity by recalling the power of naming. Just as Ticey
became Jane, who later clung to the surname Pittman out of honor, the
same way Ned adopted Douglass as a symbolic surname, Jane describes
Tee Bob's efforts as emerging from the same motive, suggesting that he
wants to give his name to Mary Agnes. But she resists because she knows
"you can't give something you don't own yourself," and he doesn't even
own his own name. The Samsons gave it, and they can take it away (MJP
175).

The symbolic power of naming is further reinforced when one considers the names Gaines selected for these two characters. Both have strong
biblical resonance. Mary Agnes's names recalls both the Virgin and the
prostitute (familiar tropes for circumscribing black female identity) and,
in Agnes, the sacrificial lamb of God. Tee Bob's childish nickname stands
in stark contrast to his surname, Samson, which conjures images of the
biblical Samson. The biblical Samson was distinguished by the fact that
although he served as God's agent, he was primarily an individualistic hero
who stood alone, not consciously fighting for the liberation of his particular
tribe or of Israel and without any sense of obligation to God. Nevertheless, God's spirit worked through Samson, just as ultimately a liberative
spirit worked through the naive but passionate Tee Bob.

Despite her attempts to calm and reason with him, Mary Agnes is un-
successful in her effort to convince Tee Bob that they can have nothing
together. At this point the story breaks off—Jane no longer presuming to
know what transpired between Mary Agnes and Tee Bob—and continues
with reports of Tee Bob running from Mary Agnes's cabin. Eventually we
learn along with Jane that Mary Agnes has survived her confrontation with
Tee Bob, but that Tee Bob has killed himself in remorse, leaving behind a
letter whose contents are never fully revealed except by Jules Raynard, who
picks up the story where Jane left off. Whatever was in the letter is
insufficient to prevent the Samson family from blaming Mary Agnes and
wanting to seek revenge until Raynard intercedes with a threat, reminding them that, after a fashion, they all killed Tee Bob.

Rather than laying personal blame on anyone, Raynard instructs them
on the systemic hate that led to the tragic outcome. Tee Bob, Raynard
observes, could not live by "the rules we been living by ever since we been

here" (MJP 190). When Jane thanks Raynard for his intercession on be-half of Mary Agnes, like others living the story he reverts to biblical pre-cedent, claiming that the rules Tee Bob was given to follow "just ain't old enough, Jane" (MJP 193). Raynard undermines the presumed religiosity of the Samsons and demonstrates that the rules of segregated society are not derived from the past of a liberative scripture but are new rules cre-ated by humanity to oppress. All this Raynard claims is the "gospel truth" (MJP 195). It is gospel because it ultimately points to the good news: the possibility of a new covenant between black and white. As Craig Werner observes, Raynard's comment is the "most profound statement of the need for a common black–white vocabulary in American literature" (39) and makes clear that "in this version of history no one need be, or can be, ig-nored as 'other'" (61).

The consequences of this story are shared and understood not by one population alone, but by both black and white, represented in Jane and Jules. In a world that still held that "the white man was God," Tee Bob could see only death as a solution. And in a library that "wouldn't let him forget" because its shelves were full of books on slavery, Tee Bob killed himself "for our sins" (MJP 196), once again indexing those who resist the status quo with the actions of Christ.

The implication here is that had the original gospel really been practiced or had Miss Jane's textimony and others like hers been the books on the shelves, perhaps Tee Bob would not have to escape history or himself. Both Mary Agnes and Tee Bob are young idealists who try to avoid "going back," but they are eventually reclaimed by the past, represented by the books in the library. Their story evokes the spirit of skepticism about progress conveyed throughout the novel, a skepticism that is recapitulated by the actions of Jimmy in the narrative's final episode. But what is differ-ent in this final encounter related by Jane is that this time the whole com-munity responds, not just Miss Jane or a well-intentioned white man like Jules Raynard. In the book's concluding passages, all the efforts undertaken by determined people such as Big Laura, Joe, Ned, Huey Long, Tee Bob, and Mary Agnes become incorporated into the lives of African Americans, who finally act as one on behalf of their own (and others') liberation.

Book Four, "The Quarters," is unlike the previous books because it is not a string of stories that pop in and out of Miss Jane's consciousness, but one extended recitation of a decisive event in the lives of all the people in the Quarters. Jane has moved out of the "big house" and back to the Quarters, thereby making this story, more than any of the others, truly from, of, and for the Quarters—not just a story told by Jane about her individual experiences and impressions, but one that was created by all the people who populate it. However, it is not a story told and understood by both black and white, as the reader might expect following the cooperative narration of Jane and Jules. This story belongs to the black people who finally claim their voices as true and don't need any corroboration. This is a slave narrative that confidently asserts its own authority without a white editor's assistance or approval. Also charged with biblical allusions, this story is not just rooted in scripture, but becomes the new scripture or sacred text that firmly establishes rules for not just enduring, but living and creating: The people fully imagine their grace.

Biblical history is indexed with living reality in the person of Jimmy, a child born in the Quarters and designated by the community as "the One." Jimmy is understood by the community as possessing a conflation or composite of traits characteristic of Moses and Jesus. Jimmy becomes the savior about whom they sang in spirituals. In these first expressions of African-American religion, Moses and Jesus were viewed as together possessing the necessary traits to lead people to liberation. In the Old Testament story of the enslavement of Hebrews by the Egyptians, enslaved people found a story like their own. In the figure of Jesus Christ, they found someone who had suffered as they had suffered, someone who understood and who offered them rest from their suffering. Combined, the two figures represent the complete aspect of the African-American spiritual quest: collective deliverance as a people and redemption from their terrible personal sufferings. Through imaginative power—and the "Lord," who "has always obliged in some way or another" (MJP 199)—Moses and Jesus became one, and in the minds and hearts of the people, Jimmy is the One. As Jane relates, "People's always looking for somebody to come lead them. Go to the Old Testament; go to the New. They did it in slavery; after the war they did it; they did it in the hard times people want to call Reconstruction; they did it in the Depression . . . they have always done it" (MJP 199).

Parentless, Jimmy is raised by the entire community of the Quarters, who felt that he was special, the one who was needed to "carry part of our cross" (MJP 199). Jimmy's reputation extends throughout the parish, but he becomes the special favorite of the people on the Samson plantation, whom he serves by reading papers and writing letters. Jane, in particular, appreciates that Jimmy can read her the sports pages (and edit them when they contain news he thinks might upset her) and keep her abreast of her heroes, Joe Louis and Jackie Robinson, whom she believes were sent by God, just as Jimmy was, to "lift the colored people's heart" (MJP 203). What Jane appreciates about these athletes is not just their talent, but the moral and spiritual insights their actions demonstrate. For example, Jane interprets Joe Louis's loss to the racist symbol Schmelling by saying, "That was just to teach us a lesson. To show us Joe was just a man, not a super-man. And to show us we could take just a little bit more hardship than we thought we could take at first" (MJP 203). And when Louis does beat Smelling, Jane sees the intervention of God, responding to people's prayers. Jane's ability to locate liberating power and spiritual guidance in these secular figures—to find character embodied in new characteristics—pre-pares her to appreciate the role Jimmy Aaron will come to play in her community.

Having anointed him at birth as the unofficial religious leader and com-munity ideal and reared him in the church to serve this role, the people try to repress all of Jimmy's natural development. They do not allow him to play with others, experiment sexually, or doubt his religious calling. Essentially, they try to make him what they believe him to be. But through stories related by Jane, Jimmy learns to counter these attempts to control him. Jane tells him the history of his people, personal and historical sto-ries about slavery, Big Laura, Ned, and the high waters that are critical for Jimmy's development because the character of the Quarters has changed considerably.

Samson has divided the plantation into shares, Cajuns have moved in, and many black people have left. Those who remain adopt for themselves the same attitude Samson espouses for them, waiting to leave or die. Jimmy, like Ned before him, inevitably leaves because of what he describes as "something like a tiger in my chest, just gnawing and gnawing and want come out. I want rip my chest open and let it free. I pray to God to take it out, but look like the Lord don't hear me. This things gnaw and gnaw at me and I want to scream. . . . Something in me want come out, Miss Jane, but I don't know how to get it out. Nobody helps me, not even the Lord" (MJP 215).

While Jimmy is away the people begin to feel the changes wrought by the emerging civil rights movement, or the "trouble," as it is described by some of the people who fear its implications. In recounting the lore of the movement, Jane recites a familiar litany of abuse and resistance and even confesses to her own "mean" thoughts about whites. What consoles her and turns her to forgiveness may have emerged from Ned's ideas, but she casts it nonetheless in conventional religious terms: "No matter what hap-pens, He's not asleep. He sees what we does; it's all written down" (MJP 219). The effect of civil rights is soon felt in the Quarters when Samson makes good on his threat to evict anyone caught demonstrating, reinforced by the warning, "Anybody 'round here think he needs more freedom than he already got is free to pack up and leave now" (MJP 220). Yoko and her family are evicted because of the civil rights activity of her son, but rather than meekly slipping away, they take the opportunity to stage their own act of resistance, posting a sign on their departing wagon proclaiming what Samson had done. As the people watch the sad procession, Jane notices that Yoko's chifforobe glass flashes all over the place, blinding witnesses with this cruel reality. Here the reader is indicted along with the community because "it flashed on you, too, if you didn't get out of the way" (MJP 221–22).

Rather than reflect on their own complicity, however, the people do "get out of the way" and are too shaken to receive what Jimmy brings them on "Termination Sunday." When he returns to assume his mantle as the One, it is not in a way the people appreciate. Now he is more political than religious, not a preacher as they had imagined, but a social activist. He comes to testify before the people, but not as he did at age 13, when he adopted their religion. Rather than offering a religious testimony, Jimmy implores the community to become involved in the civil rights struggle he has joined. Jimmy tries to link the emerging black political movement with the enduring psychological and spiritual resources of the community. Thus he chooses the day set aside for celebrating determination in one's spiritual quest—"when you tell the church you still carrying the cross and you want meet them 'cross the River Jordan when you die" (MJP 223)—to redefine the context of black humanity's cross-bearing. Using the rhetoric of a second coming, "casting his socio-political mission in the accouterments of the folk spiritual and heroic traditions" (Andrews, "We Ain't Going" 149), Jimmy seeks to raise and expand the consciousness of his people and prepare them for their final triumph.

Although he has left the church, Jimmy, the last to testify, begins by reminding the people of what happened to Yoko, linking this local humiliation with the efforts of the civil rights movement. In asking for the people's help, he tries to assure the people that he respects their religious identity and the strength it possesses. Jimmy implores, "Even now I don't feel worthy standing here before y'all . . . because I'm so weak. And I'm here because you are strong. I need you because my body is not strong enough to stand out there by myself." The people may not have guns or money, but "we have just the strength of our people, our Christian people. That's why I'm here. I left the church, but that don't mean I left my people. I care much for you now as I ever did—and every last one of you in here know me" (MJP 225).

But the people don't really know Jimmy, and his efforts are met with resistance, born of fear about the nature of progress he envisions. Although he appreciates Jimmy's youthful enthusiasm, Elder Banks reminds Jimmy that his congregation is old, and they just want to die in peace. "I can't tell my church to go with you. If they want to go, that's up to them; but I won't tell them go and they have no place to come back to. . . . What happened in Birmingham, what happened in Atlanta, can't happen here" (MJP 226). Echoing a sentiment first held and then dispelled by Jane, Elder Banks cites freedom and opportunity as residing in a geographic place. What Jane has learned, which she later transmits to Jimmy, is that the place where freedom and opportunity reside is not to be found on a map but rather in the people's minds and hearts; it must be actualized there before it can be effected in their immediate social situation. To reach that place inside them, Jimmy first needs to reach the people where they live. As Jane tells us, "I told him I could understand what he was trying to do because my boy had tried to do the same thing long before he was born" (MJP 228).

But Jane also warns Jimmy that people "ain't ready yet . . . something got to get in the air first. Something got to start floating out there and they got to feel it. It got to seep all through their flesh, and all through their bones." Now nothing is there but "white hate and nigger fear," and fear, she insists, is the only way the people know to keep going, until they realize that fear is worse than death (MJP 228). Although Jimmy has experienced his own kind of oppression, only a generation away from slavery he does not appreciate the way the experience has scarred people; by his own admission (and using a familiar trope in the slave narrative tradition), he is "veiled" about the ongoing implications of slavery. Jane's effort to explain slavery's insidious legacy to Jimmy's generation is symbolic of what Gaines accomplishes when he exposes her textimony to a wider audience.

What Jane understands that neither the community nor Jimmy fully understands is the role Jimmy must play as the One. He must learn to reach the people at the site of their deepest pain, a pain he only intensifies when he tries to make them see themselves "as good as another" because they have been told for years that they are not. And even though they believed initially that God had answered their prayers with Jimmy, they do not yet appreciate how, in his secular guise, he can be the agent of their redemption. "They want you to cure the ache, but they want you to do it and don't give them pain" (MJP 236). Jane has come further than the rest of the community, and after a quiet night of reflection she decides to join Jimmy in his protest in Bayonne, even though she knows Samson may kick her off the plantation. Although she assumes that she will go alone, as she prepares the next morning to take the bus to the demonstration, gradually many people from the Quarters emerge to join her. When one woman announces that she will sing songs to turn the counterdemonstration protesters back, Jane describes both the continuity and the progress charted by the slave narrative tradition when she announces, "I got a feeling them things in Bayonne go'n want more than just spirituals today" (MJP 242). Their departure is arrested when Robert Samson arrives to reassert his threat of eviction and to convey the news that Jimmy is dead. But Jane simply replies, "Just a little piece of him is dead. The rest of him is waiting for us in Bayonne" (MJP 245), and stares at Robert as she walks past him. The slow and winding tale of Jane ends abruptly and the reader is left to assume from the fact that the narrative was recorded at all that the demonstration was a success and none of the people were evicted. How this could have happened, given what we know about Samson, remains a mystery for the reader, but essentially it is not a speculative question. Rather, it is a direct interrogation to consider whether the reader, like Samson, might finally have heard a liberating message in the people's actions and might finally do something liberating in response. Just as actions say things, words do things. That the editor does not resolve this mystery suggests that he, along with the reader, has come to appreciate the ultimate value of Jane's textimony: that "not only political action but narrative itself must take the form of resistance" (Byerman, *Fingering the Jagged* 94).

When Jane, in faith, chooses to join Jimmy in an act of social justice, she negates the forces that have killed Laura, Ned, and Jimmy and links their rebellion to the slave narrative tradition. Her actions say that she is open to new experience while her narrative acts as a testament to triumph. Jane's actions and her story memorialize the liberative spirit of Jimmy and all who preceded him, who are "reborn in their spiritual consciousness in 'the place where they live'" (Andrews, "We Ain't Going" 149). Herman Beavers observes how the novel reveals "the sacred and secular in a state of conceptual overlap" (156), particularly in the figure of Miss Jane, who represents "an awareness of the way spirituality affects the secular world" and likewise is "imbued with the ability to see the latter's effect on the spiritual life of the community" (157).

Even though heroic figures stand out as liberating forces, Miss Jane's life and her text demonstrate that what finally happened in Bayonne, as in Montgomery, was something the people had been preparing for all their lives. What Jimmy finally hears and sees to make him the One is precisely what the reader hears and sees in reading the novel, which itself stimulates the reader to become one of Jimmy's followers. Jane's act of telling her story becomes elevated to ritual, a process of bearing formal witness to the call-and-response ethic through the act of textimony. Jane calls white Americans to imaginative participation in the past and present lives of Africans Americans, whose story, like Jane's narrative, has not ended neatly. Jane trusts the reader to collaborate with her and to write the rest of her story—the story of her people—by participating in the slave narrative tradition through continued engagement with the cause of liberation.

℘   ℘   ℘

> No one who is flesh and bones wants to be thought of as a saint . . . unless the definition of a saint is a sinner who keeps on trying.
> —Nelson Mandela

At the time *The Autobiography of Miss Jane Pittman* was written, prevailing African-American ideologies privileged black activism over an ethic of endurance and did not create a welcome place for a character like Miss Jane. In creating Miss Jane, Gaines was well aware that he was going against the trends of his time and that most people thought he should be writing something more contemporary. "But I stuck to my ground—to writing my particular book. I felt I had already set the goals for my writing, and I intended to go on. I followed the work of the sixties, read a lot of it—criticized a lot of it. But I established my direction before they started." Making specific and allusive reference to Richard Wright, Gaines insists that the "blueprint for Black literature is not *Native Son*," stressing instead the need to go back further to the same past from which both he and Wright emerged, back to the slave narrative tradition (Doyle, "A MELUS Interview" 60). But unlike Wright, Gaines wanted to tell a story from that specific point of original location without the ideological distortions of present-day realities and thus to link contemporary literary efforts at liberation with the tradition of rebellion from which they emerged.

By establishing this link, Gaines hoped to elicit from his reading community a recognition that freedom is not an abstraction or a pure quality; it is a concrete part of the human experience that must be understood in tension with necessity, however that necessity has been manifest. By showing history as something happening in and through Jane Pittman and her community—as they struggle in their daily lives and continue to dream of freedom—he reorients his readers away from historical abstractions and toward character. Like the proud individualists about whom he writes, Gaines had his own reasons for writing about people like Miss Jane that had to do with his own existential search for meaning. But he also had a broader motive: "I'm trying to write about a people I feel are worth writing about, to make the world aware of them, make them aware of themselves. They've always thought that literature is written about someone else, and it's hard to convince them that they are worthy of literature" (Doyle, "A MELUS Interview" 61).

They are worthy of literature because they respond creatively to the kinds of social realities the novel explores, the ongoing oppression born of slavery. As demonstrated in the example of Tee Bob and Mary Agnes, this oppression structures even the most intimate relationships, revealing that there are few possibilities for stepping outside the historically determined reality. Although Gaines reveals that blacks suffer most from these conditions, he also shows how whites are imprisoned within this order and, like Tee Bob's parents, must suffer loss because of an unjust system their ancestors created and they maintain. Yet in bringing the consequences of the social order to bear on the lives of his characters in intimate ways, Gaines also points to ways in which we might begin to redress and restructure the social order, not by challenging the system but by changing ourselves.

One of the most compelling and effective means of self-transformation for the African-American characters is found in religion, the fundamental source of value for this community. Most of the characters, at least initially, believe that what happens is the will of God, or as Jane remarks, "If it's not the Lord keeping me going, what is?" (MJP 211). As in many other Southern black communities, the local church is the center of their world, and the rest of life is read in terms of its symbols. When Jane has her religious conversion, she appropriately describes her encounter in a sanctified form of religious testimony, and the church accepts this story as evidence of her "comin' through" because it validates their view of life. But her conversion narrative also reveals that her spiritual transformation has not been effected by religion alone. Religion may be the form on which she shapes her new perspective, but her conversion is also shaped by Ned's beliefs in social change, just as her spiritual posture is further refined by Jimmy's beliefs and actions. When she is "saved," her present life is invested with a new moral value and her position "in the middle" comes to carry a heightened authority.

In Jane's narrative, she is both the primary agent who speaks for the religious community from which leaders such as Ned and Jimmy emerge and the brave voice that takes the secular message of its leaders back to the community and translates it into religious terms. Situated in the middle of every conflict—between black and white, progressive and conservative, religious and secular, traditional and modern—Jane can be a mother to Ned but also the friend of Albert Cluveau, she can raise Tee Bob while she shares her house with Mary Agnes, and she can defend Jimmy before a resistant congregation but also explains to him why the people are unwilling to participate in his plan. As Keith Byerman observes, Jane's "placement at the center of competing forces makes each of these a concrete, human, historicized conflict, dramatizing the fact that tensions of race, politics, religion, and economics are not abstractions but everyday realities handled by ordinary people" ("'A Slow to Anger'" 116). Moreover, Jane's involvement on all sides allows the author to make each side comprehensible to all readers; however they enter the story, they are bound to see themselves represented.

Gaines's own self-described religious posture explains a great deal about why he positioned his protagonist as occupying a middle ground. In a 1973 interview with the *New Orleans Review,* the author describes his religious background and the idiosyncratic faith he developed out of that experience. Indoctrinated into the Baptist religion when he was quite young, at the same time Gaines was attending a Catholic school. By the time he started writing, these experiences and others led him to assert that "any religion or none at all were equal to just about the same thing. Not any of them are gonna really cure things, or solve all our problems. . . . I don't think religions solve anything. It's good to believe, because I think people must believe in religion. For you to survive you must have something greater than what you are, whether it's religion or communism, or capitalism or something else, but it must be something above what you are. But as of right now, I don't think orthodox religion has solved anybody's problems. Even in *The Autobiography of Miss Jane Pittman,* you know, Miss Jane would prefer listening to the Dodgers play the Giants on Sunday. She's religious, but she can catch up with that next Sunday" ("On the Verge" 343).

The kind of religion Miss Jane espouses, which is endorsed by Gaines, is a liberating theology that engages her in life rather than removing her from it. Jane finds religion her own way and does not manufacture an easy conversion; once converted, she does not simply conform to what her friends believe. Her religious "travels" reveal her as engaged in a process of accommodating her spirituality to encompass the dominant religious institution in her community, but her challenges to the church elders, her desire to listen to baseball on Sunday morning, and her conversations with trees also demonstrate that she can adjust her religious posture to fit her personal needs. In her account of her "travels," Jane understands the need to justify her full entry into the church, that central institution of the black community. But she also acknowledges a responsibility that goes beyond giving her life over to God in perfunctory ways. By recalling the deceptive images of Joe and Ned, she comes to appreciate the role she has played in shaping the major events in her life, including the times she has evaded responsibility. By entering the world of the church she demonstrates humanity's need for fixed values, but her subsequent posture as church mother who would prefer to listen to a baseball game rather than a sermon also displays her ambivalence about religious structures.

Jane peppers her narrative with comments that demonstrate that her spirituality does not eliminate secular or noncanonical elements as ineffective in creating a religious perspective. Jane incorporates noncanonical representations of religious ideas—in conjure and hoodoo beliefs and practices, in dreams, and in her respect for nature—all of which have shown her that "it's not craziness" to talk to trees or put faith in dreams, it's just a different kind of "respect" for alternative forms of spiritual empowerment (MJP 148). These alternatives to conventional worship point the community and the reader to other sites of meaning and create opportunities for appreciating the liberating work of people who, in the words of Nelson Mandela, are not "saints" but "sinners who keep on trying." And it is in the people—the characters whom she characterizes as sacred but who are not theologically sanctioned, such as Huey Long, Jackie Robinson, or Jimmy—that she locates for the community and the reader compelling sources of empowerment outside the traditional church. In highlighting the lives of these people in her text, she demonstrates in words what she observes in actions: that there are many ways to serve the Lord that don't involve "pious kneeling in prayer" (MJP 225).

Rather than highlighting the actions of "world-historical individuals," the novel foregrounds the stories of Big Laura, Ned Douglass, Tee Bob, Mary Agnes, and Jimmy Aaron, revealing how their brave actions emerge from the values of the community—family, education, and freedom—of which religion is a part, but in the lives of these characters not the dominating motivation. What each of these characters eventually learns (and only Jimmy finally is effective in communicating) is that the people must transcend their own fearful self-protectiveness—including their spiritual cowardice—in order to progress. Jane's textimony suggests that the liberative spirit is not abstract or ahistorical or even transcendent, but is specific to its social context and historical moment. The values embodied in people such as Ned and Jimmy become part of the history of the people because they are concrete validations of their ideals, demonstrating Jane's observation that a leader emerges from the people, but not always as the preacher they might have imagined him to be. And once the leader emerges from the community that shaped him, he in turn gives shape to its experience, including its religious experience. In the process the people and the reader learn to shift their gaze away from traditional religious institutions and figures to uncover the liberating activity of God or whatever power they identify as sacred.

The same personal interpretation Jane gives to history she also gives to traditional Christian religion. Although she is a spiritual woman, she is not awed by religious conventions. She would rather sit before the radio and listen to Jackie Robinson play baseball on Sunday than go to church. Her reverence for religion and its symbols is balanced by day-to-day realism, and she keenly feels that worship should not be divorced from life. Jane is a realist who places liberation above confession. She sees that the stories of the Bible are meant to be relevant examples, not restrictive dogma. Still, it is only through the life and death of Jimmy that Jane and the community come to fully understand the impact of religious ideology and social action and their necessarily intertwined relationship to the cause of liberation. Because the people read the world as biblical allegory, they initially see Jimmy as a sign of God's blessing. When he fails to function in the way they envisioned—as a sanctified savior in their traditional theological drama—they risk appreciating the role he can still play in their lives as the One. But because they do eventually assent to his call and participate freely in social action, not only have they empowered themselves and their community, they have established new theological terms by which to appreciate the workings of the sacred in their lives.

How radical a change this is for the community has been debated by many who have read the novel. Audrey Vinson, for example, sees little deviation from traditional Christian theology in the community's religious posture. She identifies a typical morality embraced by the characters that is expressed in a common motif of sacrifice. Vinson advances the argument that any change in the world inhabited by Miss Jane and her people is effected only because of the "great sacrifice by men who may be called deliverers by virtue of the trials they undergo and the far-reaching implications of the results" (35). In her scheme, any significant social change that occurs is born of the courage of characters who accept responsibility for change and thereby adopt a sacrificial quality. "Social changes won by those willing to take risks are the vehicles through which Gaines reveals his high regard for sacrifices made in social activism. The gains per se are given little attention, while their motivation and implementation are the points of focus" (35). It is only through individual sacrifice, Vinson maintains, that subsequent social gains are conferred on the community.

Vinson's argument is supported by the dominant biblical imagery woven through the novel. This imagery is appropriate not only for Miss Jane's interpretation of reality, but for her people, and her time, and their circumstances. Jack Hicks's reading of the novel explores the folk religion or spirituality in which Jane's story is contextualized. He cites numerous examples of the method of this religion, which succeeds in influencing people not by argument but by demonstration. They may not remember the text of Ned's sermon by the river, but they cherish the lumber stained with his blood. They may not understand the physics and politics of the levee system, but they remember the devastation wrought by the high waters. This folk religion functions in two ways: As it presents alternative sources of power, it also serves a structural role in the black community.

This structure is born of traditional religious sources: the spirituals the community sings and the sermons that, however secular in content, are patterned on black preaching; scripture that serves as the most recurrent source for imaging events, as when escape from slavery is cast as an exodus and the drama of Tee Bob and Mary Agnes is identified with Adam and Eve; and the slave narratives that identified the moral implications of bondage and the great devastation slavery created. Hicks sees all of these folk elements coming together in Ned's sermon by the river, which not only recalls Jesus's Sermon on the Mount, but is an adaptation from the book of the prophet Ezekiel (37:11), a myth that taught that words can bring a past to life, put flesh on bone and seed in the soil (19). As Hicks explains, the "bones of [Gaines's] book are communal, oral and rhetorical: spirituals, black folk sermons, slave narratives, biblical parables, folk tales and primitive myths. These are spoken, declaimed forms, issuing from a collective human voice" (16).

Lee Papa attempts to register a different interpretation of the function of religion in the text, identifying what he calls a "new religion" or "new text of religiosity" advanced by the novel that presents itself in opposition to traditional Christianity. But in so doing Papa falls prey to an easy and typical analysis of the church as functioning to "codif[y] a system of oppression" (188). There is no doubt that the same Gaines who expresses considerable ambivalence and skepticism about religion has demonstrated the ways in which religious institutions and ideas can inhibit a liberative spirit. But Gaines is also careful to demonstrate that people need something to believe in. The same religion that often obstructs also sustains the people and can be seen as preparing them for their initiation into social action. The connection between religion and liberation has been made implicitly all along, but it becomes concrete when the community does not just talk the biblical talk of liberation, but literally walks the walk.

Although I agree with Papa that religion assumes a prominent role in the lives of blacks attempting to attain freedom in Gaines's fiction, that "although he rarely addresses religion explicitly, religion becomes the means through which Gaines's characters are defined or define themselves" (187), I cannot accept his view that any notion of sacrificial faith they demonstrate is born of an acquiescence "to the religion forced on the slaves" (187). Papa is correct in appreciating that the characters must "reassess and reappropriate religion in order to accept it on their terms"—indeed, this is a central tenet of all liberating theologies—but I believe he goes too far when he dismisses African-American religion as "a system of white oppression" and suggests that freedom is possible only through a "denial of the church" (187).

It is true that Jimmy Aaron, Papa's primary example of this thesis, confesses to having abandoned his belief in God, but he does not leave the church because he knows it is from the church that his strength originates—the church as the people, not as some abstract institution or system of oppression. Jimmy's name, Aaron, suggests that he will not function as the biblical Moses the people wish him to be, but will be like Moses' brother, Aaron, a man who also strayed from his faith but was spared to continue God's work in liberating the people of Israel. Furthermore, it was Aaron, not Moses, who was eventually associated with the establishment of God's own blessing of his people: "The Lord bless you and keep you; the Lord make his face to shine upon you and be gracious to you; the Lord lift up his countenance upon you, and give you peace" (Numbers 6:27).

The ways in which African Americans have divined God's blessing are part of the truth Miss Jane remembers and that Gaines seeks to reveal in his novel. His ambivalence about the role of religion in his life has not prevented Gaines from respecting the role of religion in building the character of African Americans by giving them a text in which they could become the lead characters in a social drama. This role has changed over time because, as Benjamin Mays observes, "the Negro's ideas of God grow out of the social situation in which he finds himself" (preface). In typical slave narratives and the works that came immediately after Emancipation, African Americans are motivated by the way they feel about God. From that time to the present, however, the themes are sometimes "radically different" (Bradford 20). As the needs of the people changed, so did their understanding of God. By the 1920s, black literature focused on a protest against the "white man's God" and repudiated the faith of former days (Mays 242). But in the 1950s, when the civil rights movement began to emerge and the church was once again a vital force in the social situation African Americans faced, the literature reflects a new appreciation of the religious forms out of which this social action grew.

This pattern is reflected in the spiritual travels of Miss Jane, a journey that began long before her formal conversion. By showing us the span of Miss Jane's spiritual development and how it reflects a larger social movement, Gaines directs us to adopt a tolerance about how we define, and indeed accept, what is theological. When he professes that "what religion did do was say to me you didn't have to believe in one religion or another" (Gaudet and Wooten 70), Gaines reflects a postmodern skepticism about these kinds of fluctuations in religious belief, just as he expresses a doubt about the efficacy of religion to transform people's lives. Even though he recognizes that the changes in contemporary culture have removed religion from its role of primary importance in the quest for identity and freedom, he respects that any kind of liberating activity would not be possible had it not been for the faith of people like Miss Jane.

Gaines's view of religion, as embodied in Miss Jane, who reveres the old and accommodates the new, underscores a foundational principle of a liberating theology. As an institution religion must be actively engaged in the work of fighting oppression, but it must also be flexible enough to accommodate the unique spiritual accents of African-American believers, including folk and secular contributions that emphasize a practical insistence on survival and creation. In his depiction of traditional religion in *The Autobiography of Miss Jane Pittman,* Gaines reveals it as an integral and complex part of black culture. There is both a need for religious faith and a questioning of that faith, including a mistrust of organized religion, black preachers, and others who profess to be religious. Although God and prayer are the first source the people turn to for help and compassion, traditional religion is often inadequate to meet their needs. However, the people continue to express a need for faith, and when they finally learn to accommodate the "secular" Jimmy Aaron in their spiritual quest for liberation, they demonstrate an awareness of what is truly liberating about faith: that although the church failed to keep up with their changes and lost a position of centrality in their lives, it got them where they needed to go and prepared them for their final triumph.

The need for faith, or what Gaines describes as "something higher to believe in," is reinforced by the novel's historical sweep, which celebrates the faith that was such a vital aspect of the world Gaines wants to resurrect. When asked by an interviewer whether there were things he wished could be retained from the past, Gaines replied, "Yes, I would think a faith in God is one thing. . . . But it seems that when we change, we plow the whole damned thing up. We destroy the barn to get rid of the mouse in the barn . . . we have not reached a point yet in our lives of knowing how to keep this and make the changes, too" (Gaudet and Wooten 49). Although Gaines appreciates the need for change, he realizes that it must be accompanied by an appreciation for what may be lost. Religious faith must be questioned, but not to the point at which one loses faith in what remains. As Marcia Gaudet observes, "Gaines presents religion as one of the things caught in the interstices between the need to change the social situation and the need to hold on to and preserve things of value" (Gaudet, "The Failure" 88).

There is no simple formula for how we accomplish this balance between change and preservation. As Gaines is fond of remarking, we are "on the verge" ("On the Verge" 339), and it is too easy to retreat into bitterness. For himself, Gaines insists, "I'm concerned with humanity rather than being bitter. Oh I don't like racism; I don't like bigotry; I don't like many things. But when it comes to my work, the important thing to me is to get out a piece of work that I feel is art . . . and art that is as perfectly round as you can get it. I can't let anything get in the way of that . . . everything I write shows what a man is. Although my characters might be black it doesn't meant that they represent only black people. But for anybody to make it, he might have to become an individual, and not depend on anyone else to do it for him. So a white kid growing up in a completely racist family or society, maybe he has to come out there and become that individual and face it. I think we're always on the verge of things . . . on the verge of going a little bit farther" ("On the Verge" 341).

Helping readers to "face it" is precisely what the slave narrative tradition accomplishes by imagination. Gaines encourages his readers to follow the same advice he follows as a writer. Just as Gaines writes from both "direct experience and vicarious experience" (Doyle, "A MELUS Interview" 62) as he initiates himself into the slave narrative tradition—agitating for both change and preservation—the reader must use his or her own direct experience as an entry into the vicarious experiences of people like Miss Jane. This kind of surrender is something Gaines himself experienced while writing the novel. As he explains, Miss Jane "took over" and there was no way he could change the course of the novel. "There is no way in the world I could have kept that little old lady from trying to get to Ohio.

I knew she would never get there, but I couldn't keep her from going. She had to go as far as she did till she got very, very tired, and I couldn't do anything about that" (Doyle, "A MELUS Interview" 65).

The reasons Gaines couldn't stop Miss Jane are the same reasons why his text is such a sacred text for a liberating theology: his careful interplay of character and characterization. As he explains, "I think the best writers of the present are those who concentrate on the people very closely. And I do try to develop characters to make them as real as possible. My aim in literature is to develop character, not only the character in the book, but my character as well as yours, so that if you pick up the book, you will see something you feel is true, something not seen before, that will help develop your character from that day forward" (Doyle, "A MELUS Interview" 66). Developing character does not mean one will arrive at immediate understanding or even an entirely hopeful perspective. *The Autobiography of Miss Jane Pittman,* though mostly optimistic, is shaded by ambiguity and tentative projections for a better future.

Gaines tries to encourage his readers to adopt the same attitude as his characters: "'I will make it, I will make it, I will make it,'" even though for the ten percent or so who do "make it, the other ninety percent don't. For every Miss Jane Pittman who made it, nine other Black women either went insane or died inside long before they were physically dead and put in the ground. It is the ten percent I choose to write about. That's why most of my leading characters are super brave and must take risks—to help themselves or others, even though the risk may cause his or her death" (Doyle, "A MELUS Interview" 67). Once again, the solution is not the solution, but the process is the solution. As Jane's friend Mary instructed the editor while he was collecting Miss Jane's story, "Well, you don't tie up all the loose ends all the time" (MJP vii).

The process for Miss Jane is the same process Ernest Gaines undertook in writing about her and a process to which he initiates the reader. It's a process of "going back" to understand who we have become by learning who we were. As he describes in the essay "Miss Jane and I," to ask who Miss Jane is is to ask first who Ernest J. Gaines is (24). In so doing Gaines came to understand the complexities of freedom. Although he grew up in world of "de facto slavery," there were times when he was "the freest kid in the world. . . . I was freer than any white kid, and at the same time, not free at all. What a paradox" (Ringle D2). He could not discover the reason for this paradox in years of reading through "great writers" because they did not describe him, a man who had emerged from the people who "regardless of what time of year it was, under whatever conditions . . .

would find something to talk about." Instead, he had to go "back, back, back into our experiences in this country to find some kind of meaning to our present lives. No, Miss Jane is not the end of my travelling into the past—she is only another step back so that I can see some meaning in the present" (Gaines, "Miss Jane" 34). Gaines describes the meaning of the present he uncovered in the past when he writes,

> I wanted to smell that Louisiana earth, feel that Louisiana sun, sit under the shade of one of those Louisiana oaks. . . . I wanted to see on paper those Louisiana black children walking to school on cold days while yellow Louisiana buses passed them by . . . black parents going to work before the sun came up and coming back home to look after their children after the sun went down . . . to see on paper the small country churches (schools during the week), and I wanted to hear those simple religious songs, those simple prayers—that true devotion. (It was Faulkner, I think, who said that if God were to stay alive in the country, the black would have to keep Him so.) . . . I wanted to read about the true relationship between whites and blacks—about the people that I had known. ("Miss Jane" 28)

Although when Gaines began writing *The Autobiography of Miss Jane Pittman* he had no "intention towards polemics," the acts of civil rights workers such as James Meredith inspired him. "I told myself that if James Meredith can go through all this—not only for himself, but for his race (and that included me as well)—then I, too, should go back to the source that I was trying to write about" ("Miss Jane" 31). It was then that Gaines realized that Miss Jane represents more than a capsule of history because "Miss Jane is Miss Jane. She is not my aunt, she is not any one person— she is Miss Jane." But as he reminds us,

> You have seen Miss Jane, too. She is that old lady who lives up the block, who comes out every Sunday to go to church when the rheumatism does not keep her in. She is the old lady who calls a child to her door and asks him to go to the store for a can of coffee. She sits on a screened-in porch fanning herself in the summer, and in the winter she sits by the heater or the stove and thinks about the dead . . . she knows much—she has lived long. Sometimes she's impatient, but most times she's just the opposite. If you take time to ask her a question you will find her to be quite dogmatic. You will say, "But that's not it, that's not it, that's not it." And she will stick to her beliefs. If you go to the history books, you will find that most of them would not agree with what she has told you. But if you read more closely you will also notice that these great minds don't even agree with each other. Truth to Miss Jane is what she remembers. Truth to me is what people like Miss Jane remember. ("Miss Jane" 37)

What Miss Jane remembers and what she tells is what initiated and sustains the slave narrative tradition. It begins with "an idea, this point, this fact: some time in the past we were brought from Africa in chains, put in Louisiana to work the rice, cane, and cotton fields. Some kind of way we survived. God? Luck? Soul Food? Threats of Death? Superstition? I suppose all of these have played their part. If I asked a white historian what happened, he would not tell it the same way a black historian would. If I asked a black historian, he would not tell it the same way a black field worker would. So I ask them all. And I try in some way to get the answer. But I'm afraid I have not gotten it yet. Maybe in the next book, or the one after, or the one after. Maybe" ("Miss Jane" 38).

But Gaines has gotten the point, despite his claims otherwise, because his writing answers his questions by showing us where to look: toward character, toward the people who were his childhood heroes because they would "get up and go to work every damn day, and see himself not accomplishing much that day or maybe the next day, but will get up anyway and try it again, against the odds, to make life a little bit better. People ask me what I learned from Faulkner, but the real question is what Faulkner learned from Ernie Gaines and his people" (Ringle D2). What Faulkner learned is also what Hemingway learned: that in the stories of people like Miss Jane are examples of grace under pressure. As Gaines insists, there is no better example of grace under pressure than "our people for the last 300 years" (Ringle D2). And to write about grace under pressure does not mean one capitulates to notions of what a black novel must be. As Gaines observes, "If Faulkner had just written about racism he wouldn't have been the genius we recognize today. And yet race was a large part of most everything he wrote" (Ringle D2).

Gaines accepts that race plays a part in understanding and developing the American character, but he also believes that we must look for truths and life lessons not in stereotypes and racial designations but in the depths and mysteries of the human heart. "That's the only place that really matters. That's where each of us discovers who we really are" (Ringle D2). That discovery, as Gaines himself has experienced, may involve confrontation with racism, both black and white, but when that happens, Gaines claims the most liberating power available to him as a form of resistance and says, "to hell with it," and he goes home to "try to write a better paragraph" (Ringle D2). This response is why critics such as Jack Hicks recognize that Gaines's appreciation of the immense power in language instructs him that its use is a "sacred trust" (Hicks 19). In the "better paragraphs" that ultimately and finally break down barriers between the author and his characters and between the reader and his characters, Gaines reaffirms the liberating theology expressed by Miss Jane when she observes, "Religion raises the heart, makes you noble, it don't make you crazy" (MJP 213).

When Jimmy comes to appreciate the noble qualities of religion and how it has sustained his people is also when the people finally learn that their spirituality need not be expressed only on Sunday. Jimmy's recognition, through Jane, of the need to involve the entire community in the quest for freedom becomes a call not just to his immediate community, but to the reader as well. The final action of the people ultimately reassures the reader that to enter into this space of identification is not futile. There is a possibility for change.

NOTES

1. All references to *The Autobiography of Miss Jane Pittman* appear in the text with the abbreviation MJP.

2. Initially the many narrative voices suggested to him that he needed to use a multiple point of view, but he eventually discarded it, realizing that Miss Jane was not just his "straight line" and that he "had fallen in love with my little character, and I thought she could tell the story of her life much better than anyone else" ("Miss Jane" 37).

3. Jones's discussion is situated in a larger framework that situates the thought of Awiakta and Toni Morrison alongside Dietrich Bonhoeffer's theology, thereby making an implicit multicultural connection while she interrogates the practical realities of teaching religion and literature in a postmodern world.

4 Disembarking the Past: Glenn Ligon

Art is a social construct. A work of art is what an artist
says is a work of art, and is considered great when, over
time, it manages to transcend the circumstances of its
making and its expression.
—David Ross

Until recently, Montgomery, Alabama was a tourist site for two discrete
constituencies: those interested in its distinction as the first capital of
the Confederacy and those who wanted to be where Martin Luther King
began his career as a minister and activist. Now, between Jefferson Davis's
confederate "White House" and the Dexter Avenue Baptist Church is the
Civil Rights Memorial, a new sacred space that seeks symbolically to unite
these two different classes of tourists, just as the movement itself tried to
accomplish the same. Maya Lin designed the memorial to try to encompass the whole civil rights movement and the era it spawned while recognizing that although it was "very much a people's movement," in the generic sense, it was made possible by the contributions and sacrifices of many
particular individuals who had been forgotten (Zinsser 33).

The memorial stands at the site of the offices of the Southern Poverty
Law Center, which continues the work of the movement by acting to ensure civil rights for the oppressed. The center also tracks the activities of
hate groups and episodes of ethnic violence and draws from its extensive
archive information pertinent for teaching tolerance. When she became
aware of the center's mission to continue vigilance for civil rights, Lin realized that "if you stop remembering, you can quickly slide backward into
prejudicial ways" (Zinsser 33). Lin's way to evoke remembrance of the
movement and the people who participated in it was to center her design
around rock and water.

The memorial has two components, both of black granite. The first part is a nine-foot-high wall on which are carved words drawn from a verse in the Book of Amos that Martin Luther King used at the beginning of the bus boycott and the march on Washington: "We will not be satisfied until justice rolls down like waters and righteousness like a mighty stream." Lin chose to begin the quote at "until" because she wanted the Civil Rights Memorial to deal "not only with the past but with the future—with how far we still have to go in a continuing struggle" (37), a sentiment reinforced by water that spills down the wall.

The second part of the memorial, resting on an asymmetrical pedestal nearby, is a circular tabletop almost twelve feet in diameter. Around its perimeter, carved in the stone (somewhat in the manner of a sundial) is a chronological listing of the movement's major events and its individual deaths. Fifty-three brief entries dramatically show how individual lives make up and influence history. Extra space after King's entry shows that this is where the story ends on the memorial, but not where it ends in actuality. Visitors touch the names beneath water that arises from a hole in the tabletop and flows over it. Only 31 inches high, the table is accessible to all.

As Lin explains, "the water is as slow as I could get it. It remains very still until you touch it. Your hand causes ripples, which transform and alter the piece, just as reading the words completes the piece" (Zinsser 38). The soothing sound of water combined with the words evokes righteous cleansing and adds another sensory element to the design. Like Lin's Vietnam Memorial, the Civil Rights Memorial invites visitors to touch the names, thereby bringing some part of themselves to the act of honoring the martyred. What the designer did not anticipate is what power the words joined with water would generate, how the memorial would provoke people to cry so that their tears would become part of the memorial, too (Zinsser 38).

Although it honors a movement, the memorial casts in vivid relief the sacrifices of ordinary people who accepted the call of Martin Luther King Jr. to apply biblical righteousness in working for social justice. Just as the memorial compels people to touch beneath its surfaces—through the water and deep into the carved stone—it also urges people to go beyond a mere surface response to injustice and to probe the depths of what civil rights were and are. And because of its circularity, visitors have an experience that is both private and shared; as they move around the table or pause to read and touch the names of the dead, they also touch one another—in actuality, in fragments of conversation, or in silent witness—and remember that the struggle is never-ending but circumscribes daily existence in profound and illuminating ways.

Recalling the past for edification and redemption, resurrecting people lost to history, creating a sacred space for reflecting on liberation, and amplifying the relationship between word and image are also characteristic of *To Disembark,* Glenn Ligon's 1994 installation at the Hirshhorn Gallery in Washington, D.C. The title alludes to the title of a book of poetry by Gwendolyn Brooks. *To Disembark* functions in both works to evoke the recognition that African Americans are still coping with the remnants of slavery and its ongoing manifestation in racism. The title also functions for both artists to suggest the arrival at the end of a physical journey that, recast in literature, often serves as a motif for a journey into one's self. Ligon's journey does not begin with the civil rights movement, but goes all the way back to slavery.

Ligon "boxes" black experience by creating a series of packing crates modeled on the one described by ex-slave Henry "Box" Brown in his *Narrative of Henry Box Brown—Who Escaped from Slavery Enclosed in a Box 3 Feet Long and 2 Wide.* From each crate a different sound issues, such as a heartbeat or music spanning early African-American musical forms such as spirituals to contemporary rap music. Surrounding these boxes are posters in which the artist characterizes himself, in words and period images, as a runaway slave. The framed posters resemble nineteenth-century broadsheets circulated to advertise for the return of fugitive slaves. Following this is a series of stencils painted on the wall whose text is derived from an essay by the African-American writer Zora Neale Hurston titled "How It Feels to Be Colored Me." Read from top to bottom, the stencils repeat but increasingly obscure significant passages from Hurston's essay.

The last element in this installation relies on the literary genre of slave narratives as its primary resource. In a series of framed etchings hanging side by side on the gallery wall, Ligon has reproduced in authentic typescript and form frontispieces that would introduce the published narrative of an ex-slave. By assuming another series of ironic identities—as the author on a series of title pages from nineteenth-century slave narratives—Ligon demonstrates that African Americans are still trying to disembark. This sentiment is further reinforced by inclusion of the works of contemporary black writers to supplant traditional "sacred" texts such as Bible verses or supporting testimony from distinguished white people customarily presented on the title pages of ex-slave narratives. By positioning himself as a fugitive slave or an ex-slave narrator and by including contemporary writings against the background of a traditional genre, Ligon demonstrates that a slave narrative tradition of textimony is ongoing in its formation in literal, literary, and visual ways. By exploring slavery's painful past Glenn Ligon hopes to understand his own. Furthermore, he gives viewers an imaginative way to participate in the same process of self/ historical construction.

Provoking imaginative identification is the motive behind Glenn Ligon's *To Disembark*. Despite Lucius Matlock's assertion that slave narratives were "a monument more enduring than marble," thus setting up the literary form as more potent than the visual form, one contemporary African-American artist has seized the possibility of uniting the visual with the literary in reconsidering the topic of slavery. In this installation Ligon asks us to consider anew the same issues slave narratives once forced people to confront. Regarding the construction of history and representations of identity, he asks, who sees, who names, who records? As Ligon puts it, "Who are the other 'masters' from which we flee?"[1]

Through various media, the artist suggests that issues of identity are best understood as structured by context, not essence. Just as slave narratives often began with "I was born a slave" and went on to show how the author achieved a new identity through fuller participation in a larger social context (rather than by some internal change in his or her essential being), Ligon shows how identity is socially constructed. Ligon's exhibit demonstrates that self is composed of many narratives that are read differently, depending on who is given voice. He also demonstrates that sacred texts or textimony, while retaining their narrative element, are recorded and read in ways other than literal or literary. Formerly an abstract expressionist, he also challenges the notion that pure form is "rich enough to deal with what's going on."

The issues *To Disembark* urge us to confront move between constructed dualities, most obviously between black and white, self and other, past and present. Gay and straight could also be construed as a set of dualities *To Disembark* urges us to confront. Ligon makes reference to his sexual orientation in three of the nine title pages. Although his investigation into construction of identities centers largely on racial issues, his sexual orientation is clearly also a dimension of self-construction that functions in a similar way. The dualities of these social designators are further exploited in aesthetic and theological terms, between word and image, absence and presence, spiritual and material, visible and invisible—and finally between essence and context. Ultimately, Ligon creates in this installation a "transgressive narrative self" (Marren 45) whose existence challenges readers/ viewers to scrutinize the social structures that support identity.[2]

By interrogating the culturally organized boundaries that separate apparently distinct and oppositional categories, Ligon forces us toward a basic consideration of how identity is constructed, a consideration that also characterizes the efforts of ex-slave narrators. Ligon's work therefore represents a further extension of the slave narrative tradition whereby written textimonies become the basis for visual textimony. He uses both the classic literary convention of the bearer of the word motif set forth in slave narratives and the contemporary visual word-as-image tradition to address matters of race and liberation. Ligon possesses a modern sensibility that explores the aesthetic significance of typographical forms as symbols of communication and as basic formal design elements, but he also possesses a historical memory against which he positions himself to find "connections between it and who I am."

Ligon's desire to reach back to slavery as a way to find connections is representative of a broader contemporary phenomenon. The fact that Ligon wants to take this journey is not unique. As noted earlier in this study, the slave narrative tradition in American letters is booming with works motivated by an impulse similar to Ligon's. One African-American historian, Anthony Cohen, has even undertaken an actual journey to keep alive the memories and experiences of enslaved people. He is traveling the route of the Underground Railroad taken by many escaped slaves, going so far as to have himself, like Henry "Box" Brown, crated and shipped by train from Philadelphia to New York. Cohen explains that he was bothered because, although "slavery and its effects are . . . the national obsession, nobody can talk about it" (Fletcher). Cohen, who hopes to publish the journal of his travels as a book, encourages the media attention he has received along the way because it has helped him to bring the conversation about slavery into the mainstream while opening the way for a broader appreciation of the Underground Railroad as a major humanitarian movement.

In so doing, Cohen underscores an important feature of the slave narrative tradition. Beyond the need to rehearse the past of slavery is the need to understand it, especially its paradoxical nature, wherein the Underground Railroad represents "one of the most positive aspects of our heritage" even though "it grew out of one of the most insidious chapters of our history" (Fletcher). Cohen has been pleased to discover that along any of the routes of the railroad he encountered "communities where the heritage is preserved," but he has been disheartened to recognize apparent acts of racism that are committed in these same locations, leading him to reflect, "This still goes on. . . . It is amazing to me how constantly on this trip the past has been meeting the present" (Fletcher). Finding the resources and energy to undertake this kind of personal journey is not an option for most of us, which is why the slave narrative tradition provides readers and viewers ways in which to empathetically undergo a representative experience in order to find connections to the past and point a direction for the future.

Transforming the "chains of past" into "spiritual links that willingly bind us together now and into the future" is how painter Tom Feelings describes his own manipulation of word and image around the subject of slavery. Not long after Ligon exhibited *To Disembark,* Feelings published *The Middle Passage,* a portfolio book that tells the story of the journey enslaved Africans took across the Atlantic in sixty-four paintings. Like Ligon and Cohen, Feelings describes his efforts as born of a need to make a psychological and spiritual journey into the past, as he explains when he paraphrases Paule Marshall: "You have to engage the past and deal with it if you are going to shape a future that reflects you" (*The Middle*). And like Cohen, Feelings tried to arrive at the past by taking actual journeys from his home in Brooklyn, physically tracing a trail from Africa through and into the diaspora. It was from these travels that, back home in Brooklyn, he began the twenty-year enterprise that resulted in *The Middle Passage,* a work he describes as a way to tell a story as an artist: "What could be more challenging than this powerful, profound dramatic history, probing the memory, fueling the imagination, maybe even becoming a vehicle for creative growth?" (*The Middle*).

When he began to draft the artwork, Feelings conducted extensive research. But he arrived at a very different conclusion from the one that Ligon reached after his own research. A trained children's book illustrator who appreciates the power of picture books, Feelings believed that an illustrated narrative could function more evocatively in a traditional African way. Unlike Ligon, who found text a more appropriate and accurate way to represent the experience of enslavement, Feelings judged that the texts that dealt with the experience of slavery were too tainted by racial assumptions and social influences and therefore could not provide a trustworthy passage into the experience.

Feelings crafted paintings, rendered in white, black, and shades of gray, to graphically depict all the horrors endured by enslaved people. Feelings resists the clarity Ligon achieves in typographical forms, substituting instead "rhythmic lines of motion, like a drumbeat . . . and a style that incorporated dance consciousness surfaced" (*The Middle*). Although both Feelings and Ligon appreciate that much of the pain of the present is rooted in the past, Ligon's work demonstrates an appreciation for not just the way in which Africans were brought to this continent, but the ongoing implications of their creative struggle to live in this country. After the Middle Passage came the challenge to disembark, a journey that continues to be played out in new forms that, although they may have derived from Africa, demonstrate the requirement for a unique adaptation and improvisation. A significant part of that adaptation and improvisation involves the manipulation of language. Ligon appreciates the transformative and transgressive possibilities provided by an exploration of the complexities of narrative. Rather than dismissing language in favor of "pure" image, Ligon positions himself in the slave narrative tradition of textimony as a way to find an appropriate image of self and a voice of one's own.

Ligon travels not back to Africa, but back to the plantation. He reverses the actual route enslaved people took when they journeyed "up" to freedom in the North—a classic vertical migration that denoted a corresponding elevation in character. But he takes the same path ex-slave narrators took when, by virtue of memory, they traveled back to their enslaved circumstances in order to write about them. In doing so he discovers that by going back, or "down," to African Americans' past experiences is the only way for him to rise in contemporary American culture. Along his journey into the past Ligon pays homage to both visual and literary African and African-American aesthetic traditions. He explores the possibilities provided by an African worldview in which the arts are intertwined in a complex way. He demonstrates his awareness of the found art or folk art tradition that first reflected the creative energies of African Americans. And finally, he is part of a tradition in African-American art that takes black life as a topic for creative reflection and expression and sees the redemptive possibilities of creating art to address social conditions of racism and oppression. In the process he creates art that, precisely because it is so grounded in experience and tradition, appeals to concepts of identity universal to the human condition. The resulting textimony of *To Disembark* is a postmodern expression of a liberating theology.

◎ ◎ ◎

Art does not reproduce the visible, but makes visible.
—Paul Klee

Writing for *The Washington Post,* Jo Ann Lewis observes that voices from black history appear often in Glenn Ligon's art, most of which is concerned with the experience of being black in a white society. Ligon's interest in black history and literature began when he was growing up in the Bronx. The ease with which he assumes other people's identities began when, because of his parents' wish that they have a better education than was provided by the Bronx public school system, he and his brother commuted from their housing project to the private, progressive Walden school in Manhattan. Later Ligon attended the Rhode Island School of Design and Wesleyan College. Initially he launched a career as an abstract painter until his experience in the Whitney Museum's Independent Study program introduced him to theory and helped transform him into a conceptual artist. Although some conceptual art has the effect of distancing an artist from the public, Ligon's art is distinguished by the way it invites the observer to participate, never allowing the content to outweigh the effect. Indeed, Ligon's New York dealer, Max Protetch, affirms that "what makes Glenn different from others doing socially engaged work is that he makes art from his ideas . . . and he's making conceptual art that draws on his personal experience which is why it touches me" (J. Lewis G6).

Ligon sets a new standard for conceptual artists who, in their desire to attain what E. H. Gombrich calls a "kind of purity," have formally sought "freedom of the image from the intrusion or indeed the contamination of words" (213). Ligon rejects this "uncontaminated" concept of purity by making words the primary focus of his visual work. He shows a new way of turning the word itself into an image of its meaning. In the process he demonstrates a vital distinction that has concerned philosophers since the days of Plato, a distinction between universals and particulars. Unlike images, language can make the vital distinctions and can specify what images cannot. But as Gombrich further observes, this is in "curious contrast to the fact that images are concrete, vivid, and inexhaustibly rich in sensory qualities, while language is abstract and purely conventional" (220–21). No image can be the equivalent of a verbal statement unless some directing text or familiar cultural reference that possesses a narrative component accompanies it. When the artist cannot rely on cultural knowledge—as Ligon cannot because so few people are versed in African-American history—he has to offer instructions for reading that mobilize our memory and require us to confront the knowledge presented in a particular text or a story.

In *To Disembark,* Ligon takes a general experience of oppression and search for identity and particularizes it by invoking the slave narratives. He further particularizes this experience by casting himself as the enslaved person under consideration. The viewer is then enjoined to find the link between image and idea, universal and particular, a link that leads through metaphor—seeing self as someone else or the other. The wider the distance the greater the challenge to effect this link, but Ligon's art makes the distance seem not so formidable. He transforms a historical literary mode into a private and personal idiom and then back into a contemporary public statement. Just when we think we are comfortable with the status of African Americans and the arrangement of our social order, he creates a shock of dislocation for the viewing public by his identification of an educated and accomplished contemporary African American with a nineteenth-century slave. The resulting experience is liberating, just as the previous model of the slave narratives was liberating for the new way it imaged people of African descent.

The universal dimension of Ligon's art, while firmly rooted in historical African-American experience, reaches out to everyone because of the way he perceives identity as socially constructed. As the show's curator, Phyllis Rosenzweig, emphasizes, the artist is "looking at how that history, including slavery, affects all of us personally" (Lewis G6). If African Americans are still trying to disembark, then many of us are still on the shore, waiting to affix a price. But the effect Ligon achieves by forcing this awareness is lyrical rather than didactic, provocative rather than confrontational. He thereby invites a broad spectrum of the public to consider the implications of identity formation and representation by positioning one's self in the role of an enslaved person, just as the writers of ex-slave narratives achieved the same effect. Although the artist concedes that his art is not "easy" because there is a lot of text, he hopes that viewers will "come in, spend some time, and think about the issues" (Lewis G6). Through his visual recreation of narratives of slavery—the stories captured in detail by writers or episodically rendered in advertisements for runaway slaves— Ligon forces us to read the texts that we would overlook in a literary enterprise and to become aware of how many narratives—actual texts or contexts—structure our social system and contribute to our identity constructions.

Ligon seems prepared for the risk involved in an enterprise that is so autobiographical. But he also notes that paintings are read as far more personal than *To Disembark* because they are so identified with the artist's hand, whereas his work "plays with the idea of unmediated access to the artist." Ultimately the reproductions and stencils of other people's texts enable him to explore "the border between what is mechanical, repetitive, and impersonal and what is autobiographical." This observation points to a feature of the slave narratives that long troubled historians and literary critics: their patterned and repetitious form and content. Ligon acknowledges this feature when in an interview he makes reference to Toni Morrison's comment from the essay "The Site of Memory," where she observes that writers of slave narratives often stopped short of really describing the horrors of slavery because they feared public response.

Morrison describes this characteristic with a phrase often found in the narratives themselves when authors claim the need to "drop a veil" over their interior lives. Ligon's work is an attempt to explore contemporary examples of this same phenomenon. What is it that audiences do not want to hear and how should African Americans be represented by themselves or others? Observing the changes in Frederick Douglass's autobiographical attempts from the first to the third version, Ligon became interested "in the idea of invention and self-invention in autobiography as it speaks to counteracting essentialist notions of black identity. The 'one' that I am is composed of narratives that overlap, run parallel to, and often contradict one another."

Ligon first received wide attention when he was selected to participate in the 1991 Whitney Biennial. He was also featured in the controversial 1993 Biennial at the Whitney, where the exhibits were attacked by critics as preachy and ill-conceived art that abandoned aesthetic goals in favor of polemics on social and political issues. Ligon's own contribution was an installation titled *Notes on the Margins of "The Black Book,"* which juxtaposed Robert Mapplethorpe's photographs of black male nudes with comments on Mapplethorpe's work. As Ligon explained to me in a letter, this piece "was an exploration of how the variables of race, gender, sexuality and class intersect and form varying and often conflicting readings of Mapplethorpe's images." The artist recalls as an example of this fact that black gay patrons at a particular bar read Mapplethorpe's photographs taken there as "documentation of friends," thereby outweighing discussions of the "fetishic nature of the images." Ligon defends the show and his role in it because he sees this kind of art and his own as responding to crisis. As he says, "there's urgency in the culture to grapple with these issues." He goes on to explain that he sees social and political subject matter as "crucial" to his own life and "important to a national debate that needs to go on." Although he admits to some insecurity about the appropriateness of art as a vehicle for social critique and expression, he insists that rather than saying "art is art and life is life, I like to say that they're joined and inextricable" (Lewis G6).

To Disembark has four discrete elements or "sacred spaces" that are also "joined and inextricable." One first encounters nine wooden boxes or packing crates on which are stamped international symbols that denote fragility. These symbols remind us to "handle with care" the people who will be represented and to take note of what is common to humanity. The boxes vary in size and construction method, but all take their proportions from the one in which Henry "Box" Brown had himself shipped from slavery in Richmond, Virginia to freedom in Philadelphia in 1849. In his narrative, Henry Brown describes his boxed experience as if he were feeling the physical effects of dying, a sensation he "preferred to slavery." At that moment, while boxed and presumably dying, Brown resolves to "submit to the will of God." When the box arrived at its destination a friend knocked to see whether Brown was still alive, and at that moment Brown's death was transformed into his rebirth, his "resurrection from the grave of slavery. I rose a free man" (61–62).

The trope of dying to slavery and being reborn to freedom is a common theme in ex-slave narratives that Ligon exploits for its contemporary implications. "The idea for this came from seeing an illustration of Henry coming out of the crate," Ligon explains (Lewis G6). While digging through files at the New York Public Library, Ligon repeatedly confronted this image and it led him to the text or word found in ex-slave narratives. "I thought it would be interesting to explore the idea of the person in the box, and how someone would survive that ordeal." Just as Henry Brown describes a moment of revelation when "suddenly, as if from above, there darted into my mind these words, 'Go and get a box, and put yourself in it'" (59), so too did Ligon come to a vivid realization of the symbolic potential inherent in Brown's act. As he further explains, the box "in some sense became an extension" of Brown's body, just as any social construction becomes an extension of an essential self. Just as Henry was boxed in order to enter a new space where he could articulate his identity, so too does Ligon box black experience and move it into a gallery for public consideration, all the while demonstrating that identity or self cannot be contained in such a way. In doing so, Ligon also forces us to reconsider what other social forces or boxes operate like slavery to both inhibit and create possibilities for dying into a new life of freedom.

From each box issues a barely audible sound, a weak but enduring presence that, like so many African-American voices, speaks from the margins and is heard if one listens carefully. These human sounds—including a heartbeat and a song—perform an ironic inversion of a time when human lives were considered cargo. Each discrete sound contributes to an eclectic but meaningful gathering of music. Billie Holiday sings "Strange Fruit," a lyrical elegy to a lynched man. KRS One is also represented in the rap anthem "Sound of da Police," a rhythmic response to institutional brutality. Yet also of a rhythmic order is the music of the McIntosh County shouters. These shout songs, which are sung with the accompaniment of

Untitled, 1993. Three wood and mixed-media boxes, each approximately 76.2 x 91.4 x 61.0 cm (36 x 30 x 24 in.). Collection of the artist. Photo by Dennis Cowley.

only a broom handle beat on the floor, are the antecedents of the spirituals and the musical style that most clearly identifies African retentions in American musical forms. A spiritual sung by Paul Robeson, "Didn't My Lord Deliver Daniel," is also featured.

Less expressive of African forms than the shout songs, the spiritual is like the shout songs in displaying the unique cross-fertilization characteristic of African-American cultural forms. This blending of traditions reveals different historical and cultural influences, but also shows a persistent quality of uniting the sacred and the profane in African-American aesthetic forms. The themes or topics of these songs usually are taken from biblical sources and contain some reference to liberation, construed as both this-worldly and otherworldly, both material and spiritual. Bob Marley's "Redemption Song" is a contemporary expression of the same desire for freedom that shout songs and spirituals articulated, but thematically adds to Ligon's exploration into black identity a pan-African perspective, uniting the concerns of diaspora blacks with those of North American continental blacks. Levity and an uncomplicated celebration of life are interjected with Royal House's disco song "Can You Party," and Nina Simone's ballad "Four Women" speaks to the essential aspect of gender that also complicates and energizes the process of identity formation under consideration.

In the same gallery surrounding the boxes are lithographs imitating nineteenth-century advertisements for the return of escaped slaves. Rather than tacked on a tree or a post, as they would have been in their original use, the advertisements are meticulously rendered and framed for gallery walls. All name and describe the artist himself. Ligon asked friends to describe him without giving a reason and used their descriptions to create the prints. In every case he is the runaway slave described in the texts. Most of the comments are limited to physical descriptions, which is typical of how African Americans were regarded by slaveholders; their value was located in their morphological construction. For example, one ad reads, "Ran away, Glenn, a black male, 5'8", very short hair, nearly completely shaved, stocky build, 155–165 lbs., medium complexion (not 'light skinned,' not 'dark skinned,' slightly orange)."

Not surprisingly, or perhaps ironically, one comment describes Ligon as having "nice teeth," which was something slaveholders looked at before they purchased a new slave, much as horsetraders open an animal's mouth for inspection. Also included are a few comments that speak beyond objectifying descriptions and include a range of characteristics identified with humanity—some noble and some suspicious—that hint at the personality or spirit behind the material. Ligon is described as "very articulate, seemingly well-educated," but also as one who "does not look at you straight in the eye when talking to you" or as "socially very adept, yet, paradoxically, he's somewhat of a loner."

Included on each poster to accompany the text is a characteristic period image of an African American, ranging from the classic "Am I not a man and a brother?" figure promoted in abolitionist publications to caricature black men who are running scared. There is even one female figure, also on the run toting a rucksack of personal belongings, accompanied by the description "lately I've noticed he refers to himself as a 'mother.'" These posters represent an extension of the boxing theme, but it is Ligon's own identity that has been boxed in these lithographs. As the artist explained to me, "the lithos and the boxes are about the relationship between the individuals who I know and the context in which we live. The question is: What does it mean to suggest that one's friends have a similar relationship to you that a slave owner would have had with a slave? What does it say about the society in which those friendships are formed and the position of blacks in it?"

Untitled, 1993. Offset lithograph on paper, 40.6 x 30.5 cm (16 x 12 in.). Collection of the artist. Photo by Dennis Cowley.

In another part of the exhibition, four quotes from Zora Neale Hurston's famous essay, "How It Feels to Be Colored Me," are stenciled directly on the walls. The stenciling forms a six-foot-tall stack of black words on a white wall. As John Robertson points out, Ligon chose dimensions that corresponded to "the human scale of doors—our bodies walk through them, and they open and close on so many chapters of our lives" (159). The words are meticulously drawn in black Paintstik, letter by letter, repeating evocative language from Hurston's essay. In this essay Hurston laments how blackness is discussed only in oppositional terms to whiteness. She attempts to dispel the notion of whiteness as an appropriate or necessary point of reference in constructing black identity. Hurston was criticized for continually emphasizing her uniqueness in human or spiritual terms rather than in racial terms, and Ligon appears to appreciate her struggle to move away from binary representations of identity. He makes this point visually: As he works from top to bottom, the grease from the stick thickens, increasingly obscuring the letters.

The cumulative effect of these stencils is set forth in the way the black words eventually blur and smudge with each repetition so that at the bottom of each stencil the white background is barely distinguishable from the black words. "What these pieces are about," the artist explains, "is the idea of race as a social category. Race is not something inherent to one's being: One does feel more or less colored, depending on the situation" (Lewis G6). Here Ligon reads textual content in painterly terms. As the background darkens and text and background become indistinguishable, it is apparent that as language and context near the same color value, the language disappears, as do customary racial ways of assigning identity to people. The black and white duality of text and page becomes a metaphor of racial relations and how we construct oppositional categories of identity. But as Robertson points out, the stencils reveal that "color always—or almost always—does matter for Hurston, for Ligon, for the viewer, and for blacks and whites alike. Our attempts to deny its importance—as Hurston's text appears to do—only reinforces its power" (159).

The quotes from Hurston's essay that Ligon selected to stencil for *To Disembark,* are the following: "I feel most colored when I am thrown against a sharp white background," "I remember the very day that I became colored," "I am not tragically colored," and "I do not always feel colored." Ligon found Hurston's writing pertinent because of the way she explores the idea of race as a concept that is structured by context rather than essence. He plays with the notion of being colored and how that becoming obscures meaning (obscures the text) and also creates an abstract

Untitled, 1990. Oilstick and gesso on wood, 203.2 x 76.2 cm (80 x 30 in.). Collection of the artist. The painting is from Ligon's first series of works using sentences from Zora Neale Hurston's essay "How It Feels to Be Colored Me" (in this case, "I feel most colored when I am thrown against a sharp white background"). Photo by Dennis Cowley.

object. As he explains, "One can 'become colored.' One is not born black; 'blackness' is a social construction." Again, Ligon traces this idea back to the ex-slave narratives in which the writers identified as one of their tasks the effort to convince people that there was nothing inherent in black people to justify their enslavement. He describes Frederick Douglass's famous sentence in the narrative, "You have seen how a man was made a slave, now you shall see how a slave was made a man," as an "important intervention of the idea that blacks were subhuman by birth." Just as the Bible was used to support such essentialist claims, Ligon substitutes this sacred text with a new sacred text from Hurston's canon that offers a different perspective.[3]

Ligon remarks on the motives and intentions behind this part of the installation by describing how his forays into abstract art led him to a "crisis" because he was looking for a way to incorporate into his visual art ideas culled from theoretical and literary texts. He came upon stencils as an economical, efficient, and durable solution that allowed him to use "text as the work itself," something paint would not allow. He began with painterly backgrounds but eventually settled on a white background—the way we are used to seeing text—but he repeated the quotes. As he explains "I was interested in what happened if you broke a sentence down in terms of its legibility and the meaning of its individual parts, and how the line breaks and the accumulation of paint on the stencil teased the traces of other meanings out of the sentences."

This part of the installation has its origins in a show Ligon presented late in 1990 that used the same quotes and the same technique. Also predating To Disembark is a 1992 show in which Ligon used the same technique but took as his text lines from Jean Genet. Like To Disembark, the title Prisoner of Love is taken from a work of literature. It is also the title of Genet's memoir, in which the author describes his involvement with the Black Panthers near the end of his life. The sentence Ligon selects to "break down" is ripe with multiple meanings even before he begins his process of deconstruction. It reads, "They are the ink that gives the white page a meaning." This panel is accompanied by three others that are formally similar, but the sentence varies: "We are the ink that gives the white page a meaning" and the interrogative "Why must we be the ink that gives the white page a meaning?" Finally, echoing Genet's own qualification, the last quote cautions, "When I said that we were the ink that gives the white page a meaning, that was too easy an image." Ligon subverts the outsider designation "they" when he uses the pronoun "we," thereby repersonalizing the text.

By resisting a fixed meaning assigned to a given text, Ligon draws attention to locations of power in the dominant culture that would determine how black life is read. As Ken Johnson notes in his review of this show for *Art in America*, "Despite the apparent simplicity of the text-page, black-white analogy, the installation produces considerable philosophical and expressive complexity. The way Ligon embodies Genet's thought in an austerely sensual object, giving it visual and material as well as verbal expression, is compelling" (131). Johnson goes on to describe the repetition of the sentences as like "chanting" that builds to the point of suggesting a pent-up anger or an accumulative deepening of thought. Moreover, the way the panels hang in space creates a kind of chapel-like or sacred space for contemplating race, art, and language.

In another series Ligon uses text by James Baldwin. In an entirely black work on paper with raised, barely legible letters, the quote he selects deals with the paradox that black people must use the language of the white majority to describe their own experience. It begins, "I was black and was expected to write from that perspective. Yet I had to realize that the black perspective was dictated by the white imagination." This sentiment resonates with Hurston's description of whiteness being used as a category by which to assess blackness. As Ken Johnson notes, "Here the blackness of both text and page suggests the dream of speaking in a language and out of a cultural background from which the black artist is not alienated. That this remains impossible is of the essence for Ligon; for it is the schizoid relationship of the African-American to a predominantly white culture—a culture he can neither wholly accept nor completely reject—that is fundamentally at stake" (131).

In a similar series of prints Ligon repeats the black on black theme with the first lines of Ralph Ellison's novel *Invisible Man:* "I am an invisible man." In this statement Ellison's unnamed protagonist is both proclaiming his identity in essential terms as "a man" and undercutting this declaration with the socially constructed modifier "invisible." As Ligon explains in *The Print Collector's Newsletter,* "Ellison uses the metaphor of invisibility to describe the position of blacks in this country—as ghost, present and real but, because of the blindness of racism, remaining unseen" ("Prints and Photographs"). Ligon uses the same metaphor in this work. The raised text creates the impression that it is rendered in Braille, further reinforcing that when people are blind to what is visible—as whites are when they do not see "invisible" blacks—they must "feel" their way into seeing, the tactile act becoming symbolic of the emotional effort required. Furthermore, as in similar works, the seemingly endless repetition of Ellison's phrases become incantatory, conjuring the visible out of what is perceived as invisible.

Finally, in a piece on permanent display at the Hirshhorn, *Black Like Me #2*, Ligon further complicates issues of racial identity by using the same stencil technique to consider lines from John Howard Griffin's *Black Like Me*. As discussed earlier, in the late 1950s Griffin, a white man, had his pigment altered so he would appear black and traveled throughout the segregated South in order to try to experience what life was like for African Americans who lived there. Although today the book seems almost romantic in its endeavor and its pious air of awakening and plea for racial tolerance, at the time it was published it was revolutionary. It established in a concrete way the need to understand oppression by making an imaginative identification, and Ligon's choice to use this text as a source, despite its current ambivalent status, is significant. The text Ligon chose, "All Traces of the Griffin I Had Been Were Wiped from Existence," states that Griffin, the white man he had been, was eliminated by his act of coloring his skin.

But as Robertson points out, "the pattern of smudges—different in each of Ligon's works—belies that claim. As one reads down the canvas, the black smudges are heavier and appear sooner than in other works. But many streaks of white remain, negating Griffin's claim that his whiteness had been wiped from existence" (161). Robertson interprets Ligon's meaning to suggest that race need not be so utterly defining as Griffin's text asserts and that a core of identity may exist apart from racial categories. Despite the ultimate failure of Griffin to totally erase his whiteness or to assume a black identity, Ligon also believes that the experience of transgression along racial lines—in this case a white man disguised as a black man—can lead to an understanding of a sense of otherness that "changes his life after he returns to the white world as well as while he is disguised as black."

After the stencils one encounters the final element in the installation *To Disembark*: nine etchings with a chine collé (a thin piece of high-quality paper glued to a less expensive backing paper) that mimic frontispieces of the nineteenth-century narratives. Although Ligon could not reproduce the entire text of ex-slave narratives in his exhibit, the specific role a title page can play is illuminated by L. Tongiorgi Tomasi in her analysis of image, symbol, and word on the title pages and frontispieces of scientific books from the sixteenth and seventeenth centuries. This seemingly remote historical context of the Renaissance shares with antebellum America two characteristic "nodal points." In the Renaissance period, the search for truth and the birth of new learning arising out of a critical revival of the old was paramount, just as in antebellum America veracity and liberation were the goals writers and abolitionists addressed. In both periods artists and intellectuals desired to introduce to the public a new cognitive aspect and a different way to perceive reality.

Tomasi also demonstrates how Renaissance title pages were carefully crafted and "gradually came to assume the form of a 'summa' and 'memoria' of the book" (372–73). Thus the title pages provide a synthesis and commentary on the ideas expounded in the book. Ligon exploits this quality of title pages to achieve an economy of form and space in his exhibit. Furthermore, the Renaissance title pages were designed to stimulate the curiosity of the reader, thus urging one to turn to the text to gain a complete understanding of the puzzle. Ligon, I believe, is also aware of how his title pages will tease the viewer into consulting the remaining texts he cannot include, be they actual ex-slave narratives or any variation on the slave narrative tradition.

This kind of attention to historical detail and precedent is evidenced in the fact that all the etchings of title pages are composed in nineteenth-century American literary vernacular and presented in authentic typefaces that Ligon researched carefully. Most of the text included on the title pages was composed by Ligon, just as an ex-slave would have written her own text. But Ligon replaces the Bible verses, antislavery poems, and white testimony that often appeared on the title pages of the narratives—documents culled from the dominant culture that served to vouch for the literacy, and by implication selfhood, of the black writer—with quotes from contemporary black authors such as bell hooks and Derek Walcott. Interspersing quotes from famous black personages with writings and comments of his own, Ligon reemphasizes that African Americans are still trying to disembark and that his experiences and attempts at identity construction are part of an ongoing process. Furthermore, his decision to supplant Euro-American authenticating text with African-American-authored validation has an interesting parallel in the work of Gwendolyn Brooks, the poet whose writing Ligon honored in the title of his installation.

At first Ligon's intention in alluding to Brooks is ambiguous, indeed almost ironic. Brooks's volume of poetry of the same title carries throughout it a theme that prioritizes the essential and the pan-African character and quality of black experience and identity, whereas Ligon's installation seeks to explore how African-American racial identity is uniquely a product of American experience and is socially constructed. An example of sentiments expressed throughout this volume of poems is the comment,

TO DISEMBARK

The Price
of the
Ticket

COMPRISING AN ACCOUNT OF THE AUTHOR'S BIRTH, PARENTAGE,
HIS EARLY YEARS, AND THE MANY HARDSHIPS AND SUFFERINGS HE ENDURES
ON HIS JOURNEY TOWARD FREEDOM

TO THE READER,
I have tried to present the truth, to lay
before the race a cross section of my own
life, to view my colored heart at close range.
If this effort may avail to stir myself and others to a more active pursuit of freedom and
self-love, then the object in sending it forth
will be accomplished.

G.L.

NEW YORK

1993

Untitled, 1993. Etching and chine collé, 71.1 x 53.3 cm (28 x 21 in.). Collection of the artist. Photo by Dennis Cowley.

"The blunt/blackness. That is the real thing" (28). Ligon's installation resists blunt descriptions of blackness even as he invokes their historical
presence to make his point that many features, racial and otherwise, are
present in the complex construction of character. But just as the title page
format points the viewer toward a fuller reading of the texts of slavery
embodied in the slave narrative tradition, his allusion to Brooks points us
to a deeper reading of her work, not just her poetry but her autobiographical writing as well.

Ligon's allusion to Brooks does not end with an appreciation of this
particular title and the poems of this volume. Searching Brooks's oeuvre
of writing reveals that in 1972 she wrote an autobiography, *Report from
Part One,* and that this text, as much as the volume of poems, provided a
model for this part of Ligon's installation. Brooks's own writings amount
to the process Ligon has narratively distilled into title pages in *To Disembark:* the process of on-going identity construction. In this autobiography,
Brooks describes herself in "the kindergarten of new consciousness" (86),
defining it in the explicitly black nationalist terms by which much of her
later work, including *To Disembark,* is identified.

In 1972, Brooks was just beginning to confront the implications of what
she saw as her uncritical acceptance of Euro-American literacy. In this
autobiography Brooks no longer accepts the authority of white models and
"masters." Structurally she questions the relationship between self and
literary conventions implicit in slave narratives, and in one section, "Prefaces," she mimics the slave narrative convention for providing authenticating documents from Euro-American culture but does so in African-
American terms. In place of white testimony, Brooks includes statements
from politically committed black intellectuals Haki Madhubutí and George
Kent, vouching for the reality of her "black consciousness."

Clearly Brooks's structural design and the political and aesthetic points
she makes through this design are paralleled in Ligon's own autobiographical enterprise. The runaway posters give details about his physical appearance and aspects, but the title pages are far more revealing. These etchings amount to an autobiography. Each different title—many of which
make use of actual titles chosen by ex-slave narrators and even titles of
contemporary works—reinforces Ligon's point about our life stories being composed of parallel and overlapping narratives. Some titles suggest
a thrilling or entertaining tale such as "The Life and Adventures of Glenn
Ligon, a Negro," or "Folks and Places Abroad." Another title page, "Incidents in the Life of a Snow Queen," reveals a more aesthetically shaped
sense of novelistic selection, a feature characteristic of the narrative Ligon

honors in this title, Harriet Jacobs's *Incidents in the Life of a Slave Girl.* "Pilgrimage to My Mother's Land" is also an allusive title, signifying on Robert Campbell's 1861 *A Pilgrimage to My Motherland. An Account of a Journey among Egbas and Yorubas of Central Africa, in 1859–1860;* but to the uninformed viewer this title implies a reverential homage. Several of the titles incorporate very modern and direct phrases within the nineteenth-century language, such as "Black Rage: How I Got Over: Sketches of the Life and Labors of Glenn Ligon" or "Black Like Me or the Authentic Narrative of Glenn Ligon." One title repeats the title of the installation and adds an element from the writings of James Baldwin, "To Disembark or The Price of the Ticket."

All reveal, as one proclaims, "some aspect of the author's birth, parentage, his early years, and the many hardships and sufferings he endures on his journey toward freedom." Each page also describes a different chapter of Ligon's life, including his actual confrontation with the influence of a dominant white culture that would define him: "The Life and Adventures of Glenn Ligon, a Negro who was sent to be educated amongst white people in the year 1966 . . . and has continued to fraternize with them to the present time." One particularly poignant example adds sexual orientation to the list of components of self used in identity construction and reads: "The Narrative of the Life and Uncommon Sufferings of Glenn Ligon, a colored man, who at a tender age discovered his affection for the bodies of other men, and has endured scorn and tribulations ever since." On several occasions Ligon comically signifies on his efforts as presenting a "panorama/mirror of oppression" or as the "commodification of the horrors of black life into art objects for the public's enjoyment." The cumulative result of the entire installation, though it has signifying moments of humor, is very poignant.

On these title pages Ligon sometimes names himself as author and sometimes iterates the convention slave narrators adopted in the interest of privacy and protection by proclaiming "Written by Himself," as a partial, if anonymous, declaration of identity. The most veiled self-portrait is "Incidents in the Life of a Snow Queen," where Ligon locates authorship as "Related by Herself." *Snow queen* is a term for black gay men who date white men exclusively. The accompanying description describes an "episode of blindness" as the result of the "fall of snow," a metaphor for a kind of fascination with whiteness implied by the term *snow queen.* Eventually her "ability to perceive light and dark" is restored. Ligon does not condemn interracial relationships but suggests some of the problems of blind fascination and the difficulty of maintaining these relationships in this society. What comes through clearly in this title page is Ligon's belief, reinforced by his inclusion of Hilton Als's comment that "every love affair is an act of conversion," that individual love between people of different color is a force of great "potential and hope" and also of "failure."

Ligon seems prepared to risk failure. On one title page he includes a typical address "To the Reader," in which he states his intention to risk, to present the "truth . . . to view my colored heart at close range." He continues by expressing hope: "If this effort may avail to stir myself and others to a more active pursuit of freedom and self-love, then the object in sending it forth will be accomplished." Individual conversion away from conventional stereotypes of identity is perhaps where we begin and it is this movement that Ligon's installation effects for the viewer.

What Ligon achieves through his contemporary reconstruction of slave narratives is precisely what ex-slave narrators hoped to achieve: He bridges the distance between other and self and forces us to consider how we and others construct their selves. As he writes at one point—in the role of a white person giving testimony—his presentation of "real life-like scenes presented in the PANORAMA are admirably calculated to make an unfading impression upon the heart and memory such as no lectures or books or colloquial expressions can produce." This disingenuous claim, while it appears to set his efforts above those of the original ex-slave narrators, actually points us back to the past for understanding. How we get there is offered up by Derek Walcott in a quote Ligon includes on one title page: "I had no nation now but the imagination."

ⓠ ⓠ ⓠ

> I strive to create an image that all mankind can personally relate to and to see his dreams and ideals mirrored with hope and dignity.
> —Charles White

Ligon's contribution of *To Disembark* to our cultural discourse on race and identity is especially significant when one appreciates that unlike the productive literary tradition, the representation of slavery in African-American visual arts is not common. In the history of African-American art as set forth by Romare Bearden and Harry Henderson in *A History of African-American Artists: From 1792 to the Present,* few artists are featured for having taken slavery as a specific topic for concern. But in nearly every instance there is a revealed relationship between words and images that underscore Glenn Ligon's later efforts.

The circulation in the mid-1800s of gross caricatures to depict black people made African-American artists sensitive to the issue of image portrayal. These caricatures were an attempt on the part of slaveholders and those who shared their beliefs to counter the abolitionists' efforts to demonstrate the humanity of African Americans through the literacy skills they displayed in writing slave narratives. It is these kinds of images, along with images crafted for abolitionist publications, that Ligon reproduces on the runaway slave posters. By including this range of imagery on his posters, Ligon does not distinguish for the viewer what original function each image served in different polemical contexts, but again points us away from the visual and toward the literary for complete understanding.

Still, *To Disembark* reinforces the fact that early in African-American history, image often was used in opposition to text and each represented the poles of the argument for and against slavery. As Bearden and Henderson point out, these insulting caricatures reached a flood-tide after the Civil War and became "a major instrument of achieving social and political control in both the South and the North, conveying their prejudicial message instantly to millions who would not have read a book or pamphlet or listened to a discussion" (xv). One reason why these images were such an effective tool for manipulating public opinion is that many white people who assumed they were superior also lacked literacy skills. Although this observation by Bearden and Henderson speaks loudly to the power of the image over the power of the word, it also presents for the artist the problem of the need to carefully and correctly convey images of an African-American self.

Ligon gets around the problems presented by this sensitivity to visual images by taking his cue from the literary slave narrative tradition. Ex-slave narrators, as bearers of the word, hearken back to the gospel writer John's imaging of Jesus as "the Word." Casting God as the Word becomes a literal or literary construction that Ligon transforms back into an image, but without the customary physical representation of humanity. In this sense he makes a further theological statement that acknowledges the scriptural reluctance to image or describe in physical terms the being of God. The spiritual representation of identity is set above the material representation of identity; but at the same time the artist shows how the spiritual and the material are inseparable in constructing human identity. The actual physical experiences of black humans are presented in all their heroic and painful reality, thereby forcing us to question how we could treat spiritual beings in such a way, an issue the poet David Dabydeen also raises by manipulating word and image, but from a very different perspective.

In "Turner," Dabydeen takes J. M. W. Turner's painting *The Slave Ship* as his inspiration, but unlike Ligon he does not set out to honor a neglected aesthetic tradition but to expose the colonial legacies of the canonical Western art tradition. In 1840, when abolitionist sentiment was gaining strength in America and abroad, Turner exhibited at the Royal Academy in London his finest painting in what is known as the sublime style: *Slavers Throwing Overboard the Dead and Dying,* commonly known as *Slave Ship.* He depicts a common scene in which ship captains ordered the drowning of sick slaves in order to claim their insurance value on the basis of goods lost at sea. As Dabydeen explains in his preface to *Turner: New and Selected Poems,* when John Ruskin reviewed the painting he praised it as representing "the noblest sea that Turner ever painted . . . the noblest certainly ever painted by man" (ix). Ruskin wrote a detailed account of the composition of the painting, dwelling on the genius with which Turner illuminated sea and sky, and claimed that "If I were to rest Turner's immortality upon any single work, I should choose this" (ix).

But as Dabydeen notes, "the shackling and drowning of Africans, was relegated to a brief footnote in Ruskin's essay. The footnote reads like an afterthought, something tossed overboard" (ix). So Dabydeen seeks, in picturesque words and striking images, to represent what is missing from Ruskin's prose and what is neglected in Turner's brushstrokes: the submerged head of the African in the foreground of the painting. That human figure, as Dabydeen comments "has been drowned in Turner's (and other artists') sea for centuries" (ix). In his poem Dabydeen awakens the figure and invents a biography, illustrating the difficulties in escaping Turner's representation of Africans as "exotic and sublime victims" (x).[4]

Throughout history African-American artists have used various strategies in their effort to represent black people as something other than "exotic and sublime victims." They became proficient in Western canonical styles and techniques while challenging them by using slavery as a thematic source or focal point for their artistic statements. Many abolitionists welcomed the assistance of sympathetic artists in their pursuit to represent people of African descent in a positive light in order to rally support for their cause, but their use of art as a vehicle to sway public opinion focused on portraiture. Artist and historian Richard J. Powell observes that after the *Amistad* case drew support for abolition, the demand for a reproduction of leader Cinque's image fueled an already established market for abolitionist imagery. As Powell remarks, "The idea that a portrait of a renegade slave could transcend topicality and symbolize human enfranchisement was an unlikely hypothesis, but by the 1840s this concept seemed not only feasible, but fitting" (G2).

Attempts to capture Cinque's image ranged from the earnest to the ridiculous. Among the more outrageous attempts to link image and character among people of African descent, Powell says that within a week of their incarceration, Cinque and his fellow Africans became the subjects of a phrenologist, who took measurements of their heads and gave detailed interpretations of each captive's character and personality. Plans were made for exhibiting not just the portraits but also the real Cinque and his fellow Africans. Although this was a common practice in nineteenth-century America and Europe, Powell maintains that in their displays of people of color, the abolitionists presented "black women and men who could talk, sing, read from Scripture and give testimony to lives lived under slavery's yoke as well as under the banner of freedom" (G2).

Powell cites some evidence that a "radical portrait tradition" that included many other black (and white) figures significant to the abolitionist cause was effective in counterbalancing their perceived characterization as members of a "lunatic fringe" and establishing them as "men and women worthy of cultural canonization" (G2). Ligon seems to appreciate both the exploitive and the redemptive quality of these early attempts to rehabilitate the image of people of color and uses both in his contemporary effort to explore slavery's ongoing influence. Although his work does not go so far as to propose himself as worthy of cultural canonization, the risk he takes by exposing his own identity and character and offering himself up as a new candidate for reconsideration places him directly in line with his enslaved ancestors and forces us to consider not just the issues his work brings to the fore but the very methods by which one is compelled to do so.

Apart from the portraiture tradition, most visual representations of slavery have been subtle. Among the first to evoke slavery as a trope was Robert S. Duncanson (b. 1823), who settled in Cincinnati, where his style became associated with the Hudson River School of painting. His most important work that considers slavery is *The Land of the Lotos-Eaters,* an allegorical painting inspired by a Tennyson poem. In "The Lotos-Eaters," the poet renders Odysseus's voyage after the Trojan War. He describes how the warriors, once they had found a peaceful island, never wanted to go home. Duncanson saw that for enslaved people the American wilderness was analogous to the land of the lotos-eaters. Positioned in Cincinnati, perched on the edge of slavery as the war loomed, he expressed in this painting the desire for peace and freedom from struggle and war. In other words, although this painting was informed by the experience of slavery, it recasts the experience to express the conflict in imaginative terms through the portrayal of another world that held allure and promise. Thus Duncanson participates in the word-as-image tradition in a unique way by taking the historical texts of Homer and Tennyson and using them as the basis for creating an image of a place where African Americans could live in freedom and peace.

Other artists who commented on slavery also did so in oblique but connected ways. Edward Bannister (b. 1828) painted portraits of black and white people who were significant participants in the struggle for emancipation. Edmonia Lewis (b. 1845), through the medium of sculpture, also honored important freedom fighters such as John Brown. To commemorate the Emancipation Proclamation—a text—she sculpted the work *Forever Free,* setting another precedent for the relationship between word and image. Henry Tanner (b. 1859) composed biblical paintings that made historical identification between the enslaved Israelites and enslaved Africans and thus participated in the word-as-image tradition by using the potential of recorded scriptural or narrative history to cast light on present circumstances.

By the time of the Harlem Renaissance, when formal slavery had been abolished, the notion prevailed that the resulting prejudice against African Americans could be reduced and alleviated by art. This belief was a more extended declaration of the humanity of African Americans than was offered for evidence by the slave narrative authors who excelled in literary skill. In describing this period, one of its exponents, James Weldon Johnson, exclaimed, "Through his artistic efforts the Negro is smashing [an] immoral stereotype faster than he has ever done . . . impressing upon the national mind the conviction that he is a creator as well as a creature . . . helping to form American civilization" (283–84). Johnson's comment displays an awareness on the part of African Americans that having settled the issue of their actual humanity in the struggle over slavery, African Americans had to establish their full entitlement to this humanity, which culture judges not by essential status alone but also by one's intellectual and aesthetic production. In this way, African-American artists of the Harlem Renaissance were engaged in a process Arthur Schomburg explains in the definitive text of the period, Alain Locke's anthology *The New Negro:* "History must restore what slavery took away" (231).

Aaron Douglass's (b. 1899) most powerful representation of slavery also points in the direction of its ongoing implications. In the murals he created for the Countee Cullen Branch of the New York Public Library, four panels depict aspects of the history of African Americans. The first panel focuses on the African legacy and its rhythmic dynamic. The second panel spans slavery and Reconstruction, figured in human images revealing the change from an enslaved person's doubt and uncertainty to his exaltation at the reading of the Emancipation Proclamation. From here it celebrates outstanding leaders from the African-American community who tried to seize the potential generated by the boon of freedom, but quickly moves into a depiction of union soldiers departing from the South as the Ku Klux Klan moves into view. In the last panel African Americans are shown fleeing north yet again, culminating in images that depict both the will for self-expression embodied in the Harlem Renaissance and the later confusion and frustration wrought by the Depression.

Hale Woodruff (b. 1900) also explored slavery as a historical topic for murals when he created the *Amistad* series, which gave tribute to the most famous episode of Africans who mutinied while being transported to slavery. Jacob Lawrence (b. 1917) has devoted a considerable portion of his efforts to chronicling in paint aspects of African-American history and created graphic portrayals of slavery in, for example, a children's book on Harriet Tubman. Around 1960, some African Americans in New York began gathering to discuss the notion of a black visual aesthetic. Led by Romare Bearden, Hale Woodruff, and others, they were inspired by the civil rights movement to begin articulating the role of the artist in addressing social conditions. They named their group Spiral, to denote progress, and created this forum to force "recognition of aesthetic aspirations and problems related to African-American artists' search for identity" (Bearden and Henderson 403).

As a group they never quite succeeded in generating a specific definition or articulation of a black aesthetic because they could not overcome the diverse viewpoints that reflected a dynamic characteristic of African-American public experience and private needs. Should art uplift and ennoble the race and treat topics specific to the African-American community, or should it be broad and inclusive enough to accommodate European and other influences and the idiosyncrasies of creative genius? In their search for an identifying style, they agreed that it should not be limited to black subject matter, but beyond this they came no closer to resolving the African-American identity crisis than W. E. B. Du Bois did when he formulated the notion of a double-consciousness. Between these poles of African and American, between essential and sociocultural constructs of self, is where African-American artists such as Glenn Ligon continue to find themselves.

However, throughout the development of African-American art and aesthetics—as it has been set forth by conventional standards of aesthetic judgment such as those rendered by Bearden and Henderson—black artists have been creating in forms and participating in traditions not customarily recognized by arbiters of aesthetic judgment. The folk art tradition in African-American culture is its oldest and most enduring. It testifies to a sensibility in which the perils attendant on double-consciousness and other binary constructions of identity are inconsequential.

The reason this bifurcation was not as keenly felt by folk artists is the transcendent component that informed and inspired much of their work. Creating out of what they found and responding to the movement of the spirit within, these "ordinary" artists carried on a tradition in which aesthetic sensibility was informed more by an African perspective of unity than by a Western consciousness of duality. These artists made beauty out of everyday objects—in pottery, textiles, wood carvings, ironwork, architecture, and funeral monuments—and further demonstrated that the creative spirit is not bound by social constructs but can manipulate context to serve a creative purpose. Neither racial and social status nor economic prosperity inhibited these artists. The work of these artists also preserved in more verifiable ways the retention of African aesthetic forms and beliefs.

As Dan Ben-Amos points out, relations between the arts have a particular poignancy in nonliterate traditional Africa. In such a society, he explains, "words do not have visual presence, images do not refer to canonic texts, script does not explicate pictures nor do pictures ironize verbal propositions. A whole set of relations between words and images which has been explored in literate societies is simply beyond the range of possibilities in traditional Africa" (223). Paradoxically, one finds in traditional African culture that in use and in performance, the verbal and visual arts are constantly intertwined. As Ben-Amos explains, "Rituals have both masks and myths, movements and songs. Oral narratives create, or build upon, known images in the mind, and proverbs could be the solutions for visual metaphoric enigmas. Artistic messages are both verbal and visual, and affect and meaning are expressed through the interdependence of words and images, sound and sight" (223). This kind of complex relationship among the arts, characteristic of traditional Africa, is also present in African-American folk art. The retention of African forms and ideas testifies to an enduring sense of identity that is essential in human terms and that persists despite and because of the complexities of societal constructions and influences.

To Disembark shares in this same spirit of shifting the inquiry into identity from an essentialist or socially constructed perspective by revealing how many contexts make up American social and historical constructs. In the process Ligon raises new explorative questions and pays homage, in indirect ways, to African and several African-American aesthetic traditions at once. His technical proficiency and recognition of the formal possibilities of manipulating text as image demonstrate his position in a postmodern aesthetic, but his very use of text as image and the inseparability of genres of expression derive from traditional African worldviews.

Abstract ideas about life and art play a crucial role in the relations between verbal and visual expression embodied in both African art and Ligon's installation. As in traditional African forms, words and images are on the same level of abstraction and embody a relationship not only to each other but also to the creative energy they embody. One distinctive form of creative energy is nommo, whereby the correct naming of a thing brings it into existence. As ex-slave narrators named themselves and brought their identities into articulate awareness by writing their texts, Glenn Ligon names himself and seeks to explore the elements of self that name him or that others would use to name him. He demonstrates the acquisition of this creative energy when his installation moves from "other" descriptions of himself found on the runaway slave posters to his self-descriptions when he casts himself as the author of slave narratives.

Ligon positions himself in a tradition evocative of African forms in which the aesthetic and the sacred cannot be distinguished from the prosaic and secular and it finds voice in the sounds Ligon selects to issue forth from the boxes. Ligon's use of sounds in the box component of the exhibit emphasizes the complex relationships among arts in traditional African culture, which are further reinforced by his selection of music that owes much in terms of rhythm and content to retained African ritual forms. The rhythmic and thematic emphasis is picked up again in the chanting effect created by the repetition of phrases on the stencils.

In a sacred space Ligon has created for the benefit of museum visitors, the sounds, both actual and silent, that chant to the viewer become a kind of incantation, calling forth a higher power to help one to participate in the ritual process of viewing (hearing and reading) the exhibit. Furthermore, his use of found words (such as those culled from the Hurston essay) and found formats from the past (runaway slave posters and title pages from nineteenth-century slave narratives) ties him to the folk art tradition, where one creates out of what is available and relevant in one's own culture or environment.

In addition to these general cultural and historical influences on Ligon's installation, there is also the specific precedent in the work of Charles White. Although Ligon does not acknowledge this influence, one can trace back to Charles White—particularly his portfolio collection of drawings known as the "Wanted Poster Series," published by the Heritage Gallery in Los Angeles in 1970—a direct antecedent for *To Disembark*. This corollary ties Ligon to both the visual folk and low-art and the high-art ends of his African-American heritage and its literary and visual traditions. Charles White was an accomplished draftsman who was committed to applying his talents in such a way that his art would be made available to millions.

Moreover, as Romare Bearden and Harry Henderson point out, "White sought to make a universal statement about the heroic efforts of humankind to be free of oppression" (405). During the civil rights struggle, White created moving portraits of black men and women against a background of old runaway slave "wanted" posters as one attempt to comment on oppression. In discussing the origins of this series, White describes an experience similar to Ligon's discovery of the image of Henry "Box" Brown. He came across some pre–Civil War posters advertising slave auctions and "wanted" posters for runaway slaves. He then took these found objects and used them as an image by which to search for past feelings and created a "Wanted Portrait Series."

White found the posters highly evocative and used them, complete with wrinkles and folds, as backgrounds for portraits of contemporary black Americans. One has a portrait of a twelve-year-old boy who could be purchased for thirty dollars. He rendered these images in a thin oil wash, combining sepia and black tones to create a startling clarity. The historical element, he realized, gives a haunting impact to these contemporary likenesses and asks us to consider what value we place on black life. Bearden and Henderson note that critics and art historians have largely ignored this series. Ligon's attempt to reintroduce the same historical context as a setting for exploring similar issues may compel us to take another look at the work of Charles White. Ligon's success may rest on the fact that unlike Charles White, he is not dependent on the actual representation of image in using this found source. For Ligon, the words themselves become the image and force us to consider in more literal and literary ways how we image black identity and constructions of self.

White, who wanted to create images that all humankind can personally relate to, saw his work as striving "to take shape around images and ideas that are centered within the vortex of the life experience of a Negro" (Fax 78). He selected this perspective because he found in "the life of my people . . . the fountainhead of challenging themes and monumental concepts." These specific themes and concepts, in turn, represent universal human conflicts, dreams, and ideals. The social and economic dislocation one uncovers in African-American experience White renders in his art as universally accessible because of his "stubborn, elusive, romantic belief that the people of this land cannot always be insensible to the dictates of justice or deaf to the voice of humanity" (Fax 78).

Ligon, who describes *To Disembark* as his first show "based on a single set of ideas" (Rubinstein 124), shares in the social and aesthetic concerns articulated by Charles White. Although Ligon's interest in slave narratives is recent and born of his fascination with their mode of address and "the conditions under which they were written," he sees in this historical model or context "certain parallels to my questions about audiences and cultural authority." Ligon traces a relationship between the conditions under which slave narratives were composed and "contemporary traces" in the current state of black representation in other media. He asks, "What are the conditions under which works by black artists enter the museum? Do we enter only when our 'visible difference' is evident? Why do many shows with works by colored people (and rarely whites) have titles that include 'race' and 'identity'?" Who is my work for and what do different audiences demand of it?"

In asking these questions Ligon confronts issues of cultural literacy in a postmodern world where deconstructive inquires into meaning hold sway and resist any fixed notion or closure about intended meaning. By manipulating two modes of literacy at once—the visual and the textual—he is exploring the historical process by which we have imaged and continue to image humanity. Literacy customarily is defined as the assigned meaning of a body of information that a group shares. What Ligon realizes is that what passes for literacy in contemporary culture is now more visual than it is verbal. To see has come to mean understanding, and the process of seeing has broad implications, especially for an artist who uses verbal texts as the basis for his visual work.

Ligon appreciates, as ex-slave narrators did, that once language literacy was developed, writing was seen as higher than visual and tactile modes. *Logos* began to carry the collateral meaning of thought and reason in the English word derived from it, *logic*. Noam Chomsky explores this collateral meaning in his analysis of language that defines deep structure as biologically innate but verbal literacy as something learned. It was this elevation of the written word that slave narrators seized in making their case. Knowing that on an essential level they were part of the human community, ex-slave narrators also understood how literacy is associated with higher development and used this association in their defense of their humanity.

However, thinking in concepts emerged from thinking in images by way of abstraction and symbolization, just as phonetic script emerged from hieroglyphics. The language of vision remains more universal than the language of words because it can create more possibilities for communicating ideas than the more than 3,000 languages currently in use. "Language," as one theorist has observed, "separates, nationalizes; the visual anneals" (Dondis 66). An inherent tension in the relationship between word and image arises out of our dualistic formations that ascribe different values to each mode during different phases of history.

Going back to the prophetic analyses of McLuhan and Koestler, we realize that despite our elevation of language as representative of a higher state, we have nonetheless become far more visual than literary in how we apprehend and perceive reality. McLuhan notes that this is true because as word order came to be substituted for inflection as a principle of grammatical syntax, there persisted, especially after the development of printing, a shift from the audible to the visual. Moreover, with the rise of industrialism and improved means of creating printed matter that included visual as well as literary elements, such materials were given new meaning and functions (Dondis x).

Advertising, which originally began as a way to inform, became a way to persuade. Ligon's use of advertisements for runaway slaves exploits both functions. He demonstrates how the existence of the posters also persuaded people to take a position on slavery: to either assist or resist the recapture of a fugitive. By moving this form into a gallery, he seeks to inform viewers of social conditions by first and loudly advertising their presence. However, these new forms and functions, along with the proliferation of printed images (and the impact of moving forms), made visual efforts far less effective. However, Ligon has exploited the potential in printing as one of an artist's tools by showing that it can be much more than a duplication process. By using styles and formats from the past and adapting them to his own vocabulary, he has reversed the usual filter-down process of form and style from the fine to the popular arts.

Ligon underscores the dominance of the visual, the notion that "our language culture has moved perceptibly toward the iconic. Most of what we know and learn, what we buy and believe, what we recognize and desire, is determined by the domination of the human psyche by the photograph" (Dondis 7). But Ligon also appreciates that although this state of affairs is a feature of contemporary life, it is also, as Koestler notes, a throwback. As Koestler writes, "Thinking in pictures dominates the manifestations of the unconscious, the dream, the hypnogogic half dream, the psychotic's hallucinations, the artist's vision. The visionary prophet seems to have been a visualizer, and not a verbalizer; the highest compliment we pay to those who trade in verbal currency is to call them 'visionary think-ers'" (Dondis 7). Ligon understands that this connection between elevated visionary thinkers and visual representation has all but been lost. As Tom Wolfe observed several decades ago, much of modern art is rendered in forms that require an accompanying text (usually in the form of art criti-cism or theory) to explain to the viewer what he or she sees, thereby cre-ating a climate of distrust rather than confidence between the artist and the viewing public.

Wolfe's concept of "the painted word," a comment on both the relation-ship between word and image and the relationship between the artist and the public, is one Ligon deconstructs in *To Disembark*. Ligon's turn away from abstract expressionism to conceptual art may be an expression of how pure form "isn't rich enough to deal with what's going on," but it may also be an expression of our circumstances wherein we no longer read or un-derstand the kind of visionary truth presented in narratives, especially slave narratives. *To Disembark* suggests that we can begin to learn to reread liberating texts by first seeing them. In the process he is making a state-ment about the change in art now recognized as a hallmark of early mod-ernism, a movement William Rubin describes as a change from narrative to iconic works.

Rubin remarks that after Picasso's rejection of narrative, style differences within paintings came to substitute for the articulations that had been provided by narrative. James Elkins, in his essay "On the Impossibility of Stories: The Anti-Narrative and Non-Narrative Impulse in Modern Paint-ing," suggests that narratives do survive in contemporary art but in "frag-mentary, oblique, and elliptical" constructions, "more like parts of a story or parts of many stories than like 'full' storied narratives" (348). Ligon rescues the narrative possibilities for visual arts that, though they bear traces of the fragmentary quality Elkins describes, as in the posters and title pages, also embody narrative in a full way because he points us back to narrative as a strategy to overcome both our mistrust of and uncompli-cated acceptance of iconic forms.

In *To Disembark*, Ligon gives us a new model for textimony. In creat-ing a literary and figurative form in which "linguistic and iconographic expression coexist and form a coherent whole" (Tomasi 373), he finds an alternative strategy for storytelling. He goes back to a traditional Ameri-can literary genre and recasts this form in an iconic representation. In so doing, he fills in the gaps of memory that would separate us from these forgotten and partially concealed textimonies. The icons he creates depend on narratives, both in an actual sense of derivation of form and in a thematic sense of content. He creates in the process what Elkins speculates might be "a special poetics" (364) that enables us to understand the narratives buried in ostensibly nonnarrative icons. Elkins cites a general mistrust on the part of the postmodern sensibility not with narrative per se but with its "directness, unity, and chronology" (364), features present in the slave narratives that kept them for so long out of the American literary canon. Our tendency is to judge direct, unified, and chronological narratives as somehow false, shallow, or naive. We are suspicious of narrative, just as we are suspicious of religious claims of human equality.

But Ligon shows us that narrative is where we begin to understand both the past and the present. In making the invisible past of slavery what our present imagination strives to see, Ligon affirms an observation made by Toni Morrison in her Nobel lecture that "narrative is radical, creating us at the very moment it is being created" (27). Revealing how a liberating theology can emerge from the most unexpected places and squarely positioned in the African-American aesthetic tradition, Ligon's art calls for a response from the viewing public. Between thing and concept, between reality and imagination, and between icon and word, Ligon reaches toward and personalizes the unknown or other. He reveals others to be just like him or just like us because of the essential narrative way we image humanity and despite the complicated contexts from which our identities emerge.

NOTES

1. Unless otherwise noted, quotes by Glenn Ligon are taken from the brochure prepared by the Hirshhorn for the exhibit of *To Disembark* (November 11, 1993–February 20, 1994) or personal correspondence between the author and the artist.

2. Ligon's entire oeuvre is characterized by a deeply personal engagement with the question of how African Americans' presence has been recorded, represented, and written into history, both by themselves and by others. Since mounting *To Disembark,* Ligon has exhibited several shows that further complicate issues of identity with a particular emphasis on black male constructs. The installation *Skin Tight* (1995) uses the form of a standard punching bag, juxtaposing the iconography of rap singers such as Tupac Shakur and Ice Cube with text by Muhammad Ali and Leon Spinks to examine boxing as an arena full of conflicted representations of black masculinity. The punching bag becomes the site where the black body is metaphorically worked with and worked over. Themes of sexuality, economy, race, and class are all evoked by this installation. In 1996 Ligon mounted a show at the San Francisco Museum of Modern Art that consisted of a three-part rumination on self-portraiture and the individual in relationship to collective histories and notions of group identity. Including images from the Million Man March, self-portraits, and news

clippings, journal notes, and other documents, each element is distinct yet related, reflecting both conceptually and visually the ways in which images of the self and the group are constructed and deployed and for what purpose.

3. The guard who was attending the exhibit when I viewed it noticed my intense fascination and my effort to scribble down notes and engaged me in conversation. A mature African-American man, he was quite moved by the exhibit and described for me how he watched the artist installing it. He was especially proud to show me something he had noticed that the artist (and I) had missed. In the sequence of stenciled lettering that spelled out "I am not tragically colored," in one of the repetitions of the phrase, the artist had omitted the negative modifier *not*. After the guard drew this fact to Ligon's attention, the artist declined to redo the stencil work. The guard, in telling me this, smiled a knowing smile and implied that the omission may have been a further comment on Ligon's enterprise that came not from his studied, conscious reflection, but from deep in his unconscious feelings.

4. Although not as emotionally charged as Dabydeen's poem, another interesting example of the subtle subversion of liberating black presence in favor of white voices is the exhibit "Words Like Freedom," mounted by the New York Public Library in 1989. This exhibit featured manuscripts, first editions, and personal letters that, because of their association with famous authors, have achieved a kind of iconic status for the word. Although the title is drawn from a poem by Langston Hughes, who along with a few other prominent African Americans is included in the exhibit, the bulk of the exhibit that proclaims to be about "Afro-American books and manuscripts residing in the Berg Collection," features the work of what the curator calls "classic writers" who are white. Furthermore, the curator claims that the Berg Collection, with its "specialization" on English and American texts, is an "unlikely" source for black writing. See Richard Newman's *Words Like Freedom* (New York: New York Public Library, 1989).

5 Negotiating the Differences: Anna Deavere Smith

See what a scourge is laid upon your hate.
That heaven finds means to kill your joys with love.
—William Shakespeare

On the same day in September 1993 on which Yasser Arafat and Yitzhak Rabin shook hands on the White House lawn, members of a Palestinian and an Israeli theater group shook hands in an agreement to stage an unprecedented collaborative production of Shakespeare's *Romeo and Juliet*. They chose the story of the doomed lovers because, as Israeli director Eran Baniel explained, the play sends a critical message: "There is only one alternative to peace—death" (Blumenfeld C1). As the group worked to achieve its goal, ironies deep inside Shakespeare's text took on their own dramatic life and small symbols became potent reminders of the perils inherent in collaboration. Conflicts over the appropriate site to stage the production led to an unsatisfactory compromise to hold the play in an old warehouse in Jewish West Jerusalem. Doves inhabited the warehouse when the company first moved in. Unable to trap or scare away the noisy and messy birds, they finally called in an exterminator. When the actors arrived the next morning for their peace project, they found the doves, wings twitching, dying on the stage.

Cultural differences necessitated that every aspect of the production be discussed and negotiated. They decided that the Montague and Capulet families would be represented by Arabs and Jews, respectively, and each family would speak in its native tongue among each other, but when speaking outside the family all would speak Hebrew, the language of the occupation. Weapons used during the Intifada would be used during fight scenes. For the ending they decided that in lieu of the reconciliation scene between the families, the cast would gather and repeat the compelling words of the prologue. This change suggested recognition on the part of the actors that although their gesture in mounting the play was significant, there are no simple solutions to the problems that for so long have divided these people. For unlike the "two households, both alike in dignity" who from their children's death learned to "bury their . . . strife" (Shakespeare 41), the actors knew from experience that the tragedy of Romeo and Juliet was bound to be repeated as it had been for many years.

Despite financial problems and opposition from both Israelis and Palestinians, including death threats issued from both sides, the group continued and eventually mounted a production in the summer of 1994. Although we may never know what effect this production had on the people for whom it was performed—indeed, even members of the cast claimed to still be unable to set aside preexisting hostilities and prejudices—the show went on and a message was sent. For the most part, critics were unimpressed with the aesthetic merits of the production, but the cast clung to their belief that their efforts were successful if only in bringing together the actors. Those involved in the production held onto the hope that they might have had a personal effect on those who viewed the production by bringing people out together and by causing them to think about what their toil strove to mend, what our impatient ears tend to miss.

Sending such a message is also the motive behind the theatrical work of Anna Deavere Smith, who once remarked, "I went to an acting class and saw somebody change before my very eyes. And I thought people can change. I know social change is possible because I see this individual changing right before my eyes" (Thacher 8). A devout student of Shakespeare, in interviews Smith repeatedly draws attention to the fact that "if it hadn't been for Shakespeare, I wouldn't be where I am because it was my Shakespeare teacher who got to me" (C. Martin 55). Through her study of Shakespeare, Smith became fascinated with how the spoken word works in relationship to a person's psychology. "It's the manipulation of the words that creates the character, not just the words, not just the emotions. . . . In Shakespeare, the words held not just the psyche of the person but also the psyche of the time" (Lahr 90). She also describes her encounter with Shakespeare in religious terms as a kind of epiphany or "transcendental experience" that combined both terror and mystery (C. Martin 56). A search to recreate this experience of mysterium tremendum led her to continually explore language and its effects, leading Barbara Lewis to observe that "Talk, the word, is central to Smith's theatre" (55).

Smith admits that she never duplicated her epiphenomenal experience in actual ways, but she describes how she came to make connections between language and the desire to explain her feelings. For example, while she was reciting dialogue of the nurse in "Romeo and Juliet"—a character who "goes all around the block to say a simple thing"—what struck her was how the nurse remembers Juliet's age by remembering the expression on Juliet's face when she no longer wanted to breastfeed.[1] Reciting the lines impressed upon Smith the recognition that "the process of being in the world is a process of learning the world as a place full of attractive and unattractive and warm and frightful things. The power of life is that we're always in that friction. It's never heaven. If there's a heaven, it's never pure bliss" (B. Lewis 59).[2]

Smith's attempts to explore the relationship between words and human psychology are best represented in the series of theater or performance pieces she has written, produced, and performed all across America for over a decade titled *On the Road: A Search for American Character.* Smith creates the pieces by interviewing people in select locales and later performing them using their own words. As she describes it, her goal "has been to find American character in the ways that people speak" (*Fires* xxiii). She believes that if she can find a way to "inhabit the words of those around me" then she can "learn about the spirit, the imagination, and the challenges of my own time, firsthand" (*Fires* xxv). Her desire is to hold a mirror up to diverse groups to expose the motives and meanings behind their association and in the process to generate for the public what Gayle Wald calls "theatrical compassion" (8).

Smith's choice of *On the Road* as the title for her enterprise elaborates and extends two familiar endeavors associated with the same title: the novel by Jack Kerouac and the television program created by Charles Kerault. Her work has also been compared to the documentary writings of Studs Terkel. But she goes beyond the exploratory hedonism of Kerouac, the nostalgia of Kerault, and the reportage of Terkel to investigate in her liberating "theatre of testimony" not just issues of ethnicity and American character, but fundamental issues of identity that underlie all these investigations. "Art is transformative" (Thacher 8), Smith believes. And she demonstrates her belief when she takes the words of other people and repeats them to audiences all over the country while transforming herself into the author of those words.[3]

An associate professor of drama at Stanford, Anna Deavere Smith comes from a fairly conventional background. She was born in Baltimore, Maryland, the first of five children in a solidly middle-class family. Smith claims that although she was a mimic as a child, she never wanted to grow up to be a movie star. Rather, she pursued acting because she was "interested in social change," and unwittingly ended up in acting class, where she was "stunned at how the process of acting was about transformation." Part of her exploratory personality she attributes to growing up the "experiment" of integration (B. Lewis 62). She learned that the world can be an indifferent place and that even in the communities of the academy and the theater, where she is most at home, "the dominant culture decides when we will be hidden and when we will be seen" (B. Lewis 62). After college she made her way to New York. It was there, while supporting herself with sporadic appearances on soap operas, that Smith began conducting acting workshops, developing her method and discovering her mission.

Smith developed the method that would lead to *On the Road* as exercises to teach students to experience language more fully. She began approaching people she encountered who resembled participants in her workshop, hoping they would agree to be interviewed so their words could be used or spoken by her students. In exchange, the interviewees were invited to see themselves performed. In her first such experiment there were twenty people on stage and twenty people in the audience.

Smith continued to use the interviewing technique, but rather than asking a troupe of players or students to create each character, she began to assemble one-woman shows in which she played all the parts herself. Despite her singular presence, Smith maintained a sense of inclusion by using the pronouns *us* and *we* in relation to everybody for two reasons: to avoid appearing confrontational and to force the audience to "feel that it's you and me. My experience of the interviews I included was that there was an 'us' before I left" (C. Martin 48). From these simple exercises, her ambition has evolved into an enterprise wherein she seeks to "capture the personality of a place by attempting to embody its varied population and varied points of view in one person—myself" (C. Martin 48).

Smith describes the goal of *On the Road* as creating a kind of theater "that would have a different relationship to the community than most of the theatre I was seeing. It would be a kind of theatre that could be current . . . capture a moment and as quickly as possible give that moment back to the people" (Kaufman G11). In developing pieces for *On the Road,* she observed how "inhibitions affect our ability to empathize" and traced this inhibition to the lack of vision engendered by racism and prejudice (*Fires* xxvii). Smith is blunt in her refusal to allow any standard of privilege—be it race, class, or gender—to relieve people of the responsibility to see clearly, and she believes that the theater despite its sometimes exclusionary practices, is an ideal place to confront these issues. By opening up the world of the theater to new voices and visions, Smith makes a larger statement about the quality of democracy in America. As she writes,

> If only a man can speak for a man, a woman for a woman, a Black person for all Black people, then we, once again, inhibit the spirit of the theatre, which lives in the bridge that makes unlikely aspects seem connected. The bridge doesn't make them the same, it merely displays how two unlikely aspects are related. These relationships of the unlikely, these connections of things that don't fit together are crucial to American theatre and culture if theatre and culture plan to help us assemble our obvious differences. (*Fires* xxix)

One especially useful way to appreciate Smith's enterprise is offered by Victor Turner's concept of "social dramas." In his anthropological study of symbolic human action in society, Turner probed the ways in which social actions of various kinds acquire form through "the metaphors and paradigms in their actors' heads (put there by explicit teaching and implicit generalization from social experience)," which in certain intensive or conflict-ridden circumstances generate new forms and metaphors to reflect social concerns (13). These intensive periods arise when society is "betwixt and between" agreed-upon systems of order or in a state Turner defines as liminality. In a liminal state one can stand outside personal and social positions to formulate alternative social arrangements and encourage others to assent to innovation. Furthermore, as these times invite innovation, they also become occasions to reaffirm "root paradigms" of culture—ideals such as liberty, justice, and equality—and to reinvest them with new meaning.

The social dramas that emerge in liminal times do so from abstract cultural domains or "fields" where paradigms are formulated, established, and come into conflict, but it is in specific "arenas" or concrete settings that abstract paradigms are transformed into symbolic metaphors by the actions of "lead actors" in these social dramas. The desired result of such actions is the generation of a new feeling of commitment, where the persistence of cherished values is recognized as "a striking aspect of change" (32). The liminality of episodes of conflict therefore is a "sacred" time in Turner's formulation because it provides the opportunity for self-conscious reexpression of theological and philosophical values—root paradigms—that people lose sight of when society is stable and complacent. "Communitas or social antistructure" is the creative alternative to structure, and it is generated by conflict, which is the other side of cohesion. "Structure is all that holds people apart, defines their differences, and constrains their actions," whereas communitas is "often a sacred condition or can become one" (47). The coherence of a completed social drama is a function of communitas, and that is what Anna Deavere Smith provides in the domain of theater.

Smith saw the episodes of conflict that erupted in Crown Heights and Los Angeles and determined that these locations were appropriate arenas for her to go to in search of American character.[4] Out of these incidents she created the communitas of *Fires in the Mirror* and *Twilight*. Both plays explore ethnic relations, reveal our "root metaphors," and demonstrate how in America "identity is always being negotiated" (*Fires* xxxiii). In Crown Heights in particular, Smith saw two clearly different groups of people who were "defining in every breath they took the melting pot idea of American character" (Kaufman G11). Smith also observed that in Crown Heights "everyone wears their beliefs on their bodies—their costumes. You can't pass," and came to the seemingly paradoxical conclusion that "Crown Heights is not melting pot and I really respect that" (C. Martin 46).

Taken together, these remarks underscore the basic tension between individuals and their communities that her dramas explore in contemporary settings but that emerge from historical conditions and eternal human conflicts. Both incidents are essentially social dramas, narratives that reveal "more known traditions that we can draw from—for example, [in Crown Heights] the language of African Americans that draws up images of slavery and the language of the Lubavitcher that draws up images of the Holocaust. And the whole nation understood those images" (Kaufman G11). In Los Angeles the community is more diverse, with Latinos and Korean Americans as participants in the drama. It is also more spread out geographically. Furthermore, as Smith notes, there are "many more twists and turns to the story . . . although the uprising was spurred on because a black man was beaten, you also have the reverse image, with the beating of Reginald Denny" (Kaufman G11).

In each play Smith tries to display authentically the apparent ethnicity of people as a way to underscore the basic humanity of people in all their differences. By showing how issues of race and difference figure in the character equation of creating identity, Smith demonstrates that she understands the condition author Thomas Keneally describes when he observes that in the natural and necessary process of self-definition we tend to locate ourselves as members of a particular "tribe" with its own mores and find ourselves "tempted to believe in the inferiority of the culture and mores of other groups." Keneally thus concludes that "prejudice is the hairy backside of what we all need: a sense of identity" (Keneally, "Holocaust" 7).

Smith's efforts in both these endeavors are directed not just at observation but at solution. Her notion of giving back to the community is her version what Charlayne Hunter-Gault calls "a creative approach to issues we're all struggling to handle" (Kaufman G11). But Smith is careful not to set herself up as one with the answers. Her interest lies in revealing "the complexity of the issue, not trying to solve it" (Kaufman G11). Her goal is to engage people, to get them to pay attention to each other and, if possible, get them talking and able to reconsider attitudes. "What I want to do is to invite people to listen differently. I want to have people in the same room who normally would not spend five minutes with each other. It's important that people come together to do this thing called theatre" (Kaufman G11). Smith is trying to present a standard of "truth" that is not actual in a metaphysical sense, but representational in a contextual sense. By drawing our attention to different perspectives on truth, she also shows us what is possible in terms of social justice and action. The critic John Lahr asserts that "in this heroic undertaking, she is conducting one of the most sophisticated dialogues about race in contemporary America" (90).

Smith's "dialogue" is also significant for what it shares with the slave narrative tradition. She describes her work as not just theater, but also "community work . . . low anthropology, low journalism; it's a bit documentary" (B. Lewis 56). Accordingly, she has been characterized as a performance artist, a cultural anthropologist, a documentarian, and a biographer. The director at the Mark Taper auditorium even calls her "the closest thing to a professional athlete I know. There's a willingness to go out into the field of play and just do it" (Lahr 92). By creating this eclectic mix, she evokes many of the formal and effective features of the slave narrative tradition: blending dry reportage of actual incidents with emotional appeals in creating an aesthetic work, turning a public venue over to the private world of the disenfranchised to give them voice, and revealing how people use language, as ex-slave narrators did, to describe things often forbidden or veiled not only in public discourse but also in literature or the theater.

Richard Hornby observes that her work has also reinvigorated the concept of a regional theater, further empowering those traditionally distanced from mass influence. Hornby notes that in the late nineteenth century the theater began developing a star system in which stock companies disappeared and regional theaters booked a succession of touring plays. Smith's work, which developed out of a regional theater setting, does not rely on the star system and in this sense also parallels the slave narrative tradition, in which individual performers do not matter so much as the roles they play; star quality is subsumed in the presentation of characters who force a recognition of their character. Finally, as one who gives voice to the voice-less, Smith functions like the editors and amanuenses of original slave narratives, or like Miss Jane's editor, who searches out a story he believes needs to be told. In the process we are given, as ex-slave narrators once gave us, a new framework from which to assess race and class in Ameri-can culture and a different standard by which to evaluate the canon of American literature.

Smith believes that "the process of creating literature is natural. It isn't dependent on a pen and paper. It's a person using their voice and the making of words to come to the consciousness of what they know" (Lahr 90). Convinced that everyone has a poem in them, she interviews subjects for as long as it takes for them to "come into character . . . to discover their own personal literature" (Kaufman G11). She views her method as col-laboration, actually writing a poem with her characters; that is how she sets down dialogue for publication, falling unpunctuated down the page.[5]

All the people she depicts are actual people who played some role in the social dramas she explores and whose words she has collected in interviews she speaks verbatim. Although she relies on "the kindness of strangers" to willingly offer up their stories, Smith found that everyone she interviewed wanted to talk: "Everybody felt there was something unsaid" (Kaufman G11), indicating their need to express their feelings and also testifying to Smith's interviewing skill, which "like the Billie Holiday song . . . asks heartache to come in and sit down" (Lahr 90).

When Smith conducts interviews, her interest lies not so much in what is said as in how it comes out. She rehearses with earphones on and plays back unedited talk and speaks the words until images and gestures emerge from rhythms. Smith's performances are meticulous as she assumes not just the actual speech of her characters but also their speech patterns and mannerisms, believing that "speech is a physical act" and that "the body has a memory just as the mind does" (*Fires* xxv). Her investigation into how different characters embody or inhabit language differently creates a style of performance Carol Martin calls "hypernaturalistic mimesis—in which she replicates not only the words of different individuals but their bodily style as well" (45).

Yet Smith does not consider herself an impersonator or impressionist. "The big difference," she explains, "is that when you impersonate some-one . . . you give an intelligence to what may seem to be random gestures, and once you point out to the audience that the person does this or that, an impersonator is going to be tempted to exaggerate. . . . I don't do that.

What I try to do is create a kind of document of what the person said, and the physical part follows" (Kaufman G11). Just as she "wears" characters' words and mannerisms, in her productions she relies on scant props and minimal clothing changes to symbolically convey something about the characters she represents. A change in headgear may be all it takes to transform her from a Lubavitch rebbe to a rapper.

Smith's theatrical method is a cultural transformation. It sets her in the locations, mannerisms, and speech of the subjects and shows the audience where the subjects come from, what they do, how they speak, and what they feel. Smith's enterprise is risky, for as she candidly admits, she cannot afford to have an opinion and must strive to show all sides while favoring none. To have an opinion would diminish, perhaps even silence, the very voices she is trying to amplify. And there is also the personal risk that her "willingness to walk in other communities will reflect badly on me in my own community" (Kaufman G11). How Smith honors her community is evidenced in the way she aligns herself with several African-American aesthetic traditions.

Like a folk artist, she creates out of what is available, using found objects such as dialogue culled from interviews or basic elements of wardrobe. She animates the subjects that are too often perceived as objects and reveals the spirits within. She takes the lives that society would throw away or ignore and invests them with value. Like a quiltmaker, she creates a verbal patchwork of pieces that she sews together with her own constant bodily presence. But despite the temptation to surrender the everyday use of these quilts to become museum pieces, her quilts retain their intended function, becoming a cover that envelops in intimate conversation characters and audience members who probably would never share the same room together.

As one critic explains, "In making the audience hear the characters, Smith is also showing it how to listen to the strangers in its midst. She creates a climate of intimacy by acknowledging the equality of the other" (Lahr 93). Finally, like a jazz musician, Smith adopts an improvisational style as each performance of *On the Road* and each subject she tackles "comps on the head" or improvises on the theme of identity and difference. She adds or subtracts characters to suit the needs of particular audiences or her own evolving ideas so that each performance is unique and cannot be duplicated fully. Like jazz compositions, her performances are always works in progress.

In apparent contrast to what goes on "outside" the theater, Smith creates a sacred space for equal representation wherein concepts of identity are broken down and customary distinctions between high and low art are deconstructed. She replaces the stylized language of the theater with the no less stylized language of everyday speech. Although Smith could be perceived as using a technique that involves theft—the appropriation of other's voices—she can also be perceived as practicing the art of giving, re-presenting or returning others' voices to them as textimony.

The words she amplifies are precisely those that are lost in journalistic accounts and those that describe events that result when words themselves do not suffice. Smith's theater pulls the audience into a reexamination of events they have seen only through the media, to see the events anew through the stories of the participants. In the process of eliciting everyone's personal literature, Smith is also making a larger statement about the condition of those traditionally seen as oppressed. Often we deny that those who are oppressed need to seek opportunities for imaginative expression, assuming that mere survival constitutes the whole focus of their lives. By revealing the hidden poetry that emerges out of the most conflict-ridden situations, Smith shows us that this assumption is just another way to objectify the oppressed and deny them full humanity.

To fully appreciate what Anna Deavere Smith contributes to our cultural dialogue, her mission and method must be viewed as inextricably bound. Her missionary zeal is rooted in a complex and thoughtful appreciation of aesthetic theory and dramatic performance techniques. She describes her fascination with and repeated references to the relationship between language and character as the attempt by a photographer to capture a character in physical image; she wants "to capture character linguistically, to capture what the spoken word has to offer us about character" (Kaufman G11). The basis for her notion of theater is rooted in speech-act theory and her own Africanized or spiritualized version of method acting. The result is a liberating theology of theater.

While developing her liberating theater of textimony, Smith encountered Stanislavsky and applied some of his theories of method acting; for example, she describes her goal as an interviewer as persisting until a psychological through-line is reflected in language. But she also resists what she sees as the limitations of this approach. "The through-line always made me feel bad in teaching, reading, and trying to write plays" (C. Martin 50). She objected in particular to aspects of Stanislavsky's technique in which objectives—little and super—are graphed with straight lines and arrows. Smith came to appreciate that method acting locks identity into place instead of letting it breathe and transform, as it does in real life. Method acting and psychological realism require actors to look inside themselves and build a character through their experiences.

To Smith, this kind of exercise is narcissistic (Thacher 9) and prevents her from creating a theatrical form that is socially engaged and not ego-centric. The reasons for her discomfort with this form of acting became fully apparent to Smith when she began reading a book about African philosophical systems "and saw a picture of a wheel that had all these little spikes with arrows pointing towards the center. I knew than that I wanted to try to find a way of thinking or a structure that was more like that" (C. Martin 51).

Smith connects this circular structure with the black church in America, which she sees as "not only about speaking to one God. The whole thing is supposed to be an occasion to evoke a spirit" (C. Martin 51). In resisting the linear through-line, she refined her method and began to see her thought processes as more organic and circular. Remembering her grandfather's words, "that if you say a word often enough it becomes you" (C. Martin 51), Smith believes her power as an artist comes from not just what people tell her but how they tell her something that makes a whole-soul impression on her psyche, an experience she describes as becoming "possessed, so to speak, of the person" (C. Martin 51).

Her theories on acting parallel and serve as a model for what I am suggesting a liberating theology can accomplish because acting "is becoming the other," using the other rather than the self as a frame of reference. Smith's technique, which strives to begin with the other and come to self, empowers the other, in contrast to method acting techniques that "come to a spiritual halt" precisely because they are so self-oriented and see self "as the ultimate home of the character. To me, the search for character is constantly in motion. It is a quest that moves back and forth between the self and the other" (*Fires* xxvi–xxvii).

What Smith is after is "not psychological realism. I don't want to own the character and endow the character with my own experience. It's the opposite of that. What has to exist in order to try to allow the other to be is separation between the actor's self and the other" (C. Martin 52). This kind of enterprise involves struggle, Smith reminds us,

> as well it should—the struggle that the speaker has when he or she speaks to me, the struggle that he or she has to shift through language to come through. . . . Psychological technique is built on metaphors for a reason. I believe it's quite organic. You listen to some of the characters and you begin to identify with them. Because I'm saying the stuff over and over again every night, part of me is becoming them through repetition—by doing their performance of themselves that they do. I become the 'them' that they present to the world. For all of us, the performance of ourselves has very much to do with the self of ourselves. That's

what we're articulating in language and in flesh—something we feel inside as we develop an identity. (C. Martin 57)

Her final goal is that somehow the transference she experiences as a performer will be passed on to the audience. How this transference might be accomplished Smith explains by speech-act theory: "Theatre is action, but in the beginning was the word. And the word was all. And speech is action. Theatre is action. . . . The way action happens in the theatre is through the propulsion of words. The text is spoken to push action forward. . . . And on a less obvious level, on a less literal level, there's a visceral action that's going on so that the words you hear in the theater don't just go to your head, but they go into your whole system, and if there's a catharsis it's because the words get into you" (B. Lewis 58).

Smith appreciates a concept central to speech-act theory: that words do things and actions say things. Words are "expressions whose function is not to inform or describe but to carry out a 'performance,' to accomplish an act" (Felman 12). Furthermore, she observes that the power of the speech of people backed up by crowds can frighten people, as they did in Crown Heights and Los Angeles. People with the power of the word know that their words cause action, so theater is speech as action, but in a context where individuals have agreed to participate in the language of the other, a communal language.

Still, Smith believes "that at the same time we speak communally, we also speak specifically," and that the specificity of individual voices must not be lost or appropriated. As she explains, "Part of the glory of humanity is the potential for understanding the specific and coming together around it. If we kept our ears clean, we could speak more in the specific and wouldn't have to think that the only way to speak is in this communal way" (B. Lewis 58). What Smith tries to offer everyone is a way to read the texts that are implicated in ways of seeing, believing, and feeling. Events such as those that occurred in Crown Heights and Los Angeles require an interpretive framework that allows for both individual expression and communal understanding. As she says, she is "trying to find the tools for thinking about difference as a very active negotiation rather than an image of all of us holding hands" (C. Martin 53).

Smith shares with Edward Said a profound recognition of how identities that emerge out of specific contexts travel by way of text. It is only by understanding how text "travels"—how it remains contextual and nonneutral, as Said asserts—that any theory or method can be applied to the most volatile struggles for cultural hegemony. In *The World, the Text, and the Critic,* Said observes that "texts have ways of existing that even in the most rarefied form are always enmeshed in circumstance, time, place, and society—in short, they are in the world, hence worldly" (35). His concept of borrowed or "traveling theory" therefore is an acknowledgment that ideas can and do move from place to place and across boundaries of time, but it also describes what happens when the formulations of an activist witness and participant in a particular historical event pass into the realm of pure academic discourse. These formulations run the risk of being watered down or entirely disconnected from the human life that created them.

Because Said identifies himself as an "exile," one who is not at home in his own culture of origin nor in his present location, he believes his view engenders a complex mode of identity that can tolerate the polyphony of many voices playing off against each other without the need to reconcile them. Accordingly, Smith strives to close the historical and actual gaps between people without destroying the differences between each moment and between individuals. Like Said, Smith uses images of motion as she attempts to discern who can move in space, how people pass between borders of identity, at one point even recalling an image that was especially liberating for enslaved people in America: the Underground Railroad (C. Martin 54). In the process she articulates a central problem inherent to the slave narrative tradition as it functions for liberating theology when she observes that "in terms of passing up and passing down, it's probably harder for a white person to pass in" (C. Martin 55).

Smith's performative mimicry is designed to show us how to pass in by diminishing the critical detachment that prevents one from seeking direct engagement with others. In the process, she indicts those who do not recognize that "the dominant 'I' needs the coded 'other' to function" (Snead 4). By facilitating a radical empathy, she enables the viewer a transformative slippage across socially produced identities of race, nation, gender, and class. Or as she expresses her intent in the introduction to *Fires in the Mirror,* "The spirit of acting is the travel from self to the other" (xxxvi).

Travel from self to the other requires that all voices be heard, but few hear any but their own voices or the voices of their chosen representatives. Still, the very boundaries that divide people also provide them safe support and valuable constructs of identity, so taking them down is not always easy or even desired. Like Said, Smith suggests we select a mode of being that develops "multifaceted identities" and a more "complex language" because her liberation theater has convinced her that "identity is in some ways a process towards character. It is not character itself" (*Twilight* xxv).[6]

Said's call for a fluid identity that can tolerate and initiate change while also being bound to time and circumstance is embodied in Smith's theater. Whereas her notion of identity is performative and shifting, constructed in and by identifications and articulated in narrative as a kind of affiliation or re-presentation of what we encounter, her singular presence serves as a metaphor for how such diversity can also be grounded and unified, so that what we encounter can be incorporated into self. By activating her imagination, she identifies with others in such a way that she can reproduce the historical specificity of the feelings she engages without descending into distant discourse. In so doing, she establishes herself as working soundly within the conventions of the slave narrative tradition of textimony. Furthermore, the challenge of representing identity as fluid, or as character in process, she claims as a spiritual commitment by using language characteristic of an African-American theological aesthetic: call and response. She sees her work as "a call to the community" whereby she can be part of the examination of their problems by demonstrating the need for eclectic groups of people to actively "break the silence" about race and participate in dialogue (*Twilight* xxiv).

Like many secular artists considered in this study, Smith turned to the African-American religious experience to achieve this aim. She draws on her experiences "as a girl in the Black church . . . not just talking back to the preacher, but talking to God" (Cain 66). Smith advances her technique by associating her enterprise with the slave narrative tradition of textimony, emphasizing further the need to "lift the veil" in order to engage the oppressed in their own liberation and to wake the oppressor to a new way of seeing reality. Indeed, by using a call-and-response method to "provoke a lot of other people to create theatre that inspires the audience to participate," she hopes her work "will also inspire people who don't come to the theater to come to the theater" (Cain 66). By ritualizing empathy, Smith urges all who view her dramas to see self as other, but also to change the way they see self. And if those who enjoy entitlements are willing to pay the price of the ticket, they can participate in the same experience.

Her reliance on the movement of spirit, her belief in the transformative power of language, and her affirmation of the healing aspects of ritualistic, performative experience all point to a liberating theology that characterizes the slave narrative tradition. It is no surprise that critics and scholars use religious terms to describe Smith's work. Carol Martin describes Smith's performative language as "conjuring" (46) and her method as that of a "spirit doctor" who "brings ancestors or other spirits in contact with the living—in the presence of the community of the audience" (45). Richard Schechner writes that Smith's way of working is less like that of a "conventional, Euro-American actor" and more like that of an African, Native American, or Asian "ritualist" or "shaman" ("Anna Deavere Smith" 63). Schechner explains that he see Smith working "by means of a deep mimesis, a process opposite to that of 'pretend.' To incorporate means to be possessed by, to open oneself up thoroughly and deeply to another being" ("Anna Deavere Smith" 63).

Thus Schechner finds the language of spiritual healing the most appropriate to describe how Smith's drama operates. Schechner is prominent among drama critics for applying ritual analysis to the theater. His approach to theater, centering on the ideas of environment and performance, depends on studies in traditional religion, especially shamanism, and his work does much to illuminate the meaning of rite as an orchestration of symbols. In *Environmental Theatre*, Schechner emphasizes the theatrical experience as a total experience or "total immersion" that becomes transformative for cast and audience alike. For there to be total environment, the audience cannot just be spectators outside the drama but must be participants, a part of the environment that makes the drama. Smith's work provides Schechner a classic case study for the kind of interpretation he advances.

As Schechner describes her method, Smith composes her performances much as a ritual shaman might investigate and heal a patient. By closely consulting with the "patients"—opening to their intimacy and listening and looking closely at those she interviews—Smith goes beyond the process of interviewing to create a more spiritual encounter. She shows respect and looks and listens with empathy, a sensibility Schechner describes as "going beyond sympathy . . . the ability to allow the other in, to feel what the other is feeling" (64). In the process of elaborating how Smith "heals" her audiences, Schechner makes a critical connection between her enterprise and the enterprise of all those who created and continue to participate in the slave narrative tradition. The imaginative impulse that motivates the slave narrative tradition reaches its fullest liberating potential when an aesthetic production enables an audience to imagine itself as the protagonist who desires liberation.

Smith affirms this principle when she remarks, "It's crucial that whites in the audience find points of identification" (Lahr 90). In a memo Smith wrote to one of the dramaturges of *Twilight,* she explained that she was seeking to create for her audience "points of empathy with themselves. . . . To create a situation where they merely empathize with those less fortunate than themselves is another kind of theatre. . . . My political problem is this: Privilege is often masked, hidden, guarded. This guarded, fortressed privilege is exactly what has led us to the catastrophe of non-dialogue in which we find ourselves. I'm not talking about economic privilege. I'm talking about the basic privilege of white skin which is the foundation of our rare vocabulary" (Lahr 90).

The philosopher and theologian Cornel West, in his introduction to *Fires in the Mirror*, reaffirms the role of imaginative empathy in Smith's dramas when he observes that they "force us to examine critically our own complicity in cultural stereotypes that imprison our imaginations" (xvii). His observations are affirmed by John Lahr, who describes witnessing one of her performances in the following way: "In a provocative and involving displacement, the audience assumed the part of Anna Deavere Smith as she in turn took on the role of the interviewee. Placed in this position, we are asked to read the text of the situation as closely as she has, to see what is really there, not what we have imagined or what has been fed to us by the media. Her success in creating a dialogue between different races, though contained within herself, offers a blueprint for racial harmony, an invitation to, as she as said 'negotiate the differences'" (Lahr 119).

That Smith not only engenders this response but also generates and embodies it herself is what makes her work unique. Because she and the people she portrays all remain visible, individuality is asserted while difference is called into question. In the process, she forces us to reconsider what constitutes not just theater, but also literature and text itself. For her, the texts to be studied are not preexisting literature but other human beings. By finding the poetry in people's everyday speech and shaping it into textimony, she redirects our studied theater gazes back out to the streets from which it emerged.

Smith demonstrates this imaginative empathy not just in her investigative techniques, but in her performance: the way she absorbs the gestures, the tone of voice, the look, and all the details of the personalities of those she interviews. Accomplishing this effect without parody or insult is not easy, but that Smith does so is evidence of her fine technique and her genuine commitment. As Schechner concludes in his review of *Fires in the Mirror*, "Smith's shamanic invocation is her ability to bring into existence the wondrous 'doubling' that marks great performances. This doubling is the simultaneous presence of performer and performed. Because of this doubling Smith's audiences—consciously perhaps, unconsciously certainly—learn to 'let the other in,' to accomplish in their own way what Smith so masterfully achieves" (64). Double-consciousness, of course, is not a new concept when applied to African Americans. But Smith's theater reveals a new aspect or way to interpret the crisis Du Bois identified—to negotiate the difference and use the tension for creative result rather than paralysis—and in the process she teaches us something new about ourselves.

Still, the final line of "Anonymous Young Man #2—Bad Boy" in *Fires in the Mirror* serves as caveat for Smith and her entire enterprise and to those who seek entrance into liberating action by way of imagination. When Bad Boy tries to explain to Smith "how it is," he says, "That's between me and my creator." As Smith observes in this statement, Bad Boy is asserting his dignity. "He doesn't appropriate his own culture" (C. Martin 59). Although Smith proudly claims an African-American identity and demonstrates and celebrates in her work a profound knowledge of African-American and African cultural traditions, she is sensitive not only to her own temptation to appropriate aspects of this culture but to how she may lead others to do the same.

It is only through her uncanny ability to make connections with other cultural and ethnic influences, to allow anything that comes into her orbit to enrich and deepen her perception of the human condition, that Smith both honors and challenges the people she strives to represent. As Cornel West describes her efforts, Smith demonstrates how art can constitute an empowering public space because she functions as a citizen who knows that we cannot address problems of ethnic strife "without a vital public sphere and that there can be no vital public sphere without genuine bonds of trust." She functions as an artist who knows that "public performance has a unique capacity to bring us together—to take us out of our tribal mentalities—for self-critical examination and artistic pleasure" (*Fires* xxii). Like Miss Jane Pittman does in her kitchen, Anna Deavere Smith uses her stage to create opportunities for others' stories to be told.

ꔷ ꔷ ꔷ

> People are people through other people.
> —Xhosa proverb

Fires in the Mirror: Crown Heights, Brooklyn and Other Identities was scheduled to open in New York on April 29, 1992, the same day of the uprising in Los Angeles that followed the verdict in the trial of police officers charged with beating Rodney King. The opening was canceled and Smith joined demonstrators in Times Square to protest the verdict. While Los Angeles burned, the images of fire and light that surround the text of *Fires in the Mirror* took on a wider meaning. The musings of A. M. Bernstein, an MIT physicist whom Smith interviewed and portrays in the play, became especially pertinent. Imagining the idea of a mirror large enough to accurately reflect the true nature of the universe, he says that if you want to focus on the stars without getting caught in a circle of confusion, you need a telescope big enough to gather in a lot of light. Gathering enough light to see through a dark scene becomes the metaphor for Smith's enterprise in this piece.

Mirrors are a recurrent image in the play, but as the author points out, "there isn't just one mirror." She goes on to explain that "we don't stand on a surface like a chorus line, all going across with the same legs. We've got different lengths and many different mirrors. The reason I use the image of the mirror is that we think of the stage as the mirror of society, the thing that shows us back what we are, that shows us our identity, and right now fire is in the mirror. There are plural fires, not just one fire; fires are in the mirror" (B. Lewis 57). Thus, another metaphor Smith adopts is the image of a fire truck answering distress calls and making many stops but never quite attending all the needs. "They're just putting out the little fires" (B. Lewis 57). Fire is light, power, warmth, and, like a mirror, a reflective agency.

Smith sees "the fires of social unrest that we've had as evidence of power secreting, power insisting, power igniting, power that has been dormant coming up and surfacing. Whether it's bad power or good power, or disruptive or not, it's power. It's voice. It's also danger, because its the result of friction" (B. Lewis 57). To underscore the relevance of these metaphors of reflection, fire and light, the set for *Fires* was highlighted with mirror fragments in which the audience was reflected. Large screens were also used to project the characters' names, and halfway through the piece a montage of photographs taking during the riots was shown. These technical adaptations are part of Smith's entire theatrical enterprise that is aimed at casting as much light as possible while recognizing the virtue of putting out the little fires.

Fires in the Mirror concerns the racial conflict that erupted in the Brooklyn neighborhood of Crown Heights in August 1991. Smith interviewed six hundred people in just eight days—two months after the violence abated—and from the gathered recollections she crafted her performance. Blacks and Jews had clashed following a car accident in which a Jewish van driver—steering one of the cars in a procession carrying the Lubavitcher Hasidic rebbe believed by his followers to be the Messiah— ran a red light, hit another car, and swerved onto the sidewalk. The car struck and killed a young black child, Gavin Cato, and seriously injured his cousin. Further aggravating the situation in the minds of the black residents were rumors that the children had been left lying on the sidewalk while a private Jewish ambulance helped the driver and his passengers.

That evening, a group of young black men fatally stabbed Yankel Rosenbaum, a twenty-nine-year-old Hasidic scholar from Australia. The three-day riots that followed were a culmination of years of resentment between the Orthodox Jewish sect and Crown Heights's black majority. Blacks cited white racism as playing a critical role in the conflict. Many believed that the Lubavitchers had received preferential treatment from police and other city agencies, and blacks reported that some Lubavitchers threatened and harassed them. According to Jews, black anti-Semitism also played a role, as Jews cited reports that they were frequent victims of black street crime and taunts such as "Heil Hitler" or "Kill the Jews."

The conflict also reflected the pain, oppression, and discrimination these groups have historically experienced outside their own communities. Many in the Crown Heights black community were Caribbean immigrants who faced discrimination because of their color and their national origin. Their identity could not be conventionally affirmed as African-American in the local sense, but only in the more complicated diaspora sense, where old and new worlds were more readily in tension. And the Lubavitchers, members of a 250-year-old messianic Hasidic sect that fled the Nazi genocide in Europe, were particularly vulnerable to anti-Jewish stereotyping because of their religious style of dress and insular community. The resulting trials—in which no one directly involved was convicted of a crime—and the media coverage, which polarized the people involved, made it difficult, as Smith writes, "for people to develop an understanding of the Crown Heights situation that acknowledges the experiences of all people involved" (*Fires* xiv).

The tension between these two groups Smith identifies as inevitable in America because it is "the tension of identity in motion, the tension of identity which is in contest with an old idea, but a resonant idea of America" (*Fires* xxxiv). Yet this characteristic tension was not moving identity forward in a collective way. As Smith explains, the prevailing idea of American character may have been developed initially by white men, but marginal populations have constantly adapted it. The tension that results when different notions of American character come into conflict present an opportunity she describes in the following metaphor of motion that recalls at once the historical success of the Underground Railroad and the present failure of the Crown Heights episode: "Like a train [it] can pick up passengers and take them to their destination . . . or be derailed onto a sidewalk where some innocents are waiting to get struck down" (*Fires* xxxiv).

In accordance with her notion of adapting concepts of American character, Smith structures her text in such a way that issues related to character and identity formation are investigated in a circular fashion, from the general to the particular. The first two sections, "Identity" and "Mirrors," offer broad and speculative reflections on not just identity but how one sees the reality in which identities are constructed. From there Smith locates specific issues of "Hair," "Race," "Rhythm," and "Seven Verses" (a biblical allusion) to structure the dialogue pertaining to how the African Americans and Jews of the community describe and define themselves and each other. The drama concludes with the unambiguous "Crown Heights, Brooklyn, August 1991" section, which offers different perspectives on the actual events and their meanings.

Smith performs in simple garb that is accentuated for each character by some distinctive addition—a yarmulke, a Kente cloth cap, a glittery sweater, a wig—that marks her transition from character to character. Because each character is based on an actual person who speaks his or her own lines, "there were unresolvable contradictions in the multiple versions of truth," but this "did not diminish the conviction of each character that what they said was true" (C. Martin 45). Each character gives voice to a multitude of feelings seldom expressed and rarely in the same space. But as the drama moves from general reflection to the specific issues that led to the incident documented, the audience confronts more difficult discussions of specific racist attitudes and the "reification of those ideas" (Laris 119). It is only the continuity of Smith's presence that undercuts the authority of one group over another or one individual over another. She functions as a diviner through whom many voices travel; all the characters speak together while their presence and words, as Carol Martin observes, "mark the absence and silence of the two people around whom the drama revolves, Gavin Cato and Yankel Rosenbaum" (46).

Smith begins the play with Ntozake Shange because she recognizes that although the play is about race and difference, it is also about identity. Shange's definition of identity—knowing who and what you are regardless of where you are—Smith found especially relevant. As she explains, "Who owns what of what culture and how that becomes part of another culture is in many ways at the bottom line of how we negotiate who and where we are" (B. Lewis 55). Smith's use of Shange is also a way for her to symbolically tap into all Shange represents in terms of the theater, the way she declared her own identity and made a place for herself in American theater with her groundbreaking portrayal of black women in *For Colored Girls*. Still, Smith is careful to distinguish herself from any specific tradition, identifying herself as one who has "always been on the outside . . . an observer who steps in and then steps back out" (B. Lewis 56).

Following Shange, Smith steps into two characters who discuss their own painful struggles with the social conventions that would define their identity. An anonymous Lubavitcher woman relates how an orthodox injunction prohibiting her from turning off the radio on the Sabbath affects her young black neighbor's view of her. The usually articulate director George C. Wolfe is portrayed stumbling his way through a recollection of how, as a child, segregation prevented him from seeing a Disney movie. From this early recognition of how race circumscribed his identity, he reflects on how his blackness affects other people's perceptions of him, ranging from the "insignificant" to the "extraordinary." His own "confused, complex, demonic, ridiculous," perception of himself is revealed in his stuttering speech as he tries to articulate that his blackness "does not exist in relationship to your whiteness" (10).

Smith then moves to portray characters whose sense of identity is clearly articulated and expressed by their external characteristics, particularly by their relationships to their own hair—people who reveal human commonalities in small details of personal style.[7] Basic concerns of appearance and identity are vital to a thirteen-year-old black girl gazing at herself in a mirror. She is utterly satisfied with her blackness and her appearance and chastises others—black, Puerto Rican, and white girls—who don't seem to be able to develop their own style but "bite off" (17) or appropriate the style of others. Al Sharpton describes somewhat defensively his allegiance to James Brown, which he honors by wearing the same hairstyle. Noting that the once-fashionable look is now associated largely with him and Brown, Sharpton claims it as a badge of honor, a "personal thing between me and James Brown" (21) and a way for him to pay tribute to the man who played a significant paternal role in Sharpton's life. Finally, Rivkah Siegal confesses her discomfort with the artificiality inherent in her religion's mandate for wigs. She says that wearing them is "fake . . . not me" (25), yet she continues to do so, to displace her own individual sense of self in honor of a larger communal identity, despite her apparent discomfort.

In a section titled "Race," Smith steps back from the particular and portrays Angela Davis articulating her own evolving attitude about the idea of racial communities. Davis observes that once race and community were synonymous, but she now sees that race is an obsolete way of constructing communities. Race, she believes, emerged from racism, so she uses the term "in quotes." Recalling divisions in the black community, she asserts that she is looking for new ways "of coming together in a different way." To explain her vision, she uses the metaphor of a rope that is attached to an anchor of community, but she cautions that the rope "should be long enough to allow us to move into other communities to understand and to learn" (32).

The next section, "Rhythm," introduces a young rap artist who offers another strategy for survival. Big Mo is unsparing in her criticism of the sexism that permeates the black community, which also plays a role in the declining African-American sense of community Davis observed. Big Mo articulates her response in her chosen art form, rap, which breaks down rhythm and poetry in order to create a particular kind of expression wherein self-esteem is bolstered in one's attempts to become "def," a slang expression for "the epitome of the experience . . . and you have to be def by your very presence" (38–39).

Following these examples of contemporary responses to the systemic problems of racism, in "Seven Verses" Smith includes the reflections of leading African-American and Jewish cultural critics, who provide an important historical context for what transpired in Crown Heights. She begins by portraying controversial university professor Leonard Jefferies, whose promotion of an Afrocentric perspective on history has been challenged for being anti-Semitic. Jefferies is firm and unapologetic in claiming his position, willing to take on not just whites and Jews but other African Americans as well.

Reflecting on his role as an advisor to the television production of Alex Haley's *Roots,* Jefferies cites it as an example of Jewish media control over the representation of black history. The anti-Semitism and the images of slavery recalled by Jefferies are picked up in Smith's portrayal of Minister Conrad, a Muslim who graphically describes the Middle Passage and the historical suffering of blacks, which he contrasts with the Holocaust, claiming that it in "no way compares with the slavery of our people" (54). Conrad cites as the most egregious crime the way slavery robbed black people of their identity by cutting them off from knowledge and their past so that only indigenous blacks have a "contextual understanding of what identity is" (55). He concludes with the statement that the Muslim claim to be the chosen people of God is more valid than that of the Jews, who base their claim on only "seven verses" in the Bible.

What the covenant between God and humanity offers in actual terms, how chosenness is expressed in history, is complicated by the fact of slavery and the Holocaust. This is where feminist writer Letty Cottin Pogrebin steps in, citing the role Jews have played in black liberation movements and pointing out how Jews have constantly been picked as scapegoats. In a moving recollection of her cousin Isaac's Holocaust experience and resulting death, Pogrebin offers his experience as a metaphor for how we fail in advancing liberation. After physically surviving the Holocaust, Isaac died once he had "spoken the unspeakable" to all who would listen to his story.

In this instance, Pogrebin calls into question not just what survival means, but also the effectiveness of textimony, of storytelling as a strategy for creative endurance. Her worry is summed up in the comment that "we're trotting out our Holocaust stories too regularly . . . we're going to inure each other to the truth of them" (59). The role of language in both advancing and obstructing conflict resolution is also articulated by Robert Sherman, a city bureaucrat who was not at all surprised by the episode in Crown Heights. His observations of the community reveal not a simple cultural conflict or black/Jewish dichotomy but what he calls a "soup of bias—prejudice, racism, and discrimination" (64). This murky soup is the result of "lousy language" that does not clearly identify the complexity of the social problems America faces.

It is this "lousy language" that Smith attempts to rehabilitate, without denying its presence and effect. The ingredients of the "soup of bias" are revealed in the final section, which explores from a variety of perspectives actual reflections on the incident itself. From theorizing and reflecting on the systemic conditions that generate the ingredients for a soup of bias, Smith's portrayals of different people involved demonstrate how these ingredients were blended in Crown Heights. Among those chosen to speak are several clerics of different faiths, social workers and community organizers, and anonymous residents who observed the conflict at various stages of its development, from the incident itself to the resulting riots, rallies, and funerals.

Each character's recollection is informed by some past experience or opinion, emphasizing that the conflict was not just a spontaneous outburst but the result of perceived and ongoing oppression of one group or another. Tribal loyalties come to the fore in allusions to prior episodes of justice denied or favors proffered to one group or another. The distances between people that at first seemed academic and diffuse become actual and precise in these textimonies, and seldom is a note of ambiguity interjected in the comments of any of the characters.

What also becomes apparent is that those who become the spokespeople for one position or another are conferred this privilege by their ability to manipulate language to create the specific effect of uniting people in a particular formulation of their identity. Sharpton's defiant challenge on behalf of the black community that "If you piss in my face I'm gonna call it piss, I'm not gonna call it rain" (116), and the assertion by Norman Rosenbaum, the Jewish victim's brother, that "I'm here, I'm not going home, until there is justice" (96), drown out the calmer observations of Rabbi Hecht that "we're all children of God" (111) and Richard Green's pledge to "pray on both sides of the fence" (118). What all the characters share is a recognition of difference and an unwillingness to give up individual aspects and expressions of identity that define who they are. This attitude is best expressed in the continuous historical references by Jews to images of the Holocaust (pogroms and ovens) and the repeated references by blacks to slavery (its origin and its ongoing effects) that are not fully understood even by those who possess the greatest rage.

It is Carmel Cato, the father of the child who was killed and the final character portrayed by Smith, who most overwhelms one with his ability to use language as a way to focus on the locus of identity. Smith remarks that precisely because he "crossed so many worlds" (B. Lewis 64), he is able to make a "journey in language across so many realms of experience" (C. Martin 52), an accomplishment the others don't seem to be able to achieve. As Smith remembers her interview with Cato, he began giving facts but soon moved into his own belief system, drawing on his own sensitivity and spiritual power to discuss his premonition that his son's death "was upon us" (B. Lewis 64). Unable to eat or function normally, Cato felt "something is wrong somewhere but I didn't want to see, I didn't want to accept. . . . I could feel it, but I didn't want to see" (137–138).

Smith observes that here Cato is speaking not just about his own personal tragedy and loss but also about the denial that pervades society. In this regard he is seeing for all of us. By ending his comments with a description of the circumstances of his birth—being born feet first, which he believes makes him a "special person" who cannot be overpowered— Cato's speech is structured "in the way classical drama is structured. It crosses different worlds, different feelings, and articulates his view of his existence in a really short span of time" (B. Lewis 64). There is also an African element to this structure that, by ending with reflections on birth, affirms the myth of eternal return where the cycle of life renews itself, suggesting that even out of the ashes of Crown Heights, a new mode of existence could rise.

Sonny Carson, who recognizes that "tonight by nighttime it could all change for me," suggests that a new existence might rise. "I'm always aware of that, and that's what keeps me going today and each day" (105).

Carson's comment anticipates the new perspective offered by *Twilight: Los Angeles, 1992,* another title ripe with metaphoric possibilities. Twilight is the chosen name of one of Smith's characters, Twilight Bey, who hoped to organize a truce between the gangs of Los Angeles and whose poetic interpretation of his name gave Smith the idea for her title. The concept of twilight is both the introduction to and the coda for the limbo Smith explores in this drama, and the character Twilight Bey himself functions as a surrogate for Smith's voice—one who speaks or communicates across seemingly insurmountable lines of hierarchy and difference. The metaphoric potential of twilight paradoxically recalls a time of danger and obscured vision, but also one of liminality and creativity. In *Twilight,* the bright light of fires reflected in a mirror become the dim light of a day ending, revealing new truths about identity but also new ambiguities.

Like *Fires in the Mirror, Twilight* brings the political into the realm of the personal. The effect of the individual personality, along with her or his ethnic history and economic status, is given an importance that neither media nor history books customarily elaborate. Also like *Fires,* the textimony of *Twilight* concerns a recent social uprising that generated national attention. In 1992 Los Angeles experienced some of the worst violence in U.S. history as the result of a protracted sequence of perceived injustices. In the spring of 1991, Rodney King, a black man, was severely beaten by four Los Angeles police officers after a high-speed chase in which King was pursued for speeding. A nearby resident videotaped the beating from his balcony, and when the tape was broadcast on national television there was an immediate outcry from the community. The next year, when the police officers who beat King were tried and found not guilty, the city exploded with fury over the surprising verdict. Three days of burning, looting, and killing followed the announcement.

The role of "lousy language" in social discourse becomes apparent again in the ways these events are perceived and described. "Riot," "uprising," and "rebellion" have all been used to denote the events of April 1992. But as Smith points out in her introduction to the drama, "beneath this surface explanation is a sea of associated causes" (xviii). A declining economy, a growing hostility between the police and people of color, and the increased development of marginalized ethnic communities all contributed to the preexisting tension. These factors and others reveal that the story of race in America is much larger and more complex than a story of black and white, involving not just a variety of ethnic divisions, but divisions within ethnic groups themselves.

Despite her success with *Fires,* in creating *Twilight* Smith felt what she describes as an "increased humility" about her enterprise and "a greater understanding of the limitations of theatre to reflect society" (xxii). Although she still had confidence in her theories about the relationship between character and language (citing, for example, how jurors in the police officer's trial felt a greater impact when, viewing the video of Rodney King's beating, they did not just see images but heard King's cries), the sheer number and diversity of voices she needed to represent overwhelmed her. So she decided to develop the drama in collaboration with four other people of various races who functioned as dramaturges who would bring their own experiences to bear on the work. In doing so, Smith hoped to "make theatre a more responsible partner in the growth of communities" (xxiii).

Twilight therefore presented a multidimensioned challenge to Smith and her entire theatrical enterprise. The dispersed geography, the layered economic classes, and the multiple ethnic associations complicated her search for identity and put at risk her notions of how theater could clarify social problems. Furthermore, the proximity of Hollywood, whose major industry is enchantment, presented an ironic context for a play that so clearly is intended to make people uncomfortable. In preparing *Twilight,* Smith became more aware of "how little there is in culture or education that encourages the development of a unifying voice" (xxv).

The absence of a unified voice is illustrated in the set Smith designed: a haphazard clutter of chairs and tables in front of a large, undecorated gray backdrop. At the center of the wall was a recess that became, variously, a TV split screen, a hodgepodge of graffiti, and an office window. As in *Fires,* Smith structured the testimony of *Twilight* in sections, giving each a thematic title, usually drawn from the conversation of one of her characters but also evocative of more universal circumstances. "The Territory" offers general assessments of the conditions that led to the uprising. "Here's a Nobody" traces different reactions to the beating of Rodney King and the resulting trial of the police officers involved. "War Zone" gives graphic renditions of the uprising itself, and "Twilight" and "Justice" deal with the aftermath and attempts to rebuild the community physically and psychologically.

The play concludes by circling back to the same issues raised in the Prologue by the sculptor Rudy Salas when he traces a familial history of minority victimization. From his grandfather, who died resisting "gringos" in Mexico, to his son, a Stanford student who was harassed by the police for no apparent offense, Salas gives a compelling demonstration of the dynamics of the slave narrative tradition, showing by his own family's experience that oppression and resisting it has become a kind of tradition in American life. He also enunciates the key elements that engender the tradition: the fear felt by both people of color and whites about the other and how this fear descends into hate on the part of both the oppressor and the oppressed. Despite his own uncle's reminder that "to hate is to waste energy and you mess with the man upstairs" (3), hate remains because fear has not been eliminated; it is only disguised by masks people put on in order to resist interaction with the other. The result is that the other is continually objectified as "my enemy" (3).

The role of masks in social dramas is a repeated motif in *Twilight*. An anonymous gang member, in describing the masked identity he gets from his association with a gang, betrays its presumed benefits when, in unacknowledged irony, he cites his favorite song as "Am I Dreamin'?" and describes his contention that it is advisable to shoot people in broad daylight because observers will be too scared to "identify you" (26). Theresa Allison, who became a community activist because of her own family's victimization by gang violence, shows how ineffective gangs are at providing precisely what the gang member seeks and how they destroy already intact ties to family and community.

Recalling Salas's description of the masks people wear for protection, she unconsciously connects the mask gang members wear with the one worn by police officers who, when they take off their uniforms, are "the same as you and I" (39). Even a preacher describes how he used his clerical collar to hide, as a symbol for protection rather than as the symbol of Christian proclamation it was meant to be. Eventually he took off his collar when he visited the violence-wracked part of the city and describes this initiative as creating in him a feeling of warmth that led to "a discovery . . . if there's any protection I needed it was just whatever love I had.in my heart to share with people that proved to be enough, the love that God has taught me to share. That is what came out in the end for me" (203).[8]

The theologian Cornel West expands on the symbolism of masks to include the generative myth that gives the symbol meaning. He offers an analysis of American history that attempts to explain why people feel the need to mask themselves out of fear or for protection. The myth of the American frontier and the patriarchal mode of conquest it engendered are behind people's belief that they can manipulate their identities and the identities of others. In their interviews with Smith, many characters invoke the civil rights movement as a model for how they envision society, but West invokes the model of the Black Panthers, whom he believes set forth a moral vision that, though grounded in racial pride, accented humanness and an international and multiracial perspective. The qualities he ascribes to the Black Panther movement recall principles of liberation theology and invoke its imaginative imperative, wherein one acknowledges "the role of all whosoever will identify with poor people and working people" (47).

"The Territory" continues what began in the Prologue. Specific episodes of police brutality or unmanageable neighborhoods are offered by a variety of involved parties. What is interesting is that each character portrayed in this section reveals a profound awareness—arrived at by experience or reflection—of the problems and needs that beset the community. The dialogue continually circles back to the same points, articulated from different perspectives, with recurrent observations that include the desire for community or family, a perceived sense of alienation for people of color or entitlement for white people, and an inability to know or understand the other. In other words, few people are willing to surrender their masks.

Representing the police, Stanley Sheinbaum defends them as abused by the city, but admits that these same officers seldom talk to "these curious people" (15) whom they are charged to serve. His own attempt to get to know residents met with his fellow officers' resistance, leading him to the realization that the problem between police and the community was one of the perceived need to "take a side" (15). This posture is recalled in a black resident's claim that hostility between blacks and Koreans is caused by the fact that Korean shop owners don't take the time to get to know the people who come into their stores (129). One resident, Michael Zinzun, who was blinded as the result of police brutality, describes how he used his financial settlement to take a side, to "further the struggle" (20) by exposing police brutality. Some residents, such as Jason Sanford, who are protected by white entitlement from the indignities people such as Zinzun have experienced, express a recognition of their entitlement, which they identify, as Sheinbaum did, as the result of seeing others as objectified "theys."

Although they admit their privileged status and even, as in the case of Mike Davis, nostalgically allude to the civil rights movement with the hope that "black kids can be surfers, too" (30), they neither claim personal responsibility for changing the structure of society nor imagine what a black child might be in terms other than those pertinent to their own lifestyles. As a woman who sought refuge at the Polo Lounge says, they just "put it out of their minds" (152). Later this posture is described by an affluent white businessman as "generic guilt" (136); he also uses the "we/they" formulation to describe the attitude of his friends and peers. Insulated by wealth or, as another character describes it, the "fortress" (155) of Beverly Hills, he moves toward accountability by recognizing that despite his personal beliefs, he knows the rioters were "victims of the system" and la-

ments that they burnt down not the neighborhood of their presumed oppressors, but their own homes.

The resulting conditions such attitudes foster are represented in anec-
dotes related by two characters later in the play. Elvira Evers, a cashier who
was pregnant when a stray bullet struck her and lodged in the elbow of
the fetus (her daughter, who survived), offers unflappable optimism in the
face of adversity. But her tale is also cautionary when she observes that
even in the womb, her child had to protect herself, to catch the bullet in
her arm: "See? So it's like open your eyes, watch what is goin' on" (123).
Beyond even the need to protect is the condition described by the former
range manager of the Beverly Hills Gun Club, who remarks that after the
uprising, sales went up by 50 percent because people are looking not just
for protection but for "an opportunity to defend themselves" (224).

"Here's a Nobody" elaborates further personal struggles but focuses
more specifically on the dynamics of the beating of Rodney King and the
subsequent trial. Each personal story highlights how misperceptions esca-
late until dialogue between groups is nearly impossible, thus setting the
stage for the resulting violence. What emerges in this section is the understanding that what happened in Los Angeles was not just about Rodney
King or Reginald Denny but about a whole history of oppression, either
actual or perceived, that had been internalized by all who were effected
by the events. Assuming the role of family spokesperson, King's aunt recalls an episode in Rodney's life when he caught a fish with his bare hands.
She describes her nephew as acting like a "wild African," unwittingly invoking a stereotypical image many whites might have in mind, particularly
the police officers when they tried to subdue the agitated King. In her assessment of the situation, Ms. King makes a distinction between those with
religious concerns and those who seek justice, and identifies herself with
the latter. This distinction points to the alienation of an African-American religious sensibility from one of its distinguishing characteristics and
dramatically illustrates the declining role religion has played in liberation
agendas.

Police Sargent Duke describes the use of force in his work and how,
through a series of well-intentioned bureaucratic maneuvers that eliminated
other forms of control, the police may have aggressively used their batons
in subduing King as a form of retribution. Josie Morales describes witnessing
the actual beating and says that despite her husband's pleas to not watch
(he had seen many similar episodes in his native Mexico), she felt compelled
to watch because "this is wrong" (67). Although she was eager to serve as
a witness at the trial, she was never called; she dreamt of the acquittal and

because she believes dreams are "made of some kind of indelible substance" (69), she was not surprised when the verdict was announced.

Morales' dream, while possessing the substantial quality of Martin Luther King's dream, stands in counterpoint as it imagines a different kind of world, and sadly it is hers that is fulfilled. Just as Rodney King is recalled as a wild African, even by his own aunt, another disturbing stereotype comes to light when one juror recalls how, after the verdict, along with all the threats and harassment he received, the Ku Klux Klan wrote to offer their support and to claim him as one of their own. The juror recoiled in horror at the assumption that the role he played in this trial made him appear racist (73). This kind of assumed identification is further clarified by district attorney Garcetti, who assesses the verdict by claiming that jurors naturally identify more with the police than with King. He describes the influence and identification with police as a kind of "magic" (74) that conveys reassurance to fearful people who need to believe that police officers are truthful.

"War Zone" gives many accounts of the actual uprisings themselves and, more than any other section, highlights the complex and multicultural character of the Los Angeles neighborhood where the violence occurred.[9] The Koreans and whites who were near the uprising describe the events in graphic detail and often use metaphors of war to express how they felt. Chung Lee, a store owner and leader of a Korean victims' association, admits that once the riots began they had to "give up any sense of attachment to our possessions" (84). Although this posture is theologically correct from a liberationist point of view, in this context it is unspeakably poignant. Anger is the overriding emotion detailed in this section, usually couched in apologies in which the speakers also claim a tolerant viewpoint that "people are people" but are unable to extend that belief in trying to absorb their own experiences. The anger builds to the point, as reporter Judith Tur remarks, that she "hates to be angry" (98), yet even from her professional, objective stance she cannot contain her anger or the fear that created it.

From a liberation point of view, Big Al, an ex–gang member now working for a truce, reveals the ignored dynamics of power that create the conditions for such a situation: "Anything is never a problem 'til the black man gets his hands on it" (101), using as an example a comparison of the responses to the King and Denny beatings wherein the sympathy for the white victim shows "how a black person gets treated in his community" (100). Paul Parker, who organized a committee to defend those accused of beating Reginald Denny, affirms Big Al's observation when he remarks on the irony of blacks being expected to feel for whites. "We supposed to have some empathy or some sympathy toward this one white man? It's like well, how 'bout the empathy and the sympathy toward blacks?" (173). He invokes images of slavery he became aware of by viewing *Roots*, and claims his actions are "for Kunta, Kizzy and Chicken George." His self-proclaimed motto is, "No Justice No Peace," and he, quite ironically, reflects a sentiment Reginald Denny also expresses: the desire to set aside a room to memorialize the events in Los Angeles in 1992 for instructional purposes.

Whereas Denny wants to convert other whites, Parker sees his role in parental terms, helping his children to see what it takes and what you have to do for your people. He says, "When God calls you, this is what you gotta do. You either stand or you fall. You either be black or you die" (178). Parker echoes the sentiments of James Baldwin and a principal feature of this study when he observes that until African Americans assume this posture, there will be no peace or peace of mind, even for whites. So he continues his strategy of "one brother doing the work of one brother," believing it is "the best that I can do. It's educational. It's a blessing. It's a gift from God" (179). To do this work, in the words of Big Al, one must "live here to see what's goin' on" (101). Big Al advances the reminder that Smith's theater attempts to demonstrate. Whether a theater experience can completely substitute for lived experience in generating a disposition toward human liberation is both challenged and affirmed by Reginald Denny.

Denny's description of his attitude before his beating reveals a posture common for those in positions of privilege: "I didn't pay any attention to that because that was somebody else's problem" (105). But once the problem became his, Denny did not recoil in anger or fear. The greatest discomfort he expresses is in meeting the people who saved his life, a feeling of awkwardness that vanished when "strangers" immediately became his "buddies" (108). What he describes as "a weird common thread in our lives" (108) is precisely what Smith wants people to come to appreciate. And just as she memorializes this sentiment in her theater, Denny prays, "Lord willing," that he will fulfill the desire to create a sacred space in his own home, not a "sad" room but a "happy room" where he will gather reminders of his ordeal and where "there won't be a color problem" (111). He further elaborates the paradox of those who, despite the opportunities to learn and value the lives of others, will remain "bad-ass" white guys. It is these people Denny wants to shake and say to them, "You fool, you selfish little shit." He wants people to "wake up" and realize, "it's not a color, it's a person" (112).

Personhood and character, the qualities Smith tries to animate and demystify, take on a special poignancy in the dialogue of the Park family. Each member takes a turn describing the stoic silence their culture urges them to adopt, even in the face of life-changing events. But this very silence—hiding things out of love—recalls the donning of masks and, however well intentioned, leads to incomplete resolutions even in the same family. This incompleteness of character takes on a symbolic presence in the person of Walter Park, the family patriarch and a gunshot victim who had to undergo a partial lobectomy that destroyed, as his stepson relates, "your basic character" (146). In contrast to the posture of the Park family, the Korean liquor store owner Young-Soon Han displays her anger, constantly beating the table as she talks and rhetorically inquires where or what justice is. Her claim of sympathy for African Americans is somewhat belied in her reference to "them," and although she tries to swallow her bitterness and be happy, there is "too much differences. . . . The fire is still there and can burst out anytime" (249).

Among the most powerful characters Smith portrays is Maxine Waters, the congresswoman from the district where the uprisings occurred. She expresses her assessment of this social drama in aesthetic and theological terms, citing a lack of ritual or customary and socially understood ways of communicating as the root of the problem, not just in Los Angeles, but also in the District of Columbia, where government powers try to address the issues raised by such episodes. Although the government does observe "ritual and custom," it does so in a manner that does not contribute to communitas because those in power "really don't see it . . . don't see their lives in relationship to solving these kinds of problems" (164). The cold reality of the coroner's description that occurs later confirms Waters's evaluation of the need for ritual when he describes his frustration over being unable to locate human remains, recognizing as he does people's need for closure that a funeral burial allows. Like Waters, he compares an individual's need for an appropriate ritual to what the country needs: resolution.

This sense of resolution is an ongoing struggle for America, as Waters observes when she laments that the most recent uprising is not new but one more example in history of rage, of injustice overflowing into violence, which causes "good people" to react in "strange ways" (161). Rioting is "the voice of the unheard" (162), a destructive yet redemptive act for unempowered people. The sense of absence Waters cites, where people do not see their lives in relationship, is especially amplified by the comments of Los Angeles police chief Daryl Gates. His language continually betrays him as each phrase is loaded with signification, revealing attitudes he isn't even aware he is expressing, although they describe accurately how his actions are perceived by many.

For example, when he says, "I was almost there" (181), he means to indicate that he was actually out of town, but given the relationship between the people and the police, his comment carries an entirely different meaning. Because he appears most concerned with issues of image—another variation on the masking theme—he is especially sensitive to criticism directed toward him as symbol of police oppression, but he seems utterly unaware of the image his words create as when he describes the initial episode that led to the uprisings as "the Rodney thing" (187). He unwittingly objectifies King in speech as he apparently did in life.

Despite the fact that Los Angeles was actually consumed by fire, the recurring image invoked by several characters is not of brightly burning flames but of the slow recession of daylight into twilight. The characters reveal in this image a subtle awareness that simply casting a bright light onto the issues considered is not enough. Only twilight, evoking liminal states and contradictory conditions, can represent what the fires of unrest mean. The concluding sections of *Twilight* offer from a variety of perspectives several assessments of the meaning behind the events in Los Angeles in 1992 and even go so far as to suggest prescriptions for change.

What all the characters share in their assessments is a recognition of the systemic nature of the problems and the connectedness of the human community that is too often ignored or denied. Director Peter Sellars compares America to a stingy landlord who won't replace burned-out light bulbs in his rental units. People need only a light bulb, but they are ignored because the landlord is concerned only with providing for his own family. Sellars sees the events in Los Angeles as a reminder that the landlord's house is "our house" and that "we can't live, our own house is burning. This isn't somebody else's house, it's our own house" (200).

This recognition of implicit connectedness is affirmed by Paula Weinstein, a movie producer whose awareness of the systemic problems underlying the uprising causes her to feel "extreme impotence" (204) about what to do. She describes the entertainment industry's response and, like Waters, notes the differences between the strategies of the street and party politics, the latter being more concerned with the success and failure of political agendas rather than representing genuine efforts to struggle and tell the truth that street politics represent. Although she cites what she describes as a "Jungian collective unconscious" (208) among the younger generation of citizens who work in her industry, she also observes that there has been nowhere for them to address their social justice concerns and that they have had no real experience in the affected neighborhoods even though they live only blocks away. It was only when they organized volunteer cleanup efforts after the uprisings that the young people began to confront what had been absent from their experience.

Weinstein's description of the work these young people performed in South Central neighborhoods after the violence shares many of the same qualities of both promise and futility that characterize Smith's own enterprise in theater. Like Smith's experiments, the people engaged were multicultural and multiracial, together creating a kind of "street theatre" (209) and expressing a palpable sense of collective responsibility. In their ritual work, the volunteers felt the possibility that circumstances could actually change because, as in Smith's plays, "the language was there, and all the big gestures" (211). But also like a theater experience that is limited in its temporal inclusion, their efforts didn't change much because they lasted only four days. Although she laments that "the euphoria" they felt was "fake" (212), correlative to the evocative power of a theater experience, she concedes that the experience did provide a glimpse of what could be, just as Smith hopes her theater will accomplish the same.

Senator Bill Bradley's examination of the question of responsibility and who should assume it resonates with the prior claims. His assertion that moral power must be exercised and that "all of us have responsibility to try to improve the circumstances among the races of this country" (216), from teenage mothers to corporate executives, is qualified by the recognition that there has to be long-term commitment. While working to instill this kind of commitment we need to be patient and resolute, try not to give up. There is always hope, Bradley asserts, but no easy answers. Like Cornel West, Elaine Brown invokes the model of the Black Panthers, who had plan and moral purpose, and believes that gangs can be redeemed to function in a similar way.

That they do not do so today is because they are not conscious of what they are doing and how ineffective they are in bringing about change, how ultimately powerless they are before systems that can suppress opposition; she explains with the rhetorical refrain, "ask Saddam Hussein about who is bad . . . talk to the Vietnamese people, and the Nicaraguans and El Salvadorans and people in South Africa" (230). If they want to effect change for people, Brown asserts, they must make a commitment based on love, not hate, and do it for a lifetime. Gangs' ignorance of the real forces they mean to contend with and their concern with their own egos simply represents another variation on the shallow obsession with image represented by Chief Gates.

Homi Bhabha, in his enunciation of the qualities of twilight, explains why gang members on one side and affluent Hollywood kids on the other are ineffective. People who retreat to distinct modes of light—its absence or its presence—cannot appreciate that they both occupy the same space and moment of twilight, "an in-between moment. It's the moment of dusk. It's the moment of ambivalence and ambiguity. The inclarity, the enigma, the ambivalences in what happened in the LA uprisings are precisely what we want to get hold of" (232), Bhabha asserts. The hard outlines of what we see in daylight, which make it easy for us to order daylight, disappear in twilight and people are left without ritual order. As boundaries fade and intersections appear that daylight obscured, we have to interpret more in twilight "to make ourselves part of the act" (233). This condition challenges us to be aware "of how we are projecting onto the event itself" (233) and creates possibilities for us to be more interpretive and creative. Artist Bettye Saar also invokes twilight images and limbo time, describing it as magical but cautioning that "magic is not always good" (236).

The call for moral commitment expressed by Waters, Bradley, and Brown is answered and embodied in liberation theologian Gladis Sibrian, a nun from El Salvador who cites her own faith and conviction that people have the power within themselves to change things. She deliberately chose as her nom de guerre Lucia, which means light, hoping that her organized efforts to transform society—to enlighten—will inspire others to pursue similar actions before other "social explosions" (252) erupt, as they did in Los Angeles. Twilight Bey, the final character represented in Smith's *Twilight,* also chose a kind of nom de guerre associated with light.

In his stunning final speech, Twilight Bey discourses about his name, probing both language and life and embodying the aspect of twilight when its harder to see, but when more creativity is allowed because you have to participate more. He chose his name because it reflected his temporal habits—he stays up to see what activity in the daytime creates at night—and to signify his position in the community as one who possessed "two times the wisdom," or twice the light of wisdom. His assessment of the events in Los Angeles resonates with others' as he perceives society stuck in limbo. But he is aware that "to be a true human being I can't forever dwell in darkness, I can't forever dwell in the idea of just identifying with people like me and understanding me and mine" (255). Moving beyond exclusive forms of identification is what Smith hopes to accomplish in her theater, and although her particular form may be unique, her motive has roots in the liberating theology of the slave narrative tradition through which, quoting from Benjamin Banneker and the Book of Job, one learns to "put your souls in their souls' stead."

ଵ ଵ ଵ

> The theatre is the most powerful pulpit of our times.
> —Leo Tolstoy

Established in 1963, The Free Southern Theatre (FST) was the only cultural institution that sprang directly from the civil rights movement, and it provided for Anna Deavere Smith a recent historical precedent for the liberating potential inherent in theater arts. Although by 1970 the theater had disbanded because of the conflicting ideologies of its members, its origin and development exemplify what is necessary for art to incite the imagination of people toward liberation. Among the principles affirmed by the FST was that activists in a liberation movement are most successful when they become part of the community and learn from the values, customs, and lifestyles of the very people they attempt to enlighten. Just as Smith tries to capture the unique ethos and perspective of the communities she explores, the leaders of the FST were most successful in advancing a liberation agenda when the content and form of their productions sprang directly from referents within the culture of the black South. Whereas for Smith a specific concept of theater preceded her agenda for social change, the idea for the FST sprang from people actively engaged in the Southern liberation movement.

In their 1969 preface to the documentary account of what the creators identify as "the South's radical black theatre," Thomas C. Dent, Richard Schechner, John O'Neal, and Gilbert Moses declare that the FST "is not finished. It is neither washed up nor fully realized. The theatre continues" (*The Free Southern* xi). Although it is true that FST as an institution no longer exists, two decades later the spirit of the theater has been revitalized and its purposes continued in Smith's work. Indeed, Smith identifies her early goal for the *On the Road* series as having "a traveling troupe of actors based on the model of the Free Southern Theatre" (Kaufman G11). Although Smith's reluctance to solicit funds or even apply for grants forced her to scale back her project and *On the Road* became a one-woman show, this decision saved her from the very problems that beset and eventually undid the actual FST. But Smith also pays a price for her individuality and independence. As she explains, without a troupe or organization like the FST, "people don't always know where you're coming from, and you're alone" (B. Lewis 56).

Still, a consideration of the FST illuminates what motivates and inspires Smith. It also puts in perspective what she has been able to accomplish. The FST's history shows how even the best and most idealistic intentions are ruined by basic human conflicts. FST's origin and demise raise pertinent issues about not just how to achieve liberation through artistic expression, but how we define liberation itself. The FST also offers an interesting case study of the dialectic characteristic of African-American culture throughout its history: the dialectic between integrationism and nationalism. The resulting tension or "black identity crisis" this dialectic fosters and its ongoing implications are part of what Smith explores in her search for American character.

In her study *Mirror of the Movement: A History of the Free Southern Theatre as a Microcosm of the Civil Rights and Black Power Movements, 1963–1978*, Clarissa Myrick-Harris sees the theater as a microcosm for black liberation struggles, the triumphs and setbacks that are part of "the ongoing quest by African-Americans for liberation, self-definition and self-determination" (2). Myrick-Harris identifies four distinct phases of the theater that correspond to the dialectic she has identified, phases that move from the initial integrationist idealism of the movement to a more complicated awareness and articulation of double-consciousness to a full-fledged black consciousness that led to power struggles and the eventual dispersion of the troupe. What Myrick-Harris makes abundantly clear is that the tension between integrationist and nationalist ideologies, between the desire to establish an integrated troupe and the desire to develop a black aesthetic, was evident from the beginning and present throughout the FST's history. Or as Larry Neal describes the fate of the FST, the chief problem was "its constant inability to understand what it should be about" (170). Also present, in one form or another, was the belief "that moral suasion could conquer all" (*The Free Southern* 28).

At its most successful, the FST offered Smith not just a cautionary tale but also an instructive model for the kind of theater she attempts to promote. It established and affirmed the power of art in general and theater in particular to function as an agent of social change and a shaper of identity. It reaffirmed a function of artists as being responsible and accountable for the political as well as the aesthetic consequences of their efforts. It dignified black art forms and celebrated the contributions ordinary people and everyday experience can bring to an aesthetic experience. It recognized the presence of slavery as a persistent motif in African-American expressions of oppression and liberation. It lauded and promoted an African as opposed to a European sensibility regarding the ritual function of performance. In essence, the FST offered productions that "in them-selves, were acts of liberation" (Myrick-Harris, *Mirror* 90).

The FST was established by Gilbert Moses, John O'Neal, and Doris Derby in the spring of 1963 to provide a form in which "the theatricality of the black church, the black freedom movement, black music, black militancy—black power in its widest and deepest sense—can be made into myth, allegory, public performance" (*The Free Southern* xi–xii). To say the FST was seen as a sacred calling to the creators would not be an overstate-ment. Indeed, Geneviève Fabre explains that the black church served as "the principal model" for the FST because in this institution "ceremonies of all sorts were staged, mingling theatricality, ritual, and improvisation, enlisting the participation of the congregation" (55).

Among the issues the growing civil rights movement needed to address, the creators identified a lack of imagination. The FST was developed to fill a need to articulate the experience of the liberation struggle because "there is something in the human spirit that is reflective, that asks for some-one to 'tell it like it is'" (*The Free Southern* xii). Furthermore, the creators were insistent that part of their agenda was to serve not just the artists and actors and directors who wanted to say something, but the audience, which "cries to express itself" (*The Free Southern* xii). The members of the FST consistently affirmed that the audience was "the most important and ex-pressive element" in their performances (*The Free Southern* xii).

In the group's prospectus, they identify as their fundamental objective "to stimulate creative and reflective thought among Negroes in Mississippi and other Southern states by the establishment of a legitimate theatre, thereby providing the opportunity for involvement in the theatre and the associated art forms" (*The Free Southern* 3). They liken their efforts and imagine their development as being similar in origin to those of blues and jazz. The theater, they hoped, would open a new area of protest that would promote the development of black arts and artists, permit the growth and "self-knowledge" of a black audience, and supplement the existing struggle for freedom. From its inception the FST was to be by and for the black community, employing black artists, exploring themes that related to prob-lems in the black community, and conducted for black audiences. The cre-ators envisioned a primarily pedagogical role. The FST would fill an edu-cational and cultural void by educating African Americans of the South about their history and the civil rights movement.

Although it was conceived and conducted by blacks for blacks, as Stu-dent Nonviolent Coordinating Committee member Gilbert Moses remarks, the political aims of FST also "reflected the political aims of the Movement at that time: integration" because "one of the first steps of rebelling against the Southern society . . . was to make an effort to integrate anything" (*The Free Southern* 9). Blacks and whites were expected to work together in the theater as they did in the movement. Thus, one of the things the FST believed they could accomplish was to "promote the growth and self-knowledge of a new Southern audience of Negroes and whites" while "liberating creative talent that had been denied the opportunity of development and expression" (*The Free Southern* 11). These goals would be accomplished by emphasizing "the universality of the problems of the Negro people" (*The Free Southern* 12).

The early recruitment and participation of a white professor of drama, Richard Schechner (who later reviewed *Fires in the Mirror*), was a demonstration of the FST's commitment to an integrationist vision. Financial and professional support also came from integrated sources, largely the Northern theater community. Many distinguished black and white actors, including Harry Belafonte, Paul Newman, Ruby Dee, and Rod Steiger, lent their talents toward fund-raising and ensuring that FST's activities were being reported in leading New York publications. FST also received major funding in the form of a Rockefeller grant. Because support was coming from both black and white Americans, the group decided that, whenever possible, they would perform for integrated audiences. The venues would be any available space, from churches to barns. Participants would also include people from the local communities. Essentially, the goal of the FST was to "act as a stimulus to the critical thought necessary for effective participation in a democratic society" (*The Free Southern* 11). What these creators recognized especially is that a cultural and educational dimension was needed in the Southern freedom movement because, as they asserted, "self-knowledge and creativity are the foundations of human dignity" (*The Free Southern* 12).

"You are the actors." This is how John O'Neal, one of the founders of FST, addressed his first audience. Although FST's productions did not always make use of the actual words of participants in the struggle, as Anna Deavere Smith's work does, they did draw on the general cultural expressions characteristic of Southern African-American culture, "such as the Black Church sermon and music," to convey messages about the struggle (Myrick-Harris, *Mirror* 42). The troupe also held discussions after the plays to solicit the community's response and to help them articulate the connection between their theater experience and their actual lives. Just as Smith's plays derive much of their power from their text—the actual words of people living through culturally divisive conflicts—the members of the

FST recognized that "relevance in the theatre finally depends on the plays. While there is a sense in which all good plays (art) are universal, therefore relevant to all human experience, each of us finds most full that particular reflection of ourselves and our own experience" (*The Free Southern* 177). As Fabre reminds us, "the scripts created by the FST were written not as literary texts" but mainly "to create a theatrical experience: and to establish a forceful means of communication with the audience" (59).[10]

A large portion of the plays performed drew on the resources of the slave narrative tradition in actual or evocative ways. One of the first such original productions was *In White America,* a dramatic reading of black history based on historical documents dating back to the slave trade written by a white, Northern history professor, Martin Duberman. FST added to the historical readings the singing of freedom songs as a way to encourage audience participation. Also written and performed by the FST was *Where Is the Blood of Your Fathers?* which examines enslaved people's struggles against oppression before the Civil War. Using a variety of documents—including the narratives of Frederick Douglass and William Wells Brown, newspaper clippings, addresses, journals, letters, sermons, and songs—the play dramatized episodes of slave life through an alternation of vignettes, dramatic episodes, and narrative and rhetorical sequences.

Slave Ship, an impressionistic drama by Leroi Jones (Amiri Baraka), was another significant original production. *Slave Ship* portrayed the kidnapping of Africans by European slavers and the horrific journey of the Middle Passage. As Myrick-Harris points out, the play was staged with a "modal approach to theatre," denoting an arrangement in which objects and beings from various time frames coexist. Rather than focusing on the creation of a concrete scene, this kind of theater aims to activate emotions and images. The producer Gilbert Moses used symbols of African cosmology and integrated jazz music with the acting. The ultimate effect Moses wanted to create was "the same effect that church can have" (Myrick-Harris, *Mirror* 146). The audience response was overwhelming as they enthusiastically connected with the drama and waved fists and sang along with the actors. The performance, which combined the history, traditions, and symbols of African and African-American culture, "became a cathartic experience with spiritual dimensions. Few left the performance unmoved" (Myrick-Harris, *Mirror* 147).

Also performed were improvisational dramas that depicted recent real-life struggles in two Louisiana towns—Jonesboro and Bouglusa—much as Smith drew on episodes in Crown Heights and Los Angeles. These dramatizations drew on traditional theatrical forms of African cultures. Characteristics of traditional West African dramatic forms discussed by Ossie Onuora Enekwe include a recognition that the theater's "communal nature is related to its social function as a stabilizing factor. . . . Since this theatre deals with the life of the community, the audience is spontaneously led to participate. Such theatre is doubly entertaining because it is not averse to relishing life while commenting on it" (66). Like traditional African dramatic events, the FST pieces were communal and utilitarian as well as entertaining.

Furthermore, Myrick-Harris explains, "like African oral art forms, [the plays] had the potential to be cathartic, for the community people who helped create and tell the stories of their own lives could unleash some of the anger and hostility they carried silently within them. For the people in the audience such a dramatization could not only bring about catharsis, but also create psychological distance so that they could perhaps see themselves and their situation more objectively and even begin to determine ways of changing the storylines of their real lives. Also traditional in African dramatic forms, [the improvisational plays] encouraged overt audience response and participation through their laughter, cries and shouts of affirmation" (*Mirror* 45–46).[11] These same terms of analysis apply to the theater of Anna Deavere Smith, linking her historically and formally to traditions extending back through the record of African-American liberation movements, beyond the civil rights struggle, and all the way back to slavery and its African antecedents.

As early as 1964, in an interview with *The Nation* John O'Neal remarked about the few whites who attended the FST performances that "our idea that the whites might have come to the play out of some desire for understanding and communication was neatly punctured" (*The Free Southern* 28). At the same time an integrationist agenda was being challenged within the FST itself. Concerned about the implications of this challenge, O'Neal warned in a letter to his colleagues in 1966, as he was leaving the FST to perform alternative military service, that "'black' and 'white' are dysfunctional categories" and encouraged the members that to move toward an exclusively "black" theater "would not be the FST. It would contradict the values of those people who are the theatre; it would not issue from the dynamic of the group relating to itself or from the group or any individuals in the group and their relationship to the community; it would not satisfy the aim of the theater to be a liberating influence on the people who participate in the experience of the theatre" (*The Free Southern* 99). However, O'Neal's plea was soon drowned out by other voices, and with the departure of Richard Schechner, the theater was run exclusively by African Americans.

The troupe's continuous worry over logistical and financial requirements led to fear that the FST would succumb to establishment structures in order to sustain itself. Yet as the documented history of the group attests, what eventually pulled the FST apart was not financial or logistical worries or the external hostility of whites or the fear and disinterest of blacks, but philosophical divisions deep within the troupe itself.[12] In 1985, seventeen years after the dissolution of the FST, it was laid to rest in a traditional New Orleans jazz funeral. The funeral ended a three-day conference (or wake) in which the leaders and former members of the FST conjured up scenes from the past in order to understand the significance of their institution. It seems fitting that the final comment on the conference was not a formal analysis or manifesto but a performed ritual.

What the FST affirmed that remains pertinent to this study is that no liberation movement is complete unless it includes a recognition and use of the imagination of its participants. As the chroniclers of the FST remark, "As a matter of essential form, the theater, all the arts in fact, are political" (*The Free Southern* 174). But in challenging whose political interests are served by acts of imagination, the FST reminds us of an issue as old as the slave narrative tradition itself. As Tom Dent says,

> When the black artist speaks to a critical audience that is not also black, he speaks from one set of cultural and political interests and experience to an audience with different, sometimes hostile priorities and contradicting experience. The black artist, in order to communicate across that gap, becomes an explainer. He must interpret how his own experience relates to the "human experience" of white people so they can understand it. His time is spent in pursuit of more effective explanations of characters or images. That process takes him away from his legitimate work as an artist. . . . The more seriously the black artist tries to affect the white consciousness, the more explicative he must become. The more explicative he becomes, the less attention he gives to the essential of his art. A kind of negative value field is established. Racism systematically verifies itself when the slave can only break free by imitating the master: by contradicting his own reality. (*The Free Southern* 174–75)

Anna Deavere Smith negotiates the communication gap identified by Dent by striving to let people speak for themselves so that the only "masters" whose voices are heard are the people she interviews. Her success as a political artist and a liberating theologian rests largely on her ability to allow ideas to travel without surrendering her aesthetic vision that art is not larger than life, it is life. She understands what ex-slave narrators and those who participate in the slave narrative tradition understand: that the conditions of oppression and the struggle for liberation have their own dramatic merits that do not require exaggeration to be understood or appreciated. What they do require is expression and an opportunity to be heard—to be transformed from testimony to textimony. Creation in the midst of endurance is what constitutes genuine survival and transforms both victim and oppressor into characters entitled to the fullest measure of humanity. When those on the margins dance to the center and those at the center relinquish their space, the result can be community rather than chaos because "American character lives not in one place or the other, but in the gaps between the places, and in our struggle to be together in our differences" (*Fires* xli).

NOTES

1. Act 1, scene 3: "And she was weaned (I never shall forget it), / Of all the days of the year, upon that day; / For I had then laid wormwood to my dug, / Sitting in the sun under the dovehouse wall. / My lord and you were then at Mantua. / Nay, I do bear a brain. But, as I said, / When it did taste the wormwood on the nipple / Of my dug and felt it bitter, pretty fool, / To see it tetchy and fall out with the dug!"

2. Smith connects the experience of Juliet's nurse with what black children feel when they first discover their skin color. This childhood discovery is a persistent trope in slave narratives—a recognition of difference that the author almost always records with painful awareness.

3. "Theatre of testimony" is how playwright and director Emily Mann characterizes her documentary dramas, which are similar in form and function to Smith's work. Although Mann (who directed the world premiere of *Twilight* at the Mark Taper Forum) does not play all the roles herself, like Smith she conducts interviews and uses the actual conversation of involved people to consider issues such as the Vietnam War, the murder of gay activist Harvey Milk, the Holocaust, and most recently her celebrated adaptation of the reminiscences of Sadie and Bessie Delany, *Having Our Say,* all of which she hopes have something to contribute to healing and reconciliation in America. See "The Delany Sisters, Having Their Say." *Washington Post* 14 May 1995: G1, G4.

4. Smith recently mounted another production in the ripe arena of the District of Columbia. *House Arrest: First Edition* focuses on the relationship between the press and the presidency and how our images of America are embodied in the presidency. *House Arrest* includes allusions to slavery, among them modern and historical characters who discuss the relationship between Sally Hemings and Thomas Jefferson. This complicated and expensive production, which required the support of four regional theaters and several grants, is unusual for Smith in that she does not perform in it. An ensemble cast of actors, all using Smith's technique, plays the parts of actual people Smith interviewed. *House Arrest* premiered at Arena Stage

in Washington, D.C., in 1997 to mixed reviews. Like all of Smith's work, it remains in process and will be adapted as it travels to different venues throughout the country.

5. For the purposes of clarity and conservation of space, I reproduce Smith's dialogue not in the poetic form she uses but as punctuated dialogue.

6. When asked to comment on the character of O. J. Simpson, the "lead actor" in another celebrated trial of the decade, philosopher Richard Rorty observed, "I think 'Which is the real person?' is really a bad question. All of us are three or four or sixteen people, because there are that many coherent stories you can tell about our lives" (*Washington Post Magazine* 19 March 1995: 29).

7. Although hair may seem an insignificant attribute around which to develop profound notions of identity, curators at the U.S. Holocaust Memorial Museum recently discovered otherwise. Among the items sent to them by the State Museum of Auschwitz-Birkenau for inclusion in the new museum's exhibitions was a box containing approximately twenty pounds of human hair. Jacek Nowakowski, the curator in charge of acquiring objects, admits that when they first received the hair "we regarded it as just another artifact for the museum," but when "the Content Committee met to discuss the best way to display it, it became clear that the members viewed human hair differently from the other objects." The ensuing discussions about what to do with the hair were among the most sensitive deliberations of the entire project because "hair is a highly personal matter. It is not only part of the human body; it is also part of the human personality—part of one's identity. How you wear your hair tells a lot about you as a person. Hair is so simple—but it is so fundamental." For a fuller discussion of this problem faced by the museum (and its exponential extension for the museum in Poland), see Timothy W. Ryback, "Evidence of Evil." *New Yorker* 15 November 1993: 68–69.

8. Another example of masking—this time where masks are deliberately avoided—is detailed by the captain of the Compton fire department, who tells how his firefighters are denied bulletproof vests because the city council doesn't want to "telegraph the message" that Compton is dangerous (*Twilight* 116).

9. Smith amplifies this quality by including, along with the English dialogue of Korean characters, their words rendered in their native tongue.

10. Accordingly, the FST also initiated the Community Workshop Program, a year-round program geared specifically to the participation of local people.

11. Works considered classic in the Euro-American tradition were also performed, including Bertolt Brecht's play about the Spanish Civil War, *The Rifles of Señora Carra,* and Samuel Beckett's *Waiting for Godot.* Although some members of the troupe considered the performance of these plays a violation of the agenda of the FST to promote a black aesthetic, the plays had a surprising impact on the audience. Audiences made connections between their own liberation struggles and those occurring in other parts of the world in different eras.

12. The theater eventually dissolved and was revived in small coffeehouse performances and community youth programs. For three years (1972–75), some of

the participants staged the television program *Nation Time,* a combination of news analysis, documentaries, and performances. But when this show was canceled it became apparent that the FST could not endure because the participants could not reconcile the deep divisions between art and politics that first engendered the enterprise.

6 Improvising on the Feeling: Charlie Haden

It all comes from our memory, from our past, and from our imagination.
—Richard Davis

One of the most famous accounts of a white person's recognition of his complicity in the system of slavery—when a person comes to honestly reflect on his own character and how he has characterized others—is the story of John Newton, whose hymn "Amazing Grace" went on to become an anthem for civil rights struggles all over the world. Born in 1725, Newton was the son of a seafaring father and devoted and religious mother. A rebellious and contentious teenager, as a young man he lived a debauched life, drinking and gambling. His pious mother's death when he was seven apparently left him with a scorn for things spiritual and he eventually adopted the trade of his father and became a sailor, usually as a member of the crew on a slave ship. Despite a record he kept in journals of his continual struggle with alcohol and his shame over his belligerent and blasphemous acts, he did not change until 1754.

At the time Newton was on a slave vessel that was wracked by a violent storm. Although he survived the storm in the same body, his soul changed when the confrontation with death forced him to reevaluate how he was living his life as an alcoholic and a slave trader. During that storm, when he did not know whether he would live or die, he composed the words of the song that was to become an international anthem of hope. This transformational, spiritual experience led to Newton's decision to become a preacher, a composer of hymns, and a vocal opponent of slavery: "Disagreeable I had always found it; but I think I should have quitted it sooner had I considered it as I now do, to be unlawful and wrong. I hope it will always be a subject of humiliating reflection to me, that I was once an active instrument in a business at which my heart now shudders" (Collins 8).

Newton's personal story of spiritual transformation amplifies the already compelling text of his hymn that insists on the possibility of grace. How one might imagine the grace that "could save a wretch" like Newton, and how it could make others similarly blind "now see," is what energizes the slave narrative tradition and its unique blend of cultural memory and individual imagination. Understood in context with Newton's own story, the song "Amazing Grace" directly linked an abolitionist impulse with a belief in saving grace, but the subsequent broad application of Newton's musical message to struggles for freedom worldwide shows how a liberating theology cast in a compelling aesthetic form can inspire even nonbelievers to confront the slave trader in all of us.

Despite its obvious religious tone, "Amazing Grace" has drawn into its wake many who were nonreligious, irreligious, and even antireligious. "Amazing Grace," as Maurice Jackson observes, "has been used as a song by anyone in need of hope regardless of color or creed."[1] Although it captures for Christians the liberative aspect of God, its concept of liberating grace is accessible to anyone. Given the biographical history associated with the song's composition, one might even assume that the song has had conversional effects, turning people toward a concept of a saving grace that is available to all with the imagination and the will to envision freedom.

As the slave narrative tradition developed, receding further from the historical context of its origination, its liberating impact has remained constant, but slavery as a point of reference has become more broadly construed, serving a function more metaphorical than factual. Likewise, the tradition's religious elements have changed, moving away from strictly theistic and Christian categories to encompass a more expansive notion of spirituality. It is the combination of "memory," "past," and "imagination" that jazz bassist Richard Davis cites as the source of his music, which is also used by contemporary artists who are exploring further dimensions of the slave narrative tradition: a memory acquired from textimony and a past made present through imagination.

Always inclusive in its vision of liberation, the slave narrative tradition of textimony now serves as a model for nonblacks and non-Christians who also want to honor the tradition and explore its many dimensions. Newton's story is an early example of how nonblack people have enhanced the mission of the slave narrative tradition and extended its influence into secular arenas by applying it to various struggles, both private and public. Furthermore, the ways in which Newton's song points us back to his personal story and forward to the universal ramifications of that story demonstrate that textimony can reside in and find full expression in ostensibly nonnarrative and nonblack forms.

Among the nonblack artists whose work could be included in a canon of slave narrative textimony is Charlie Haden, who appreciates how music has narrative dimensions that can tell stories to advance social justice. An amazing grace issues forth from the music he performs as leader of the Liberation Music Orchestra (LMO), what one reviewer cites as "his voice of conscience" (Levenson 24). Designed to express his solidarity with progressive political movements throughout the world, Haden's twelve-member jazz band gathers diverse musicians from multicultural backgrounds to perform "music that comes from people struggling to keep their freedom" (Zipkin 171) that makes a statement about how to initiate and celebrate liberating change.

By extending the slave narrative tradition of textimony to include stories from around the world, Haden underscores a feature of not just textimony but the jazz form in which he chooses to cast it. For jazz, as Fred Wei-han Ho insists, "is the revolutionary music of the 20th century—not just for America, but for the planet as well" because it is "fundamentally rooted to the world's division between oppressor. . . and the liberation struggle of the oppressed" (Ho 284). Through the works they perform and the cooperation they display, the LMO stands as a model for the kind of community and commitment this study explores.

Haden's inclusion in this study may strike some readers as an inappropriate choice, given my early caveats about "black like me" testimonies. But I chose Haden to conclude this study because his presence underscores several significant themes I have been trying to advance. Among them is the posture Haden, as a nonblack, assumes before the African-American tradition. Haden does not presume to appropriate black experience as a way to characterize himself, but he has learned from it ways to develop his character.

Haden embodies what saxophonist Archie Shepp means when he observes that "black as a color doesn't determine blackness. Blackness, that's an attitude, an identity" (Putschögl 276). As explained by Ornette Coleman, one of Haden's most important inspirations and collaborators, Haden acquired this attitude and became the "most natural" of all white bass players Coleman has encountered because he paid his dues. Coleman explains that in the beginning of Haden's career, "the only thing that got Charlie confused was that he finally became aware that he was playing with

Negroes and that made him paranoid, as if the situation were reversed, you know. He hadn't had enough experience as a man to know the difference between his talent and his origin" (Spellman 141–42).

Initially Haden's consciousness of his "origin," coupled with his respect for African-American music and performers, was so profound it was almost paralyzing, but he wasn't the first nonblack jazz musician to experience this feeling. In his autobiography, *Live at the Village Vanguard,* Max Gordon describes how during a performance at the Vanguard, Sonny Rollins walked out after the first set because he "couldn't take" the "blond trumpet player" who sounded great when they played together in California but terrible in this celebrated New York venue. When Gordon asked the other musicians how a player could sound so different on different coasts, pianist Al Dailey replied, "It's the vibes, man, the vibes. . . . Coltrane, Miles, Coleman Hawkins, Bill Evans, Mingus, and Sonny himself, cats who've played here and left their vibes here, man! . . . That blond cat didn't belong in this company. The vibes scared the hell out of him" (Balliet, "Rollins" 58).

But Haden never ran away from the vibes. Instead, he combined his talent with a respect for the music's origins and chose to participate in the liberative and creative strains of African-American culture; in so doing, he establishes a model for nonblack participation in the slave narrative tradition. His presence in this study is presented as an act of hope about what the slave narrative tradition can achieve: Ideally performed, the slave narrative tradition works toward its own extinction, and inviting nonblack participation in the tradition is one step in achieving that goal.

The appearance of a nonblack artist coming at the conclusion of a study of the slave narrative tradition provides symmetry. For just as white abolitionists often functioned as amanuenses and editors of the first slave narratives, Haden functions in the LMO as one who amplifies the voices of the voiceless. Haden does not assume the guise of author or creator of the textimonies of the oppressed, but like the abolitionists who preceded him, Haden facilitates the emergence of their textimonies. Or as he simply puts it, "I play music that I think is important for people to hear" (Mandel, "Charlie Haden's" 21).

Finally, because Haden does not publicly align himself with any specific religious orientation but nonetheless affirms a spiritual dimension in his life and work, he reinforces my contention that however untraditionally one locates the divine and imagines grace, one can still profess a liberating theology. Haden locates his spirituality in the same space occupied by all those whose work has been considered in this study—in relation to self, to others, to craft—and in so doing emphasizes the dialogic nature of liberating cultural production and what it is meant to accomplish. Simply put, his work embodies the call-and-response ethic.

The LMO, like the slave narrative tradition, began as a way to document one person's outrage. Like the original participants in the slave narrative tradition, who were responding to the dominant example of oppression in their time, Haden's involvement with the LMO began at the height of the Vietnam War when he began to lament that so much was spent "killing innocent people in Viet Nam" while "major problems in our own country are being neglected—poverty, civil rights, mental illness, drug addiction, unemployment." Furthermore he was angry that "in this, the richest country in the world . . . most creative artists can't live on what they earn from their art." Haden is aware that "this has all been said before," but he still maintains that "no change can begin to take place if everyone remains silent" (Morgenstern 42).

Because Haden refused to remain silent, the LMO, like the slave narrative tradition, has been successful because a white person used his influence and access to amplify the voices that go unheard. And like the slave narrative tradition, the LMO stands as a witness to an ongoing individual and communal concern with the interfaces of art and social conscience. Through the music he performs with the LMO, Haden upholds the transformative potential of the slave narrative tradition and a function of art recently appraised by critic Robert Hughes in the following way: "The arts are the field on which we place our own dreams, thoughts, and desires alongside those of others, so that solitudes can meet, to their joy sometimes, or to their surprise, and sometimes to their disgust. When you boil it all down, that is the social purpose of art: the creation of mutuality, the passage from feeling into shared meaning" (34). Ornette Coleman characterizes Haden's music in terms similar to those advocated by Hughes: "Charlie Haden's music has its roots in Viva la humans. It is not Capitalistic, Communistic, or Socialistic. His music does not dictate. . . . Charlie's music brings one stranger to another and they laugh, cry, and help each other to stay happy" (Litweiler 171).

In creating the LMO, Haden set art in creative opposition to the world of political and social injustice as a way to take his listeners on a passage from feeling to shared meaning. Art, Haden demonstrates, creates a place where one can do some good for the oppressed by putting cultural productions in the context of social pressures and needs. He claims he had little choice in selecting the form his witness would take, remarking that "music is my life. I never had a choice of what I wanted to be when I grew up." However, his experiments with the jazz aesthetic of improvisation led him to adapt it to express his ethics: "It can touch the creative powers in everyone and help make a better world" (Weinstein 55). An aesthetic sense is not all that motivates Haden. Guitarist Pat Metheny describes Haden's music as "very deeply spiritual . . . but that is really just a reflection of who he is. He manifests in sound who he is as a person, and that's the ultimate compliment I think you can give a musician" (Brace C2).

In manifesting his spirituality in sound, Haden is also bringing forth a liberative strain that is part of the jazz aesthetic to which he is committed. It might be said that for most jazz musicians, the very act of being is a liberating statement. As Eric Lott demonstrates in his essay "Double V, Double Time: Bebop's Politics of Style," militancy and jazz music are often "undergirded by the same social facts; the music attempted to resolve at the level of style what the militancy fought out in the streets" (246). In the case of bebop that Lott cites, the music "was about making disciplined imagination alive and answerable to the social change of its time" (243). Although Haden demurs about how he identifies his role, recognizing that he is "a musician and not a politician" (Woodard, "A Healthy" 20–21), he also admits that part of the inspiration behind assembling the LMO was his frustration over systemic oppression. "I felt that I had to do something about it in my own way. . . . I think that every artist dedicated to their art form is really politically motivated, because what they're really doing is bringing beauty to the world against all odds" (Woodard, "A Healthy" 20–21). In American culture, however, jazz is unique in fulfilling this role. Jazz, as Archie Shepp describes it, "'is the lily in spite of the swamp.' It is the triumph of the human spirit, of spirituality and ethicality in the midst of cannibalistic and corrupting capitalism" (Ho 289).

Although many argue that the term *jazz* is an insult to a musical form created by African Americans—a term coined by oppressors[2]—the ways in which the term has been reappropriated (or, in the words of Albert Murray, "extended, elaborated, and refined" to the point where it defines an "Omni-American" aesthetic) reveal a great deal about how the form continues to serve multicultural and revolutionary platforms such as the one articulated by Charlie Haden.[3] In *Playing the Changes*, Craig Werner analyzes how jazz, as a form of "cultural negotiation," engages basic postmodern concerns, including the difficulty of defining or even experiencing the self, the fragmentation of public discourse, and the problematic meaning of tradition. "The jazz impulse engages the question of how to communicate visions of new possibilities—psychological, aesthetic, or political—to audiences and communities that frequently seek release from the dislocations of (post)modern life by retreating to superficially reassuring, if fundamentally outmoded and often counterproductive, cultural attitudes and forms" (xvii).

Haden clearly appreciates these extramusical qualities of jazz that embody ethical, spiritual, and sociopolitical dimensions and exploits the potential in the jazz impulse as a way of defining or creating self as he comes to appreciate others—as he sees himself in relation to a multicultural community and tradition. He understands what Ralph Ellison observed when he wrote that "true jazz is an act of individual assertion within and against the group. Each true jazz moment . . . springs from a contest in which each artist challenges all the rest; each solo flight, or improvisation, represents (like the successive canvases of a painter) a definition of his identity: as individual, as member of the collectivity and as a link in the chain of tradition" (*Shadow and Act* 234). Because jazz possesses a "'spiritualizing' quality" that can "revolutionize the consciousness, values, aesthetics and actions of the people" (Ho 290), it serves as an appropriate form for the mission of Charlie Haden.

In an interview with Josef Woodard, Haden and guitarist Pat Metheny discussed the revolutionary heritage of jazz and how their encounter with it helps prepare them to "push against things." Metheny, in offering advice to young musicians, stressed how important it is "to have a deep understanding of what has preceded them," claiming that all the important jazz musicians were people who had "a healthy dose of disrespect." Concurring with Metheny's assessment of jazz as "the music of rebellion," Haden continues to explain that the quality of rebellion is "rare in all art forms—when someone challenges the art form and challenges the world and take risks to express the passion or the vision inside them," but adds that to do so is both a "responsibility" and a "mission" (Woodard, "A Healthy" 20).

How Haden extends the revolutionary potential of the jazz form and unites it with a responsibility to a mission can be appreciated in the ensemble character of his LMO, but its contribution to our cultural discourse still derives from one person's vision and personal triumph in exploiting his privileged status to link the music and literature of oppressed people with the energy and creativity of the American avant-garde. A prolific musician (who has recorded albums over four decades), Haden is also a composer (who has been awarded a Guggenheim Fellowship and a National Endowment for the Arts grant) and teacher at the California Institute of the Arts in Los Angles (where he founded a jazz program in 1982). All of these aspects of his character are shaped by the same liberative impulse that characterizes those who work within the slave narrative tradition. Haden honors and extends the tradition through his appreciation of the power of musical textimony to address issues of liberation pertinent to African Americans and others seeking justice worldwide. As his frequent collaborator, Carla Bley, explains, "Problems always exist in the human race. . . . I accept them. Charlie doesn't, he's outraged by them" (Carey 7).

In contrast to Haden's outrage and bold stance for liberation is an attitude he displays as a prominent feature of his playing style. Since his New York debut with the Ornette Coleman Quartet, when all the jazz luminaries intimidated him, Haden has always closed his eyes while performing. He also assumes a clearly reverential posture, bending himself around the bass and lowering until his head is almost at the bottom of the bridge (Roberts 45). Howard Mandel describes Haden's playing posture in the following way: "He leans into [the bass] as though the wood whispers a secret message from its core. Sometimes he holds it far away, as a square dance partner do-se-dos—sometimes he bends low, as though his bass embraces and comforts him, then he plucks at the gut strings beneath its bridge to wring out its cries. . . . He plays bass with a dedication and intensity of feeling that marks an artist in any medium" ("Charlie Haden's" 21). Obeisant before the music and the instrument, he visually expresses what he identifies as a necessary element of artistic creation and human contentment. Outrage and passion, he understands, must be disciplined by humility.

As an instructor to students of advanced improvisation, Haden "talk[s] about what happens spiritually when you play, not what happens technically. I talk about the spiritual connection to the creative process" (Schuster 17–18). He tries "to show the musicians how to discover their voices," and he helps them to accomplish this by preaching that they adopt a spiritual posture whereby they create the conditions to find the "music inside you" and learn a spiritual discipline that will enable them to "reach" it and "bring it to your instrument" (Schuster 47).

Although there are many different ways to accomplish this goal, Haden recommends to his students that they "begin with complete silence and contemplate the state of your spiritual self. Then, when you begin to play, it's almost like walking into a cathedral" (Schuster 16). Haden's advice is tantamount to promoting a meditative or prayerful state wherein "there's no yesterday or tomorrow, there's only right now. And in that moment you have to see your insignificance and unimportance to the rest of the universe before you can see your significance or importance" (Schuster 16). This entire process of finding one's spiritual self and expressing it musically cannot be done, Haden insists, "without having humility and respect for beauty. The musician who is best able to make this happen is the one who says, 'Thank you for my gift, for what I've been given. I want to give this back'" (Schuster 47).

Haden teaches humility to his students because that is what music has taught him. And when he affirms that "the secret of playing music in a powerful and beautiful way is to have humility" (Schuster 16), he is advancing a kind of theology of music, of losing one's life in order to find it. Correspondingly, adopting this spiritual posture and the requirement it demands— to "play music at the level of freedom, of beauty"—obliges one to accept the ethical imperative to "play as if you're willing to risk your life for every note you're playing. As if you're on the front lines" (Schuster 17).

Haden is essentially recommending to his students that they care for their souls and the souls of others: "It's especially important to strive to become a great human being, and if you work on that, then you'll be a great musician. I think the secret of this art form . . . is to discover your soul. No two people hear music the same way, just as no two people have the same fingerprints. Every person is unique. I help each student to discover their sound, their melodies, and their harmonies. The whole purpose is to get people to go into the world and play their music" (Schuster 17–18).

Haden's understanding of humility is perhaps also informed by his own attempts "to go into the world" and exercise his imagination in ways that carried with them a special kind of risk. As critic Michael Zipkin observed in 1978, a decade after the founding of LMO, "The master bass player has always been upfront in his feelings, statements and actions—musically, politically and otherwise" because he is "a true survivor, and his survival as an artist, political activist, father, husband and concerned human being becomes all the more potent when one considers that, for many of his twenty years of playing jazz, Charlie has been involved in the use of opiates" (27–28).

Haden's compassion has been deepened by his own direct link to conditions of vulnerability exposed by his drug addiction. He used what he learned through bouts with addiction and by being educated in oppression of others in order to understand a feature of black performance Ornette Coleman describes in the following way: "I think black people in America have a superior sense when it comes to expressing their own convictions through music. Most whites tend to think that it's below their dignity to just show suffering and just show any other meaning that has to do with feeling and not with technique or analysis or whatever you call it" (Spellman 142).

Haden's humility informs his specific approach to jazz, which does not make style paramount but allows many things to influence his creation. Haden resists people's attempts "to put music in categories" (Morgenstern 42). Unlike many musicians, who are wedded to performing and identifying themselves in strict stylistic categories, Haden is remarkably democratic in his tastes and musical partners. All he asks of his collaborators is that they allow him to "follow my convictions" (Mandel, "Charlie Haden's" 22). Accordingly, he will play with anyone whom he believes shares the way he hears his music and sees life. For example, once while he was playing with the legendary Roy Eldridge, the trumpeter asked Haden, "How can you play music with both Ornette Coleman and me?" and Haden replied, "Easy. You're both playing beautiful music" (Mandel, "Charlie Haden's" 22). As Haden explains, "It's all beautiful music. Coleman Hawkins played just as free and deep as Ornette, because they approach music at this level of giving their life for it" (Woodard, "A Healthy" 18).

His diverse musical associations indicate a great deal about Haden's open mind and his insistence that "when music is played from a person's heart, it's true. Wisdom includes both the old and the new, merged. I play the way I play no matter who I'm with" (Morgenstern 42). Haden elaborates his point by moving beyond jazz and reaching toward not just other musical forms but other aesthetic forms. As he explains, "I get the same good feeling from listening to all sorts of music, from Bach to Bird, from seeing a painting by a beautiful painter" because "it all comes from the same place—the place where all creation comes from. In a categorical sense, perhaps things have to be labeled, studied, analyzed. . . . But in the end, as a poet has said, 'Word knowledge is but a shadow of wordless knowledge'—feeling came first, words later" (Morgenstern 42).

Although Haden's adoption of a spiritual intuition and approach to making music that is founded on feeling rather than a rigorous analytical approach may seem to undermine the potential effectiveness of his social justice strategies, he does not see a conflict between how he plays and what he can accomplish by way of liberation. As he explains, both are grounded in a sense of commitment: "So many things have been written and said about the political, economic, and cultural state of our country, that one would almost feel inclined to avoid the issues completely, giving in to a sense of futility. But I'm unable to do this, because, after all, it is my country, too, and I feel very concerned" (Morgenstern 42).

Haden demonstrates his concern by concentrating on how he plays the notes because "every note is as important as the next, and I put my whole life's energy into every note I play" (Brace C2). Possessing what one critic cites as a "head-long dedication to creative expression to music" (Zipkin

27), over the years Haden has waged an equally involved struggle for more universal freedom of expression. Haden's unlikely source for the LMO's communal and wide-ranging effort is rooted in his own early experimentation and proficiency in what many see as jazz's most idiosyncratic and alienating form: free jazz.

Yet in "The Making of Free Jazz," Haden's descriptions of the improvisation that is at the heart of free jazz, his discourses on the technique of this avant garde form are tantamount to a theology: Free jazz offers both a way of life and reason to live. It is not surprising, therefore, that Haden's introduction to the form occurred in the manner of a revelation: "It was like someone had said, 'This is the way it should be'" (Mandel, "Charlie Haden's" 21). Free jazz prophet Ornette Coleman became an influential guide in his life. When he met Coleman in 1957, the saxophonist told him that "the way that he was hearing music was to improvise on the feeling and the inspiration of a song rather than on a chord structure" (Haden, "The Making" 29). And just as there are many feelings, so too can result "so many different ways to improvise." But at the bottom of all this diversity is a commitment: "It's all about honesty and beauty and communicating beautiful music. And how you go about it is what's inside you" (Haden, "The Making" 29).

According to Haden, the ethic of free jazz insists that one remain "open to discovery, experimenting, and playing free"; as Ornette told him, "'Just listen and your roles will come to you'" (Haden, "The Making" 30). Technically speaking, free jazz is a constant modulation in the improvisation that is taken "from the direction of the composition, and from the direction inside the musician, and from listening to each other" (Haden, "The Making" 30). Free jazz therefore became more than a new way of playing; it was also a new way of hearing. It embodied a kind of performance ethic whereby the height of individual expression was achieved by listening "to one another very intensely and very closely . . . completely" (Zipkin 28).

Haden found that the discipline of listening with "my whole being" required by free jazz lifted him to "another level of consciousness that doesn't have that much to do with everyday thinking. It's as if you could imagine life before there were words" (Zipkin 28). Again, Haden finds one aesthetic example insufficient to explain the dimensions of his principle when he continues, "Once you realize the technical aspects of any art—as a painter, it's perspective; as a dancer, the different steps—it becomes a part of you and you don't think about it anymore. I tried to get into that as completely as I could while I was playing" (Zipkin 56).

Exploring style in a variety of contexts while taking inspiration from the entire composition requires nothing less than a religious response, a whole-soul commitment to change and transcendence. In essence, the ongoing spirit of free jazz is "to create something that's never been before in a way that's going to change the world and is something that you do with your whole life's energy" (Haden, "The Making" 30). But as avant-garde as this approach may have seemed at the time, Haden understands that it is sim-ply an extension of the creative imperatives that characterize African-American aesthetic forms in which one, like Charlie Parker, is appreciated for "risking his life with every note he played . . . to create something that's never been before, on a level that's way above the normal level of life. That's what Ornette's music is about, that lasting way of improvising, that des-peration to create something that's never been before" (Haden, "The Making" 30). Although this risk may appear to be utterly solipsistic and taken solely for the pleasure of the musician, the way Haden and Coleman see the potential of improvisation is not just in what it creates, but in the effect it has; musicians may "play it as if you never heard music before, creating it for the first time," but "as for the audience, they know they are going to be challenged, and that they're going to have an experience they'll never forget" (Haden, "The Making" 30).

Thus it is Haden's spirituality—a combination of outrage and passion, humility and vulnerability, experimentation and commitment to the cre-ative process—that allowed him eventually to overcome the vibes of his ancestors and to learn how to give back to the tradition to which he was indebted. As he explains, "I have a feeling as far as I myself am concerned and my own dedication to playing creative music, as also being a part of the first people to have dedicated their lives to this art form" (Palmer 17). Haden made this remark in a 1972 interview with Robert Palmer in which he describes how he tried to "imagine what it was like in the beginnings of jazz playing." In his imaginative reconstruction, Haden not only dem-onstrates his debt to and appreciation of the form's origin, but also reveals the ways in which it parallels the slave narrative tradition, where "a mu-sical expression and language evolved from life or from an experience of a people . . . the black people. And as that evolved, the beautiful thing, I thought, was young people all of a sudden finding themselves with a need inside to be a part of that new language. . . . And it actually happened right here in our own—if you want to call it our own—country" (Palmer 17).

Haden's qualification of "our own country," is significant because he is aware that those responsible for creating the American art form of jazz have not been fully appreciated, either musically or in terms of human rights. Haden observes that his African-American musical ancestors have been exploited, most recently by rock musicians, whom he charges with imitating "black peoples' music" in such a way that it robs African Americans of their identity and prevents them from profiting from their talent (Palmer 45). Comparing this trend to blackface minstrelsy, Haden cites such actions as "not accepting any social responsibility" (Palmer 45). It is not surprising, therefore, that Haden's interviews often include some reverential remark about a jazz ancestor.

Haden once related to Josef Woodard an incident that occurred in 1973 when he was playing in Miami at the same time as legendary bassist Charlie Mingus. Mingus gave Haden the nickname "Bass" and, by identifying Haden with the instrument over which Mingus was expert, conferred upon him a distinct honor that Haden fully appreciated. When Mingus asked Haden whether he could borrow his instrument, Haden offered to give it to him as a symbol of respect. Mingus did play the instrument but returned it; still, Haden was so overcome by the fact that the instrument had been played by Mingus that he "didn't touch that fingerboard for about four weeks after that" (Woodard, "A Healthy" 17). Similarly, in recalling Charlie Parker, Haden laments they never had the opportunity to play together, but describes with a mystical confidence his elation over realizing that in 1937 Bird had played in bands near where Haden was living, often taking spells to practice in the surrounding woods where Haden played as a child. "I mean, we were probably in the same place. It's unbelievable" (Woodard, "A Healthy" 19), Haden recalls with the enthusiasm one might feel after having visited the site of a miracle.

Accordingly, Haden advises his students to appreciate the great tradition from which they are emerging, reminding them that although many of the great jazz performers began young, they all learned about the values attached to what they were playing. He laments that so many young jazz musicians have "self-esteem, but not humility and respect. . . . The fact is they should consider themselves honored and lucky to be able to play with musicians the caliber of a Sonny Rollins, Hank Jones, Max Roach," all of whom understand that "it takes humility to become a great musician" (Schuster 19). Haden's regrets that jazz forebears are not fully appreciated leads him to assess this lack of respect as a way of devaluing the art form itself. If he had his way, "there wouldn't be any money charged for people to hear music, because creative music in its true sense is supposed to be given to people and communicated to people, and having to pay money somehow takes away from that in all of its aspects . . . the profit motive isn't conducive to creativity" (Palmer 17).

The economics of the music industry also prevent jazz from reaching the wider audience Haden is convinced jazz deserves. Haden tried for a while to influence musical corporations to be responsive to the jazz community. "I went to executives and said, 'Man, it is very important for a lot of people to listen to this music because it's going to educate them, and bring them closer to the creativity inside themselves.' But nobody would listen to me" (Zipkin 27). Haden took on this challenge because, as he explains, "Every white middle-class generation in this country has had a racist conditioning which includes not only being against the black man and any other race except their own white race but being against anything that's meaningful or that's beautiful or that's creative, it's all the same" (Palmer 17). Linking his social justice concerns about racial struggles in America to a broader notion of the liberation of the artistic spirit, Haden hopes that what he presents will contribute to people's education about creativity. For like all those who participate in the slave narrative tradition, Haden insists that one way to advance social justice is to open people's minds to "the importance of life and of creative art" (Palmer 17).

In Haden's estimation, what stifles creativity is the same thing that leads to the world's problems; it all "stems from racism, from men thinking about money and material gain, the governments wanting more territories, more wealth in other countries, more people under their thumb, world resources" (Palmer 17). That is why artists who are confident about their creativity have a responsibility to create conditions conducive to developing the imaginations of others. In turn, society should value the contributions of artists and provide conditions whereby they can pursue their craft and vision. Although Haden knows that art can emerge out of oppression, the goal of all creative effort should also include the belief that "everybody's supposed to have a good place to live, everyone's supposed to have good food to eat, there's not supposed to be any poverty, malnutrition. And I think when that begins to happen, there will be an intelligence and an awareness in human beings that's going to start developing, and more and more people will be developing themselves to their full potential, and then they will appreciate everything that comes natural to appreciate which includes the art forms in this country and everything will be the way it should be" (Palmer 17). Haden's description of the way it should be is not unlike Victor Anderson's notion of the "cultural fulfillment" to which theology should aim.

How Haden strives to make "everything the way it should be" is demonstrated in his ability to "improvise on the feeling"—the feeling of rage and humility, of justice and hope. In remarks he made after successfully managing his eight-year narcotic addiction but just before he created the

LMO, Haden describes his own experience of amazing grace when he had a kind of conversion, a feeling that "right now it's like beginning all over again for me. Every experience is a new one, and every day something new happens to me," which led him to give priority in his life to his creative impulses "and make a living as a side effect from that" (Morgenstern 42). His desire to express himself creatively and to use his talents responsibly is what saved Haden from a life of addiction. It also led him to other challenges that he saw as part of his creative mission: to study his instrument, to learn more about history and government, in effect to "know the society I live in" and to do all the things that "are included in becoming a more fully aware human being, and developing oneself to the greatest potential, becoming a productive person" (Morgenstern 42). This discipline and creativity amount to his belief that one should strive to open one's self to other people. "People think only of themselves. I'm trying to open myself up to interaction with others, to asking and thinking and giving—not only with musicians but everyone" (Morgenstern 42).

Haden's "everyone," whom he represents in the LMO, extends the pan-African scope of the slave narrative tradition, connecting its historical implications with other struggles for freedom worldwide. Yet by chronicling through music significant events that have marked the movement toward freedom, Haden both records and creates history, charting the universal truths that remain constant. As he explains, "The truth that came from Charlie Parker and Billie Holiday, and that which comes from the creative musicians today, is equal in truth to that of the poet, painter, sculptor, and composer of the past and present. Both truths are spelled as one and come from the same place" (Morgenstern 42). Furthermore, his music allows him to exploit more completely a function of art characteristic of the slave narrative tradition that "even when most pessimistic and bitter, arise[s] out of an impulse to celebrate human life" (Ellison, *Shadow and Act* 114). Although Haden's attempts to celebrate human life occur within a musical context, his performance with the LMO is supported and enhanced by a literary tradition of textimony as he draws inspiration and lyrics from writings by people as diverse as an anonymous freedom fighter in El Salvador or poet Langston Hughes.

The LMO's first album, *Liberation Music Orchestra* (1969), was Haden's response to the nation's involvement in Vietnam and its growing discontent with the foreign policies of Richard Nixon. Their second album, *The Ballad of the Fallen* (1983), emerged after Ronald Reagan was elected and began ordering military excursions into Central America. And the LMO's last album, *Dream Keeper* (1991), appeared just as George Bush began

American's incursion into the Middle East. The ensemble's energy and repertoire fill in not just the gaps of time between their performances and recordings but also gaps in history, giving an account of recent and past events from a perspective not always included in customary reporting and accounts.

Musically the group offers a patchwork of styles and attitudes, from folk melodies to free play, from brooding laments to carousing marches, making resourceful use of music from a variety of settings and styles. Their repertoire includes folk songs from the Spanish Civil War, Salvadoran melodies, the African National Congress (ANC) anthem, and original compositions inspired by events such as the Democratic Convention of 1968 and the civil rights action of Martin Luther King Jr. As Haden explains, "We're playing what's going on in the world. The way I play music is to make the people a part of the music to the point where they question what's happening in the world" (Brace C2).

Because of the economics of the music business and the other professional commitments of the LMO musicians, the group performs and records infrequently. An anomaly among jazz bands, the LMO has issued just three albums in twenty years. Because recording companies do not welcome large aggregates with an overtly political message, the LMO has recorded on three different labels across as many continents in order to parcel out the cost of production and distribution. Furthermore, the LMO's first album has the distinction of being the object of an attempt by the record company's shareholders to withdraw it from the catalogue because of its "anti-American" content (Brace C2). But as social conditions continue to deteriorate, Haden keeps relighting the revolutionary spark that inspired this first effort in 1969. Blending contemporary politics with avant garde music, Haden, in the words of Josef Woodard, "meld[s] the anthemic voice of solidarity found in revolutionary songs with the anguished and soaring individual expression of fluent jazz soloists" while maintaining "an abiding respect for the people's material," which the LMO "adapts and renders universal" ("Charlie Haden" 71–72). Although the issues Haden confronts in his music may change, the struggle for liberation, whatever the context, remains relevant.

Described by Joe Carey as "one of the few jazz artists to successfully espouse active political consciousness on record and in person" (7), Haden has "been labeled everything from 'radical' to 'Communist' even though his impassioned music and polemics are primarily directed at institutions that repress the individual's right to creativity and freedom" (Carey 7). Haden's commitment to growth encompasses not only the musician or artist but "all people because he sees his music as a way for all people to share in the creative process, to 'bring people closer to meaningfulness in life'" (Zipkin 28). His dedication to creative expression in music parallels his involved struggle for a more universal freedom of expression through social justice. Haden admits that "it's very hard to play the music you believe in, music that you know should be good, and do good" because in the same way people are conditioned by racism, "people are taught what to like, and what's important; they are taught their taste in everything, and pattern their lives after a talk show . . . from their clothes to their thoughts and opinions and values" (Zipkin 27).

In his own life, Haden strives to avoid being conditioned and to spiritually and creatively find his own path. He paid his dues to get to this point, and his eclectic background—emerging from a musical Midwestern family that performed folk and country music on local radio shows—contributes to his ability to see the whole composition behind the different musical contexts and the whole human being in different cultural contexts. How a child raised on country music grew up to challenge the structure of music, how a child who began performing at age two grew into a man who indicted the music industry, how a middle-class white child came to identify with the oppression of African Americans, Haden explains in the following way:

> That music isn't that far apart. . . . They both are about finding a voice to express all the heartache and sorrow of trying to maintain dignity while working to pull yourself out of extreme poverty. The art form of jazz was formed from the African slaves' struggle for freedom . . . and country and western music was born in poverty. Mountain people playing on washboards, and tubs with broomsticks sticking out of them with a string, and jugs, blowing on jugs. I mean we used to have a whiskey jug, man, that my dad played. My grandpa played the fiddle on his chest, not under his chin. I'm talking about people living in extreme poverty just the way African people were after slavery. If you listen, you'll hear the similar themes. (Brace C1–C2)

Finding similar themes and promoting the ways in which oppressed people do not just survive and endure but create and appreciate is the mission of the LMO. Through their blend of avant-garde technique and traditional folk material, Haden and the LMO musically articulate the connections between different struggles for freedom and use their imaginations to transmit beauty, to give back to the world, and to agitate for social justice. Haden understands that his wish that "everybody could get together and talk sometime" to discuss what they can do to make life "more meaningful" (Zipkin 57) is unlikely to be fulfilled, so he counts on his music to accomplish something similar. Haden worries that "the natural sensitivity of most human beings is stifled along the paths of their lives" (Zipkin 57), so he perseveres in his musical mission to reawaken people's sensitivities. Like Wright and Gaines before him, he also hopes to reach young people before they have a chance to be stifled.

To circumvent the racist and social conditioning Haden finds so destructive, he suggests as "one of the most important ways of changing from the shallow values to creative values" the education of children "because a child has a natural creative being. It's very important to surround children with creative thought, and teachers, and to impress upon them the importance and reverence of life" (Zipkin 57). Haden's music may not reach children in his audiences, but it may reach the child inside of each of us, "the creativity that is inside us," so that we can raise ourselves the way we want to raise our children: as "brilliant, majestic and sacred human beings, who are capable of making a world where people use their intelligence for the good of humanity" (Zipkin 57).

ⓠ ⓠ ⓠ

> Each of us, helplessly and forever, contains the other—male in female, female in male, white in black, black in white. We are part of each other.
> —James Baldwin

In a 1987 profile, Howard Mandel describes Charlie Haden as a "compulsive, though hardly innocent, idealist" who provides a "link between our vanishing rural culture and today's pan-ethnic improvisatory jazz" (20). His family of professional singers and musicians began with The Grand Old Opry and toured churches and state fairs, eventually settling into *The Haden Family Radio Show*. A popular feature on Midwest airwaves in the late 1930s and early 1940s, the show was broadcast live every day out of the family home in Shenandoah, Iowa, where Haden was born in 1937. Neither Charlie nor his family had any formal musical training; all were self-taught musicians. By age two he was being introduced by his father as "the yodelin' cowboy" during the morning and afternoon radio shows the family performed. "Everything I know about music I learned from singing on the radio every day from the time I'm two until 15" (Brace C1). Although this lifestyle didn't necessarily offer a context for Haden's radical politics to emerge, it did influence his lifelong interest in folk material and the rich, melodic quality of his sensitive bass lines, both of which he put in service of his social justice imperatives after he encountered free jazz.

Haden began playing bass after a bout of polio at fifteen left his face temporarily paralyzed and ended his singing career. Although he quickly became sufficiently skilled to win a scholarship to Oberlin, he chose to attend West Lake College of Modern Music in Los Angeles. There he tried to learn to play by first learning how to read music. "Up to that point, music to me was just my ear, and hearing. Putting it out, connecting it with your insides, your brain and heart, and singing. Listening, not thinking about theory or fundamentals. Reading was a shock to me. But I got over it" (Mandel, "Charlie Haden's" 21).

Haden soon abandoned formal schooling to learn by praxis, attending nightclubs where jazz was played. Eventually he was invited to sit in and perform with the musicians. He learned more about music at this informal "night school" than he did in a conventional classroom; not surprisingly, he connects this praxis approach with other forms of learning and awareness. "[It's] the same way you develop your mind, your feelings about politics or about music. I never felt I had a choice—all I thought about was playing first with records, then with musicians. Your sound develops after your ears tell you, 'You're gonna play better if you sound good.' And so you learn how you want the instrument to sound" (Mandel, "Charlie Haden's 21). In the early 1950s, playing with Art Pepper and Hampton Hawes, Haden experienced what racism was like for African Americans. He recalls vivid memories of driving around Los Angeles with pianist Elmo Hope curled up in the back seat because in those days even interracial mixes among musicians were taboo (Carey 7).

Haden ignored these taboos, and his search for how to expand what his instrument could do led him to the then-unknown African-American saxophonist Ornette Coleman, who was supporting himself as an elevator operator. Along the way Haden also made brief forays into commercial music, playing jingles on an electric bass, but he came home "depressed, sad, sick, and nauseous. I felt I was perpetuating values, spiritually and musically, I didn't believe in. I felt I was aiding and abetting the enemy. I realized I was miserable, so I decided never to do that again" (Mandel, "Charlie Haden's" 21). Coleman helped turn Haden around and gave him the support to pursue his vision, to say what he wanted to say on his instrument by radically shifting "the whole sound and direction" (Mandel, "Charlie Haden's" 21).

This transformation Haden describes as happening in a "natural way," the "way it was supposed to be" (Mandel, "Charlie Haden's" 21), and to play this way became nothing less than "a mission" (Woodard, "Charlie Haden" 20). Haden recalls, "Before I met Ornette I would sometimes feel to play not on the changes of the song, sometimes I would feel to play on the inspiration and the feeling of the song, and create a new chord structure to it in my solo. Whenever I tried to do that, whoever I was playing with would get very upset because they didn't know where I was. And I would have to bring the melody back in, so everybody would know where to come back in. So I had to be careful who I did this with. And the first time I played with Ornette, he was doing that, I said, 'Man, Finally!'" (Litweiler 60).

Thus, in Los Angeles in the late 1950s, free jazz was born. Together with Don Cherry on trumpet and Billy Higgins on drums, Coleman and Haden formed a quartet that changed the musical landscape forever by tossing out song structure and throwing into question melodies and tempos. To this effort Haden's own contribution was a method of juxtaposing independent bass lines against the lines of the soloist. He abandoned conventional bass positions and reacted to the free flow of the horn lines in such a way that the bass remained a harmonic cornerstone for the group while still providing the beat and offering solos that were on an equal melodic terms with the horns. Haden impressed Ornette Coleman because he came with an important blend of attributes: a strong sense of responsibility to the communal process, willingness to listen to the suggestions of other musicians about the role he should play in the group, and a peculiar ear that was already developing its own idiosyncratic genius (Spellman 123).

The bold challenge to music offered by the Ornette Coleman Quartet is best expressed in the titles of their first two recordings for Atlantic Records: *The Shape of Jazz to Come* and *Change of the Century*. Haden's own contribution to the free jazz movement was "a constant modulation in the improvising that was taken from the direction of the composition, and from the direction inside the musician, and from listening to each other" (Litweiler 148). Haden's technique, as described by Robert Palmer, is significant because of the way he conjures so much out of so little, elaborating "on the minimal materials of the fanfare—a handful of chromatic intervals and a single melodic skip that might imply a modulation or chord change. With nothing more to work from, Haden begins to sketch dimensions of a new world . . . he is improvising from the flavor and feeling of the horn's introduction, and not from any regular chord structure. The solo is pure melodic exposition, but the relationships between the notes are closer to blues singing than they are to the fixed intervals of the piano keyboard" (Schuster 16–17). What Haden has accomplished by playing this way Joachim Berendt evaluates as nothing less than a "revolution" of "the harmonic concept of bass playing in jazz." He was the first bassist who created a solid harmonic foundation out of the passage of independent melodies. In technical terms, Haden isn't a virtuoso but his "virtuosity lies on a higher level" as a "master of simplicity, which is among the most difficult things to achieve" (Schuster 17).

In creating and promoting free jazz and his own contribution to the movement, Haden was demonstrating a principle he finds paramount to his musical ethic. He explains, "One of the most important things in this music is to create something that's never been heard before, but not just for the sake of doing it, but because it's a priority in your life. To experience that moment when the music allows you to touch it and be close to it, that's what it's all about" (Brace C2). Haden's experimentation was not limited to music, however, and several times in his career his addiction to narcotics stalled him. In 1961 Haden's involvement with drugs led to his losing his New York cabaret card, effectively denying him participation in the music he helped to create. He broke his probation in 1966 while "trying to stay clean by drinking" but admits that he was "like a walking dead person, doing nothing constructive, not playing anymore" (Morgenstern 20).

Haden detoxified his system but soon relapsed. It was only when he joined Synanon House, an independent, unorthodox narcotics rehabilitation community in Santa Monica, that he made progress, in part by seeing how others had changed and by working at menial chores. After a year of taking the cure, he started to play again. He eventually helped established a Synanon House in New York City and continues to endorse the program's methods (Morgenstern 20). These repeated encounters with his own vulnerability and the vulnerability of others similarly oppressed by addiction have obviously played a role in enhancing Haden's empathetic powers. At San Francisco's Delancey Street Foundation rehabilitation center in 1977, Haden learned what "prepares people of all age groups and races, with many different problems, to go back out into society to continue whatever goals they have in life" (Zipkin 27).

When Haden finally succeeded in managing his addiction, he welcomed his instrument back in his life like he was "meeting an old friend" (Zipkin 28). This experience led him to include addiction as one of the forces of oppression that he targets in his challenge to society. The profit motive that maintains the drug trade Haden sees as leveled primarily at those who are already oppressed because "the people who control the economy have to have addiction to hold down the people in the ghettos. As long as a person has a needle in his arm, he's not going to threaten the people who are exploiting him" (Palmer 47). More intimately, Haden understands that

"people who are addicted to drugs are not in control of their lives at all—
its impossible for them to create to their fullest potential" (Zipkin 57).

The ways in which addiction affected all parts of his life led him to conclude that music could be more than a form of entertainment and a personal experience. As he explains, "I know it's idealistic-sounding, but the
first time I got healthy, I discovered inside me that I felt personally responsible for making everything better—not only for me, but for everyone I
knew, and for human beings everywhere. And, as I started a family, I
wanted it to be good for them, too. The way I had to do that better than
any other way was through music; you communicate to thousands of
people through recordings and concerts. And that communication is a vital
part of the creative process. One of the most important things in life is being
able to share, to continue that thing you yourself experienced originally,
from the beginning" (Zipkin 57).

Music provided the model for how Haden could get close to people, creating the same kind of imaginative transformation the slave narrative tradition effects. "There comes a point when you play music together, that you
get very close to one another—not only musically, but spiritually and as
other human beings, too. You just flow and go with the flow of the music;
you're very sure of it. For an artist, it's important for these things to happen in other parts of one's life, beyond the act of creating—with other human beings, or alone. It is experiencing something in a way that brings tears
to your eyes, it's so beautiful. That's the way I try to live every day. It isn't
a conscious trying; it's just the way I wake up every morning" (Zipkin 57).

After years of risking his life "physically, emotionally, and spiritually"
(Zipkin 57) in his use of narcotics, Haden became steeled toward other
kinds of risks, but this time took on challenges other than self-destruction,
challenges that were part of his self re-creation because they put something
larger at stake and embodied his quest to connect with other people. For
example, as recounted in nearly all the articles written about Haden, his
initiation of a small symbolic act of solidarity with the oppressed led to
an international incident. In 1971, Haden was arrested in Portugal while
performing with the Ornette Coleman quartet in Europe as part of a four-
teen-country tour of Europe with a Newport Jazz Festival package that
included many prominent musicians. Haden had not premeditated his act,
but admits that every time he performs he hopes he won't have to play
somewhere with a government with "whose politics I didn't agree" (Zipkin
57). When he realized that the tour with Coleman's quartet meant a last
stop in Portugal, he began to figure out "what I was going to do to make
my feelings felt" (Zipkin 57).

At that time Portugal was ruled by a dictatorship that was still attempt-ing to maintain a hold on what was left of its colonial empire. As Haden remarks, "The guys who were recruited in Portugal to go fight the black liberation armies in Africa refused to fight, like the guys [Americans] who go to Canada here [rather than fight in the Vietnam War]. If they refused to fight, they weren't put in jail—they were put on the front lines to be killed" (Litweiler 142–43). Not wanting "to leave Ornette in an uptight position" (Zipkin 57), he chose a course that would allow him to play and not involve anybody else in his personal statement. The group concluded their performance by playing Haden's "Song for Che," which Haden per-sonally dedicated to "the black liberation movements in Mozambique, Angola, and Guinea-Bissau." Haden describes the scene that followed: "You couldn't hear, there was such a cheer. There were about 20,000 people there, a lot of them students who were against the government, and the cheering continued through most of the song" (Zipkin 57).

Among those attending the concert were many students who opposed government policies. The group played an encore and at the conclusion of the set Haden, Dewey Redman, and Ed Blackwell gave a raised-fist sa-lute. After that fights broke out in the audience and Haden was warned not to stay alone that night. The rest of the festival was canceled and Haden left his hotel just as the police arrived to get him. He was formally arrested at the airport and taken to the Lisbon prison, where he was kept alone in a room for several hours. After that he went through several hours of in-terrogation and was finally forced to sign a statement in Portuguese that he did not understand. While the Portuguese officials were interrogating him, they were also trying to persuade him by showing him photos and brochures of their African colonies that explained "all the good things they were doing for black people there" (Litweiler 143).

Through Coleman's intervention, a cultural attaché from the U.S. Embassy eventually came to get Haden. Recalling the episode, Haden remarks, "I'll tell you something, man, it was a drag. But I've thought about it alot after-wards, and I know I would do the same thing if I was put in that position again. People have to act on what they believe in, or nothing's ever going to change. If someone was changed by what happened, that was worth it to me, because their children will be changed as a result, and there will be more of us" (Zipkin 57). How effective Haden's act was in encouraging change will never be known, but after the government changed, he was invited back to Portugal for the 1978 Avante festival, an all-cultural event with artists from different countries, where he played to an audience of 40,000 who began chanting his name when he appeared on stage (Zipkin 57).

The recognition he received on his return was gratifying to Haden, but not the reason why he acted that night back in 1971. As he explains, "I've been concerned all my life about human rights and racial equality. I knew I had to do something" (Roberts 41), leading one critic to conclude that "this courageous decision typifies Haden's remarkable career: his dedication to creative music has always been matched by an equally fierce commitment to the cause of human rights" (Roberts 41). Haden admits, "I never sat down and said, 'Well, I'm going to become politically involved.' I grew up in the Midwest and South, and all around was evidence of racism. I felt the injustice, and I just followed my feelings and tried to tell people how I felt" (Roberts 41). And nowhere is this urge to tell people how he feels more apparent than in the stories he tells through the LMO, which performs challenging and inspiring music with a conscience and a soul.

Haden's LMO recordings share qualities ascribed to all works considered in this study: They possess and express the rage and lyricism of Richard Wright; they tell stories with an episodic approach to unrecorded history that characterizes the narrative of Miss Jane; like the work of Anna Deavere Smith, they bring the talk and the energy of the people into the service of cultural production for the sake of negotiating differences; and like Glenn Ligon's work, they affirm a collaborative approach to meaning by structuring different artistic modes of expression as dependent on and conversant with one another. Just as it is not easy to separate the music from the message and motive when considering the LMO, it is not easy to separate the various artistic forms in which Haden casts his vision. An important feature of all of the LMO's recordings is the way in which Haden has set forth a cultural production that reveals how the arts are intertwined in significant and reciprocal ways.

Narrative dominates each form. Lyrics to songs performed by the LMO are almost always reproduced for the listener to read, even if the lyrics are not sung in every composition. In addition, Haden offers extensive liner notes that are an important commentary on the narratives told by the music, providing background information on the songs' performance and history. In his liner notes Haden clearly articulates his own liberative mission and aesthetic vision and elaborates in words on what stories are told by the music and, as with Newton's "Amazing Grace," often adds another level of narrative meaning that makes the whole story more compelling.

Visual images that accompany each recording also describe what the music and words relate. A photograph of the entire ensemble holding a roughly rendered banner proclaiming the group's identity illustrates the first album, *Liberation Music Orchestra*. The picture captures its era and symbolizes it at the same time. In the late 1960s, when the album was created, protesters carried signs in marches for civil rights and against the Vietnam War. It was also a time when the rapid proliferation of photographic images in the media brought home to the public a representation of the suffering of soldiers and civilians that was so intense they could not comfortably hide from the experience.

Ballad of the Fallen includes a photograph of the group also, but in a staged studio portrait, signifying a kind of institutionalization of the movement the group had begun. But this recording is also accompanied by a painting by a Salvadoran refugee. Hung in the Manuel Franco Refugee Center in Managua, Nicaragua, the painting could be by a child or a primitive artist, bearing qualities of innocence and visionary talent that is poignantly challenged by the text included in the painting. The inscriptions read, "No to U.S. intervention; Yankee invader out of El Salvador—Our only crime is that we are poor—We are tired of so many bullets sent by Ronald Reagan."

A painting is also presented on the cover of the group's final album, *Dream Keeper*. Created especially for this project, the painting *The Dream Searcher* is stylized and abstract. It depicts the profile of a black human head on a background of geometric forms of purple and blue. The figure has full lips, also purple, and a multicolored eye from which issues a strong line of different colors. Almost African in inspiration, the painting suggests that we focus our vision—our spiritual eye—in the direction that the music provides. Danny Johnson created *The Dream Searcher*. He was a friend of Haden who often sat in on his gigs, playing triangle and bells. Haden later discovered that Johnson was an accomplished sculptor and painter (his sculpture honoring civil rights activist and Nobel Peace Prize winner Ralph Bunche is in front of the United Nations building) and eventually invited him to paint *The Dream Searcher* for the album. Perhaps recognizing the diversity in unity and how the LMO had grown beyond Haden's own private inspiration, the group's photographs shown on this last album are individual portraits. Just as the slave narrative tradition developed, the LMO increasingly provided for individual representation while still maintaining a commitment to corporate responsibility.

Given that these cultural productions rely on the collaboration of sound, words, and images, it is not surprising that one reviewer extends the trope to include a religious dimension by describing the LMO's actual performances as "musical/political 'rites'" (Carey 7). Nor is it inappropriate that in assessing Haden's lifelong interest in the role music can play in a advancing social justice, the critic Robert Palmer cast his impressions as "Charlie Haden's Creed." Haden's creed includes a description of how he sees himself extending a great tradition of creative resistance:

> Since I started thinking about playing and writing music about the reality that's happening around us, I wanted to meet other musicians and other artists who had the same feeling. There've been artists and musicians from all over the world throughout history who have done that, playing or writing or dancing or painting about political movements or about political realities or starvation or whatever, and I have in the last five years or so met a few people in this country and people in other countries who are doing that now. I feel that I can't write or play music about joy and love and closeness as long as there is racism and starvation and men who are causing starvation and perpetuating racism and conditioning it in other human beings. I feel that I have to make people aware that that's what's happening, and hope that they see it for what it is and try to do something about it. I've never been one to join any kind of movement or political organization, I feel that I have my own organization inside me, just like I have my own philosophy and direction inside me. So I have to say what I say in my music, and I feel right now that I have no choice, I have to play and write about this reality in a very powerful way that's going to have an impact on someone. (Palmer 17–18)

Like most artists who participate in such a tradition, Haden is aware that his efforts may not be contributing much toward effecting social change because "when I look at the little piddling music I'm trying to play and write," as compared to what activists do, he appreciates that they are "laying their lives out for their beliefs knowing that they can be killed at any moment" (Palmer 18). But in his own way, Haden, who admires, instructs, and embodies a particular musical ethic of playing "as if you're risking your life for every note you're playing" (Brace C2), does lay his beliefs on the line. As he continues, "I'm playing because I have music inside me that I need to express, that I want people to hear. I want to try to give back the gift that I've been given, try to give it back to the world and to try to transmit as much beauty as I can on this planet" (Brace C2). Described by Joe Carey as "the most potent platform he's ever had to carry out his wide-ranging artistic/humanistic vision" (7), the LMO is Haden's chief vehicle for giving back and transforming society.

Haden's entire career is characterized by challenges to the establishment—in playing and listening to music as well as in other areas—and his musical perspective provides an extremely appealing tool for advancing social justice (Woodard, "A Healthy" 18). But the actual impetus for the group's assembling was the climate of unrest of the late 1960s, a time rife with political consciousness, Vietnam backlash, and angry, awakening black-self realization. Haden's consciousness of the tradition of resistance in black art forms and his own experimentation with the seeming rebelliousness of free jazz also played a part. As he explains his vision, "I wanted to voice my concern, and I had some folk music from the Spanish Civil War that I thought was beautiful, as is most music that comes from a people's struggle to live in a free society. I envisioned great jazz musicians being inspired by this folk music and improvising on it, which had never been done before" (Schuster 18).

Thus was born the LMO, out of Haden's distaste with the "insane reactionary direction" of the United States in 1969: "First with Kennedy, then Johnson and then Nixon . . . a senseless, stupid, wasteful thing was happening. I got this feeling of futility and helplessness, but what can you do? Vietnam was at its peak, Che Guevara was murdered, the Vietnam Minority Plank was defeated on the Chicago National Democratic Convention floor . . . it was all frightening to me, and I tried to make a visual happening of it" (Carey 7). In trying to fashion what he describes as a "visual happening," Haden stretched back further into history, back to music of the Spanish Civil War he had encountered years before. As he explains, "I envisioned an album where a person could be communicating a message about that war. I had always wanted to record the folk songs of that period and was waiting for the right time" (Carey 7).

Haden also had to find the right means to spread his message and faced a difficult decision over whom they would record for; going with a large label for him was tantamount to complicity, "actually aiding and abetting the very system that is stifling creativity. I thought recording for a large corporation would completely destroy the meaning of the album," but he was also aware that "I had to think about getting the album out to where people would be able to know about it and to hear it" (Palmer 18). The irony of Haden's dilemma became apparent when he had difficulty in peddling the project—"every record company I went to refused me"—but eventually ABC/Impulse decided to take a chance (Carey 7). The first LMO album was recorded in New York on three successive days in late April 1969.

Combining emotional political content with stirring arrangements for large ensemble, it was a milestone in recorded jazz. While recording before live audiences there were intense personality clashes among the musicians, and things did not go as planned, but the group never abandoned their enterprise and they managed to complete the album. Included in the first gathering of LMO were Don Cherry, Gato Barbieri, Rosewall Rudd, Dewey Redman, Paul Motian, Sam Brown, Perry Robinson, Mike Mantler, and Carla Bley. Proclaimed a "potent musical document" by *Down Beat* editor Dan Morgenstern (Carey 7), the recording reaped numerous jazz laurels. Despite these accolades, the group made only two public appearances and for various reasons was soon forced to disband. At the time Haden lamented that the group never went on a tour: "We wanted to play, but we also wanted to do it in the right situation" (Carey 7). The album was reissued in 1973, but remained an unavailable collectors' item until it was reissued on compact disc in 1996.

Superimposing third-world folk melodies, patriotic song clips, and collective free jazz work, the LMO recording emerged, in the words of Joe Carey, as a "stunning controversial tapestry of turbulent historical times" (7). Kaleidoscopic in nature and reference, the album's purpose was powered by songs of the German Democratic Republic, the Cuban revolutionary movement, the Democratic National Convention, the U.S. civil rights movement, and especially songs from the Spanish Civil War, Haden's initial musical inspiration.[4] The Spanish Civil War (1936–39) remains an important and traumatic event in history because it seemed, at the time, to be a struggle over the future of all humankind. Fueled by ethnic rage, the Spanish Civil War was the first international fight over purely ideological principles and served as a harbinger of the philosophical conflicts that were to erupt during the next half century.

That Haden chose to feature music created during this war is significant for analyzing his work as an extension of the slave narrative tradition. The Spanish Civil War's parallels to the American Civil War are striking because of the ethnic elements, its clearly liberationist/reformist defense, and the insidious role of the institutional church in defending the fascists. This war was also consequential in history because men from fifty-seven different nations went to Spain as volunteers to help defend the freedom of the democratically elected Republic. The Russians organized the International Brigades; 40,000 foreigners from more than fifty countries came to the aid of the Republicans. Included among them were more than 3,000 Americans, who named themselves the Abraham Lincoln Brigade, symbolically linking their efforts to the American Civil War for the emancipation of slaves. Only 1,600 of these Americans came back alive, and it took the combined forces of Franco, Hitler, and Mussolini to defeat the Spanish Republic. Survivors of the Abraham Lincoln Brigade were present when the first LMO album was recorded, and as Carla Bley remembers, the men were "tapping their canes" full of heartfelt admiration for the entire proceedings (Carey 7).

As Haden emphasizes, the "people's struggle for freedom lives on" in the songs that emerged from the experience, four of which he includes on the album. Thus, the first LMO album begins with a plaintive, almost dirgelike "Introduction." A lamenting tenor saxophone gives way briefly to a full and rich orchestral sound; above that, the saxophone rises in melody while a trombone moans. Abruptly, "Song of the United Front" begins, with a deliberate keyboard march, joined by horns in a crescendo of sound and a quickened tempo that soon falls and rises again and again, overridden by a woodwind melody. Eventually the short song fades out, as if the marchers had receded into battle. This song contains words by Bertolt Brecht (although uncharacteristically, Haden does not include them in his notes or in the performance).

Also included on the first side are "El Quinto Regimiento," which begins with a lyrical guitar picking out the melody in intricate fingerwork and strumming. The sounds turn slightly dissonant, a quality that increases along with the tempo when the horns and percussive instruments join in and move the piece into free play while the guitar competes for the dominant sound, eventually reestablishing its presence through the din of the free play. "Los Cuatro Generales" and "Viva La Quince Brigada" follow as part of this sequence of songs from the Spanish Civil War, and Haden uses the latter two songs with only slight changes from the original 1930s orchestra and chorus arrangements of "Los Cuatro Generales" and "Viva La Quince Brigada" as they were played on the soundtrack of the film *Mourir a Madrid* (*To Die in Madrid*). Tracks of the original are also superimposed on the improvisation the group performs on the songs. In bringing the original music into direct collaboration with the contemporary renditions of these songs, Haden is making an implicit statement that characterizes those whose work extends the slave narrative tradition: It recognizes present conditions while turning us back to the past for the full story.

On the second side, "Hasta Siempre," composed and sung by Carlos Puebla, is superimposed on the improvisation on Haden's own composition, "Song for Che." Dominated by Haden's performance on bass, the song stands in sharp contrast to all the lively and aggressive free play that precedes it. For most of the piece, the song is interrupted only by an incessant but subtle ringing of chimes or a trilling flute or shaking maracas, until a saxophone registers in a sound not unlike what Coltrane achieved in his elegy "Alabama." Haden's play in this song never recedes, but dominates the song in its intensity and focus, thereby reflecting his own personal response to the life and death of Che Guevara. As Haden explains in his liner notes, when he read of Dr. Ernesto Che Guevara's death in 1967, he wanted to write a song in his memory—for him, for his people, "and for the struggle that immortalized him."

Following "Song for Che" is Ornette Coleman's "War Orphans," a difficult piece to characterize. This album is the first time this composition was recorded. Gentle piano playing expresses much of the mood of the song, a simple, childlike melody that persists in improvisation while a muted saxophone cries in the background until the piece builds to the point where the horn sounds like a siren call and then abruptly trails off back to the piano melody and concludes with a few bass plucks. Desperately poignant, the song must have appealed to Haden in part because it recalls his emphasis on the needs of children and musically reflects the mood engendered when war makes orphans of us all.

After these emotionally and musically intense pieces, Haden includes "The Interlude (Drinking Music)," composed by Carla Bley, a silly, slow polka that he describes as a "bouncy little number to quiet the conscience by." But the quiet does not last for long: Rounding out the album is "Circus '68 '69," Haden's own composition, the idea for which came to him while he was watching the Democratic National Convention on television in the summer of 1968. After the minority plank on Vietnam was defeated in a vote taken on the convention floor, California and New York delegates spontaneously began to sing "We Shall Overcome" in protest. Unable to gain control of the floor, the rostrum instructed the orchestra to drown out the singing; they played "You're a Grand Old Flag" and "Happy Days Are Here Again" to stifle the song. As Haden explains, "To me, this told the story, in music, of what was happening in our country politically." Thus in "Circus '68 '69" Haden divides the orchestra into two separate bands in an attempt to recreate what happened on the convention floor.

Although "Circus '68 '69" begins with Haden simply plucking out a tune, it soon swells into the most lively free play expression on the entire album, evoking the strains of Spanish Civil War music while still capturing the specific mood of the contemporary event through organ music and police whistles. Echoing the delegates' spontaneous performance, the album concludes with the civil rights anthem "We Shall Overcome," played by the entire orchestra but dominated by a trombone sounding out the theme in a style that recalls a New Orleans funeral. As Haden writes in his liner notes about the entire album, the music "is dedicated to creating a better world; a world without war and killing, without racism, without poverty and exploitation; a world where men of all governments realize the vital importance of life and strive to protect rather than to destroy it. We hope to see a new society of enlightenment and wisdom where creative thought becomes the most dominant force in all people's lives."

In between their first and second recordings, the LMO achieved an "un-

derground cult status in Europe" (Carey 7). Meanwhile, Haden continued to be outraged at the atrocities and inhuman conditions brought on
by political establishments throughout history and "finally found the 'situation' he's sought to recall the group to musical 'arms': It took Reagan's
election to do it" (Carey 7). Haden had come to appreciate that the challenge LMO took on in 1969 still existed, if in a different form. As he explained at the time, "It's the same struggle against people who run the
governments of the world dictating values to the majority of people, their
quest for power and values of destruction over those of the good of humanity. If only the human mind could be used in the brilliant ways it was
meant to be, instead of by the guys who run the governments" (Carey 7).

   In recalling how the group regathered, Haden emphasizes observations
he has made about social reality in America and reaffirms principles he has
long held: "I was born and raised in this country and I'm proud to be raised
in this country, but I feel a strong commitment to improving things. It's
still a racist country in terms of the treatment of women and respect for
the rights of blacks and there's no creative appreciation of thought or
life. . . . I'm lucky I can communicate my feelings and values through my
music and that's the responsibility of anyone lucky enough to have those
qualities; to be able to communicate with good values as opposed to rac-
ist/sexist ones. If you have any sensitivity inside you at all, you have a
concern for humanity and that takes in the whole world" (Carey 12).

   Howard Mandel characterizes the second LMO as comprising "11 jazz
radicals, committed to free-spirited expressivity, expanding from meaningful traditions" who were "maintaining their commitments but adjusting
their strategies" ("The Hymn" 101). The LMO's second album, *Ballad of
the Fallen* (1982), included many musicians from the first group, among
them Cherry, Redman, Motian, Mantler, and Bley but with the addition
of Gary Valente, Steve Slagle, Sharon Freeman, Jack Jeffers, Mick Goodrick, and Jim Pepper. *Ballad of the Fallen* incorporates folk material from
a wider geographic span—"the whole world"—including El Salvador,
Spain, Nicaragua, Angola, Japan, Cuba, and Chile, as well as new compositions by Haden and Bley. Several of the traditional tunes had to be
transcribed by Carla Bley from discs half a century old and were enhanced
by the addition of traditional Hispanic folk harmonies. This time the group
performed throughout Europe before cutting an album for ECM, a label
Haden thought he could trust because they appeared to have made recording creative music a priority. After touring Europe the group returned to
New York for two sold-out concerts at the New York Public Theatre, then
"re-scattered to the jazz winds" (Carey 12).

Side One of the album begins with "Els Segadors" ("The Reapers"), another song from the Spanish Civil War, which describes the revolt of the Catalan farmers against the central power. It later became the official hymn of the Catalan Republic. Dominated by the horn section, the song is dirgelike and plaintive, and the brass eventually gives way to a bass solo that plucks an improvisation on the melody in deep, low registers. "The Ballad of the Fallen," the album's title track, is a recent song from El Salvador, based on a poem found on the body of a student who was killed when the U.S.-backed National Guard of El Salvador massacred people at a sit-in at the university in San Salvador. Like "Amazing Grace," this song tells two stories: the story of the martyred student who composed the words and the story he tells in his poem.

"The Ballad of the Fallen" is a significant liberation anthem because, characteristic of the slave narrative tradition, the character of the protagonist is established in his wish to be remembered as one of the people. As he writes,

> Don't ask me who I am
> Or if you knew me
> The dreams that I had
> Will grow even thought I'm no longer here.
> I'm not alive, but my life continues
> In that which goes on dreaming
> Others who will continue the fight
> Will grow new roses
> In the name of all these things
> You'll find my name . . .

The poet directly links his own identity to the dream for which he fought and sees his immortality embodied in a future of liberation. He also instructs through his song for others to adopt the transformative imagination displayed by the slave narrative tradition. As he writes,

> Cry with us all those who feel it
> Suffer with us all those who loved them
> Fall to the earth on your knees
> tremble with fear
> All those who on that fateful day . . . assisted in the murder.

He establishes a clear sense of justice for the righteous and the unrighteous and links his identity with the future:

My true age is the age
Of the child I have liberated
. . .
I only die
If you give up
For those who die in combat
Live on in every compañero . . .

The song expresses the urgency of the poet, with strong horns bellowing
out a sweet melody that expresses the lyricism of the poem's images while
maracas keep a gentle rhythm accompanied by the sensitive strumming of
a guitar.

Following this stirring ballad, the song segues into a march tune, "If You
Want to Write Me" ("Si Me Quieres Escribir"), another song from the
Spanish Civil War, that was sung by the Spanish Republican Armies in
battle. The music is played at a rapid tempo, invoking images of energetic
folk dancers that gives way to a searching horn solo with free play under-
neath, and eventually the rolling strums of the bass, all holding the composition together while the melody emerges and vanishes and a sputter-
ing, staccato piano pleads like a dying request. This sound gives way to
another march tune, "Grandola Vila Morena" which, as Haden explains
in liner notes, was played on Portuguese radio to signal the young enlisted
army officers to revolt against the fascist Portuguese government in 1974.

Like the spirituals, this song functioned on two levels: as an inspiration
and as a coded message. Announcing a cause in strong beats, a flute conveys a kind of urgency to join, and so the horns join in, triumphant and
celebratory, while trombones free-play in the background. "Introduction
to People" by Carla Bley is based on traditional Spanish harmonies and
serves as a passage to "The People United Will Never Be Defeated" ("El
Pueblo Unido Janas Sera Vencido!"), a song written by Sergio Ortega and
Quilapayun. The best-known political song to have emerged from Chile
since the CIA-supported coup and Pinochet dictatorship, it has become an
anthem for the Chilean resistance and in LMO's performance is given full
orchestral treatment and dignity.

Following these songs that tell specific stories about the struggle for liberation worldwide, Haden includes "Silence" because silence is "at the beginning and ending of everything in life." Dominated by a solo horn playing simple, clear notes, eventually joined by other instruments in harmony,
the entire composition is defined by a slow, steady, contemplative tone that

overrides the brief intrusion of a horn's trill, and the song descends to simple piano chords. Haden wrote the song with the thought "that there are infinite possibilities for humankind contained within the brilliance of the universe." Haden's belief in these infinite possibilities combined with his musical mission means that in some respects silence is his foe.

But here Haden is not so much admitting defeat as recognizing reality. Haden's insertion of silence on this album reflects a belief he promotes to his students. He encourages young musicians to "strive for the deepest sound they can get. You can get a deep sound out of any instrument, and when that sound comes back to you, it will inspire you to play even deeper" by beginning this process with complete silence. "When you start from silence, you're able to hear the timbre and the texture and the nuances of the music inside your soul" (Roberts 47). Silence in this respect is not an occasion of refusing to speak up, but an opportunity to cleanse, to remove previous baggage and preconceptions that might prevent one from seeing and hearing the truth revealed.

Side Two begins with "Too Late," a duet between Carla Bley on piano and Charlie Haden on bass, and is followed by "La Pasionaria," which is dedicated to Dolores Ibarruri, the renowned "La Pasionaria" who during the Spanish Civil War inspired the Spanish Republic against fascism with the slogan "No Pasaran" ("They shall not pass"). Another in a series of rousing marches, the song begins with a melodic guitar solo and maintains the melody throughout the piece until the bass improvises a solo but gives back eventually to the full orchestral sound. The last song, "La Santa Espina," is an old song from Catalonia, revived during the Spanish Civil War by the freedom fighters. A highly spirited tune, this is an upbeat march that sets the stage for the most extensive free play included on the album. The improvising in this song has an urgency and intensity—at times the horns sound like sirens—and concludes abruptly, as if the musicians were denied the opportunity for complete expression.

In reviewing *The Ballad of the Fallen* for *Down Beat,* Howard Mandel describes it as the "Hymn of the Hopeful." Noting the fourteen years between this album and Haden's first convening of the LMO, Mandel cites the new work as a "response to anyone who insists, 'There's one right way—mine'" ("The Hymn" 101). In observing that Haden is not coy about identifying his political loyalties—"Haden again appropriates themes popular with the Spanish Republican Armies and leftist parties in Chile, Portugal, and El Salvador"—Mandel describes the performances as a "rich blend of brass, reeds and acoustic touches" that create music that is "reflective" and "regret-filled" but also "leaven[s] idealism with irony" and "tempers sober dedication and sad loss with sweet pride in a swooning waltz that blossoms as though a village militia's returned" (101). In Mandel's assessment, "One needn't be a politico, though, to enjoy the beauties of this music. Without the package's poetry and painting, you might guess these settings for impassioned improvisations have some simple Pan-American purpose. Of course it's earthy—Haden at his best always firmly stands his ground. His rootedness is his strength, allowing others to soar" (101).

Mandel describes the album as "recognizable in one listen as a classic" and reflects on how the music and the message mix. In this instance Haden's music becomes an occasion to remark not only on the social efficacy of art but on how jazz is uniquely suited to serve such a role. As Mandel writes, "That's the power of jazz composition, allowing truth and beauty to flower as each individual interprets some wholly wrought tune. It's a capacity of their music jazz players believe in and defend with every improvisation, as we'll defend self-expression and self-government in principle and practice, without insisting there's just one path to their accomplishment—mine" (102). Haden's confidence in the infinite possibilities, that we shall overcome, is part of why Mandel assesses the album as an artistic achievement. As he explains, the musicians' "belief in humankind's perfectibility makes 'Ballad of the Fallen' a triumph and steels our commitment to resist and not inflict oppression. The burdened, the victims, the unequal among us may be down, but they aren't out" (102).

The critical success of the LMO's second album was exceeded only by that of *Dream Keeper,* which was an unequivocal critical smash, winning the *Down Beat* critics' and readers' polls for best jazz album of the year in 1991 (and Haden as top acoustic bassist in both polls, an award he had earned fourteen times before). Included in this assembly of the LMO were Carla Bley, Dewey Redman, and Paul Motian (all performers on each album), Sharon Freeman and Mick Goodrick (who also performed on *Ballad of the Fallen*), and Joe Lovano, Branford Marsalis, Ken McIntyre, Tom Harrell, Earl Gardner, Ray Anderson, Joe Daley, Amina Claudine Myers, Don Alias, and Juan Lazzaro Mendolas. The album was inspired by the poetry of Langston Hughes, from which Haden selected the title and commissioned original compositions by Carla Bley. As Haden explains in the album's liner notes, in 1984 he discovered Hughes's poem "As I Grew Older" in *The Dream Keeper and Other Poems.* He was "struck by how eloquently it described one person's view of racism," so he shaped an album around the inspiration the poem provided.

Haden includes the text of "As I Grew Older," which tells a story about a character denied a dream because of a slowly rising wall that,

Dimming,
Hiding,
The Light of my dream.
Rose until it touched the sky—
The wall.

What makes up the wall becomes clear in the next stanza when the speaker asserts, "Shadow / I am black." Racism has raised a wall between the speaker and his dream so that he is left to lie down in the shadow. Recalling Charley Thomas's lament over his skin color, the speaker continues by exclaiming, "My hands! / My dark hands!" while imploring them to "Break through the wall! / Find my dream! / Help me to shatter this darkness." Given Haden's often-stated belief that we must begin the work of liberation by educating children in human rights and values, it is not surprising that he would find Hughes's poem especially poignant because of the way it traces disillusionment with aging. And this same principle must have guided his imagination when he selected the Oakland Youth Chorus to participate on the compositions "Spiritual" and "Dream Keeper."

Dream Keeper is comprised of eight parts, with original compositions by Carla Bley interspersed with traditional songs from El Salvador, Venezuela, and Spain. In contextualizing liberation songs from around the world within a framework inspired by Langston Hughes's lyrical lament over racism, Haden and Bley are making an implicit statement about the universal role a tradition of creative resistance, such as the slave narrative tradition, can play in ongoing social justice work. Among the traditional songs that shape *Dream Keeper* are the vibrant "Feliciano Ama" from El Salvador, named after Jose Feliciano Ama, a revolutionary leader of Indian people during the 1930s insurrection in Izalco, El Salvador. "Canto del Pilon," from Venezuela, is presented in two parts and describes peasant women in a village who are mashing corn and talking about the events of the day while the barnyard animals make noise in the background.

Haden credits his wife, Ruth, with discovering "Hymn of the Anarchist Women's Movement" while watching a television documentary about this Spanish Civil War movement. After compiling all the songs he wanted to record, Haden sent the music and tapes to Carla Bley with a copy of Hughes's poem, which inspired her to compose the integrating and unifying transitional music, *Dream Keeper* Parts One through Five. The piece is so well integrated that it is nearly impossible to distinguish the separate parts. Continuous throughout the piece is a marchlike rhythm, accentuated by maracas and castanets, tempered by flutes and pipes that create an almost ethereal sound, all held together by guitar strumming and bass plucking and supported by choral intonations.

"Rabo De Nube" ("Tail of the Tornado"), by Cuban composer Silvio Rodriguez, describes a speaker longing for "the tail of a tornado" to sweep sorrows, pour vengeance, carry off all ugliness, and leave a place that "will look like / Our hope." Perhaps the most poignantly lyrical of any of the LMO recordings, the song is dominated by an exquisite guitar melody that rises until all the orchestra's instruments join in to create an utterly uplifting, soothing, deep, and rich sound that is perfectly balanced and nuanced by all the instruments. This selection is followed by "Nkosi Sikelel'i Afrika," formerly the anthem of the ANC and now the national anthem of South Africa. Written in Zulu, Xhosa, and Sutu, three of the predominant indigenous languages of South Africa, translated the song reads,

> Lord, bless Africa
> Let its horn be raised
> Listen also to our prayers
> Lord bless
> Lord bless
> Come Spirit
> Come Spirit
> Holy Spirit
> Lord bless Us
> We thy children.

The obvious religious elements of this anthem generate much of its universal appeal and link its sentiments to other theologically articulated liberation songs.

Although at the time the album came out South Africa had not yet moved toward democratic rule, Haden's inclusion of it was timely for his recognition that "apartheid and the continuing genocide of black South African people by a white racist government is an assault against humanity." In order to "voice a protest against this injustice," Haden chose to record the ANC anthem. In 1985 he invited Victor Mashabela from the New York offices of the ANC to come hear the orchestra and received permission to record the song on *Dream Keeper*. In LMO's performance of the song, it is first given the orchestral dignity reserved for national anthems and played in the ceremonial way such anthems are customarily heard. Soon, however, this interpretation gives way to extended free play that is not orchestral but the music of a small combo jamming during a nightclub gig.

Eventually, the song circles back to the beginning and the full orchestra completes the piece as it began. Continuing a tradition established by other LMO albums, Haden superimposed an original tape of a South African choir singing the anthem under Dewey Redman's solo. "Sandino" is an original composition by Haden that he wrote for a 1987 documentary by Academy Award–winning documentary filmmaker Deborah Schaffer. The filmmaker had approached Haden to compose the score for her documentary based on the book *Fire from the Mountain,* about the evolution of Sandinistas. "Sandino" is the title theme, introduced by guitar and bass playing off one another; the horns eventually join in to complete this gentle, pleading ballad.

The last selection, the affirmative "Spiritual," is also a Charlie Haden original, dedicated to Martin Luther King, Medgar Evers, and Malcolm X, whose contributions to the civil rights movement in the United States Haden credits with inspiring him. Recalling the sound and sentiment of gospel music, "Spiritual" self-consciously recalls the spiritual strains of the African-American musical traditions as they developed from the spirituals to gospel and even interjects a bluesy, New Orleans funeral sound while a full chorus sings beneath it all. Haden's bass solo dominates the composition as it winds down, appropriately concluding the piece in its grounding force. As for the other LMO recordings, Carla Bley was the arranger for *Dream Keeper.* Her symbiotic collaboration with Haden is long-standing and profound, and he asserts that she "hears and voices music like no other." Recorded in two days, one take each, the album came together almost by grace and issues forth a similar sentiment. As Haden expresses it, "Hopefully this album conveys the necessity for every human being to work towards appointing people to positions of government leadership who possess insight, intelligence, compassion and a commitment to human rights in order to ensure that the dream of racial and sexual equality becomes a reality throughout the world." Haden concludes his notes by invoking the refrain associated with the Reverend Jesse Jackson: "Keep the dream alive!"

In a review of *Dream Keeper,* critic Art Lange notes that although it was twenty-one years since the LMO's first recording, "its message is no less meaningful or urgent today. How rare it is to hear music—beautiful, inspiring music—with a conscience and a soul. True, music is an abstract, non-rhetorical art form. But here the themes, from El Salvador, Cuba, Venezuela, the Spanish Civil War, and South Africa, create an extramusical backdrop that helps promote an awareness of war and other social and political injustices. The LMO emphasizes involvement and cooperation in deed as well as thought. The main thrust of the music is in ensemble; the soloists blend into the fabric of the arrangements and are supported by the orchestra" (Lange 30). Unlike the first LMO recording, which experimented more with free jazz and was characterized by Lange as possessing a "boiling undercurrent of rage and near-chaos," *Dream Keeper,* substitutes a "sense of solidarity and resolve. At the center of it all is the warm, human sound of Haden's bass, soloing eloquently, and providing the foundation for the passion and intensity of saxophonists" and other musicians (Lange 30).

An interesting feature of the tour that accompanied the release of *Dream Keeper* dovetails with Haden's emphasis on young people as the source of our hope. Like Wright and Gaines, who saw redemptive possibilities in the way children are raised, Haden strives to include young people in his life and mission. Apart from the students he trains, he invites young musicians to play with him, and during LMO's 1992 tour in Europe he included Joshua Redman, the son of Dewey Redman, who joined Haden's first effort. Also unique to the LMO tour in 1994 at colleges, Haden invited the participation of local children's choirs and local musicians as a new method to embody his beliefs: "It's a very valuable experience for young musicians or singers, because if they are involved in a jazz studies program, they usually only get to play big-band charts and they're never exposed to this type of music. I try to broaden their horizons. Every time, young musicians told me I'd changed their lives or the way they thought about improvising. It's a really good feeling because that's why I'm doing what I'm doing—trying to touch people's lives" (Schuster 18).

Haden wishes he could touch more lives and he strongly advocates for broad arts education. As he explains, it's up to all of us to make sure the arts become part of everybody's education because "a society—a world—without art is doomed as far as I'm concerned. Jazz has always been a minority art form with a limited audience. That's one of the reasons why the musicians that play the music are so dedicated—because they know they're a minority and they have to persevere. Most musicians that play on the level of dedicating their lives to their music won't accept playing a type of music they don't believe in. As long as there are musicians who have a passion for spontaneity, for creating something that's never been before, the art form of jazz will flourish" (Schuster 19). In children and in musicians, as in freedom-fighters worldwide, is where Haden places his hope: "As long as there are musicians who grow up with and acquire a need to express themselves in creative improvised music, there'll always be a future" (Palmer 47).

For all that the LMO represents as a group, it is still the singular vision and commitment of Charlie Haden that provides the foundation, a position symbolized by the instrument he plays. As a bassist, Haden is uniquely poised in any jazz assembly because he is at the center, not unlike Miss Jane, who occupied a similar place in her community and used the advantages of that position to effect change. In the center Haden hears everything that is played as he provides the harmonic and rhythmic cornerstone. But having reinvented the role of bassist with his melodic improvisations, he is also leading the group in new directions.

While fulfilling the traditional role a bass serves to keep the group on time, Haden exploits this new bassist role to embody his whole-soul commitment to musical integrity and human justice: He grounds us in our steady, present reality while ushering in the lyrical strains of the oppressed. Combining his folk sensibilities, his open-mindedness and eclectic bent, and his passionate and radical commitment to social justice, Haden, in the center, energizes his Liberation Music Orchestra and keeps it, like his hope, alive. As Haden asserts, "The idea of the Orchestra . . . I don't think that will ever go. . . . Look at the history of the States, it's just not happening yet" (Carey 12). However critical and pessimistic about human nature Haden may sound at times, his actions give evidence that, as in the slave narrative tradition, hope is born of the struggle, not the success, and of the unwavering belief that free artistic expression in the midst of survival is the most liberating act of all.

ⓠ ⓠ ⓠ

> I'm a devout musician.
> —Charlie Parker

In *Jazz: Myth and Religion,* Neil Leonard writes, "No man or society exists long without some form of religion to help them come to terms with the disturbing and inexplicable. Without beliefs and practices to deal with mystery and misfortune, the cosmos seems chaotic, filled with existential isolation and anxiety. God may die, but religion does not; we forever seek ways to reinforce or replace old beliefs" (178). One of the new ways we continue this search, Leonard asserts, is through jazz, a society of rebels that works as a church, with the musicians as its prophets and the critics as its priests. Those who worship at the Church of St. John Coltrane (formerly St. John's African Orthodox Church) in San Francisco have extended this principle to its institutional limit.

A giant painting of Coltrane hangs in the chancel, where each Sunday a band plays a musical liturgy based on the saxophonist's late period. In this setting jazz and the legendary Coltrane are worshipped and John Coltrane is apotheosized as a saint, the "Divine Sound Baptist." Adherents to this religion trace their beliefs to Coltrane's spiritual awakening in 1957, when he swore off alcohol and drugs and began a final decade of composition that was dominated by sprawling pieces infused with religious passion, music of a hierophany and search for sacred experience. In liner notes for *A Love Supreme* (1964), Coltrane acknowledges his debt to God, referring to the recording as "a humble offering to Him. An attempt to say THANK YOU GOD." Those faithful to this religion refer to this album as his Sermon on the Mount. They are proud also that their church is not segregated, like so many other places of worship, and believe that it is the power of music that effects this multicultural harmony.

This phenomenon is but one of many in the history of jazz appreciation that reveals a link between the music and the religion of African Americans, a link that was forged before the slave narrative tradition exploited language for similar purposes. In his exploration of these links, Jon Michael Spencer has been led to develop a new discipline he calls "theomusicology," which is aimed at evaluating the aspects of popular music that embody the sacredness that is embedded in and forever shaping the secular.[5] In *Protest and Praise: Sacred Music of Black Religion,* Spencer demonstrates how, beginning with the spirituals, black music was established as an "archetype of protest seen later in antislavery, social gospel, and civil rights hymnody" (vii–viii). Spencer's discussion of the songs of the civil rights movement, for example, demonstrates that even a century or more after the events that inspired the creation of the spirituals, a majority of the movement's songs incorporate religious language and posit a faith in a liberating god, however abstractly that god is rendered. Functioning as "sources of spirited support" rather than "songs of faith" (J. Washington 207), the songs still culturally validated a whole "system of core beliefs that verified the providence of God," even in this secular and interfaith movement (Spencer 102).

As a "sacred motif in black culture" (Spencer 103), an ultimate concern with freedom is what energizes the spiritual force embodied in African-American music. How African-American culture continues to perceive religious truth and how its ultimate concern with liberation figures into a secular worldview is what this study has explored. Although not expressly African American, the songs performed by Charlie Haden's LMO are examples of this same phenomenon because of the ways in which they are indexed to the sacred motif of liberation in black culture. Although I have tried to demonstrate how the music of the LMO participates in the slave narrative tradition of textimony, I would be remiss if I did not extend my discussion to include the musical form that precedes even the slave narrative tradition.

For Haden's music actually circles back to beginnings of liberating theology, where narrative textimony was delivered in the spirituals. In his essay "Singing Swords: The Literary Legacy of Slavery," Melvin Dixon argues that the fabric of tradition in African-American literature and music is woven from two sources: slave narratives and spirituals. Dixon identifies these cultural forms of expression as providing the model by which African Americans have sought to create a vision of history, assess the human condition, and create heroic characters. Citing the impulse for freedom as the beginning of a change in character—when African Americans asserted their character through new characterizations of themselves and others—Dixon explains how "in song and narrative, through the unifying image and actual experience of deliverance and survival—a life-affirming ideology—the slaves themselves have defined heroic value as an essential aspect of human character" (313).

Dixon also notes that in the tradition set forth by the spirituals and the slave narratives, freedom was equated with salvation. "Thus the life of man that the spirituals and the narratives create for us is one which is grounded in concrete action and one which follows the highest moral persuasions. Man, as conceived within the slave's mythos and ethos, progresses toward spiritual regeneration" (314). The creators of spirituals and slave narratives also made this kind of spiritual regeneration possible for those who were oppressing them. Because "the slave has become free by first singing with a sword in his hand" (313), the transformative potential of cultural production has been upheld as long as the tradition itself. However far-flung or contemporary Haden's LMO may seem, its foundational principle that good art can further the ends of a human liberation agenda is grounded in the American experience going back to slavery. Thus it comes as no surprise that in 1995, Haden released "a kind of informal jazz Eucharist" (Cocks 59), a collection of spirituals, hymns, and folk songs called *Steal Away*.

Haden was inspired to do this recording after hearing Hank Jones perform a spiritual on the *Smithsonian Collection, Jazz Piano*. Haden recalled the first time he heard the music for critic Jay Cocks, who describes how the music caused Haden to slip into a spiritual state: "Haden had religion. He had the history, he had the soul" (Cocks 59). The critic goes on to report how Haden initiated him into a similar experience: "'You've got to hear this,' Charlie Haden said, passing the silvery CD as if it were a communion wafer. 'Man, you got to hear this. It's like going to church'" (Cocks 59).

The critic's own response to hearing Hank Jones play was no less em-
phatic. "If church were as blissful as this—if the world swung like this—
there would be a worldwide conversion" (Cocks 59). Haden eventually
convinced Jones to record with him, despite the pianist's initial apprehen-
sions about "how people would accept spirituals played in the same context as bebop or modern jazz" (Cocks 59). Jones and Haden overcame their
anxieties; even if there were "a couple of times we looked at each other
and said 'Forgive us, Lord, for that flatted 13th'" (Cocks 59), they trusted
the "natural approach" each took to the recording, confident that, in
Jones's words, "We didn't try and do anything different than what we had
already done in our experience" (Cocks 59).

Bringing one's own experience to bear on cultural production, in fact,
is the essence of the spirituals. The music, as Abbey Lincoln testifies in the
album's liner notes, captures "the essence of the music of the pre-indus-
try, unknown poets and composers that most of the population learned
to sing in schools and churches. The songs chosen for the album give a
historical, social profile of a nation of people. Songs of conflict and despair
and hope and reference and love and longing and separation . . . forever
songs." This album represented two returns for Haden, one that he acknowledges when he thanks the members of his family for teaching him
the old hymns and singing them with him on the radio. For it was Haden's
mother who, while they were living in Springfield, Missouri, took her son
some Sundays to the local African-American church. "We would quietly
go in the door after everybody and sit in the back and listen to the music," he remembers. "That was one of the most moving experiences of my
young life" (Cocks 59).

But the album also represents a return to the original liberation music
first created and performed in America, the spirituals. Haden, "a man with
reverence for tradition and impatience with stasis" (Cocks 59), has made
no direct mention of how this music is linked thematically or formally to
his LMO performances. But he acknowledged as much when he selected
Maurice Jackson to produce liner notes that explore the origins of the music
on the album. Jackson's narrative functions in the same way Haden's liner
notes for all the LMO recordings function: It tells the story of creation in
the midst of oppression, of liberation in the midst of bondage.

As they have come to assume a dominant presence in the canon of
American folk song and to be sung throughout the world, the spirituals
have transcended their particular context and, like the songs chosen by
LMO to record, stand symbolically to represent the hope of liberation from
oppression. As John Lovell writes, "Very rarely is a folk song taken to heart

by more than a handful of appreciators outside its original folk. Never in history has this happened when the folk were despised as slaves. But the black spiritual has outlasted, by more than a century, its original creators in the minds of Americans, without a sign of losing strength. It has also built large new communities in a great many parts of the world. It has been adopted by millions as freedom song and as a multipurposed anthem of the human spirit" (xiv).

Furthermore, the spirituals' unique formal features tell an additional story about creative improvisation. Although the spirituals are associated primarily with African-American church congregations of the antebellum South and the earlier, more informal, and sometimes clandestine gatherings of enslaved people, they also represent the result of a process of mutual influence and reciprocal borrowing. Scholars have credited all the following as all contributing to the creation of the spirituals: evangelical sermons and hymns, biblical stories, traditional African chants and praise songs, and the combined experiences of enslaved people in the South.

Thus, as Maurice Jackson writes in the liner notes, the "music slowly evolved as the many African peoples over time became African American." The spirituals are but one example in African-American history of a people taking the cultural productions that were intended to oppress them and transforming them into expressions of liberation. It is this improvisatory heritage of a creative response to survival that became an unrelenting force for liberation that Haden celebrates in the LMO and which makes his recording of the spirituals something akin to coming home.

In addition, in *Steal Away* Haden comps on the multicultural form of the spirituals, rounding out his inclusive portrait of ethnically driven music, and finds what Jay Cocks describes as "a perfect ecumenical grace" (59) by including the songs of immigrant minorities. "L'Amour de Moi," a French-Canadian folk song, and the Irish-American folk song "Danny Boy" are performed on the album. Haden's choice to include these songs still circles back to African-American culture. He selected these songs to honor Paul Robeson because he admired his music and courage and because, as Jackson explains, like Robeson, Haden "has traveled the world listening to indigenous music of the native peoples."

In addition to spirituals, hymns, and ethnic folksongs, *Steal Away* includes "We Shall Overcome," a song twice recorded by the LMO and earning special distinction because, as Maurice Jackson explains, "if there is one song that African-Americans and Whites have shared over last 30 years it is 'We Shall Overcome.'" Haden and Jones's performance of the song Cocks describes as "blow[ing] away all the encrusted sanctimony" and "rediscovering its splendor and pride" (59). When Pete Seeger adapted the song during the civil rights movement, the folksinger added the plural pronoun "we" to emphasize the collective struggle for civil rights for all Americans and for those in other lands who have identified it with their own struggles. It is the same "we" by which Charlie Haden identifies himself, a corporate identity first promoted in the slave narrative tradition.

Yet it is the sound of the spirituals—the musical counterpart to the narratives—that dominates this recording and establishes the foundation for all the songs represented here and in Haden's LMO recordings. Described by Whitney Balliet as "quiet as God's thoughts" ("The Dean" 63), each musician displays an individual improvisational talent that he combines with a respect for the source and tradition of the spirituals. While for the most part they play the music "straight," they also add "harmonic and rhythmic inflections that separate jazz from the rest of the music" (Balliet, "The Dean" 63). But what particularly distinguishes the album is the way the two men, black and white, work together.

As Balliet explains, Jones and Haden "work as one, in unison or in harmony, and the recording becomes a subtle meditation on the horrors of slavery as well as a celebration of the great songs that came to be the slaves' solace" ("The Dean" 63). Jay Cocks supports Balliet's observation of the symbiosis between the musicians when he describes how they "play off each other, against each other, flirting with the melody and firing the spirit." In the process of their collaboration, Cocks asserts, Haden and Jones "prove that it's not the context that counts as much as the soul" (59). What Haden and Jones accomplish in *Steal Away* is nothing less than establishing a model for interracial cooperation in the creation of textimony.

The ways in which the musicians apply individual talent and a jazz sensibility to performing the music of the spirituals becomes especially pertinent when one appreciates the origin of the spirituals. W. E. B. Du Bois stands for many as one of the preeminent interpreters of the spirituals. His reflections in *Souls of Black Folk* on the "sorrow songs" explain how "by fateful chance the Negro folk song—the rhythmic cry of the slave—stands today not simply as the sole American music, but as the most beautiful expression of human experience born this side of the seas" (182). At the beginning of the twentieth century, Du Bois's examination of African-American culture led him to the "sorrow songs," in which "the soul of the black slave spoke to men" as providing a model for survival and an interpretive framework for that culture.

In *The Souls of Black Folk,* Du Bois foregrounds the issue of African retentions and features the music and message of the spirituals as related to the history of black people striving for humanity in a society of oppression. As the "singular spiritual heritage of the nation and the greatest gift of the Negro people," the spirituals fascinated Du Bois because of their tension between polarities of joy and sorrow. He came to see them as reflections of the African-American struggle to merge a double self into "a better and truer self" that held out "a faith in the ultimate justice of things . . . that sometime, somewhere, men will judge men by their souls and not by their skins" (189).

Most important for interpreting the meaning of the spirituals is an appreciation of the context—social and religious—in which they were performed and the insight they lend to the extraordinary power of music to shape the experience and conscious identity of a people. In the spirituals, enslaved people critically analyzed their colonial conditions, fashioned a creative theological response, indicted their oppressors without overtly denigrating them, reasserted the influence of an African sensibility, and empowered themselves by exercising a form of resistance that would endure longer than the conditions to which they were subject.

Like the songs performed by the LMO, the spirituals created by enslaved people became a unique way to "keep on keeping on" under the physical and psychological pressures of daily life, testifying to the belief that the supernatural interacted with the natural and humanity had a decisive role to play in accomplishing liberation. As one contemporary reviewer described them, the spirituals were "God's image in Ebony." In creation as well as performance, they exhibited the essential characteristics of spontaneity, variety, and communal interchange. The form of the spirituals was flexible and improvisational, thereby able to fit an individual slave's experience into the consciousness of group, creating at once an intensely personal and vividly communal experience.

In his remarks Jackson also draws attention to the fact that the spirituals, as the cultural product of enslaved Africans, used rhythms and beats of various homelands. The distinguishing musical aesthetic of the spirituals derives from West African percussive forms, multiple meters, syncopation, extensive melodic ornamentation, a call-and-response structure, and an integration of song and movement, each involving improvisation. Call and response embodies the foundational principle behind the performance of the spirituals, denoting the ritual requirement of what is necessary for completion. The soloist in original performances of the spirituals was viewed as a mystic whose call inspired the participating group to respond. This full sense of process and communication reinforces the communal identity and its belief that art is an appropriate response to oppression. Very much a ritual act, when spirituals were sung by enslaved people they amplified their desire for liberation and created conditions of sacred space and time wherein the biblical stories of which they sang were transformed and the history of the ancient past became the history of the present.

A feature of the songs many ex-slave narrators appreciated is that they derive from a people yearning for equality and freedom, not just in the next world but in this world. Capable of communicating on more than one level, as noted by Booker T. Washington and Frederick Douglass in their auto-biographies, on occasion the spirituals functioned as coded songs to communicate information between enslaved people. Washington affirmed that the freedom in their songs meant freedom in this world, and Douglass insisted that references to Canaan implied the North. But formally and thematically, spirituals were open to change and improvisation; a spiritual in one situation might mean something else in another. In nearly every instance, however, there is an intertwining of theological and social messages, borne out in Douglass's description of how "every tone was a testimony against slavery, and a prayer to God for deliverance from chains" (*Narrative* 57–58). Their meaning, though inspired by religious faith and story, transcended an exclusively religious response to oppression and adopted a vital, liberating element that was meant to challenge the social order. Lovell provides one of the most succinct descriptions of how the spirituals functioned in the following passage from his study *Black Song: The Forge and the Flame*:

> [Spirituals] were not religious songs in the sense of a compartment of life, nor religious in the sense of the theology of the camp meeting, nor religious because they often used Biblical symbols, nor religious because the hope of heaven was substituted to solve the problems of earth, nor religious for any other such reason. They were religious and spiritual because they tried, with inspired artistry, to pose the root questions of life, of before life, and of beyond life, and to react to these questions as the aroused human being and the bestirred folk have done since the rosy dawn of literature. (17)

When the Civil War shattered the closed society to which enslaved Africans were confined and brought them in to large-scale contact with the world outside the plantation, Northerners, often agents of the federal government or missionaries, came to appreciate their distinctive music. They eventually promoted spirituals in much the same way slave narratives were promoted, establishing the precedent Charlie Haden would later follow with the LMO. As with ex-slave narratives, the African-American authorship of the spirituals was challenged at first. But in an 1867 article

published in *The Atlantic Monthly,* Thomas Wentworth Higginson, a mili-
tant New England abolitionist who commanded the first freed slave regi-
ment to fight against the Confederacy, was among the first to describe how
he heard "the choked voice of a race at last unloosed" (Sernett 111). He
diligently took down the songs sung by the First South Carolina Volunteers around evening campfires. Higginson failed to recognize all the cultural components of the slave songs, but he did appreciate the forms of
resistance articulated in their performance, describing them as a "stimulus to courage and a tie to heaven" (Sernett 131). Noting how at the out-
break of the Civil War, enslaved blacks sang "We'll soon be free / When
the Lord will call us home," Higginson confirms the layered meaning of
many spirituals, citing a drummer boy who confided in him that "Lord"
in the song was a code for the "Yankees" (Sernett 128).

Often linked in tradition with slave uprisings led by Denmark Vesey, Nat
Turner, and Gabriel Prosser, the spirituals were archetypes of protest for
actual and spiritual liberation. Synthesizing sacred and secular meaning,
creators of the spirituals drew images from the Bible to interpret their own
experience, measuring it against a wider system of theological and historical
meaning. Three themes dominate spirituals: the desire for freedom, the
desire for justice, and strategies for survival. God is a liberator who is involved in history, and as "Wade in the Water" suggests, God will "trouble
the waters" of oppression. Many spirituals, such as "Joshua Fit the Battle
of Jericho" and "Didn't My Lord Deliver Daniel?" are drawn from biblical texts that stress God's involvement in the liberation of the oppressed.
Although God's liberating work was not always concretely evident, enslaved people were confident that "You Got a Right" to "the tree of life."

The songs also stress a need for enslaved people's own participation in
God's liberation, to be "Singing with a Sword in My Hand." Enslaved
people viewed their cry of "Let My People Go" as answered with the
Emancipation Proclamation, when "Slavery Chain Done Broke at Last."
God makes justice for the righteous and the unrighteous because "All God's
Children Got Wings," but "everybody talkin' 'bout heaven ain't going
there," and anyone who stands against liberation is called to account,
"Were You There When They Crucified My Lord?" Jesus represents both
a historical savior and a helper of the oppressed. Jesus functions in a more
personal way than God does, as deliverer and comforter, because "you may
have all the world," but "Give Me Jesus." He is affirmed in both his divinity and his humanity, especially his identification with the oppressed,
who believe that "A Little Talk with Jesus Makes It Right." Hence his birth

is an occasion to "Rise Up Shepherd and Follow" and "Go Tell It on the Mountain," and his life on earth a reminder to "Rise, Mourner, Rise."

Songs such as "Steal Away" and "Let Us Praise God Together on Our Knees" may have served as a means to convene secret resistance meetings, and "Deep River, My Home is Over Jordan" may imply a wish to cross over to Africa or the North. But getting to freedom is what occupies many of the lyrics that take as a theme a tired sojourner struggling through a hostile landscape while leaning and depending on God. Portraying a struggle against oppression in a variety of metaphors, many spirituals focus on the difficult movement through space and time, but with the confidence to cheer the "Weary Traveler." Spatial and temporal metaphors of movement using a variety of methods—sailing, walking, riding, rowing, climbing—all appear for a people "Bound to Go," urging them to "Travel On."

The spirituals actually and symbolically moved a people toward liberation when they sang "We Are Climbing Jacob's Ladder," even if they could only "Keep Inching Along." Noting the threat of adverse physical conditions, the creators appropriated symbols from their own situation and describe searching for God in the wilderness, rocks, darkness, storms, and valleys. Lyrics from songs such as "O Stand the Storm," "Sinner, Please Don't Let This Harvest Pass," and "Hold On!" gave inspiration to endure. Although an enslaved person often felt "Like a Motherless Child," lost where "I Couldn't Hear Nobody Pray," and for whom "Nobody Knows the Trouble I've Seen," faith is always affirmed because "All My Troubles Will Soon Be Over." Sometimes a lonely sojourner is aided by heavenly transportation, as in "Swing Low, Sweet Chariot," or the activity of the Underground Railroad that invites "Get on Board, Little Children." But the destination is always freedom, sometimes construed as Africa, the North, or heaven, as in "Roll, Jordan, Roll." The role of the community—expressed in concepts of home in "I Got a Home in That Rock," as a heavenly reunion with family in "Band of Gideon," or as a place of safety in "There Is a Balm in Gilead"—is also reinforced.

Significant contemporary comments on the spirituals, such as James Cone's *The Spirituals and the Blues,* almost always link the power of song in the struggle for black survival with a liberating theology. Cone examines the spirituals and their secular counterpart, the blues, as cultural expressions of black people, delineating the functional techniques for cultural survival that the songs embody. John Lovell's comprehensive *Black Song: The Forge and the Flame* explores how the spirituals were "hammered out" in the forge of oppression and the subsequent social implications when, over time, their "flame" cast a liberative spirit far and wide. Emphasizing their African roots in the context of enslaved life, he demonstrates how the spirituals assisted in resistance to slavery, insisting that the songs not only project religious and otherworldly visions but were enslaved peoples' descriptions and criticism of their environment and an index to their revolutionary sentiments and desire to be free. In *Black Culture and Black Consciousness,* Lawrence Levine argues persuasively for an appreciation of the profound connection between the other world and this world in slave consciousness that the spirituals describe. Like Cone and Lovell, Levine seeks to underscore the roots of resistance behind the spirituals and to rehistoricize the experience of enslaved people, for whom religion was wrought out of an encounter with the divine in the midst of social realities.

What Charlie Haden understood when he chose to record *Steal Away* was that in evoking the spirituals he was calling forth the spirit of a people struggling to be free, a people who asserted that "Before I'll be a slave / I'll be buried in my grave / And go home to my Lord and be free." But with Hank Jones as his partner, Haden extends the slave narrative tradition and makes it relevant to a contemporary, multicultural society. Together, the two men have "drawn some history and autobiography and a little private meditation, set them deep in the spirit, then drawn them out into a jazz pilgrimage. Black spirituals, white hymns, folk tunes from Ireland and French Canada: Jones and Haden give them a singular unity and immediacy. This isn't just great music. It's healing music" (Cocks 59).

Just as the form of the sacred spirituals evolved into the secular blues and later jazz, the slave narrative has tradition has taken a similar path. What has remained constant, however, is a narrative element that foregrounds a liberating text and resists the categorization of the forms as either sacred or secular. Both the music and the narratives are textimonies that participate in a universal struggle to make sense of experience as a mode of survival, a struggle that, in turn, becomes a mode of creation and recreation—of cultural fulfillment. As the slave narrative tradition and its musical counterpart, the spirituals, have been extended, traditional forms have simply been recontextualized in order to address the complexities of the modern era. However, the inspiration has remained constant. Dialogic in form and inclusive in intent, textimony still liberates.

In *The Spirituals and the Blues,* James Cone observes that "black history is a spiritual" (33). In choosing to record the spirituals, Haden directly links not just his efforts but his identity with the legacy of liberation promoted by African Americans. In so doing he embodies an ethical posture that assumes that blackness is not a restrictive term but encompasses all who are oppressed or all who take sides with the oppressed by joining with body as well as mind in the struggle for liberation. Or as Cone writes, "To be black means that your heart, your soul, your mind, and your body are where the dispossessed are" (Cone and Wilmore, *Black Theology* 151).

Steal Away concludes with a medley of hymns often sung in both black and nonblack congregations, the last of which is "Amazing Grace," thereby providing a certain symmetry to this analysis of Haden's Liberation Music Orchestra. As a nonblack performer of the music of the oppressed, Haden is careful in offering his suggestions for how we struggle against oppression. Haden's music does not automatically open the door to social change, but it does gesture toward the door, allowing us to be moved by grace toward liberation because it is our imagination that has been awakened: It is our idea to be moved and our identity that is at stake.

Charlie Haden's music, the literature of Richard Wright and Ernest Gaines, the art of Glenn Ligon, and the drama of Anna Deavere Smith are all acts of imagination that uncover the grace that emerges out of the cultural text of slavery. Although we must accept that such acts provide no actual guarantee of liberation—that triumphs over language, art, and music do not translate directly into triumph over social and material circumstances—we can also appreciate that the slave narrative tradition of textimony is instrumental in effecting a liberating theology because of the ways it transforms our abstract feelings about a historical, social institution into an intimate engagement with actual people.

Toni Morrison observes that "language can never 'pin down' slavery," but it can still have the "force" and the "felicity" to "reach toward the ineffable" and in so doing become a "sublime activity" because it is fundamentally "generative" (*Nobel* 21–22). In this sense, our imagination is graced with the possibility, if not the fact, of liberation. The slave narrative tradition presents to the public an opportunity and the permission to experience privately—through the act of reading, viewing, or listening—both the conditions of oppression and the human spirit that flourishes, and in so doing offers people a chance to grow, to turn their faces to the other and to see their own faces reflected in it.

Although the slave narrative tradition in many respects is effective in helping us to bridge the gap between self and others, the respect for otherness it engenders also seems to release a specter of an infinite regress. Where does the self end and the other begin? This overwhelming spectrum of possibility is tempered in the slave narrative tradition by the ordering form of faith. The language, the culture, the symbols and substance of religion become important in these supposedly secular enterprises because religious inquiry resists competing claims on identity and turns us toward a consideration of what is general to the human condition and what provides ultimate orientation in individual human lives. The mythic narratives of Wright and Gaines, the ritual drama of Anna Deavere Smith, the meditative art of Glenn Ligon, and the symbolic music of Charlie Haden all reveal in their cultural specificity and their search for liberating truth the same thing that religion traditionally makes possible for people in search of meaning.

Religion in a culture of slavery, as Wright's text so dramatically demonstrates, bears much responsibility for people's suffering, but as Gaines's text reveals, it also can wrest meaning out of that suffering. Wright and Gaines both give us new histories to supplant the official histories of the oppressors, and like Smith, Ligon, and Haden, they accomplish even more: They make that history personal. The reason why all these texts function as textimony that imagines grace is that their creators also understand the ways in which their imaginations have been graced. They accept the limits of what their art can accomplish but nonetheless continue to create with a full sense of responsibility to the role they play in the tradition of textimony. Each artist's individual attempt to imagine grace is shaped by the way in which each invites his or her imagination to be graced. This posture may not be traditionally religious, but it inclines toward the religious in part because of what it shares with contemporary liberation theology; in the words of David Tracy, it insists, "Do not reduce me or anyone else to your narrative" (5).

Liberating theologies force us to reconsider the ways we think and act and, finally, the way we are. As the slave narrative tradition so effectively demonstrates, our entry point into this new reality, engendered by a recognition of otherness, is facilitated by transgression or the "ethical call of the other" (Tracy 6). As this study tries to demonstrate, the turn to the other may take many forms. In each instance of textimony, an interruption of complacency is effected, sometimes as a historical act or moment, sometimes as pure revelation, but always in the slave narrative tradition as an act of imagining grace that also graces our imaginations. Those who work within the slave narrative tradition sense that our common history can change over time to accommodate our expanding awareness of the variety of who we are and what we hold as sacred. As the central religious and moral fact in the history of our nation, slavery shows how our theology, like our identity, can expand in response to the textimony of those whose story has not always been heard. As Albert Raboteau explains,

Our nation too has ancestors. Now, as much as ever, we stand in need of their presence. We, the American people, need to hear and to listen to the stories of all our forefathers and foremothers. We need to be informed by the memories of their lives. Can't these bones live, these dry bones? If we allow them to be re-knit and re-membered. Memory, story, ritual—these are all the ways of re-membering a community broken by hate, rage, injustice, fear. Not to avenge, nor to make up for, not undoing what cannot be undone, but perhaps to heal. There are those who fear that the stories will not cohere, that they will remain a disparate set of unrelated or conflict-ridden experiences that only confirm our feelings of divisiveness, us against them. Perhaps, but I am convinced that if we listen, truly listen to the stories of others, something else will happen. We will find ourselves intrigued by the drama of these stories, moved by their poignancy and, finally, surprised at the common humanity that lies beneath their distinctive details. Finally, what we hold in common is a set of shared stories. If we seek commonality, we will discover it in the telling and listening to each other's stories, confident that an adequate history of the varied races and religions who came to dwell in this land will reflect our continually expanding American identity. ("Fire" 9)

Thus the slave narrative tradition continues to give a point of entry into understanding the radical sense of otherness that often characterizes our concepts of difference, directing us away from the center and toward the margins—toward creative acts that reveal the liberating aspect of human history in what Raboteau describes as "a set of shared stories." From these artists we learn what contemporary liberation theologians teach us: that history is the site of discovery for how people endure and create, survive and appreciate. The legacy of the slave narrative tradition of textimony is to tell the stories of our relationship to what we hold as sacred: to imagine grace.

NOTES

1. This remark by Jackson is included in the liner notes he prepared for *Steal Away*, a recording by Charlie Haden and Hank Jones discussed later in this chapter.

2. Some suggestions to replace the term *jazz* include Rasaahn Roland Kirk's "Great Black Music," Archie Shepp's "African American Instrumental Music," Max Roach's "the music of Louis Armstrong, the music of Charles Parker, etc.," and Billy Taylor's "Twentieth-Century American Music."

3. Although it is not possible here to summarize Albert Murray's immense contribution to developing a jazz aesthetic, my remarks are drawn from one of his earliest formulations, *The Omni-Americans: New Perspectives on Black Experience and American Culture* (New York: Outerbridge and Dienstfrey, 1970), where

he posits as an Omni-American one who is "fully oriented to cultural diversity" (8), and his later work, *The Blue Devils of Nada: A Contemporary American Approach to Aesthetic Statement* (New York: Pantheon, 1996), where he defines art as "the ultimate extension, elaboration, and refinement of the rituals that reenact the primary techniques (and hence reinforce the basic orientation toward experience) of a given people in a given time, place, and circumstance" (13).

4. Unless otherwise noted, Haden's remarks about the compositions for all three LMO albums are taken from liner notes he prepared for each album.

5. In a more recent study, *Re-Searching Black Music* (University of Tennessee Press, 1996), Spencer advances the notion that we have become estranged from ourselves because we maintain a doctrine of belief that situates the sacred and religious in opposition to the profane and cultural; he suggests that this polarity occurs in all forms of discourse. Recognizing this estrangement, Spencer hopes, will encourage us to seek reconciliation, and he proposes that African-American culture is uniquely qualified to help us negotiate this reconciliation.

Works Cited

Adams, Timothy Dow. *Telling Lies in Modern American Autobiography*. Chapel Hill: University of North Carolina Press, 1990.

Amirthan, Sam. *Stories Make People: Examples of Theological Work in Community*. Geneva: World Council of Churches Publications, 1989.

Amis, Martin. "Blown Away." *New Yorker* 30 May 1994.

Anderson, Victor. *Beyond Ontological Blackness: An Essay on African American Religious and Cultural Criticism*. New York: Continuum, 1995.

Andrews, William. "In Search of a Common Identity: The Self and the South in Four Mississippi Autobiographies." *Southern Review* 24.1 (1988): 47–64.

———. "The Novelization of Voice in Early African American Narrative." *PMLA* 105.1 (1990): 23–34.

———. *To Tell a Free Story: The First Century of Afro-American Autobiography, 1760–1865*. Urbana: University of Illinois Press, 1986.

———. "'We Ain't Going Back There': The Idea of Progress in *The Autobiography of Miss Jane Pittman*." *Black American Literature Forum* 11 (1977): 146–49.

Aptheker, Herbert. *Abolitionism: A Revolutionary Movement*. Boston: Twayne, 1989.

Atwood, Margaret. "Silencing the Scream." *Profession* 94 (1994): 44–47.

Babb, Valerie Melissa. *Ernest Gaines*. Boston: Twayne, 1991.

Baldwin, James. *Evidence of Things Not Seen*. New York: Henry Holt, 1985.

———. *The Fire Next Time*. New York: Dell, 1963.

Balliet, Whitney. "The Dean: Listening to Hank Jones." *New Yorker* 15 July 1996: 82–83.

———. "Rollins Rampant." *New Yorker* 29 July 1991: 58–59.

Barbour, John D. *Versions of Deconversion: Autobiography and the Loss of Faith.* Charlottesville: University Press of Virginia, 1994.

Bearden, Romare, and Harry Henderson. *A History of African-American Artists: From 1792 to the Present.* New York: Random House, 1993.

Beavers, Herman. *Wrestling Angels into Song: The Fictions of Ernest J. Gaines and James Alan McPherson.* Philadelphia: University of Pennsylvania Press, 1995.

Beckham, Barry. "Jane Pittman and Oral Tradition." *Callaloo* 1.3 (1978) 102–9.

Ben-Amos, Dan. "Introduction." *Word & Image* 3.3 (1987): 223–24.

Berubé, Michael. *Life as We Know It: A Father, a Family, and an Exceptional Child.* New York: Pantheon, 1996.

Bloom, Harold. *The American Religion: The Emergence of the Post-Christian Nation.* New York: Simon & Schuster, 1992.

Blumenfeld, Laura. "Mideast Side Story." *Washington Post* 30 June 1994: C1, C2.

Boesak, Alan Aubrey. *Farewell to Innocence: A Socio-Ethical Study on Black Theology and Power.* Maryknoll, N.Y.: Orbis, 1984.

Bonazzi, Robert. *Man in the Mirror: John Howard Griffin and the Story of Black Like Me.* Maryknoll, N.Y.: Orbis, 1997.

Brace, Eric. "The Bassist Who Set Jazz Free." *Washington Post* 2 December 1995: C1–C2.

Bradford, Ernest. "Towards a View of the Influence of Religion on Black Literature." *CLA Journal* 27 (1983): 18–29.

Brooks, Gwendolyn. *To Disembark.* Chicago: Third World Press, 1981.

———. *Report from Part One.* Detroit: Broadside Press, 1972.

Brown, Henry "Box." *Narrative of Henry "Box" Brown.* Wilmington, Del.: Scholarly Resources.

Bryant, Jerry H. "Ernest J. Gaines: Change, Growth, and History." *Southern Review* 10 (1974): 851–64.

Butterfield, Stephen. *Black Autobiography in America.* Amherst: University of Massachusetts Press, 1974.

Byerman, Keith E. *Fingering the Jagged Grain: Tradition and Form in Recent Black Fiction.* Athens: University of Georgia Press, 1985.

———. "'A Slow to Anger' People: *The Autobiography of Miss Jane Pittman* as Historical Fiction. In *Critical Reflections of the Fiction of Ernest J. Gaines.* Ed. David C. Estes. Athens: University of Georgia Press, 1994: 107–23.

Cain, Joy Duckett. "The Source of Our Magic." *Essence* May 1992: 66.

Callahan, John. "Image Making: Tradition and the Two Versions of *The Autobiography of Miss Jane Pittman.*" *Chicago Review* 29.2 (1977): 45–62.

———. *In the African-American Grain: The Pursuit of Voice in Twentieth-Century Black Fiction.* Urbana: University of Illinois Press, 1988.

Cannon, Katie. *Black Womanist Ethics.* Atlanta: Scholars Press, 1988.

Carey, Joe. "Charlie Haden Revives the Liberation Music Orchestra." *Jazz Times,* March 1983: 7, 12.

Carson, Sharon. "Shaking the Foundation: Liberation Theology in the Narrative of the Life of Frederick Douglass." *R&L* 24.2 (1992): 19–34.

Clarke, Donald. *Wishing on the Moon: The Life and Times of Billie Holiday.* New York: Viking, 1994.

Clasby, Nancy Tenfelde. "Malcolm X and Liberation Theology." *Cross Currents* 38.2 (1988): 173–84, 210.

Cocks, Jay. "That Old-Time Religion." *Time* 17 July 1995: 59.

Coles, Robert A. "Richard Wright's Synthesis." *CLA Journal* 31.4 (1988): 375–93.

Collins, Judy. *Amazing Grace.* New York: Hyperion, 1991.

Cone, James H. *Black Theology and Black Power.* New York: Seabury Press, 1969.

———. *A Black Theology of Liberation.* Philadelphia: Lippincott, 1970.

———. *For My People: Black Theology and the Black Church.* Maryknoll, N.Y.: Orbis, 1984.

———. *God of the Oppressed.* New York: Seabury Press, 1975.

———. *Martin and Malcolm and America: A Dream or a Nightmare.* Maryknoll, N.Y.: Orbis, 1991.

———. *My Soul Looks Back.* Nashville: Abingdon Press, 1982.

———. *The Spirituals and the Blues.* New York: Seabury Press, 1972.

———. "The Story Context of Black Theology." *Theology Today* 32 (1975): 144–50.

Cone, James H., and Gayraud S. Wilmore. *Black Theology: A Documentary History, 1980–1992.* Maryknoll, N.Y.: Orbis, 1993.

Couser, G. Thomas. *American Autobiography: The Prophetic Mode.* Amherst: University of Massachusetts Press, 1979.

Dabydeen, David. *Turner: New and Selected Poems.* London: Jonathan Cape, 1994.

Davis, Charles T. "From Experience to Eloquence: Richard Wright's *Black Boy* as Art." In *Chant of Saints: A Gathering of Afro-American Literature, Art, and Scholarship.* Ed. Michael S. Harper, Robert B. Stepto, and John Hope Franklin. Urbana: University of Illinois Press, 1979: 425–39.

Davis, Charles T., and Henry Louis Gates Jr., eds. *The Slave's Narrative.* New York: Oxford University Press, 1985.

Davis, Thulani. "Masterpieces for a Mixed-Up Age." *Washington Post* 1 May 1994: G3.

Dent, Thomas C., Richard Schechner, and Gilbert Moses, eds. *The Free Southern Theatre by the Free Southern Theatre.* New York: Bobbs-Merrill, 1969.

Dixon, Melvin. "Singing Swords: The Literary Legacy of Slavery." In *The Slave's Narrative.* Ed. Charles T. Davis and Henry Louis Gates Jr. New York: Oxford University Press, 1985: 298–317.

Dondis, Donis A. *Primer of Visual Literacy.* Cambridge, Mass.: MIT Press, 1973.

Dorsey, Peter A. *Sacred Estrangement: The Rhetoric of Conversion in Modern American Autobiography.* University Park: Pennsylvania State University Press, 1993.

Douglass, Frederick. *My Bondage and My Freedom*. Ed. William L. Andrews. Urbana: University of Illinois Press, 1987.

———. *Narrative of the Life of Frederick Douglass, an American Slave*. New York: Penguin, 1981.

Doyle, Mary Ellen. "The Autobiography of Miss Jane Pittman as a Fictional Edited Autobiography." In *Critical Reflections on the Fiction of Ernest Gaines*. Ed. David C. Estes. Athens: University of Georgia Press, 1994: 89–105.

———. "A MELUS Interview: Ernest J. Gaines—'Other Things to Write About.'" *MELUS* 11.2 (1984): 59–81.

Du Bois, W. E. B. *The Souls of Black Folk*. New York: Fawcett, 1961.

DuCille, Ann. "The Occult of True Black Womanhood: Critical Demeanor and Black Feminist Studies." *Signs* 19.2 (1994): 591–629.

Duke, Lynne. "This Harrowed Ground." *Washington Post Magazine* 28 August 1994: 9–13, 21–25.

Edwards, Bob. *Fridays with Red: A Radio Friendship*. New York: Simon & Schuster, 1993.

Elkins, James. "On the Impossibility of Stories: The Anti-Narrative and Non-Narrative Impulse in Modern Painting." *Word & Image* 7.4 (1991): 348–64.

Ellis, Rex. "Re-Living History: Bringing Slavery into Play." *American Visions* December/January 1993: 22–25.

Ellison, Ralph. *Going to the Territory*. New York: Vintage Books, 1987.

———. *Shadow and Act*. New York: Vintage Books, 1972.

Enekwe, Onuora. "Theatre in Nigeria: The Modern vs. the Traditional." *Yale Theatre* 8.4 (1976): 62–66.

Evans, James H., Jr. *Black Theology: A Critical Assessment and Annotated Bibliography*. Westport, Conn.: Greenwood Press, 1987.

———. "Deconstructing the Tradition: Narrative Strategies in Nascent Black Theology." *Union Seminary Quarterly Review* 44 (1990): 101–19.

———. *Spiritual Empowerment in Afro-American Literature*. Lewiston, N.Y.: Edwin Mellen Press, 1987.

———. "Toward an African-American Theology." In *Black Theology: A Documentary History, 1980–1992*. Ed. James H. Cone and Gayraud S. Wilmore. Maryknoll, N.Y.: Orbis, 1993: 26–34.

———. *We Have Been Believers: An African-American Systematic Theology*. Minneapolis: Fortress, 1992.

Fabre, Geneviève. "The Free Southern Theatre, 1963–1979." *Black American Literature Forum* 17.2 (1983): 55–59.

Fabre, Michel. *The Unfinished Quest of Richard Wright*. New York: Morrow, 1973.

Fax, Elton C. *Seventeen Black Artists*. New York: Dodd, Mead, 1971.

Feelings, Tom. *The Middle Passage*. New York: Dial, 1995.

Felman, Shoshana. *The Literary Speech Act*. Trans. Catherine Porter. Ithaca, N.Y.: Cornell University Press, 1993.

Fletcher, Michael A. "By Foot and Rail, Historian Traces Slaves' Secret Flight to Freedom." *Washington Post* 2 June 1996: A3.

Franklin, John Hope. "Truth and Fiction." *American Heritage* October 1992: 90.

Freire, Paulo. *Pedagogy of the Oppressed*. New York: Continuum, 1997.

Fulop, Timothy E., and Albert J. Raboteau, eds. *African-American Religion: Interpretive Essays in History and Culture*. New York: Routledge, 1997.

Gaines, Ernest J. *The Autobiography of Miss Jane Pittman*. New York: Bantam, 1971.

———. "Miss Jane and I." *Callaloo* 1.3 (1978): 23–38.

———. "On the Verge: An Interview with Ernest J. Gaines." *New Orleans Review* 3.4 (1973): 339–44.

———. "A Very Big Order: Reconstructing Identity." *Southern Review* 26.2 (1990): 245–53.

Gates, Henry Louis, Jr., ed. *The Classic Slave Narratives*. New York: Penguin, 1987.

Gaudet, Marcia. "The Failure of Traditional Religion in Ernest Gaines' Short Stories." *Journal of the Short Story in English* 18 (1992): 81–89.

———. "Miss Jane and Personal Experience Narrative: Ernest Gaines' *The Autobiography of Miss Jane Pittman*." *Western Folklore* 51.1 (1992): 23–32.

Gaudet, Marcia, and Carl Wooten. *Porch Talk with Ernest Gaines: Conversations on the Writer's Craft*. Baton Rouge: Louisiana State University Press, 1990.

Gombrich, E. H. "Image and Word in Twentieth Century Art." *Word & Image* 1.3 (1985): 213–41.

Graham, Maryemma, and Jerry W. Ward. "*Black Boy* (American Hunger: Freedom to Remember)." In *Censored Books, Critical Viewpoints*. Ed. Nicholas J. Karolides, Lee Burress, and John M. Kean. Metuchen, N.J.: Scarecrow Press, 1993: 109–16.

Grant, Jacquelyn. "The Sin of Servanthood and the Deliverance of Discipleship." *The Other Side* September/October 1994: 36–40, 47.

Griffin, John Howard. *Black Like Me*. New York: New American Library. 1962.

———. *Black Like Me*. New York: Houghton Mifflin, 1977.

Gunn, Janet Varner. *Autobiography: Towards a Poetics of Experience*. Philadelphia: University of Pennsylvania Press, 1982.

Haden, Charlie. "The Making of Free Jazz." *Down Beat* 59 (January 1992): 29–30.

Haden, Charlie, and Hank Jones. *Steal Away: Spirituals, Hymns, and Folk Songs*. CD. Polydor/Polygram, 1995.

Haden, Charlie, and the Liberation Music Orchestra. *The Ballad of the Fallen*. LP. ECM, 1982.

———. *Dream Keeper*. CD. Blue Note, 1991.

———. *Liberation Music Orchestra*. LP. ABC Records, Inc., 1973.

Harrington, Walt. "Rosa Parks and the Making of History." *Washington Post Magazine* 8 October 1995: 10–17, 24–30.

Hart, F. R. "Notes for an Anatomy of Modern Autobiography." *New Literary History* 1 (Spring 1970): 488.

Hicks, Jack. "To Make These Bones Live: History and Community in Ernest Gaines's Fiction." *Black American Literature Forum* 11 (1977): 9–19.

Ho, Fred Wei-han. "What Makes 'Jazz' the Revolutionary Music of the 20th Century, and Will It Be Revolutionary for the 21st Century?" *African American Review* 29.2 (1995): 283–90.

Hodges, John O. "An Apprenticeship to Life and Art: Narrative Design in Wright's *Black Boy.*" *CLA Journal* 28.4 (1985): 415–33.

Hodgson, Peter C. *Children of Freedom.* Philadelphia: Fortress, 1974.

Holiday, Billie, with William Dufty. *Lady Sings the Blues.* New York: Penguin, 1984.

hooks, bell. "The Magic of Our Moments." *The Other Side* May/June 1994: 8–11, 30.

Hopkins, Dwight N. *Shoes That Fit Our Feet: Sources for a Constructive Black Theology.* Maryknoll, N.Y.: Orbis, 1993.

Hopkins, Dwight N., and George Cummings, eds. *Cut Loose Your Stammering Tongue: Black Theology in the Slave Narratives.* Maryknoll, N.Y.: Orbis, 1991.

Hornby, Richard. "Regional Theatre Comes of Age." *Hudson Review* 46.3 (1993): 529–36.

Hughes, Robert. "The Case for Elitist Do-Gooders." *New Yorker* 27 May 1996: 33–34.

Hulbert, Ann. "Romance and Race." *New Republic* 18 May 1992: 43–48.

Hurley, Neil P. "Liberation Theology and New York City Fiction." *Thought* 48 (1973): 338–59.

Hurston, Zora Neale. "How It Feels to Be Colored Me." In *I Love Myself When I Am Laughing: A Zora Neale Hurston Reader.* Ed. Alice Walker. New York: Feminist Press, 1979: 152–56.

Jackson, Blyden. "Jane Pittman through the Years: A People's Tale." In *American Letters and the Historical Consciousness: Essays in Honor of Lewis P. Simpson.* Ed. J. Gerald Kennedy and Daniel Mark Fogel. Baton Rouge: Louisiana State University Press, 1987: 255–73.

Jacobs, Harriet A. *Incidents in the Life of a Slave Girl.* Ed. Jean Fagan Yellin. Cambridge, Mass.: Harvard University Press, 1987.

Johnson, James Weldon. *Black Manhattan.* New York: Athenaeum, 1968.

Johnson, Ken. "Glenn Ligon at Max Protetch." *Art in America* 80.11 (1992): 131.

Jones, Carolyn M. "Dietrich Bonhoeffer's Letters and Papers from Prison: Rethinking the Relationship of Theology and Arts, Literature and Religion." *Literature and Theology* 9.3 (1995): 243–59.

Jones, Gayl. *Liberating Voices: Oral Tradition in African American Literature.* Cambridge, Mass.: Harvard University Press, 1991.

Jones, William R. *Is God a White Racist?* Garden City, N.Y.: Anchor, 1973.

Kastor, Elizabeth. "Toni Morrison's 'Beloved' Country." *Washington Post* 5 October 1987: B1, B12.

Kaufman, Joanne. "Anna Deavere Smith: Passion Plays." *Washington Post* 25 April 1993: G1, G11.

Keneally, Thomas. "Faithful in His Fashion." *Washington Post Book World* 25.46 (1995): 1, 10.

———. "Holocaust Was Archetype of Race Hate Everywhere." *Daily Progress* 27 February 1994: A7.

Kinnamon, Keneth, and Michel Fabre, eds. *Conversations with Richard Wright.* Jackson: University of Mississippi Press, 1993.

Lahr, John. "Under the Skin." *New Yorker* 28 June 1993: 90–93.

Lange, Art. "Charlie Haden/Liberation Music Orchestra." *Down Beat* 58 (May 1991): 30.

Laris, Katie. "Fires in the Mirror: Crown Heights, Brooklyn, and Other Identities." *Theatre Journal* 45 (March 1993): 117–19.

Ledbetter, Mark. *Virtuous Intentions: The Religious Dimension of Narrative.* Atlanta: Scholars Press, 1989.

Leonard, Neil. *Jazz: Myth and Religion.* New York: Oxford University Press, 1987.

Levenson, Jeff. "Blue Notes: Charlie Haden Keeps the Dream Alive on a New Album (*Dream Keeper*)." *Billboard* 15 December 1990: 24.

Levine, Judith. "The Heart of Whiteness: Dismantling the Master's House." *The Voice Literary Supplement,* September 1994: 11–16.

Levine, Lawrence W. *Black Culture and Black Consciousness: Afro-American Folk Thought from Slavery to Freedom.* New York: Oxford University Press, 1978.

Lewis, Barbara. "The Circle of Confusion: A Conversation with Anna Deavere Smith." *Kenyon Review* 15.4 (1993): 54–64.

Lewis, Jo Ann. "Self-Portrait of the Artist as a Young Black Man." *Washington Post* 14 November 1993: G1, G6.

Litweiler, John. *Ornette Coleman: A Harmonologic Life.* New York: William Morrow, 1992.

Locke, Alain. *The New Negro.* New York: Athenaeum, 1968.

Lott, Eric. "Double V, Double Time: Bebop's Politics of Style." In *Jazz among the Discourses.* Ed. Krin Gabbard. Durham, N.C.: Duke University Press, 1995: 243–55.

Lovell, John, Jr. *Black Song: The Forge and the Flame.* New York: Macmillan, 1972.

Lowe, John, ed. *Conversations with Ernest Gaines.* Jackson: University Press of Mississippi, 1995.

MacKethan, Lucinda H. "*Black Boy* and Ex-Coloured Man: Version and Inversion of the Slave Narrator's Quest for Voice." *CLA Journal* 32.2 (1988): 123–47.

———. "From Fugitive Slave to Man of Letters: The Conversion of Frederick Douglass." *Journal of Narrative Technique* 16.1 (1986): 55–71.

Mackey, Nathaniel. "Other: From Noun to Verb." In *Jazz among the Discourses*. Ed. Krin Gabbard. Durham, N.C.: Duke University Press, 1995: 76–99.

Mandel, Howard. "Charlie Haden's Search for Freedom." *Down Beat* 54 (September 1987): 20–23.

———. "The Hymn of the Hopeful." *Village Voice* 28 (December 1983): 101–2.

Margolick, David. "Strange Fruit." *Vanity Fair* September 1998: 312–20.

Marren, Susan M. "Between Slavery and Freedom: The Transgressive Self in Olaudah Equiano's Autobiography." *PMLA* 108.1 (1993): 94–105.

Martin, Carol. "Anna Deavere Smith: The Word Becomes You." *Drama Review* 37.4 (1993): 45–62.

Mays, Benjamin. *The Negro's God as Reflected in His Literature*. Boston: Chapman & Grimes, 1938.

McDowell, Deborah E. "Negotiating between Tenses: Witnessing Slavery after Freedom—Dessa Rose." In *Slavery and the Literary Imagination*. Ed. Deborah E. McDowell and Arnold Rampersad. Baltimore: Johns Hopkins University Press, 1989: 144–63.

McDowell, Deborah E., and Arnold Rampersad. *Slavery and the Literary Imagination*. Baltimore: Johns Hopkins University Press, 1989.

Meier, August. *A White Scholar and the Black Community, 1945–1965: Essays and Reflections*. Amherst: University of Massachusetts Press, 1992.

Miller, R. Baxter. "Forum." *PMLA* 111.5 (1996): 1156.

Morgenstern, Dan. "Charlie Haden—From Hillbilly to Avant-Garde—A Rocky Road." *Down Beat* 34 (March 1967): 20–21, 442.

Morrison, Toni. *Beloved*. New York: Knopf, 1987.

———. *The Nobel Lecture in Literature, 1993*. New York: Knopf, 1994.

———. *Playing in the Dark: Whiteness and the Literary Imagination*. Cambridge, Mass.: Harvard University Press, 1992.

———. "The Site of Memory." In *Inventing the Truth: The Art and Craft of Memoir*. Ed. William Zinsser. Boston: Houghton Mifflin, 1987: 103–24.

Moylan, Tom. "Anticipatory Fiction: Bread and Wine and Liberation Theology." *Modern Fiction Studies* 35.1 (1989): 103–17.

Myrick-Harris, Clarissa. "Mirror of the Movement: The History of the Free Southern Theatre as a Microcosm of the Civil Rights and Black Power Movements, 1963–1978." Ph.D. Dissertation, Emory University, 1988.

Neal, Larry. "Conquest of the South." *Drama Review* 14.3 (1970): 169–74.

Neely, Mark E., Jr. *The Last Best Hope on Earth: Abraham Lincoln and the Promise of America*. Cambridge, Mass.: Harvard University Press, 1993.

Ochillo, Yvonne. "*Black Boy*: Structure as Meaning." *Griot* 6.1 (1987): 49–54.

Olney, James. "'I Was Born': Slave Narratives, Their Status as Autobiography and as Literature." *Callaloo* 7.1 (1984): 46–85.

———. "The Value of Autobiography for Comparative Studies: African vs. Western Autobiography." *Comparative Civilizations Review* 2 (1979): 52–64.

Ozick, Cynthia. "Rushdie in the Louvre." *New Yorker* 13 December 1993: 69–79.

Palmer, Bob. "Charlie Haden's Creed." *Down Beat* 39 (July 1972): 16–18, 45, 47.

Papa, Lee. "'His feet on your neck': The New Religion in the Works of Ernest J. Gaines." *African American Review* 27.2 (1993): 187–93.

Perry, Lewis. *Radical Abolitionism: Anarchy and the Government of God in Anti-slavery Thought.* Knoxville: University of Tennessee Press, 1995.

Pinn, Anthony B. *Why, Lord?: Suffering and Evil in Black Theology.* New York: Continuum, 1995.

Plasa, Carl, and Betty J. Ring, eds. *The Discourse of Slavery: Aphra Behn to Toni Morrison.* New York: Routledge, 1994.

Porter, Horace A. "The Horror and the Glory: Richard Wright's Portrait of the Artist in *Black Boy* and *American Hunger.*" In *Richard Wright: A Collection of Critical Essays.* Ed. Richard Macksey and Frank E. Moorer. Englewood Cliffs, N.J.: Prentice Hall, 1984: 55–67.

Powell, Richard J. "How Cinque Was Painted." *Washington Post* 28 December 1997: G2–G3.

"Prints and Photographs Published." *Print Collector's Newsletter* 24.1 (1993): 21.

Putschögl, Gerhard. "Black Music—Key Force in Afro-American Culture: Archie Shepp on Oral Tradition and Black Culture." In *History and Tradition in Afro-American Culture.* Ed. Gunter H. Lenz. New York: Campus Verlag, 1984: 262–76.

Raboteau, Albert J. "Fire in the Bones: African-American Christianity and Auto-biographical Reflection." *America* 170.18 (1994): 4–9.

———. "Praying the ABCs: Reflections on Faith in History." *Cross Currents* 42.3 (1992): 314–25.

Raffat, Donne. "Introduction: Boundaries of the Imagination." *Profession* 94: 41–43.

Rambo, Lewis R. *Understanding Religious Conversion.* New Haven, Conn.: Yale University Press, 1993.

Rawick, George P., ed. *The American Slave: A Composite Autobiography,* 41 vols. Westport, CT: Greenwood, 1972, 1977, 1979.

Reilly, John M., ed. *Richard Wright: The Critical Reception.* New York: Burt Franklin, 1978.

Ringle, Ken. "A Southern Road to Freedom." *Washington Post* 20 July 1993: D1–D2.

Roberts, Jim. "Charlie Haden." *Bass Player* July/August 1991: 41–47.

Robertson, John A. "On Glenn Ligon." *Reconstruction* 2.3 (1994): 158–61.

Rosenblatt, Roger. "Black Autobiography: Life as the Death Weapon." In *Auto-biography: Essays Theoretical and Critical.* Ed. James Olney. Princeton, N.J.: Princeton University Press, 1980: 169–80.

Rosenfeld, Megan. "Conversation Piece: Robbie McCauley and Audience." *Washington Post* 5 May 1994: D1, D2.

Rowell, Charles H. "'This Louisiana Thing That Drives Me': An Interview with Ernest Gaines." *Callaloo* 1.3 (1978): 39–51.

Rubinstein, Meyer Raphael. "Glenn Ligon." *Art News* 92.9 (1993): 124.

Said, Edward. *The World, the Text, and the Critic.* Cambridge, Mass.: Harvard University Press, 1983.

Schechner, Richard. "Anna Deavere Smith: Acting as Incorporation." *Drama Review* 37.4 (1993): 63–64.

———. *Environmental Theatre.* New York: Hawthorne, 1973.

Schnapp, Patrice Lorine. "The Liberation Theology of James Baldwin." Ph.D. dissertation, Bowling Green State University, 1987.

Schuster, Fred. "'Risk Your Life for Every Note.'" *Down Beat* 61 (August 1994): 16–19.

Scott, Nathan A., Jr. "The Dark and Haunted Tower of Richard Wright." In *Richard Wright: A Collection of Critical Essays.* Ed. Richard Macksey and Frank E. Moorer. Englewood Cliffs, N.J.: Prentice Hall, 1984: 149–62.

———. *Negative Capability: Studies in the New Literature and the Religious Situation.* New Haven, Conn.: Yale University Press, 1969.

Sekora, John. "'Mr. Editor, If You Please': Frederick Douglass, *My Bondage and My Freedom,* and the End of the Abolitionist Imprint." *Callaloo* 17.2 (1994): 608–26.

Sernett, Milton C. *Afro-American Religious History: A Documentary Witness.* Durham, N.C.: Duke University Press, 1985.

Shakespeare, William. *The Tragedy of Romeo and Juliet.* Ed. J. A. Bryant Jr. New York: New American Library, 1964.

Skerrett, Joseph T. "Richard Wright, Writing, and Identity." *Callaloo* 2.3 (1979): 84–94.

Smelstor, Marjorie. "Richard Wright's Beckoning Ascent and Descent." In *Richard Wright: Myths and Realities.* Ed. C. James Trotman. New York: Garland, 1988: 89–109.

Smith, Anna Deavere. *Fires in the Mirror: Crown Heights, Brooklyn, and Other Identities.* New York: Anchor, 1993.

———. *Twilight: Los Angeles, 1992.* New York: Anchor, 1994.

Smith, Sidonie Ann. "Richard Wright's *Black Boy:* The Creative Impulse as Rebellion." *Southern Literary Journal* 5.1 (1972): 123–36.

Snead, James. *White Screens: Black Images.* New York: Routledge, 1994.

Solomon, Joshua. "'Skin Deep': Reliving *Black Like Me:* My Own Journey into the Heart of Race-Conscious America." *Washington Post* 30 October 1994: C1, C4.

Somers, Pamela. "'Sally's Rape': Searing Talk about Racism." *Washington Post* 6 May 1994: B1, B8.

Sopher, David E. "The Landscape of Home: Myth, Experience, Social Meaning."

In *The Interpretation of Ordinary Landscapes: Geographical Essays*. Ed. D. W. Meining. New York: Oxford University Press, 1979: 129–49.

Spellman, A. B. *Four Lives in the Bebop Business*. New York: Limelight Editions, 1990.

Spencer, Jon Michael. *Protest and Praise: Sacred Music of Black Religion*. Philadelphia: Augsburg Fortress, 1990.

Spillers, Hortense J. "Changing the Letter: The Yokes, the Jokes of Discourse, or Mrs. Stowe, Mr. Reed." In *Slavery and the Literary Imagination*. Eds. Deborah E. McDowell and Arnold Rampersad. Baltimore: Johns Hopkins University Press, 1989: 25–61.

Stanislavsky, Constantin. *Stanislavsky's Legacy: A Collection of Comments on a Variety of Aspects of an Actor's Art and Life*. Ed. and trans. Elizabeth Reynolds Hapgood. New York: Theatre Arts Books, 1958.

Stepto, Robert B. *From Behind the Veil: A Study of Afro-American Narrative*. Urbana: University of Illinois Press, 1979.

———. "I Thought I Knew These People: Richard Wright and the Afro-American Literary Tradition." In *Chant of Saints: A Gathering of Afro-American Literature, Art, and Scholarship*. Ed. Michael S. Harper, Robert B. Stepto, and John Hope Franklin. Urbana: University of Illinois Press, 1979: 195–211.

Stone, Albert E. "Identity and Art in Frederick Douglass's Narrative." *CLA Journal* 17 (1973): 192–213.

Styron, William. "Nat Turner Revisited." *American Heritage* October 1992: 64–73.

Sundquist, Eric J. *To Wake the Nations: Race in the Making of American Literature*. Cambridge, Mass.: Harvard University Press, 1993.

"Talk of the Town." *New Yorker* 1 November 1993: 8.

Tanner, Laura E. "Self-Conscious Representation in the Slave Narrative." *Black American Literature Forum* 21.4 (1987): 415–24.

Tate, Claudia C. "*Black Boy*: Richard Wright's 'Tragic Sense of Life.'" *Black American Literature Forum* 10.4 (1976): 117–20.

Taylor, Gordon O. "Voices from the Veil: Black American Autobiography." *Georgia Review* 35.2 (1981): 341–61.

Thacher, Zachary. "American Rhythms: An Interview with Anna Deavere Smith." *Intermission* 29 February 1996: 8–9.

Thaddeus, Janice. "The Metamorphosis of Richard Wright's *Black Boy*." *American Literature* 57.2 (1985): 199–214.

Tomasi, L. Tongiorgi. "Image, Symbol and Word on the Title Pages and Frontispieces of Scientific Books from the Sixteenth and Seventeenth Centuries." *Word & Image* 4.1 (1988): 372–78.

Tracy, David. "The Hidden God: The Divine Other of Liberation." *Cross Currents* 46.1 (1996): 5–16.

Turner, Victor. *Dramas, Fields, and Metaphors: Symbolic Action in Human Society*. Ithaca, N.Y.: Cornell University Press, 1974.

Vinson, Audrey L. "The Deliverers: Ernest J. Gaines's Sacrificial Lambs." *Obsidian II* 11.1 (1987): 34–47.

Wald, Gayle. "Anna Deavere Smith's Voices at Twilight." *Postmodern Culture* 2 (1994): 1–17.

Walker, Alice. "In Search of Our Mothers' Gardens." In *Black Theology: A Documentary History, 1966–1979.* Eds. Gayraud S. Wilmore and James H. Cone. Maryknoll, N.Y.: Orbis, 1979: 434–44.

———. *Living by the Word.* New York: Harcourt Brace Jovanovich, 1988.

Washington, Booker T. *Up from Slavery.* New York: Viking Penguin, 1986.

Washington, Joseph R. *Black Religion: The Negro and Christianity.* Boston: Beacon Press, 1964.

Watkins, Mel. "James Baldwin Writing and Talking." *New York Times Book Review* 23 September 1979.

Watts, Leon W. "Caucuses and Caucasians." In *The Black Experience in Religion: A Book of Readings.* Ed. C. Eric Lincoln. Garden City, N.Y.: Doubleday, 1974: 24–36.

Weinstein, Norman. "Charlie Haden." *Down Beat* 53.6 (June 1986): 55.

Werner, Craig Hansen. *Playing the Changes: From Afro-Modernism to the Jazz Impulse.* Urbana: University of Illinois Press, 1994.

Wertheim, Albert. "Journey to Freedom: Ernest Gaines' *The Autobiography of Miss Jane Pittman.*" In *The Afro-American Novel Since 1960.* Ed. Peter Bruck and Wolfgang Karrer. Amsterdam: B. R. Gruner, 1982: 2119–235.

West, Cornel. "The Loss of Hope." *Utne Reader* September/October 1991: 54–55.

———. *Prophesy Deliverance!: An Afro-American Revolutionary Christianity.* Philadelphia: Westminster Press, 19822.

Williams, Delores S. "Black Women's Surrogacy Experience and the Christian Notion of Redemption." In *After Patriarchy: Feminist Reconstructions of the World Religions.* Ed. Paula Cooey, William R. Eakin, and Jay B. McDaniel. Maryknoll, N.Y.: Orbis, 1991: 1–14.

———. *Sisters in the Wilderness: The Challenge of Womanist God-Talk.* Maryknoll, N.Y.: Orbis, 1993.

———. "Writing Our Way Home." *The Other Side* September/October 1994: 49–50.

Wilmore, Gayraud S., and James H. Cone. *Black Theology: A Documentary History, 1966–1979.* Maryknoll, N.Y.: Orbis, 1979.

Wolfe, Tom. *The Painted Word.* New York: Farrar, Straus & Giroux, 1975.

Woodard, Josef. "Charlie Haden and the Liberation Music Orchestra." *Down Beat* 58 (December 1991): 71–72.

———. "A Healthy Dose of Disrespect." *Down Beat* 59 (August 1992): 16–21.

Wright, Richard. "Between the World and Me." *Partisan Review* July/August 1935: 18–19.

———. *Black Boy.* New York: HarperCollins, 1991.

———. "Blueprint for Negro Writing." In *Richard Wright Reader*. Ed. Ellen Wright and Michel Fabre. New York: HarperCollins, 1978.

———. *12 Million Black Voices*. New York: Viking, 1941.

Zinsser, William. "'I Realized Her Tears Were Becoming Part of the Memorial.'" *Smithsonian* September 1991: 32–43.

Zipkin, Michael. "Charlie Haden: Struggling Idealist." *Down Beat* 45 (July 1978): 27–28, 56–57.

Index

KIMBERLY RAE CONNOR has a Ph.D. degree in religion and literature from the University of Virginia. The author of *Conversions and Visions in the Writings of African-American Women* (1993), she teaches at San Francisco University High School.

Typeset in 10/13 Sabon
with Joanna Italic display
Designed by Dennis Roberts
Composed by Jim Proefrock
at the University of Illinois Press
Manufactured by Maple-Vail
Book Manufacturing Group

University of Illinois Press
1325 South Oak Street
Champaign, IL 61820-6903
www.press.uillinois.edu